THE LIFE AND DEATH OF QUERNS

THE DEPOSITION AND USE-CONTEXTS OF QUERNS IN SOUTH-WESTERN ENGLAND FROM THE NEOLITHIC TO THE IRON AGE

Susan R. Watts

HP

SOUTHAMPTON MONOGRAPHS IN ARCHAEOLOGY NEW SERIES 3

© Susan R Watts 2014

ISBN: 978-0-9926336-1-5

A CIP record for this book is available from The British Library

Published by The Highfield Press Southampton, 10 Hiltingbury Road, Chandlers Ford, SO53 5ST, United Kingdom

This book is available from Oxbow Books Ltd, 10 Hythe Bridge Street, Oxford, OX1 2EW or from David Brown Book Company, 28 Main Street, Oakville, CT06779, USA

Printed in Great Britain by imprintdigital.com

CONTENTS

	List of Figures	iv
	List of Appendices	v
	Preface	vi
Chapter 1	Introduction	1
Chapter 2	The Early Chronological Development of the Quern	17
Chapter 3	The Object Biography of Querns	25
Chapter 4	The Symbolic Properties of Querns	45
Chapter 5	An Overview of the Querns found in Structured Contexts within the Study Area	58
Chapter 6	The Neolithic Period	64
Chapter 7	The Bronze Age	74
Chapter 8	The Iron Age	102
Chapter 9	Conclusions and Future Directions	126
	Appendices	140
	Bibliography	162
	Index	184

List of Figures

1.1	Activity and refuse areas of a Rarámuri residence, Mexico
1.2	An Endo compound, Kenya
1.3	Bronze Age pit, Winnall Down, Hampshire
1.4	Neolithic pit, Upper Deal, Kent
1.5	Complete rotary quern from a pit at Danebury, Hampshire
1.6	Saddle quern and rubbing stones at Trethellan Farm, Newquay, Cornwall
1.7	Saddle quern and rubber in a pit, Etton, Cambridgeshire
1.8	Rotary querns in a pit, oppidum of Pandours à Saverne, Alsace, France
1.9	Map of the study area
1.10	Unprovenanced querns in Tresco Abbey Gardens, Isles of Scilly
2.1	Saddle quern and rotary quern
2.2	Saucer quern, saddle quern and trough quern
2.3	Rotary quern
2.4	Saddle querns at Abu Hureyra, Syria
2.5	Trough querns and saddle quern at Jarlshof, Shetland
2.6	Upper stone from Silchester, Berkshire
2.7	Two women working a quern together
2.8	Proto rotary quern
2.9	Types of beehive quern
3.1	A constellation of knowledge for the manufacture of a quern
3.2	Grinding with a saddle quern
3.3	Querns of different stone types and colours
3.4	Buckwheat quern
3.5	Broken rotary quernstone from Alderney, Channel Islands
3.6	Pair of rotary quernstones from Rossie Quarry, Perthshire
3.7	Egyptian model of a bakery
3.8	The quern as part of a social setting
3.9	Multiple saddle quern emplacement
3.10	Plan of an Iron Age dwelling at Nornour, Isles of Scilly
3.11	Rotary quernstone from Penryn, Cornwall
3.12	Rotary quernstone reused as mouldstone
3.13	Quernstone reused as a decorative building stone
4.1	Megarian bowl with milling scene relief
4.2	Contrasting coloured saddle querns from Sigwells, Somerset
4.3	Decorated querns
4.4	Interior of a reconstructed roundhouse
4.5	Japanese quern monument
5.1	Map of sites included on the main database
5.2	Graph of querns from structured contexts, unstructured site finds and find spots
5.3	Table of querns from the study area
5.4	Map of sites plus find spots
5.5	Graph showing the numbers of broad context forms by period
6.1	Map of Neolithic sites
6.2	Table of Neolithic depositional contexts
6.3	Saddle quern from Milsoms Corner, Somerset
7.1	Map of Bronze Age sites
7.2	Table of Bronze Age depositional contexts
7.3	Collections of querns in pits at Truro College and Scarcewater, Cornwall
7.4	Rhyolite quern from Sheep Slait, Dorset
7.5	Quern fragments from posthole F043 at Sigwells, Somerset
7.6	Graph showing the cardinal locations of pits and postholes with querns

7.7	Saddle quern from Holworthy, Devon and plan of the roundhouse
7.8	Pit 531 at Meacombe, Devon
7.9	Cremation burial at Chew Park, Somerset
7.10	Bant's Carn, St. Mary's, Isles of Scilly
7.11	Quern in barrow at Boscawen-un, Cornwall
8.1	Map showing location of Iron Age sites
8.2	Table of Iron Age depositional contexts
8.3	Plan of Glastonbury Lake Village showing the location of quernstones
8.4	Lower stone reused in an oven or kiln, Cadbury Castle, Somerset
8.5	Pit A at Blaise Castle Hill, Bristol
8.6	Raven burial at Sigwells, Somerset
8.7	Pit 345 at Trenowah, St. Austell, Cornwall
8.8	Quern fragments in a pit at Mount Folly, South Devon

List of Appendices

Appendix 1	List of sites included in the database
Appendix 2	List of chance finds and other sites not included in the database
Appendix 3	Tables from database
	6.1 Neolithic pits
	6.2 Other Neolithic features
	7.1 Postholes in Bronze Age roundhouses
	7.2 Pits, hearths and kilns in Bronze Age roundhouses
	7.3 Other Bronze Age pits
	7.4 Bronze Age ditches
	7.5 Bronze Age graves and barrows
	8.1 Iron Age postholes
	8.2 Iron Age gullies and drains
	8.3 Iron Age pits
	8.4 Iron Age ditches
	8.5 Iron Age funerary and human bone deposits

PREFACE

This book presents the results of a PhD thesis on the structured deposition of querns within the south-west of England submitted to the University of Exeter in 2012. My awareness of where and how querns were found in archaeological contexts was stimulated when reading *Ritual and Rubbish in the Iron Age of Wessex* (Hill 1995). I was further inspired in 2003 by a broken, trough-like saddle quern found, inverted, beneath the transverse slab at the entrance to the end chamber of the Neolithic passage grave at La Hougue Bie on Jersey. Both monument and quern are of granite but of particular interest is that the transverse slab and quern are from a different granite source to that of the other stones in the monument (Société Jersiaise 1977, 12; Information from La Hougue Bie Museum). This was surely more than coincidence. It was this that prompted me to investigate the theory that, in conjunction with their utilitarian role as milling stones, querns also had important, symbolic roles to play within the communities that used them and that as such they comprised a significant element within the apparent prehistoric practice of structured deposition.

The subject of the structured deposition of querns has been little researched on a detailed regional and chronological basis and this research fits well, therefore, into existing work on both querns and structured deposition. It is intended to demonstrate that querns are multi-functional tools, assuming both symbolic and utilitarian values through their importance to subsistence communities for grinding staple foods, values that are reflected in their use as structured deposits. In doing so, I hope to raise the awareness of the significance to prehistoric communities of what today are still often considered mundane artefacts.

Definitions
It should be noted that, unless a definitive term is given, the word 'quern' is used generically throughout this book to mean all forms of tool used for milling by hand, such as the saddle quern, rotary quern or metate. It is also used generically to indicate either or both upper and lower stones. 'Quernstone' is used in a similar way. Likewise the term 'structured deposit/deposition' is also used generically to indicate any form or category of artefactual deposition made with intent or meaning. The following points should also be noted with regard to the text. All Biblical quotations are taken from the Authorised King James Version. The Latin names of plants are given, in brackets, after the first use only. Similarly, the county location is generally given only after the first use of a site name within each chapter.

Abstract
It is now widely assumed that many artefacts found in the prehistoric archaeological record were not casually discarded as unwanted material but were deposited in features and contexts with structure and meaning. This appears to include saddle and rotary querns for they are often found whole and apparently still usable or, conversely, deliberately broken. Analysis of the structured deposition of querns in the south-west of England shows that they were deposited in features on both domestic and non-domestic sites. Furthermore, the location and state of the querns, together with the artefacts found in association with them, indicates that they were deposited with different levels and layers of meaning, even within the same type of feature. The deposition of querns appears to have pervaded all aspects of prehistoric life and death suggesting that they played a role above, but nevertheless related to, their prime task of milling. An exploration of the object biography of querns demonstrates the importance of what are often considered to be mundane tools to subsistence communities. Each quern has its own unique life history, its meaning and value determined by the reasons that gave cause for its manufacture, the material from which it was made, the use(s) to which it was put and who used it. However, all querns share points of commonality, related to their function as milling tools, their role as transformers of raw material(s) into usable products, their association with women and the production of food, and the movement of the upper stone. Through these, symbolical links can be made between querns and agricultural, human and building lifecycles, gender relations and the turning of the heavens. The reason for a quern's deposition in the archaeological record may have drawn upon one or more unique or common values.

ACKNOWLEDGEMENTS

I take this opportunity to express my thanks to everyone who helped me during the course of my research as a part-time post-graduate student at the University of Exeter. This work was helped financially by a bursary from the Archaeology Department of Exeter University and I am also most grateful to The Harold Hyam Wingate Foundation for the award of a scholarship which part-funded the first four years of my research. I especially thank my supervisor, Dr. Linda Hurcombe for her guidance and helpful and inspiring discussions and my second supervisor, Dr. Marisa Lazzari, particularly for her advice on matters pertaining to material culture. I also benefitted greatly from Dr. Carl Knappett's Masters Degree classes on material culture. My thanks are due also to my internal and external examiners, Professor Anthony Harding and Dr J.D. Hill whose rigorous reading of my research encouraged me to clarify my analysis on a number of issues. I am also grateful to Professor David Peacock, Southampton University, for his work in preparing my research for publication.

I also take this opportunity to thank all the individuals and organisations who kindly supplied photos and granted permission to use them in this publication: Dr. Stuart Blaylock, Guy Clausse, Dr. Clément Féliu, Dr. Terry Green, Mike Hall, Dr. Caroline Hamon, Peter Hill, Kenjiro Kawakami, Dr. Andrew Moore, Jocelyn Rendall, Dr. Delwyn Samuel, Dr. Richard Tabor, Dr. Eileen Wilkes, Archaeological Institute of America, Birmingham Museum of Art (Alabama, USA), Trustees of the British Museum, Cornwall Council Historic Environment Service, Exeter Archaeology, Hampshire Field Club and Archaeological Society, Headland Archaeology, North Devon Archaeological Society, Oxford Institute of Archaeology, Oxford University Press (USA), Perth Museum & Art Gallery.

My grateful thanks are due also to Henrietta Quinnell, who has freely given of her knowledge of the prehistoric south-west, Dr. Caroline Hamon for sharing details of her research in Mali with me, Ann Dick for translating German articles and Dr. Richard Sandover for the base maps, the Historic Environment Record officers who sent me details of the querns they hold information on, the staff of the Royal Cornwall Museum, Truro, the Royal Albert Memorial Museum, Exeter and the Museum of Somerset, Taunton, who allowed me access to their collections of querns, and the staff of the Somerset Record Office who willingly fetched me nearly every file and folder from the Cadbury Castle Archive. My thanks are also due to the archaeological units who shared information with me in advance of publication. I especially thank Dr. Andy Jones, James Gossip and Charlie Johns, Cornwall Council Historic Environment Service, and Dr. Richard Tabor, Cadbury Castle Environs Project. My greatest thanks, however, are to my husband, Martin, for helping with the illustrations and for his encouragement and support throughout.

1
INTRODUCTION

1.1 The Concept of Structured Deposition

The artefacts recovered from the prehistoric archaeological record are not entirely discarded rubbish, nor do they necessarily represent the unbiased, inadvertent detritus of activities and occupation. Instead many of the objects found on prehistoric sites have been intentionally placed in the positions in which they are found for reasons that had meaning to the person(s) who deposited them. This purposeful placement, which is now generally referred to as structured deposition, also appears to include querns, for they are often found whole and apparently still usable, or conversely, possibly deliberately broken. But what is structured deposition and how can it be recognised in the archaeological record?

The term 'structured deposition' itself was first used by Richards and Thomas in 1984 to explain the nature of the deposits of ceramic, faunal and lithic assemblages within the Neolithic henge monument at Durrington Walls, Wiltshire. They suggested that 'highly formalised, repetitive' modes of behaviour could be reflected in the associations and contexts of various artefacts. Such artefacts were imbued with symbolic meaning and their patterns of deposition governed by underlying cosmological rules and structures (Richards and Thomas 1984, 189, 191-192). The recognition of structured deposits has been described as 'one of the most significant developments of British later prehistoric archaeology from the 1980s' (Hamilton 2002). Structured deposition has subsequently proved key in interpreting past behavioural practices not only across the prehistoric period but also into the Roman and medieval periods (Fulford 2001; Gossip and Jones 2007, 49-50; O'Sullivan and Kenny 2008) and has been taken to cover the location of a wide range of objects whose various contexts have been described, for example, as purposeful, unusual, intentional, symbolic, ritual, formal or deliberate (Hill 1995, 95; Brudenell and Cooper 2008, 15). These words have, in turn, been used to define perceived distinctions in the nature of the deposits so described (Brudenell and Cooper 2008, 15).

Darvill (2008) defined structured deposition as 'patterning in the way that artefacts are found when uncovered through excavation which allows the suggestion that behavioural regularities underlie the way in which they were put into the ground in the first place'. Grave goods, hoards and depositions of metalwork in watery places during the prehistoric period have long been identified as examples of the practice, although the term 'structured deposit' may not have been used specifically to describe them. But it is now generally considered that many of the artefacts, both whole and fragmentary, recovered from other contexts, including those associated with the domestic sphere, and which may previously have been regarded as rubbish, were also structurally deposited (Thomas 1999, 63; Chapman 2000a, 350; Webster and Mayberry 2007, 48; Giles 2008, 343).

The main problem, however, has been how such structured deposits, particularly those on domestic sites, can be recognised in the archaeological record. Richards and Thomas (1984, 189) suggested that it is 'certain structural qualities of the material record' that are diagnostic of structured deposition. Hill (1995, 96) refers to the 'alerting quality' of a deposit. As Thomas (1999, 65) comments, particular depositions 'alert one to the likelihood that something more than the routine disposal of waste material was happening'. Pollard (2001) refers to this as the 'aesthetics of depositional practice', that the choice and deposition of certain artefacts in certain places were undertaken with care and forethought. Thus the condition, distribution and positioning of artefacts may have been as important as the objects themselves.

This rationale, however, makes the assumption that structured deposits are distinct and separate from other forms of deposit but there is a reason for the placement of every object in the archaeological record (Whittle *et al* 1999, 355-356; Brudenell and Cooper 2008; Morris 1973, xv). Daily activities, including the storage of potentially reusable items and the disposal of unwanted material can also incorporate repetitive, habitual behaviour resulting in patterns of deposition. Patterns may also arise through happenstance as well as intent or be perceived where, in fact, none were intended (Brück 1995, 254; Hill 1995, 4; Whittle *et al* 1999, 356; Brudenell and Cooper 2008, 34). Graham's work amongst the Rarámuri in northern Mexico, for example, showed that their residences included several distinct but coincidental areas of refuse (Figure 1.1) (Graham 1994).

The problem, therefore, is not simply of how structured deposition can be recognised in the archaeological record but how to distinguish between different levels of deposits, between those associated with ceremonial activities, for example, and those associated with daily practices.

1.1.1 Depositional processes and the formation of the archaeological record
Fundamental to the recognition of structured deposits is an understanding of the cultural and natural processes by which material entered the archaeological record, how it was deposited and changed over time until recovered by excavation or other means from that record. It is central to understanding the nature of those deposits, the activities, events and practices that led to them and thus the ways in which prehistoric societies related to and interacted with the world around them (Murray 1980, 490; Schiffer 1995, 171; Hill 1995, 3, 10; Darvill 2008).

The constructs of archaeological formation processes were developed by Schiffer in the 1970s and 1980s (Schiffer 1983; 1987; 1995). Inspired by the tenets of new or processual archaeology that developed in America in the 1960s, Schiffer came to reject the traditional definition of archaeology, 'the study of past societies through their material remains' and instead adopted a new statement of meaning, 'the study of the relationships between human behaviour and material culture'. This was the premise of what was to become behavioural archaeology, a particular approach to material culture that studied human behaviour with especial reference to the manufacture, use and discard of artefacts. This approach enabled Schiffer to formulate the taphonomic processes by which the archaeological record was formed (Schiffer 1995, 1-3, 10, 13).

Schiffer saw material culture as moving from a past cultural context, which encompassed the various stages of the use-life of an artefact (procurement, manufacture, use, maintenance and discard) to the archaeological context, the state of an object within the archaeological record as excavated. The creation of the archaeological record and the state of the artefact within that record, as found, were the result of formation processes caused by human and natural agencies. Schiffer referred to these agencies as cultural and non-cultural (Schiffer 1987; 1995, 25-34; Darvill 2008). Cultural formation processes (C-transforms) are human activities and events, either deliberate or accidental, such as discard,

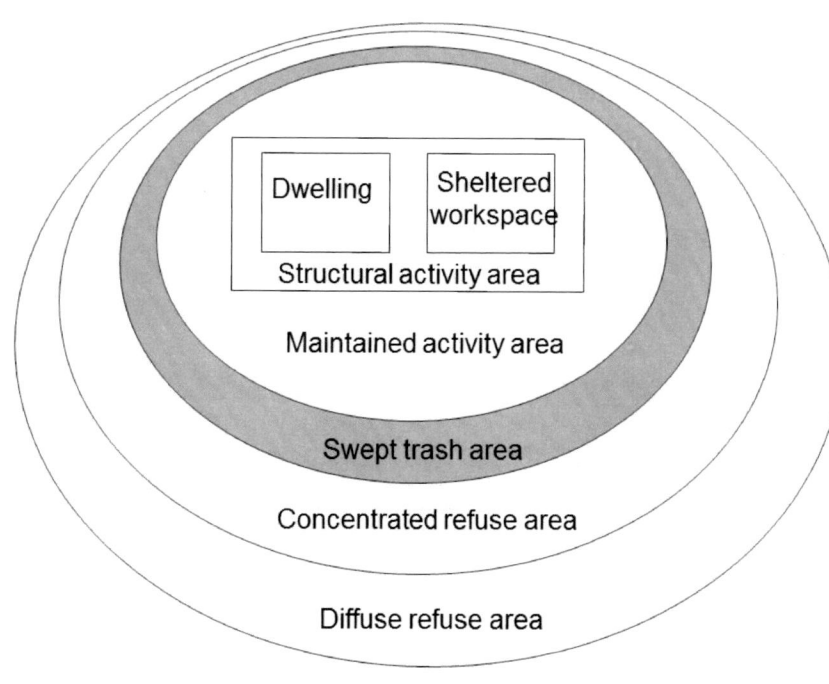

Figure 1.1: Diagrammatic representation of the main activity and refuse areas of a Rarámuri residence in north-west Mexico (S. Watts after Graham 1994, 63-72, Figure 36).

site abandonment, caching, loss or burial with the dead. Some processes such as burial in pits and ditches favour the survival and consequently the retrieval of artefacts from the archaeological record. Non-cultural processes (N-transforms) are natural processes and events such as burial of a site under wind-blown sand or volcanic ash. Again certain N-transforms such as exceptionally wet or dry conditions favour the survival of material. The majority of N-transforms, however, are post-depositional processes that affect material after it has entered the archaeological context such as rodent activity, erosion or environmental or soil conditions. C-transforms, however, such as ploughing or looting can also affect material within the archaeological record (Schiffer 1995, 48-51; Renfrew and Bahn 1996, 48-66).

Schiffer initially suggested three main means by which items entered the archaeological record; as artefacts placed in connection with the dead, loss and discarded refuse. Within the latter category he further identified primary refuse that is material discarded where it was used, secondary refuse or material discarded away from its location of use and de facto refuse which comprises those elements which enter the archaeological context without being deliberately discarded such as when a site is abandoned and material is left behind. It also encompasses site furniture and chance loss (Schiffer 1987, 89-92; Schiffer 1995, 28-31). However, as mentioned above, certain depositions of artefacts within the archaeological record appear to show a high degree of structure which is thought to reflect formalised behaviour rather than the casual disposal of refuse. This fact was subsequently acknowledged by Schiffer who further identified 'banking caches' or objects buried for safe-keeping and 'ritual caches' which he described as a 'diverse set of deposits apparently produced in a ritual and ceremonial context' (Schiffer 1987, 78-79).

1.1.2 Levels of structured deposit
The archaeological record can be seen, therefore, to bear witness to different levels and types of deposit from those arising from formal events, to those resulting from everyday domestic routine, from artefacts buried in-memoriam or for safe-keeping to objects dropped, lost or casually left. The latter, however, cannot be considered as structured deposits. Likewise, material that has been moved and redeposited within the archaeological record as a result of subsequent environmental or human disturbance is also unstructured.

It has been suggested, however, (Brück 1995, 254-255) that typological distinctions are largely academic as all aspects of daily life, both practical and esoteric, were governed by the same symbolic and cosmological formulae. As Hill (1995, 16, 30) comments, it is our modern western interpretations of rubbish and ritual that have resulted in the basic premise that deposits must be one or the other. Anthropological research, on the other hand, intimates that prehistoric peoples may not have made such firm distinctions (Brück 1995, 254-255; Bradley 2005a, 33-36). To the Endo of Kenya, for example, goat dung, and ash and chaff have male and female associations respectively. Consequently each is disposed of in a different part of the dwelling compound, both respecting the separate burial areas for men and women and at the same time reaffirming the gender differences (Figure 1.2) (Moore 1996, 109-110; Moore 2006). As Pryor (1998b, 64) believes, rubbish may have been an alien notion to prehistoric peoples; midden material being seen, for example, as a store of fertility, a territorial marker or a stock pile depending upon its context of use (Brück 1995, 255; Pryor 1998b, 64; Needham and Spence 1997, 84-85).

Whittle *et al* (1999, 356) further declared that typological distinctions may in fact hinder rather than aid interpretation and condemned the term 'structured deposition' as 'insufficiently precise'. They suggested that it should be seen as a particular form of behavioural practice undertaken in different ways for different reasons and meanings. Indeed the whole notion of structured deposits has been recently challenged. A distinct lack of formality was noted in the fill of a Late Bronze Age pit at Broom, Bedfordshire (Brudenell and Cooper 2008, 31). Although it was acknowledged that the burnt quern at the bottom of the pit may have been placed there intentionally, it was suggested that the majority of the fill comprised occupation debris and soil swept into the pit over a period of time. Likewise, examination of the fills of groups of Earlier Neolithic pits at Kilverstone, Norfolk, dated between *circa* 3670 and 2900 cal. BC led to the conclusion that the artefacts within had not been chosen or placed with any due care (contra Pollard 2001) but rather represented a mixture of occupation debris and soil (Garrow *et al* 2005, 144). That said, it was also noted that pieces from the same pot were found in each series of pits, but in diminishing numbers in a clockwise pattern around each pit group (Garrow 2007, 152). This suggests that there was, therefore, some form of structure to the deposits. The fact that artefacts do not appear to have been placed with care does not mean that the deposits were not made with meaning and purpose.

It is argued, therefore, that structured deposition also covers those intentional deposits whose nature is more mundane (Brück 1995, 254; Whittle *et al* 1999, 355-356). Furthermore, in addition to below ground deposits, structured deposition can also encompass above ground deposits (O'Sullivan and Kenny 2008). Any placement made with apparent purpose and meaning may be considered as structured but not all deposits are equally significant. Although, for example, both those deposits resulting from daily, domestic practice and those resulting from special, ceremonial events would have drawn on the same set of cosmological and symbolical principles their meaning and relative importance would have been different (Garwood *et al* 1991, viii; Hill 1995, 99). Artefacts should not be identified as structured deposits, therefore, without further consideration of the nature and context of the deposit (Brudenell and Cooper 2008, 16; Jones forthcoming). Although it may not be possible to distinguish between those deposits resulting from daily domestic practice from those that define special events, it may nevertheless be possible to recognise variations in the contexts or constitution of deposits that could be indicative of differences in level or category of meaning (Bradley 1987, 352; Needham and Spence 1997, 86-87).

Factors to be taken into consideration, therefore, in the identification of different levels or categories of structured deposit include the nature and context of deposits, the formation processes that led to their creation, the frequency with which particular deposits occur, their location, combinations of artefacts and whether artefacts are whole or fragmentary (Bradley 1987, 352; Schiffer 1987, 302; Bruck 1995, 255; Hill 1995, 3, 95-96; Needham and Spence 1997, 86-7; Thomas 1999, 62; Osborne 2004; Brudenell and Cooper 2008). The latter, as will be shown, appears to be an important facet in the structured deposition of querns.

1.2 Why Use Querns to Investigate Structured Deposition?

Quernstones are durable artefacts and frequently met with on archaeological sites. Indeed, it has been suggested that the greater proportion of all querns used on prehistoric sites may be represented in the archaeological record (Hill 1995, 2, 108, 131). They are amongst the categories of finds frequently included within structured deposits. They are often in a fragmentary condition (quernstones are not objects that break easily) but complete stones are also found. The latter may be placed upside down, in positions in which they would not have been used (Hill 1995, 108; Poole 1995, 259; Pryor 1998a, 103, 107). Synonymous with women, domestic toil and grinding grain, and yet often found outside the domestic arena, querns provide an ideal medium through which to investigate the concept of structured deposition. Are we, as Bradley (2005a, 35) suggests, seeing an artefact transcending its everyday ubiquity or is it this very characteristic, the fact that querns were used for grinding corn for the 'daily bread', that rendered them eminently suitable as structured deposits? With two contrasting aspects, querns have the potential to be a most revealing category

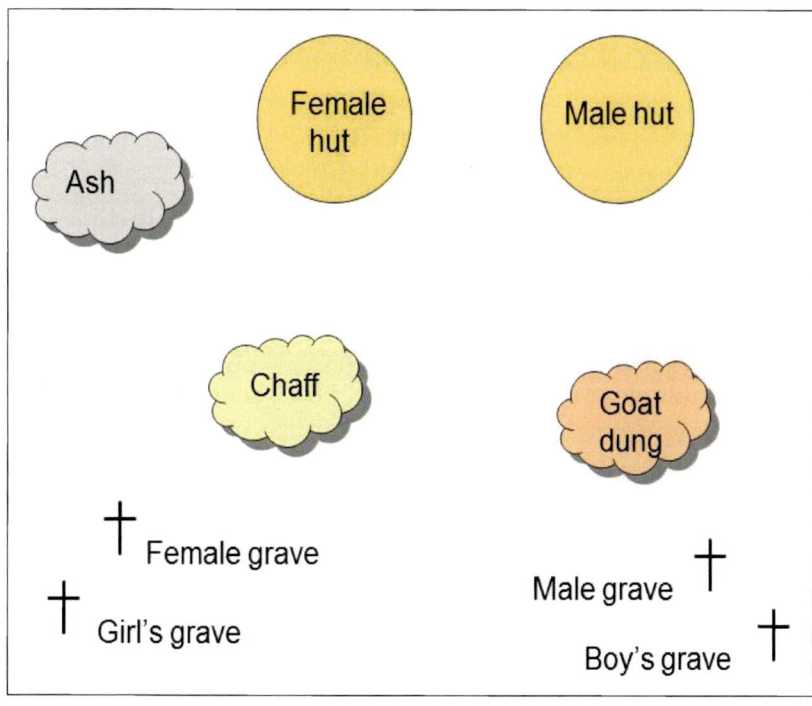

Figure 1.2: Diagrammatic representation of an Endo compound, Kenya (S. Watts after Moore 2006, Figures 3 and 4).

Introduction

of artefact. On the one hand querns have traditionally been treated as mundane, utilitarian artefacts, the toil of milling being described as one of the 'less pleasant household tasks' (Moritz 1958, xxv). On the other hand, querns have also been described as 'an excellent instance of necessary things for they grind the corn which for an agricultural people is the chief basis of life' (Crawford 1953, 98-99). This dichotomy is well demonstrated in the Old Testament within which there are several passages indicating that the grinding of flour was considered a lowly chore, fit only for slaves and prisoners (Exodus 11:5; Isaiah 47:2; Judges 16:21 (Authorised King James Version)). Yet, there is also a reference to a law prohibiting the taking of a quernstone as a pledge as that would be tantamount to taking a man's life (Deuteronomy 24:6).

Querns also have the added fillip of being long-lived artefacts with the potential of being handed down from generation to generation. They can be used for grinding products other than grain and can also have several phases of secondary use. As Gwilt and Heslop (1995, 40) point out, many decades may pass between the date of a quern's initial manufacture and use and that of its final deposition in the archaeological record. The importance and meaning of a particular quern may alter as it moves from one context of use to another and consequently its relative significance as a structured deposit may also change (after Barrett 2000, 45; Walker and Lucero 2000, 133). Querns are thus many-faceted objects with complex biographies or life histories, and multiple meanings and values. These values may be linked to the quern's role as part of a social network, be that part of domestic food processing or other craft activities and/or to its symbolical aspects related to the transforming act of grinding (Lidström Holmberg 2004, 226). There is much, therefore, that querns can reveal about past behavioural practices and the nature of structured deposition.

It has been said, however, (Heslop 2008, 73) that structured deposition cannot be fully understood through the study of a single artefact. This may be so, just as neither can it be fully appreciated through a single site, or type of feature. Structured deposition is a complex subject with many facets. Deposits may have been made, for example, with different levels of meaning and intent. There may have been local variations of practice within regional frameworks, the meaning(s) of which would have only been fully understood by members of that community and changes are also to be expected in practices over time (Bradley 1987, 351; Tilley 1999, 9; Haselgrove et al 2001, 18-19). Nevertheless, what the study of a single artefact can do is highlight particular aspects of the phenomenon thereby advancing our overall understanding of the subject. Such individual studies are like pieces of a jigsaw puzzle that gradually come together to present a fuller picture. However, although this book focuses on a single artefact type it is appreciated that quernstones are frequently placed in conjunction with a variety of other artefacts. Such contiguity in the archaeological record may reflect an association that existed in the artefacts' use lives. Each different combination of artefacts has its own story to tell.

1.3 Previous Work on the Structured Deposition of Querns

1.3.1 British literature

One of the first archaeologists to recognise that 'alerting quality', alluded to by Hill (1995, 96), in the treatment accorded to querns was E.C. Curwen who, in 1929, commented on the small size of the quern fragments found in Iron Age contexts at The Trundle, Sussex compared to those found in the Neolithic ditches. The former, he concluded, had been 'broken up so small as to make it appear that their fracture was intentional'. He subsequently proposed that they had been deliberately burnt in order to break them (Curwen 1929, 63; Curwen 1931, 145). Curwen did not advance any theories as to why this should have been and it was not until the late 1960s that the first article relating to the structured deposition of querns was published (although it was not referred to as such) (Chadwick Hawkes 1969). This ground-breaking article, on the complete and apparently still usable lower and upper stone of a Bronze Age saddle quern buried in a shallow pit on Winnall Down, Hampshire, introduced the notion of quern burials (Figure 1.3). The excavator, Chadwick Hawkes gave other examples of complete saddle querns found in pits such as at Itford Hill, Sussex concluding that these 'quern burials… were some form of religious offering made under circumstances actually unknown to us but nevertheless perfectly imaginable' (Chadwick Hawkes 1969, 8). It is perhaps surprising that neither Chadwick Hawke's concept of quern burials nor Curwen's suggestion of the deliberate breakage of querns bore fruit. These innovative theories were probably restrained, however, by the general archaeological perception of artefacts in pits and ditches as rubbish. This view prevailed until comparatively recently (Winbolt 1929-1930, 162; Bersu 1940, 53, 60; Richmond 1968, 27-28; Wainwright 1979,

Figure 1.3: Saddle quern and rubbing stone in a Bronze Age pit, Winnall Down, Winchester, Hampshire (Chadwick Hawkes 1969, Plate Ib, © Hampshire Field Club and Archaeological Society 1969).

184). One exception was Thompson's (1979, 285, 303) suggestion that the number of quern fragments recovered from the hearths and pits at Hascombe, Surrey represented deliberate breakage of the tools on abandonment of the hillfort, perhaps due to the peace terms laid down by Julius Caesar.

It was not until the 1980s, however, with the questioning attitude of post-processual archaeology towards the significance, purpose and meaning of past behavioural practices (Greene 1998, 172-173; Darvill 2008) that the subject of structured deposition in general and querns in particular came to the fore. One of the earliest publications on the subject of special deposits which mentions querns is *The Archaeology of Ritual and Magic*, a survey of superstitious customs and ritual practices from the Neolithic through to the post-medieval period (Merrifield 1987). Merrifield (1987, 33-34) notes that 'a special mystique seems to have been associated with corn-grinding stones'. He cites examples of 'ritual' deposits of querns in Iron Age pits at the hillforts of Cadbury Castle, Somerset and Danebury, Hampshire together with a Neolithic forerunner from Deal, Kent. The careful positioning of five pots at the base of the latter pit and the placement of a rubber within the central pot have that 'alerting quality' (Hill, 1995, 96), demonstrating well the phenomenon of structured deposition (Figure 1.4) (Dunning 1966, 2). These deposits, Merrifield presumes are connected with 'their importance... in providing the daily bread' (Merrifield 1987, 33-34).

Some 2,300 storage pits were found at Danebury during the course of excavations carried out between 1969 and 1988, making the site ideal for the examination of the nature and meaning of pit deposits. It was noted that many pits contained recurring groups of artefacts, including quernstones. The two halves of a quernstone placed in a similar position in two different pits (2595 and 1596) were highlighted as particularly special deposits. These fragments can be contrasted with the complete upper and lower stones deposited in the top layer of another pit, although interestingly these were not identified as important (Figure 1.5). The contrast between the two forms of deposition is clearly significant, however, implying that the depositions were made with different levels of meaning and intent. It was suggested that the pit deposits were propitiatory offerings, made to appease or thank the gods, and perhaps linked to agricultural fertility, the pits having been originally used for the storage of grain (Cunliffe 1992; Cunliffe 1995a, 5, 80, 83, 87-88; Poole 1995, 262). The notion of a pit 'belief system' *per se* has, however, been challenged as other locations such as boundary ditches also appear to have received significant depositions of material. In addition pit deposits were not made on a regular basis nor were all pits used in this way (Hill 1995, 102, 110). Moreover, it has been recently argued that pits, most notably those at hillforts, were

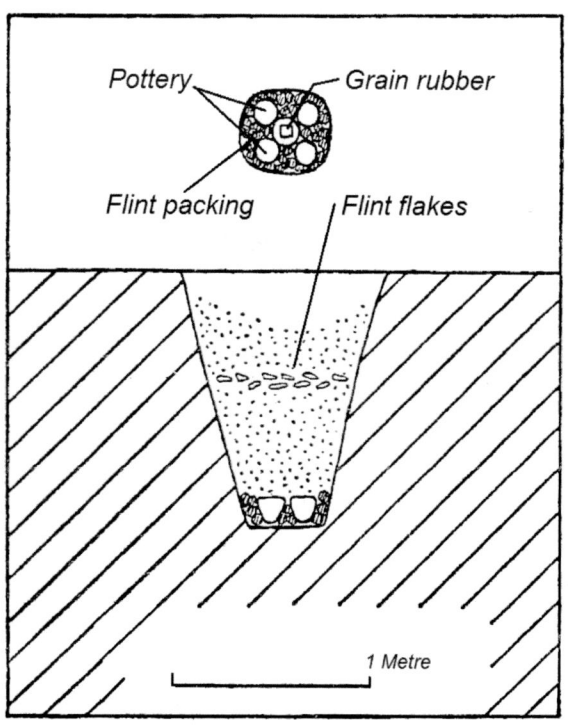

Figure 1.4: Plan and Section of a Neolithic pit, Upper Deal, Kent (M. Watts after Dunning 1966, Figure 1).

Introduction

*Figure 1.5:
Pair of quernstones in the top of pit 288, Danebury Hillfort, Hampshire (Cunliffe 1993, Figure 66, © Oxford Institute of Archaeology).*

for the storage of surplus grain, rather than seed corn, which was used for feasting and associated rituals (Van der Veen and Jones 2006). Such events, however, may also have entailed the placement of special deposits. It has also been suggested (Reynolds 1979, 76) that the lurid colours and smell of mouldy grain in a storage pit that had failed due to an inadequate seal or water penetration may have been seen as indicative of the presence of evil spirits. This is perhaps reason enough for its abandonment and the offering of propitiatory gifts (Watts, S. 1999).

The special treatment of querns was also noted at Trethellan Farm, the site of a well-preserved Middle Bronze Age settlement on the outskirts of Newquay, Cornwall, particularly during the orderly process by which the site was demolished on abandonment. Fragments of a burnt saddle quern were found strewn among the levelling layers within one of the roundhouses, and a large saddle quern laid over a collection of rubbing stones in a pit within another house was recorded as one of the final acts of abandonment (Figure 1.6) (Nowakowski 1991, 25, 73). The different treatments accorded these querns, however, creates a dichotomy of meaning that has not yet been resolved. On the one hand, the site's desertion and demolition was seen as analogous with its death and burial, an act that can be seen as both destroying and creating a 'sense of place' (Nowakowski 1991, 208; Nowakowski 2001, 141, 147). Within this scenario, the scattering of quern fragments fits well. As Brück (1999b, 155) comments the quern, symbolic of life and fertility was 'burnt, broken and buried on death'. On the other hand it was also suggested that the action of leaving a complete quern, together with the treatment of the hearths which were left relatively undisturbed, was symbolic, an indication perhaps of the inhabitants intention to return (Nowakowski 1991, 73, 208).

Nowakowski's interpretation of levelling deposits as part of the abandonment process at Trethellan Farm can be usefully compared with Seager Thomas' analysis of the stone assemblage from the settlement at Black Patch, Sussex, also of Middle Bronze Age date (Seager Thomas 1999). The site of House 1 contained a series of layers on and above the floor which contained burnt fragments from a single quernstone together with other 'common finds'. These layers, in the light of Trethellan Farm, suggest that the roundhouses at Black Patch were also subject to similar abandonment processes. However, Seager Thomas concluded that the mixing of finds did not constitute a special deposit but that the layers comprised a rubbish dump. Interestingly, Seager Thomas also suggested that the presence of the burnt quern fragments was unrelated to the quern's primary use as a milling tool but that the stone had been used for cooking or heating (Seager Thomas 1999, 46).

An article entitled *Querns in Ritual Contexts* published in the 1993 Quern Study Group Newsletter was the first article specifically devoted to the structured deposition of querns (Buckley 1993). This thought-provoking paper was prompted by the find of four complete saddle querns beneath the timbers of the Bronze Age platforms at Flag Fen near Peterborough, Cambridgeshire which Buckley, given the 'ritual' nature of the site, had no hesitation in identifying as special deposits. He cites

Figure 1.6: Saddle quern (left) over a collection of rubbing stones (right) in Pit 2027, H2001, Trethellan Farm, Newquay, Cornwall (© Historic Environment, Cornwall Council).

a number of other examples of structured deposits including seven saddle querns found in a Neolithic pit at Barford, Warwickshire and a complete lower stone of a rotary quern found in a pit at the Iron Age settlement at Gussage All Saints, Dorset. He also comments on the tendency of archaeologists to continue to treat querns as utilitarian tools. This, he says, is despite their obvious importance for grain processing and their place in exchange networks. Buckley recommends that more attention be given to the location of all quern finds, not just 'complete querns in pits'. In the light of his own recommendation it is interesting to note, therefore, that on the previous page he describes the majority of quern fragments found on Bronze Age settlement sites in Sussex as 'simply scattered pieces from broken querns' (Buckley 1993, 3). This comment aside, Buckley's article provides much food for thought, particularly the series of pertinent questions with which he concludes. For example, he asks 'if complete horse skulls in a backfilled well represent "votive deposits" is the quern found in the same context to be seen only as discarded rubbish?' (Buckley 1993, 4).

Quern use and discard was discussed by Gwilt and Heslop in their paper on *Iron Age and Roman Querns from the Tees Valley*, published as part of a series of papers in honour of Hayes and Spratt, who initiated the Yorkshire Quern Survey in the mid 1980s (Gwilt and Heslop 1995). They, like Curwen (1929, 63) before them, noted that the fragmentary nature of many beehive querns must point to deliberate breakage as they do not tend to break accidentally or as a result of wearing too thin. They also suggested that quern fragments could have potentially seen several phases of secondary use before being finally deposited in the archaeological record (Gwilt and Heslop 1995, 40). Likewise, saddle querns are also not easily broken and

at Hazleton North, Gloucestershire, where fragments were found in the midden beneath a Neolithic burial chamber, it was suggested that the quern had been broken up elsewhere and pieces selected for deposition (Saville 1990, 198). Similarly, at Ballybrowney, County Cork, Eire, the breaking up of the saddle querns found in the entrance postholes of several Bronze Age structures was considered to be intentional. The coincidence of the locations of the fragments also led to the supposition that, given the association of saddle querns with the production of food, coupled with the perceived liminality of thresholds, their placement was not a purely functional reuse of broken querns as packing stones (Cleary 2006, 20).

Querns in pits came under the scrutiny of Hill in his seminal work on *Ritual and Rubbish in the Iron Age of Wessex* (Hill 1995). This is perhaps the most important and influential work on the general subject of structured deposition. The association between the deposition of querns and the burial of human remains or animal bones and the fact that upper and lower stones, even when fragmentary, were not normally deposited together led Hill (1995, 55, 61, 65) to conclude that their deposition in disused storage pits was not 'just dumping of discarded or broken querns' (the complete quern in a pit at Danebury mentioned above is an important exception, therefore). Hill also noted that many small finds, including querns, found in structured deposits can be associated with the transformation of raw materials into usable, needful products and suggests that querns may have been symbolically linked to the preparation of food, gender and the lifecycle of the household (Hill 1995, 108, 131).

Lifecycles and transformations are the corner stones

Introduction

of Brück's research on Middle and Late Bronze Age settlements (Brück 1999a; Brück 2001; also Brück 1999b; Brück 2006). She suggests that metaphorical analogies existed between human lifecycles and those of houses and certain artefacts such as querns, pots and metal objects through which social relationships and the passage of time were comprehended. Brück's work covers much ground through which the gradual development of querns as symbols of transformation and regeneration can be seen. Thus querns, which she describes as 'essential for the preparation of food', are initially seen as 'potent symbol[s] of life, fertility and productivity'. She suggests that, like people, querns were subject to transforming rites of passage and were often 'burnt, broken and buried' at death (Brück 1999b, 155; Brück 2001, 152). Brück (2001) further suggests that this fragmentation, together with that of people, houses and other objects, was an important part of Bronze Age cosmology, the means through which death was harnessed and the cycle of life and death ensured. Brück also sees the grinding action of the quern as a particularly powerful metaphor for the transformation from life to death. Querns, therefore, she suggests 'must have been redolent with the symbolism of death and rebirth' which she says 'explains the presence of so many quernstones in event-marking deposits on Middle and Late Bronze Age settlements' (Brück 2001, 155). Brück's theories are most persuasive but as shown below there are other reasons that could account firstly for the presence of querns in the archaeological record and secondly for their fragmentation before entering that record. Moreover, not all querns were broken prior to deposition.

The apparent 'deliberate fragmentation' of querns prior to deposition is also highlighted by Chapman (2000b; Chapman and Gaydarska 2007). He considers a number of reasons to account for the presence of broken objects in the archaeological record such as post-depositional accidental breakage, the scattering of pieces to promote fertility, the burial of broken objects or the ritual killing of objects. However, the incompleteness of objects led Chapman to conclude that this breakage may have been part of an enchainment process, linking peoples and places, in which pieces were taken off site for curation and eventual deposition elsewhere. The fact that querns do not break easily and are frequently found in archaeological contexts as single fragments lends credence to Chapman's suggestion. However, although joining fragments of quern have been found from different contexts within a single site, none, to the author's knowledge have been found originating from different sites but little work has been done in this field and further research may prove Chapman's theory. But other causes, such as the deliberate breakage and dispersal of fragments through the spreading of midden material could also account for missing fragments. Likewise, the ritual killing or sacrifice of objects could also have resulted in fragmentation. These latter two theories are especially important with regard to the inherent symbolism between grain, querns and fertility.

The association between animal bone and querns highlighted by Hill, above, was also noted by Proctor (2002) in an article on a series of Late Bronze Age/Early Iron Age pits at Carshalton, Surrey. Proctor takes Buckley's comments on board regarding the arrangement of artefacts, including a horse skull and quern fragments, in one of the pits, concluding that they were 'deliberately and carefully placed' (Proctor 2002, 95). She suggests that the choice of artefacts as special deposits was determined by their importance to the community, querns being identified, for example, as essential for grinding grain. Proctor concludes that, as at Danebury, the deposit was perhaps an offering to promote fertility, made as a constituent part of an agricultural lifecycle that could easily be hit by disease and crop failure (Proctor 2002, 96-101).

Ancestors and families rather than gods provide the meaning behind Pryor's interpretation of the structured deposits of querns and other artefacts in the Neolithic causewayed enclosure at Etton, Cambridgeshire (Pryor 1998b, 61-64; Pryor 2003, 164-169). He comments particularly on a complete saddle quern placed on its side in a small pit, overlying a rubber (Figure 1.7). This he describes as 'the world turned upside down' suggesting that the quern had been 'killed' and buried for use, not in this world but the next. He further suggests that all artefacts had a symbolic as well as an everyday meaning and that consequently nothing was placed in the ground merely as unwanted material; the fragmentary quernstones found in the ditches, for example, representing the family (Pryor 1998b, 61-64; Pryor 2003, 169). However, grain is generally not considered to have been grown for everyday consumption during the Neolithic period (Richmond 1999, 42; Thomas 1999, 25; Pollard 2002, 10). Consequently, the deposition of querns at such sites is perhaps more likely to have had an esoteric meaning rather than being related to familial events.

Robinson (2007, 94-101) returns to Brück's theory of

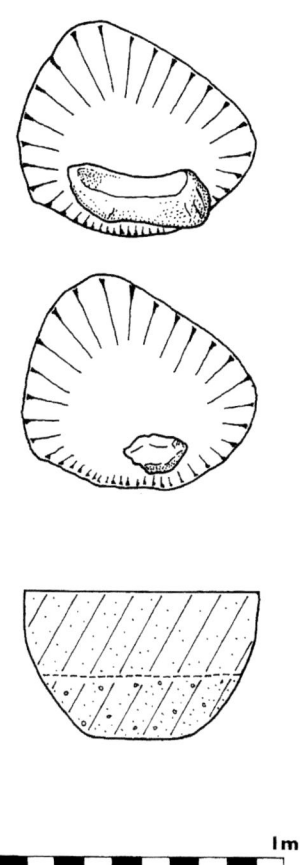

Figure 1.7: Saddle quern and rubber in Pit F711, Etton, Cambridgeshire (M. Watts after Pryor 1988a, Figure 111).

lifecycles in his commentary on structured deposition in *The Prehistoric Landscape of Scilly*. He suggests that querns, representative of the 'life of the household', were broken and used within abandonment deposits upon the death of the house. He also suggests that artefacts may have been utilised in the construction of new houses to create a link from the present to the past (Robinson 2007, 97-98).

The importance of querns to earlier Neolithic communities in Britain, as shown by their structured deposition at causewayed enclosures such as Etton, mentioned above, and also within the construction of long barrows such as Wayland's Smithy, Oxfordshire, is further highlighted by the author in an article on object biography (Watts, S. 2008a). It is suggested that the fact that querns are rarely found on later Neolithic sites, which coincides with an apparent drop in cereal cultivation, implies that the significance of querns to Neolithic communities lay in their function as tools for grinding grain. Watts follows the theory suggested by Thomas (1999, 16), Pollard (2002, 10) and others that grain is not considered to have been grown on a large scale in the Neolithic period. She consequently suggests that the symbolical association between querns, grain and fertility, life and death may have been a pre-existing belief, introduced to Britain as part of a Neolithic 'cultural package' that encompassed ideology as well as agricultural techniques and other aspects of material culture. The apparent lack of grain cultivation in the British Neolithic is now being questioned, however, by some archaeologists who have suggested that grain was in fact more important to Neolithic communities than was previously thought (Jones and Rowley-Conwy 2007). However, neither scenario detracts from the importance of querns to Neolithic communities or from the theory of an imported symbology.

Heslop also concludes that the deposition of querns was linked to propitiation of the gods and agricultural fertility in his publication on *Patterns of Quern Production, Acquisition and Deposition* (Heslop 2008, 80, 82). This comprehensive work, which presents the data collected from north Yorkshire and south Durham as part of the Yorkshire Quern Survey not only includes chapters on the morphology, petrology, quarries and distribution of beehive querns but also includes helpful sections on fragmentation and deposition. Although the book is primarily concerned with Iron Age (beehive) rotary querns, Heslop also looks briefly at the deposition of saddle querns in the light of Brück's theory of transformation and death but notes that in the Iron Age depositions associated with boundaries received increased attention. He reiterates the point that many querns were deliberately broken before their deposition and observes that each fragment appears to have been treated differently and separately, with fragments from the same quern rarely being found in the same context. He also notes a contrast between querns found on site, which tend to be fragmentary and those found off-site which tend to be complete. These he suggests represent votive deposits, placed at significant points in the landscape, with a potential mutual exclusivity between the location of iron hoards and quern deposits. Interestingly, a similar pattern has also been noted in Ireland (Heslop 2008, 68-80; Waddell 1998, 323).

Finally, in their article on early medieval quernstones, O'Sullivan and Kenny (2008) demonstrate well that the structured deposition of querns is a phenomenon that continued well beyond the prehistoric period. Using examples from early medieval Ireland, they return to Brück's theory that quernstones and other artefacts were placed in pits or foundations to mark particular

Introduction

points in the lifecycle of a house. They, like Robinson, emphasise the role of querns in household food production and suggest that broken querns symbolise a cessation of this activity. However, they also note the inclusion of quern fragments in the fabric of corn-drying kilns and suggest that in this context the reuse of querns may denote some form of votive deposit to ensure the safety of the harvest and the regeneration and continuity of life (O'Sullivan and Kenny 2008). Thus, as at Trethellan Farm, a potential dichotomy of meaning can also be seen on medieval Irish sites suggesting that querns were deposited with different levels and layers of meaning.

1.3.2 The European perspective
In addition to literature pertaining to British sites there is also a useful and growing body of published literature relating to continental sites. This shows that not only is the structured deposition of querns a pan-European phenomenon that was initiated in the Neolithic period but also that querns are to be found in structured deposits both in and beyond the domestic arena. Fendin (2000, 88), for example, notes that querns are found in wetlands, graves, ceremonial structures, wells and also within settlements, in postholes and hearths. She suggests that the deposition of querns within 'functionally odd' contexts is related to their 'special properties', that there was a metaphorical link between the action of grinding and notions of transformation, reproduction and the passage of time as manifested in human and agricultural lifecycles (Fendin 2000; Fendin 2006).

Chapman (2000b, 94), on the other hand, sees the deposition of querns as related to symbolic aspects of the home, the preparation of food and also, given their origin beyond the immediate settlement, of the wider social network. Chapman's (2000c) work in the Balkans demonstrates the deposition of querns on domestic sites well. He fully concurs with Hill (1995, 16, 30) and Brück's (1999a) assertions that interpretations of past behavioural practices are hindered by the modern western value of rubbish and that to prehistoric peoples secular and ritual activities were one and the same. He suggests that the choice of materials chosen for deposition was related to local practices, although these may have been set within wider cosmological frameworks (Chapman 2000c, 61-63). As far as the structured deposition of querns is concerned, Chapman gives an impressive example of a special deposit of 21 fragments of saddle querns placed in piles in a pit under the floor of a Copper Age house at Vermeşti, Romania (4500-4000/3700 cal. BC), with three pairs of rubbers placed on top of them. All the grinding surfaces were face downwards. Also of note are the inclusion of querns in pits with unusual collections of artefacts and the association of querns with human remains such as the lower and upper stones laid beside a child burial in a pit at Traian, Romania of similar date (Chapman 2000c, 69-76).

Lidström Holmberg also makes an association between querns and human burials in her paper on *Saddle Querns and Gendered Dynamics of the Early Neolithic in Mid Central Sweden* (Lidström Holmberg 2004). She notes the different depositional treatment of upper and lower stones and suggests that their separate placements was one of the ways through which gender relations were negotiated. As a tool with two separate but necessary parts the quern is seen as symbolic of relationships, the upper and lower stones representative (although not always) of males and females respectively (Lidström Holmberg 2004, 222-227). Conversely, Hamon's (2008a) research on Neolithic settlements in northern France and Belgium noted that lower and upper stones tended to be deposited together in specially dug pits associated with dwellings. Hamon considers a number of reasons to account for their presence but concludes that they are abandonment deposits, a symbolic expression of an agricultural, settled community.

A recent paper on *Subsistence, Social and Ritual Practices* compares the different contexts of quern deposition during the Neolithic periods in central, west and northern Europe, Britain and Greece (Graefe *et al* 2009). Using examples from domestic, communal and funereal contexts, Graefe *et al* show that points of commonality can be perceived in depositional practices across Europe despite the differences in dating and cultures. These, it is suggested, are linked to new cosmologies and identities based on the emergence of agricultural economies. The paper also introduces the concept of 'closed' and 'open deposits', highlighting the important difference between, for example, querns used as foundation deposits whose placement was intended to be permanent and irretrievable and querns that were stored in the ground with the intention of future reclamation or included within contexts that were left open for the purpose of placing further deposits. The large number of querns and fragments found in a pit in the Neolithic settlement at Makriyalos in Greece (5300-5000/4900 cal BC) which it is suggested were associated with rituals connected to a significant communal feasting event, may be seen as an example of a closed deposit. Also of note are the multiple quern deposits found in ritual wetland sites and communal burial mounds in Sweden (Graefe *et al* 2009, 89, 90, 92).

Much of the European research on the structured deposition of querns has, like the article mentioned above, tended towards the Neolithic period. Mention should also be made, therefore, of an article by Jodry and Féliu (2009) on two depositions of rotary quernstones found in recent years in the Alsace region of France; one on a site at Wiwersheim, the other within the oppidum at Pandours à Saverne. In both cases, the stones were found together with other artefacts in pits dated to the Late Iron Age (Figure 1.8). The complete manner in which the querns were deposited and the items which accompanied them led Jodry and Féliu to conclude that the deposits were ritual in nature, perhaps offerings to the relevant deities, and derived from tools and objects that best symbolised the agricultural way of life of the communities that used them.

1.3.3 A world-wide phenomenon
Finally, two publications serve to illustrate that the practice of placing querns in the ground with purpose or meaning is not solely confined to Europe. Firstly, in *The Origins of Agriculture in the Lowland Neotropics*, Piperno and Pearsall refer to a tomb lined with metates and manos and also to caches of grinding stones within the settlement at Real Alto, Ecuador dated *circa* 4000BP. These they suggest reference rituals concerned with the harvest (Piperno and Pearsall 1998, 254-255). Secondly, in an article on rotary querns in India, Sankalia (1959, 128) mentions some 60 fragments of rotary quern found on the earliest floor of a house at Sirpur dated to the 6th-7th century AD.

1.3.4 Discussion
The published literature cited above shows that, although the structured deposition of querns is becoming an increasingly featured topic, it tends to be incorporated within individual site reports and analyses or within wider thematic studies. The articles by Buckley (1993), Graefe *et al* (2009) and also O'Sullivan and Kenny (2008) are important exceptions, therefore. Heslop (2008, 73-80) also includes an overview of the depositional contexts of querns in his work on querns from North Yorkshire and South Durham. There has, however, been little in-depth research on a regional basis exclusively pertaining to the structured deposition of querns.

It must also be said that most literature tends to focus on the 'cream' of the practice and in order to investigate it more fully less obvious deposits should also be considered. As mentioned earlier there is a reason for the position and location of all artefacts within the archaeological record and, as indicated at Trethellan Farm and Danebury for example, different levels or categories of structured deposit can potentially be identified. Nevertheless, it is the prime examples that raise our awareness of the phenomenon and show that querns function on more than a purely utilitarian, practical level.

The literature also demonstrates that the structured deposition of querns is both a long-lasting and widespread practice. As the paper by Graefe *et al* (2009) shows the custom is found across Europe and appears to date back to the beginnings of cereal cultivation in the Neolithic period. This lends credence to the theory

Figure 1.8: Rotary querns in the bottom of a pit in the oppidum of Pandours à Saverne, Alsace, France (C. Féliu 2005, University of Strasbourg).

Introduction

proposed by Watts, S. (2008a, 100) that the use of querns in structured deposits was a practice introduced to Britain from the continent. However, Piperno and Pearsall's (1998, 254-255) reference to the structured depositions of querns in Ecuador *circa* 4000BP stretches the phenomenon across the world to the Americas. This may indicate that the practice is a universal norm, to be expected wherever subsistence communities who follow such customs have concerns over the harvest. On the other hand if, as suggested by Pailler and Sheridan (2009) for example, the uptake of the Neolithic culture in Britain was due in part to migrant settlers, and if cereals were not regularly grown as a subsistence crop as suggested by Thomas (1999, 16) and Pollard (2002, 10), then the possibility that the deposition of querns was an imported practice becomes more valid. In either scenario the importance of querns to early subsistence societies is highlighted.

The literature also highlights two potentially contradictory issues. Firstly, is the fact that upper and lower stones may be deposited separately or together and secondly, that querns may be broken prior to deposition or deposited whole. As Seager Thomas (1999, 45) rightly points out a quern comprises two stones, and thus the separation of the stones renders the quern inoperable. This basic tenet echoes throughout history in laws relating to querns. The laws of Moses, for example, state that one should not take an upper stone as a pledge for that would be like taking a man's life away (Deuteronomy 24:6) and under 10th century Welsh law, in the event of a divorce, the wife was to have the lower stone and the man the upper (Bennett and Elton 1898, 162). This suggests that there is a difference in meaning between depositions of complete querns and those of either upper or lower stones.

Likewise, differences in meaning are also perceived between the depositions of whole or fragmentary querns. The former can potentially be used again, the latter, on the other hand, are broken, perhaps deliberately, to permanently remove them from circulation. Several contrasting theories, however, are presented to account for their fragmentation. Chapman (2000b, 94) proposes that fragments were distributed as part of an 'enchainment process' linking peoples and places whereas Brück (1999b, 155; 2001) suggests that such fragmentation is representative of death. O'Sullivan and Kenny (2008, 11), although agreeing with Brück's interpretation in relation to houses, see the reuse of quern fragments in the context of corn drying kilns as symbolic of life and the harvest. At first glance these seemingly opposed interpretations present a confusing picture but they are in fact different although related aspects of similar underlying cosmologies. These theories also suggest that querns should not be considered simple objects with a 'one size fits all' meaning and that the traditional symbolic link between querns and agricultural lifecycles and fertility suggested by some authors is too simplistic. Generally, however, these symbolic associations are only assumed through the implication of the use of querns for grinding grain. Although Watts, S. (2008a, 100) has suggested that the clues to the origins of this symbolism may be found in mythology, this subject has received little attention. In addition to the different treatments accorded querns prior to their deposition, often within the same site, the literature also suggests a link between querns and thresholds, and deposits of human and animal bone and the use of burnt querns in abandonment deposits.

One aspect of depositionary practice found in Europe and which, on current evidence, is not generally found in mainland Britain, however, is the deposition of multiple querns and fragments, an exception being the seven saddle querns recovered from a Neolithic pit at Barford, Warwickshire (Buckley 1993, 3). This quantity, however, pales into insignificance beside the 800 complete and fragmentary querns from Makriyalos (Graefe *et al* 2009, 90). Nevertheless, the implication is that the querns from Barford, like the continental deposits are related to large communal events. Likewise, it is suggested that the concentrations of grinding stones found at Real Alto are linked to rituals connected with the harvest (Piperno and Pearsall 1998, 254-255). The fact that maize is considered to have been a ceremonial feast food at this time suggests that the deposits may have been made in a similar vein to that at Makriyalos. In this respect, it is worth further considering the proposal by Van der Veen and Jones (2006) that storage pits on hillforts were grain repositories for feasting rather than sowing. This suggests that large quantities of grain would have been processed for consumption on particular occasions and has implications for the use and deposition of querns on these sites.

The role of querns in prehistoric societies appears, therefore, to be an important consideration in furthering our understanding of their use as structured deposits. Consequently, it is necessary to better appreciate how they were used and functioned in the communities that ultimately deposited them in the archaeological record.

1.4 Research Objectives and Methodology

The main aims of this research were firstly, to investigate, through the medium of querns, the principles of structured depositon. To what extent do the querns recovered from prehistoric sites and structures appear to have been deliberately placed in structured meaningful ways as opposed to being unthinkingly discarded as useless, unwanted material?

Secondly, to demonstrate, by taking an everyday artefact, that the practice of structured deposition was not confined purely to 'exotic' items but also included domestic tools. Furthermore that these everyday items were also deposited in non-domestic contexts suggesting they had roles to play other than the utilitarian. Thirdly to consider the possible motives and meanings behind the structured deposition of querns and finally to raise the awareness of the significance to prehistoric communities of tools that today are often considered to be mundane, utilitarian artefacts.

To achieve these objectives, three avenues of approach were taken. Firstly, a fresh look at the origins and development of saddle and rotary querns and their introduction to the British Isles. Such factors would have greatly influenced their respective meanings and values within prehistoric societies. Secondly, an exploration of the object biography or life history of the quern as witnessed in the archaeological, historic and ethnographic record, in order to more fully appreciate how querns functioned within those societies on both practical and symbolic levels. Through this it was hoped to gain a better understanding of the potential meaning(s) behind the inclusion of querns in structured deposits. Thirdly, an analysis of the contexts in which querns are found on prehistoric sites in the south-west of England, looking at the distribution and type of sites on which querns are found, the numbers and general form and condition of the querns found, the different features and contexts in which they are found and the artefacts that accompanied them. Is it possible to identify different categories of deposit that could be indicative of different levels of meaning and intent? Can changes be perceived that may relate to spatial or temporal variations in practice? Can the importance of querns to prehistoric communities on both practical and symbolic levels, as presumed from historical and ethnographic evidence, be inferred from the contexts in which querns are found in the archaeological record?

1.4.1 The study area
The area chosen for the basis of this research was the south-west peninsula of England stretching from the Isles of Scilly in the far west to the valleys of the Rivers Britt, Frome and Avon in the east. The area, broadly bounded on the east by the oolitic limestone, corresponds with the counties of Cornwall, Devon, Somerset, North Somerset and Bristol together with a small piece of south-west Dorset to the west of Bridport (Figure 1.9).

Querns have generally been little studied in the area, other than for individual site reports and no overview of the region as a whole has yet been undertaken. Consequently little analysis has been done in the region on the structured deposition of querns except on an individual site basis. Such studies, however, are beginning to demonstrate well that the practice of placing objects in the ground was of some import to prehistoric communities, perhaps creating a sense of place or marking significant events. This research marks a timely opportunity, therefore, to explore through querns the concept of structured deposition across a wider region, to determine if the local patterns of deposition found are part of a broader practice.

1.4.2 Categories in the structured deposition of querns
Structured deposition may now be a widely recognised phenomenon of the prehistoric period but as suggested above not all deposits were made with the same sense of purpose or level of intent. How then can different categories of deposition be identified?

The published literature highlights two facets of quern deposition that have an important bearing on the recognition of different types of deposit. Firstly, the tendency for upper and lower stones to be deposited separately and secondly that stones may be in a complete or fragmentary state. The deposition of paired stones can be viewed as unusual and potentially significant, therefore. Likewise the deposition of complete and potentially reusable stones can also be seen as important. Both these categories of deposition have that 'alerting quality' alluded to by Hill (1995, 96) and Thomas (1999, 65). However, levels of intent can also be seen in the deposition of fragments placed with apparent care and deliberation in particular contexts or features or with unusual combinations of artefacts or made of an exotic stone. At the other end of the scale are quern fragments in deposits that have no evidence of structure, arrangement or apparent choice of artefact and which, to all intents and purposes, appear to be no more than buried rubbish or occupation detritus. There is also a raft of non-structured deposits including unstratified site finds, topsoil and general surface finds and those querns whose final resting place in the archaeological

Introduction

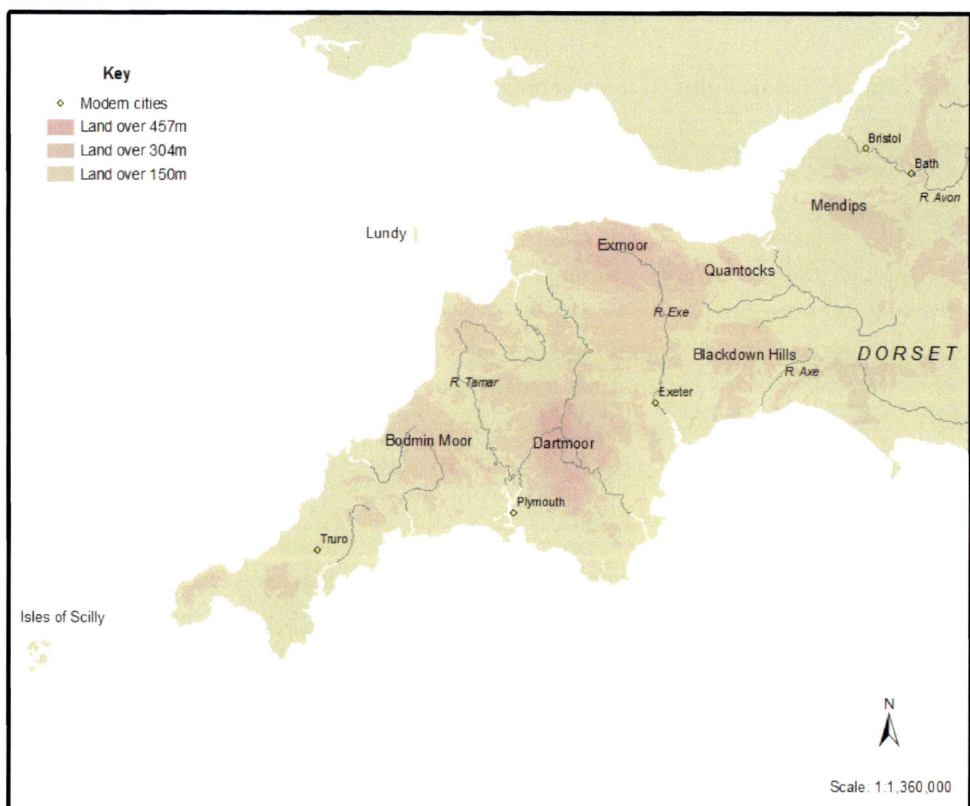

Figure 1.9: Map of study area.

record is due to post-depositional movement caused by human or environmental disturbance. These latter deposits, however, as detailed below, are not included in the analysis.

Also of import are the different contexts in which quernstones are found. Hill (1995, 110-111) has suggested that similar deposits can be found in a range of below ground features including pits, ditches and gullies and that it was the act of placing something in the ground that was important, not the location. However, each depositional location is likely to have been selected for a particular reason. Boundary ditches, for example, provide potentially different symbolic opportunities compared to storage pits or roundhouse postholes and contrasts can also be envisaged between depositions made on domestic and non-domestic sites. Thus the meaning behind each deposition, although they may include similar items, will have been different. In addition, deposits may be open, that is made with the intention of future interaction of some form, or closed and finite (Graefe *et al* 2009).

1.4.3 Collation and limitations of the data
For the analysis a database was compiled containing, as far as was possible, the contextual and statistical information for all querns found within structured deposits across the study area from the Neolithic period through to the end of the Iron Age. Data collection began in January 2005 and continued until August 2011. Information was taken from all available published and unpublished, grey and on-line, literature and included antiquarian investigations dating back to the mid 19th century and reports of individual finds. Consequently, the quality and quantity of the recorded data for each quern varies considerably. As Coles (1987, 9) points out, it is 'not possible to extract all of the kinds of information which we now seek, from a site excavated…years ago'.

The Lake Villages of Glastonbury and Meare in Somerset, primarily excavated by Arthur Bulleid and Harold St. George Gray in the period 1892-1907 and 1908-1956 respectively, are a case in point. Although the majority of finds were plotted horizontally they were not done so vertically. Also artefacts were assigned to a particular mound whether or not they actually lay within it. In addition, a number of quern fragments, particularly from Meare West, were not given small find numbers but simply grouped together as having come from a particular mound. These omissions are primarily due to the methods of excavation and recording used but also to a lack of experience on the part of Bulleid together with the nature of the sites, the speed of the work and the wealth of artefacts that poured out of the ground (Coles 1987, 15; Coles and Minnitt 2000, 24-27). As the purpose of the research was to seek out those querns with good contextual information through which to investigate the phenomenon of structured deposition, unprovenanced finds in museums, churches and private collections were not included in the main database. This proved a particular problem on the Isles of Scilly where many querns and other stone objects collected from fields and beaches now reside in gardens (Figure 1.10). Not only are there few records of whence these querns originally came but the situation is made more complicated here by the fact that querns remained in use on the Isles of Scilly until at least the 18th century (Borlase 1756, 28; Ratcliffe 1991, 67). That said, however, more recent rotary querns tend to be flatter and wider than their Iron Age and Roman counterparts. Also excluded from the main database were unstratified site finds and those recovered from topsoil deposits or which had been subject to post-depositional processes. These included 15 quernstones found on the surface just outside and within the ramparts of Berrywood Hillfort, Newton Abbot, Devon which are thought to have been collected from the interior of the hillfort when the area was cleared for a fete in 1855 (Gallant and Silvester 1985, 39, 47).

1.4.4 Dating parameters

Although as recent work demonstrates (Webster 2008) many sites in terms of material culture can be shown to lie athwart the divides of the traditional three-age system of Neolithic, Bronze and Iron Age, it was nevertheless decided to base the analysis on these three periods. There are several reasons for this decision. Firstly, although as several authors, including Griffith and Quinnell (1999a, 55) and Johns (2011), have pointed out, these divisions create artificial event horizons, the use of the three-age system remains a useful and well-known means of dividing up the time period between *circa* 4000BC and AD43. Secondly, many querns, particularly those from older excavations, are currently only broadly datable to one period or another. Thirdly, it was hoped that by encompassing the introduction of the rotary quern in the Middle Iron Age any changes in depositional patterns of saddle querns might be made more manifest. Such sites as lie on the cusp of the Neolithic-Bronze Age or Bronze-Iron Age are tended towards what is considered to be the most appropriate period.

Where no specific date is mentioned the following broad dating parameters have been assumed:

Earlier Neolithic	*circa* 4000-3000BC
Later Neolithic	*circa* 3000-2000BC
Early Bronze Age	*circa* 2000-1500BC
Middle Bronze Age	*circa* 1500-1100BC
Late Bronze Age	*circa* 1100-700BC

Figure 1.10: Unprovenanced querns in Tresco Abbey Gardens, Isles of Scilly (centimetre scale) (S. Watts).

Early Iron Age	*circa* 700-300BC
Middle Iron Age	*circa* 300-100BC
Late Iron Age	*circa* 100BC-AD43

The end of the Iron Age is traditionally taken to be the Roman invasion of AD43 although the date of the conquest of the south-west is later, from circa AD49 (Holbrook 2008, 151). On multi-period sites such as Carn Euny, Cornwall and Cadbury Castle, Somerset which saw phases of activity extending into the Roman period and beyond only those querns whose contexts can be assigned to the prehistoric period were included in the database.

Before proceeding to the results of the analysis, however, it is now considered timely to turn to the history and development of the quern and its object biography. The first is a necessary step in understanding the introduction and use of the saddle and rotary quern to Britain and their relative importance to prehistoric societies. The second complements the typological study demonstrating the important role that querns play in the lives of subsistence communities and hence why they should have been used as structured deposits during the prehistoric period.

2

THE EARLY CHRONOLOGICAL DEVELOPMENT OF THE QUERN

2.1 Introduction

A quern[1] can be defined as a hand-operated mill for grinding grain and other products. It comprises two stones, a stationary lower one and a moveable hand-operated upper one. There are two basic forms of quern, non-rotating and rotating. The earliest type is non-rotating and is generally referred to in British archaeological literature as a saddle quern, so-called for the characteristic concave shape of its upper, grinding surface on which grain was ground with a forward and back motion using a hand-held upper stone called a rubber or muller (Figure 2.1). Related to the saddle quern are saucer or basin querns which are rounder in shape and trough querns which, as the name implies, have deep, trough-like grinding surfaces and are usually much larger in size (Figure 2.2). It should be noted, however, that the grinding surfaces of some saddle querns are flat due either to the relative length of the rubber or to the fact that the stone has been less used compared to others. The Olynthus mill or hopper rubber is a sophisticated form of saddle quern mounted on a platform and operated with a lever and which is found in the Greek World in the latter half of the 1st millennium BC (Figure 4.1) (Frankel 2003).

The second form of quern is the rotary quern, (Figure 2.1, 2.3) comprising two circular stones, one of which is rotated above the other by means of a projecting handle. British Iron Age rotary querns are often referred to as beehive querns, due to their morphological resemblance to an old fashioned straw bee skep. Another form of rotary quern is the pot quern (Figure 4.3). This was introduced in the medieval period and derives its name from the shape of the lower stone which has a cylindrical recess cut within it. The upper stone turns within this recess and the ground meal is expelled through a spout in the side of the lower stone.

The quern is related to the mortar and both tools can be used to process similar materials. However, there is a fundamental difference in their method of use. Material is ground on a quern with a forwards and backwards or circular motion, that is the upper stone moves across the lower stone, whereas material is pounded in a mortar using a pestle with an up and down motion (Nesbitt and Samuel 1996, 47-48). It should also be noted that the grinding action of a quern cuts or shears the material with a scissor like-action, rather than crushing it (Horsfall 1987, 348).

Figure 2.1: Saddle quern (top) and rotary quern (bottom) (M. Watts).

---

1. The word 'quern' derives from the Saxon *cweorn* which, like the Old Norse *kvern*, comes from a pre-Teutonic stem, $g^w ern$, which may be descended from a proto-Indo-European word $k^b r\bar{a}u$ and is similar to the Russian, *zhernov*, the Latvian *dziřnus*, the Lithuanian *girnos* and the Polish, *żarna* (Simpson and Weiner 1989a, 4; Kelly 2002, 9). It is a well-established word in English literature, mentioned in the Lindisfarne Gospels and used by both Chaucer and Shakespeare. The use of the word continued into antiquarian and early archaeological literature and hence to the present day.

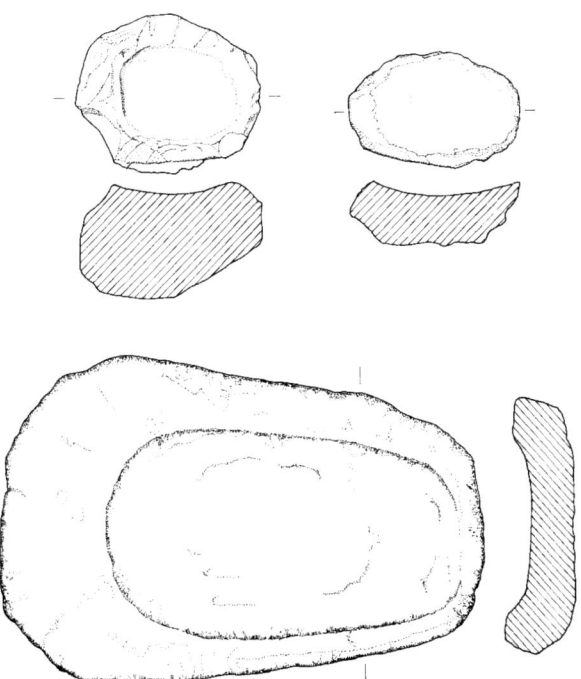

Figure 2.2: Saucer-type quern from Windmill Hill, Wiltshire (top left), saddle quern from Wayland's Smithy, Oxfordshire (top right) and trough quern from Fallaws, Angus (bottom) (M. Watts after Smith 1965, Figure 52.S16; Whittle 1991, Figure 11.10; Close-Brooks 1983, Figure 1.1).

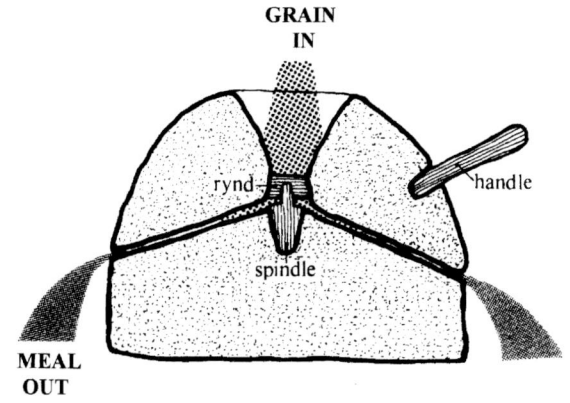

Figure 2.3: Cross-section of a rotary quern (southern/Wessex type) showing the (invisible) passage of grain between the stones and the rynd, spindle and handle (M. Watts).

2.2 The Saddle Quern

Stones have been used to grind and pound vegetable, mineral and animal products for many thousands of years. The earliest known grinding stones come from the Neanderthal occupation sites in the Dordogne, *circa* 50,000BP and from Florisbad, Orange Free State and the Bushman Rock Shelter in the eastern Transvaal, South Africa which are dated to 48,900BP and 46,950-42,950BP respectively (Beaune 2003, 21; Kraybill 1977, 495). Fragments dating to *circa* 28,000BP were found at Cuddie Springs, New South Wales, Australia and other early examples have been found at Bilancino, Italy, dated *circa* 25,000BP, at Ohalo II, Israel and Wadi Kubbaniya, Egypt dated 18,400-18,100 BP and in the Darling Basin of New South Wales, Australia dated 18,000-15,000BP (Fullagar and Field 1997; Aranguren *et al* 2007; Piperno *et al* 2004; Hamilton 1980, 14; Bloxam 2011, 46).

However, recent research on mortars and querns from a number of Natufian and Neolithic sites in the Levant, *circa* 12,800-9,300BP, suggests the beginnings of cereal cultivation in that area during that time led to an increasing use of the saddle-type quern (Dubreuil 2004; Wright 2000, 98). This development has been shown to be linked not so much to the cultivation of grain itself but to the adoption of subsistence strategies founded on meal-based products (Adams 1999). The saddle quern, with its flatter grinding surface, would have been more effective than mortar type stones for grinding grain sufficiently finely to obtain the maximum release of nutrients. It also had the advantage of being easier to manufacture (Wright 2000, 98; Dubreuil 2004, 1626). The coincidence of the potential specialisation of saddle querns for grinding grain with the beginnings of agriculture has great implications for the development of symbolic meanings associated with querns and their place in structured deposits. It is also suggested (Dubreuil 2005, 56; Haaland 1997) that the organisation and allocation of domestic tasks associated with grinding may date from this time.

Some of the earliest evidence for agricultural practice comes from Abu Hureyra, a settlement in the valley of the Euphrates in northern Syria. Here the inhabitants began to cultivate cereals and lentils alongside their foraging and hunting *circa* 11,000BP. Grain and other plant foods were processed with mortars and pestles, fine-grained basalt grinding dishes, which may also have been heated to parch the grain, and coarser grained saddle querns, two of which were found in situ on the floor of the large pit in which they had been used (Figure 2.4). Many of the querns, grinding dishes and pestles had traces of red ochre on them indicating that they were also used for grinding pigment (Moore *et al* 2000, 166-169, 492).

Grinding with a saddle quern was hard, physical work putting great strain on the back, knees and toes of the operator kneeling behind it as they applied constant and sufficient pressure to crack and grind the material. The damage caused by such labour is evident on the bones of female skeletons at Abu Hureyra (Molleson 1994). In

Figure 2.4: Two saddle querns in situ in a pit at Abu Hureyra, Syria dated c. 11,500 – 10,000BP (Moore et al 2000, Figure 5.16. By permission of Oxford University Press, USA).

some prehistoric societies the saddle quern was later set in a raised mud brick or clay emplacement which made the task more comfortable (Figure 3.2). Such quern emplacements have been found *in situ* in the Copper Age settlement at Lîga, Bulgaria, established *circa* 4400 cal BC and also in the workers' houses at Amarna in Egypt, a short-lived village founded by Akhenaten *circa* 1360BC and abandoned after his death (Albek 2005, 118; Samuel 1999).

The saddle-type quern appears to have spread with the introduction and adoption of arable farming practices across Europe between the 8th and 5th millennia BC reaching Britain in the 4th millennium BC. Comparatively few grinding tools have been found on mainland European sites dating to the preceding Mesolithic period and none have been recorded, to date, in Britain and Ireland, although stones and natural rock hollows must have been used for grinding foodstuffs and other materials such as ochre (Zvelebil 1994, 56; Woodman 2000, 246). Ethnological evidence suggests, however, that querns are not carried by nomadic communities on a regular basis, except perhaps during the harvesting season, but left at favoured or convenient locations (Gould *et al* 1971, 164; Allen 1974, 315; Hamilton 1980, 8; Gast 2003, 63). Such sites in a Mesolithic context would be most ephemeral. It is possible, therefore, given the traditional archaeological division between Mesolithic hunter-gatherers and Neolithic farmers that some isolated finds of saddle querns have been wrongly attributed to the Neolithic (Barrett 1994, 82-84; Lidström Holmberg 2008, 70). It is also possible that some early Neolithic querns may be Mesolithic in origin. However, although, as Zvelebil (1994, 56) and Lidström Holmberg (2008, 82) assert, querns may well be under-represented in the archaeological record, it must also be borne in mind that Mesolithic communities may not have regularly used querns as a means of processing foodstuffs. Seeds, for example, can be easily gathered, but the intensive labour required for their processing results in little calorific return compared to other starchy plant foods such as edible roots or tubers (Cane 1989, 111; Wright 1994, 243-245; Hardy 2007, 5). Hazelnuts may also be ground into flour but roasting them in a shallow pit results in a good food that has the added advantage of keeping well (Mears and Hillman 2007, 26). Lidström Holmberg's research in Sweden has shown that the Neolithic period saw a transition from flat or shallow bowl-shaped grinding stones used with unmodified pebbles and cobbles as multi-purpose tools for both grinding and polishing to saddle-shaped querns used with a specially shaped upper stone. She suggests (following Adams 1999) that as such technological change is not directly necessary for grinding cereals it may be the result of an increase in plant processing and/or the adoption of new foods (Lidström Holmberg 2004, 207-210; Lidström Holmberg 2008, 84-86). Indeed, use-wear and residue analyses indicate a strong link between Neolithic saddle querns and cereal cultivation, there being no certain evidence for the latter in Europe in the Mesolithic period (Hamon 2008a; Lidström Holmberg 2008, 75; Behre 2007).

In this light it is also worth considering the increase in grinding tools recorded between Mesolithic and Neolithic sites in the Sudan in the 6th millennium BP which is thought to reflect an increasing dependence on plant food and thus its cultivation (Haaland 1995, 169). In South America, the Neolithic period *circa* 3000BC saw the introduction of more elaborately shaped milling stones, used with a two-handed rather than a single-handed rubbing stone. These are also primarily associated with grinding grain. This change, it is suggested, reflects an increasing use of meal-based foods rather than simply the adoption of agriculture (Adams 1999; Katz 2003, 34).

In Britain early examples of saddle querns and rubbers have been found in the midden below Hazleton North long cairn, Gloucestershire, in the primary barrow at Waylands Smithy and in the ditches of the causewayed enclosures at Windmill Hill, Wiltshire, and Etton, Cambridgeshire, all dated to the first half of the 4th millennium cal. BC (Saville 1990, 268; Whittle 1991, 87; Smith 1965, 121-123; Prior 1998a, 257-260; Meadows *et al* 2007; Whittle *et al* 2007; Whittle *et al* 2008). The contexts and state in which the querns were found at these sites incidently demonstrates that querns were amongst the earliest artefacts used as structured deposits.

Neolithic and Early Bronze Age saddle querns vary considerably in size and shape, dependent upon the form and workability of available stone, ranging from chunky saucer or bowl-shaped querns to classically shaped saddle querns to the massive trough querns (Figure 2.2). An example of the latter stood in the inner room of a Neolithic dwelling at Knap of Howar on Papa Westray, Orkney, dated to the later 4th millennium BC. Beside it was a pile of crushed shells with two rubbers. Since the pottery fabric was found to contain shell fragments it is likely that it had been used for grinding pottery temper (Pryor 1998a, 259, 260; Ritchie 1983, 43). This is important as it shows that, in Britain as in the Near East, querns were used for grinding products other than grain from earliest times.

The Bronze Age in Britain saw the introduction of a range of small, neat saddle querns perhaps related to a specific use. Examples of these have been found across southern England at Itford Hill and New Barn Down in Sussex, Thorney Down in Wiltshire, Sigwells in Somerset and Holworthy in Devon (Figure 7.7) (Burstow and Holleyman 1957, 204; Curwen 1934, 116; Stone 1941, 132; Watts, S. 2008b; Watts, S. 2009, 78-79). Smaller saddle querns continued to be a feature of the Iron Age. At Danebury Hillfort in Hampshire, for example, two types of saddle quern were noted, small, oval stones and larger rectangular ones (Laws *et al* 1991, 396). Likewise, both small and large saddle querns were recovered from the Iron Age 'Lake Villages' at Glastonbury and Meare in Somerset and also from Gussage All Saints in Dorset (Bulleid 1917; Gray and Cotton 1966, plate LXIII; Buckley 1979, 89). In Scotland, the trough quern continued to be used, although the trough tended to become a wide, shallow scoop and by the Iron Age these trough querns were giving way to flatter types (Figure 2.5) (Close-Brooks 1983; Hamilton 1956, 49, 50). Trough type querns were also common in west Cornwall and appear to have been used throughout the prehistoric period (Ashbee 1996, 106; Pearce and Padley 1977, 37).

2.3 The Rotary Quern

The saddle quern was the main means of grinding grain and other raw materials in Britain for some three and a half thousand years but in the second half of the 1st millennium BC a new form of milling equipment was introduced, the rotary quern. As mentioned above, this comprises two circular stones, the upper one held in place by means of a spindle projecting from the lower stone and turned by means of a wooden or metal handle (Figure 2.1, 2.3). Grain (or other material) is poured into the quern through the central hole or eye in the upper stone and the ground meal expelled all around the edge between the two stones. A bridge or rynd can be wedged across the eye of the upper stone, if the size of the latter allowed, which pivots on the spindle and the distance between the two stones can be altered, if necessary, to grind coarser or finer. Unlike a saddle quern on which grain is ground due to the pressure exerted through the upper stone by the operator, the gap between the milling surfaces of the upper and lower stones of a rotary quern is fixed at a sufficiently narrow distance to catch and grind the grain. A slightly wider gap, or swallow, at the centre helps draw the grain between the two stones. The only

Figure 2.5: Bronze Age trough querns (left) and Iron Age saddle quern (right), Jarlshof, Shetland (S. Watts).

effort involved, therefore, is that of turning the upper stone, a comparatively easy task once it is in motion.

It is suggested that some rotary querns were operated with an oscillatory rather than fully rotary motion (Heslop 2008, 55; Storck and Teague 1952, 76). The provision of two opposing handle holes found on some beehive querns certainly indicates this possibility as does the shape of a handle found remaining in a quern from Silchester, Berkshire (Figure 2.6) (Thomson 1924, 608; Shaffrey 2003, 153-154). Likewise, the uneven angles of the grinding surfaces on some rotary querns also suggests that they may have been oscillated, leading to increased pressure and wear on one side of the stone. Greater pressure exerted on the nearer side of the quern while turning it can, however, also led to uneven wear. Modern experiments have also shown that it is less tiring to rotate the upper stone completely (Jørgensen 2000, 191). Furthermore, a rotary quern can be operated by more than one person, who sitting either side of the quern each take hold of the handle with one hand and alternately push and pull the upper stone around, making the task not only more companionable but easier and more efficient (Figure 2.7) (Anon 1834, 3; Thomson 1877, 526-527).

The change from the forward and back *modus operandi* of the saddle quern to the rotating motion of the rotary quern marked a great step forward in milling technology. The basic principle of rotating one stone above another was to hold throughout the future of milling with stones being subsequently adapted to animal, water and wind power (Watts, M. 2002, 28; Watts, M. 2008, 9). The origins of such a radical innovation are still open to debate, however. Storck and Teague (1952, 76) refer to 'an intellectual leap of startling abruptness', although Madureri (1984, 734) suggests that the rotary quern developed from a rudimentary version derived from the saddle quern on which the upper stone was twisted rather than being moved back and forth (Figure 2.8). If this were the case then, as Watts, M. (2002, 28) suggests, the oscillatory rotary quern may represent an intermediary stage, a method of use which, as the Silchester quern intimates, continued to find favour. According to Storck and Teague the earliest example of a rotary quern comes from the Lake Van region of Anatolia and dates to about the 8th century BC (Storck and Teague 1952, 77). However, the date is unconfirmed and the excavator was of the opinion that it was later in date and, in the absence of other examples from the vicinity, its authenticity must remain in doubt. The

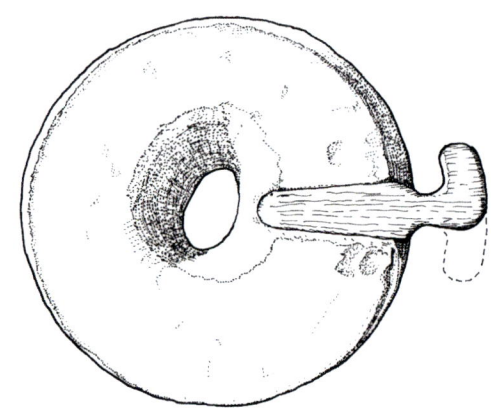

Figure 2.6: Upper stone from Silchester, Berkshire, c. 36.0cm – 37.0cm diameter, with the remains of its wooden handle (M. Watts after Thomson 1924, 608).

Figure 2.7: Women grinding lentils in Tille village, Adyaman province, Turkey (S. Blaylock).

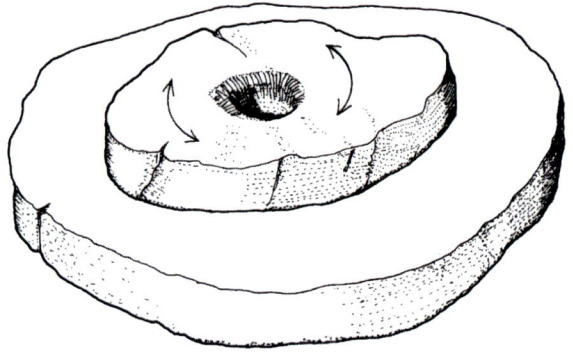

Figure 2.8: Proto rotary quern (M. Watts after Madureri 1984, Figure 49).

earliest reliably dated rotary querns are from Catalonia, Spain where they have been found in contexts dating to the 5th century BC (Alonso *et al* 2009). The rotary quern is probably, therefore, the Spanish mill, the [*molas*] *Hispaniensis unas*, mentioned by Cato in his work on agriculture written in the 1st century BC, which he recommended for an olive yard together with *molae asinariae* (donkey mills) and *molae trusitalis* (saddle querns) (Cato *On Agriculture* 10.4; Childe 1943, 21).

The first use of the rotary quern in Catalonia appears to follow the increase in grain production in the area following the establishment of the Greek trading settlement at Emporion in the 6th century BC. Fields of grain silos are particular features of the indigenous settlements in the area at that time. The appearance of the rotary quern also accords with the initial use of the potter's wheel and an increasing use of iron in that same area (Aquilué *et al* 2000, 19, 41; Alonso 1997, 15-19; Alonso 2002, 111, 122). The serendipitous concurrence of three factors – grain, rotary motion and iron tools – may have provided the need, the inspiration and the means necessary for the formulation of such an innovative process.

Datable evidence suggests that the rotary quern spread from Catalonia to other parts of Spain and eastwards into France and along the Mediterranean coast with early examples being found in the Languedoc region dating to the 4th century BC, and in Italy and Greece dating to the 3rd and 1st centuries BC respectively. It also spread up through France into central Europe reaching Germany by about the 3rd century BC (Reille 2000; Alonso 1997, 17-18; Runnels 1990). The relatively slow expansion around the Hellenistic areas of the Mediterranean may perhaps be explained by the fact that these areas were developing other forms of milling equipment, namely the Olynthus mill and the Pompeiian type donkey mill at about the same time (Frankel 2003; Runnels 1990). However, the presence of rotary querns at sites such as Gussage All Saints, Dorset, Danebury and Easton Lane, Winchester in Hampshire, Dalton Parlours in West Yorkshire, Thorpe Thewles in Cleveland, and Wanlip and Hallam Fields, Leicestershire indicate that they were already in widespread use across England by the Middle Iron Age suggesting an introduction in the 4th century BC (Buckley 1979; Cunliffe 1995a, 69; Cunliffe 1995b, 114; Fasham *et al* 1989, 107; Heslop 2008, 20; Buckley and Major 1990; Thomas 2010). Indeed evidence from Fairfield Park, Bedfordshire potentially points to an initial use as early as the 5th century BC (Shaffrey 2006). This raises the possibility that the rotary quern was introduced to Britain direct from the Iberian peninsula or that it may even have developed independently here at a time which, as in Catalonia, coincides with an increase in grain production and in the use of iron (Haselgrove 1999, 125, 129).

It has been suggested, however, that the development and diffusion of the rotary quern may owe as much to its efficiency for grinding mineral ore as milling grain (Domergue *et al* 1997, 57; Greene 1997, 227). Such diverse uses would presumably have had profound effects on the cultural significance and associated symbolism attached to particular querns (Watts, S. 2008a, 95). Saddle querns were certainly used for crushing ore in the Bronze Age, as evidenced from the mine at Cwmystwyth in North Wales and also possibly at the metalworking site at Lough Eskragh in County Tyrone and as examples from Danebury, Hampshire and St. Austell, Cornwall suggest this application continued into the Iron Age (Barber 2003, 112; Tabor 2008, 64; Williams 1978; Laws *et al* 1991, 396; Johns forthcoming).

However, although as Diodorus (3.13.2) states gold ore was ground to powder prior to smelting, such fineness was generally not necessary, particularly for iron ore. Alluvial tin ore was probably pure enough to negate the need for crushing (Craddock 1995, 161-162; Newman 1998, 30, 40; Gerrard 2000, 104). Craddock (1995, 161) suggests that for iron ore pea-sized nuggets would have been the most favourable size to enable gases to circulate within the furnace. It is likely, therefore, that most iron ore was broken up to the required size using hammerstones rather than rotary querns. Craddock (1995, 162) further suggests that many querns found on metalworking sites would not have been hard enough to grind ore and that they were probably for grinding grain. As he comments, 'even miners have to eat' (Craddock 1995, 162). Crazing mills were used in Devon and Cornwall from the medieval period until the mid 16th century for grinding ore from dry stamping mills or waste from dressing floors. They went out of use with the introduction of the wet stamp in the 16th century (Gerrard 2000, 120).

It should perhaps also be noted that, although there are exceptions such as Danebury in Hampshire, Brooklands in Surrey, Bryn y Castell in Gwynedd and Culduthel Farm near Inverness, ore crushing and smelting, particularly in the earlier part of the Iron Age, is thought to have generally taken place on sites removed from domestic settlement and, therefore, rotary querns found on the latter are perhaps more likely to have been used for food preparation (Hingley 1997, 10-11; Haselgrove 1999, 125; Pitts 2007, 6). Furthermore, much of the potential evidence for the use of the rotary quern for grinding ore dates to the later Iron Age, that is from the 3rd/2nd century BC to the 1st century BC, and the Roman period (Nash Williams 1939, 109; Burnham and Burnham 2004, 284-285; Domergue *et al* 1997, 48;

Healy 1978, 142). Nevertheless, as indicated above, there was a link between iron and rotary querns; it was the availability of iron tools that made the production of rotary querns, in particular the drilling of handle holes and eyes, possible (Watts, M. 2002, 29).

In Britain a number of regional forms of Iron Age beehive rotary quern can be identified, based on the typology initially created by Curwen in the 1930s and 1940s (Curwen 1937; 1941). Furthermore there appears to be a distinct north-south divide (Figure 2.9) (Watts, M. 2002, 31-32). Beehive querns from southern England have sloping grinding faces and wide diameter eyes whereas those from the midlands and north have flat grinding faces and narrow eyes. These different styles may be due to different points of origin and/or ethnic choices; regional pottery styles were also developing at about the same time as the introduction and spread of the rotary quern (Cunliffe 2005, 120, 122). There are, of course, exceptions to the north-south divide but these tend to be later in date. Querns from a quarry at Folkestone, Kent which appears to have flourished in the 1st century BC and 1st century AD, for example, have flat grinding surfaces. The distinctive querns of Hertfordshire Puddingstone are similarly mostly dated AD 50-100 (Keller 1989; Green 2011, 123).

Welsh rotary querns are thought to date from about the 1st century BC and broadly appear to derive from northern and southern beehive querns in the north and south of the country respectively (Watts, S. 1996, 27). Irish and southern Scottish beehive querns are related to northern type querns and, on current evidence, appear to have been introduced to those countries in the final centuries BC, perhaps as early as *circa* 200BC. In northern Scotland, however, flatter disc-shaped querns were used rather than beehive querns, although again they are thought to have been introduced about 200BC (Caulfield 1977, 125; MacKie 1971, 52-55; MacKie 1971-1972; Armit 1991, 194). The contrast between the English beehive quern and the Scottish disc quern suggests separate origins. Flatter types of rotary quern were to become more common across the whole of the British Isles in the Roman period with the lower stone frequently having a spindle hole that completely perforated the stone rather than a socket. However, as examples from Bishopstone, Sussex and Danebury show these forms were already in use in southern Britain by the later Iron Age (Curwen 1937, 142, 144; Watts, M. 2002, 34; Laws *et al* 1991, 390, 395; Bell 1977, 124). Conversely, evidence also shows that the rounded beehive form also remained in use into the Roman period, particularly in Cornwall and northern England (Watts S. 2003, 25-26; Buckley and Major 1990, 117; Gwilt and Heslop 1995, 43).

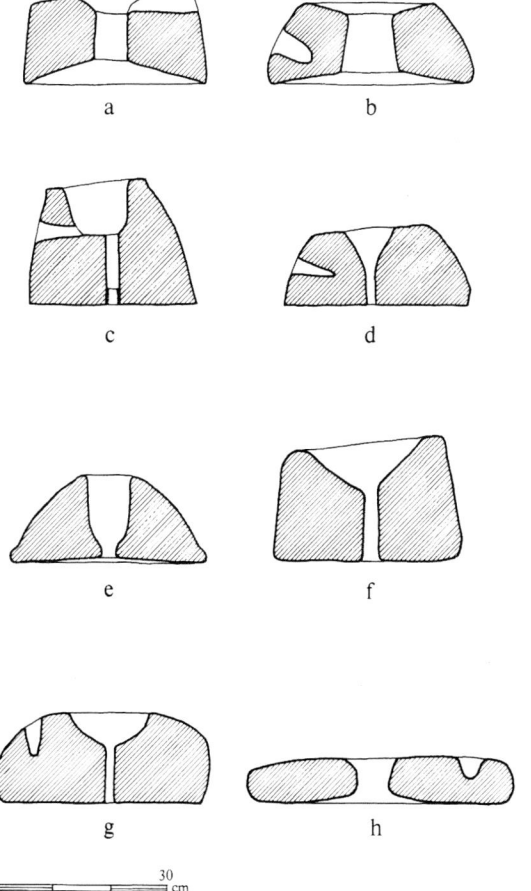

Figure 2.9: Iron Age rotary querns: Southern types Wessex (a) and Sussex (b); northern types Hunsbury (c) and Yorkshire (d); Hertfordshire puddingstone (e); Folkestone (f); Irish beehive (g); Scottish flat (h) (M. Watts after Cunliffe 1984b, Figure 7.53 (8.24); Cunliffe and Poole 1991, Figure 7.56 (8.112); Curwen 1941, Figure 5; Heslop 1987, Figure 54.5ii; Rogerson 1977, Figure 64.5; Keller 1989, Figure 3.7; Caulfield 1977, Figure 23F; MacKie 1971-1972, Figure 1d).

As with the saddle quern, the rotary quern was probably generally set on the ground for use. Examples of lower stones *in situ* have been found on both Iron Age and Roman sites such as at Gadebridge Park in Hertfordshire, Dalton Parlours in Yorkshire and Randylands Milecastle on Hadrian's Wall (Neal 2001, 111-112; Buckley and Major 1990, 117; Simpson and Richmond 1935, 240). A lower stone found at the bottom of a pit at Gussage All Saints, Dorset still had the remains of chalk mud adhering to it by which it was once steadied (Buckley 1979, 91). However, it was also to become not uncommon for the quern to be placed on a special stand or table. By using a lower stone with a completely perforating spindle hole, this allowed for the use of a longer spindle which passed through both stone and stand to pivot on an adjustable beam beneath. By slightly moving one end of the beam up or down the gap between the upper and lower stones could also be altered, an operation known as tentering.

The rotary quern did not entirely replace the saddle quern, however. Saddle querns continued to be used throughout the Iron Age and into the Roman period and later and are still used in some parts of the world today. Despite being physically more tiring to use than a rotary quern, the saddle quern has the advantage of being easier to manufacture. Indeed two surface stones of suitable size, shape and texture can suffice. However, where the two types of quern are found together on Iron Age sites in Britain such as Glastonbury Lake Village and Cadbury Castle, Somerset it is thought likely that the saddle querns were used for grinding products other than grain (Bulleid 1917; Bellamy 2000, 211; Watts M. 2002, 28). This relegation of use would have had a profound effect on the relative meaning and value of the saddle quern. However, saddle querns are more versatile than rotary querns for grinding wet as well as dry products.

2.4 The Relevance of Quern Typology to Structured Deposition

In the creation of a chronological typology artefacts tend to become divorced from the contexts in which they are found. Instead they are discussed more in terms of form and feature. This is needful, however, in order to understand the nature of the development of an object. Such typologies not only reveal regional differences and changes over time but also aid our understanding of other aspects of an object such as changes and developments in the techniques and methods by which it was manufactured. Furthermore, an examination of the typological development of an object may also highlight issues that are important considerations in furthering our understanding of its use as a structured deposit. The typology of the quern is a case in point.

On present evidence, the saddle quern appears to have been introduced to Britain, or at least its use or rather deposition in the archaeological record visibly increased, in the Neolithic period. This coincides with the introduction of grain cultivation and suggests that the practices, meaning and symbology relating to its use may have been pre-established norms with antecedents perhaps stretching back to the origins of agriculture in the Near East. The introduction of the rotary quern in the Middle Iron Age marks a significant development in milling technology and it has been suggested that the use of virtually complete but still usable saddle querns in floors and walls points to their redundancy as grinding tools (Alcock 1960, 99-100; Cool 2007, 76). However, both forms of quern are found in Middle and Late Iron Age contexts indicating that the rotary quern initially supplemented rather than supplanted the saddle quern. The reuse of saddle querns in such contexts cannot, therefore, be automatically taken as illustrative of obsolete tools. Nevertheless, the introduction of the rotary quern will have gradually affected the relative meaning and value of the saddle quern. It has also been suggested (Heslop 2008, 19) that rotary querns were initially valued as prestige items. A rotary quern, on the other hand, can be operated by two or more people working together.

There are two fundamental differences in the *modus operandi* of the two tools which may have had a great bearing on their associated symbology. Firstly, the upper stone of the saddle quern is moved across the lower stone with a forward and back motion, a movement which has sexual connotations whereas the upper stone of the rotary quern has a circular motion which can be related to the movement of the heavens and/or to the passage of time. Secondly, although saddle querns may be used in unison each is worked by one person only. A rotary quern, on the other hand, can be worked by two people, who sitting either side each take hold of the handle with one hand and alternately push and pull the upper stone around.

Finally, this chapter has touched upon the fact that querns were not only used for milling cereals but were also used for grinding other foodstuffs and products such as pottery temper and mineral ores. Again, each different use would have affected the meaning and value of that particular quern and thus, presumably its choice for inclusion in a structured deposit. It was the dynamic interaction between people and querns that ultimately determined the latters' cultural meaning and value and thus their potential as structured deposits. In order to more fully understand this particular use, therefore, it is necessary to better understand how they may have functioned within the societies that used them and the nature of the relationships that existed between quern and user. To do this one needs to explore their life history or object biography.

3

THE OBJECT BIOGRAPHY OF QUERNS

3.1 Introduction

Object biography analyses the 'life' of an artefact or other aspect of material culture in dynamic, interaction with human lives (Gosden and Marshall 1999, 65; Schamberger *et al* 2009). The concept was introduced by Kopytoff (1986) in his work on 'commoditization as process'. Using slaves as an example, Kopytoff showed that things could move in and out of a commodity state. When slaves were initially captured and sold they were treated as commodities, as objects. Although they regained their individual status upon being bought and integrated into a new social setting they nevertheless retained a commodity value and could be sold again. In the same way, Kopytoff proposed, the commoditisation of other things could also be seen as part of a process. The biographical approach taken with people could, therefore, he suggested be applied to objects with such questions as 'where does it come from and who made it? What has been its career so far...and what happens to it when it reaches the end of its usefulness?' (Kopytoff 1986, 64-67).

The notion of object biographies was developed further by Gosden and Marshall (1999) who saw objects as actively engaging in relationships with people, through which meanings were created and renegotiated. People interact with objects on several levels, both physically and mentally, utilising all the senses (Gosden 2001). Renfrew (2003, 149) talks of the 'mysterious process by which humans engage with the material world through the action of the mind as well as the hand'. People both create and react to material goods (Schiffer 1999, 4; Renfrew 2003, 159). Social relations are enabled and enacted through objects, the symbolism and meaning attached to them establishing and reaffirming those relationships. Objects can thus assume great power invoking memories and emotions, binding a community together. They can also be the way through which people define themselves (Gosden and Marshall 1999, 174; Harrison 2003, 313-314; Renfrew 2003, 109, 140-159).

Object biography, therefore, expands upon the technical and practical processes of production, use and discard as seen, for example, in Leroi Gourhan's 'châine opèratoire' and Schiffer's 'behavioural chain'. It also includes the social and symbolic aspects of those processes, taking into account the meaning and significance of the object within the social context in which it occurs (Schiffer 1995, 57, 107-108; Schiffer 1999, 16-19; Hurcombe 2007, 38-43; Tilley 2007). The same or similar objects will have different biographies in different cultural contexts, their significance, meaning and value dependent upon how they are defined and used (Kopytoff 1986, 67, 80, 90). In addition, object biography also considers, as called for by Ingold (2007), the physical, material properties of the object. These include not just what it is made of, its size, shape and colour but also its performance characteristics, such as its texture and hardness; physical parameters which can change and modify over time (Schiffer 1999, 16-19; Ingold 2007). Also of import are the 'affordances' of that object, the possibilities afforded by the characteristics, qualities or properties of an object. In other words what we perceive an object can do, not just what it was intended to do (Gibson 1986, 127, 134). A quern, for example, is a tool for grinding grain but an upturned saddle quern provides a surface for sitting on and the handy shape and weight of a rubbing stone provides an effective hand-held missile as Abimelech, an ancient King of Israel found to his cost (Judges 9:53).

In terms of object biography, however, the physical attributes and affordances of a thing should not only be considered in isolation but also in terms of their relation to the cultural contexts within which they are defined and used (Tilley 2007). The material(s) used to manufacture an object, for example, not only affect its lasting qualities but also its significance and value compared to similar objects made out of different materials. In addition, throughout their life history objects are enmeshed in a series of associations and relationships not just with people but also with other things. Thus objects not only have their own biography but are also part of the biographies of other things (Schiffer 1999, 23; Knappett and Leeuw forthcoming). In a similar way objects made of several different components or materials bring together the biographies of those components. These run in tandem for the use-life of that object but may split again when that object is finally discarded. Likewise, should an object be broken each fragment subsequently has its own biography. Nor do all similar items follow the same unilinear path of manufacture, use and discard. Some items may have been reused in a way which was not originally intended or recycled within the manufacturing process of something else thus becoming part of the biography of another object or structure. As Binford (1973, 242) comments, 'almost any item has a different life expectancy and will be discarded more in terms of its estimated utility for future reuse than as any direct reflection on its use or importance in the ongoing technology'. Of particular import in terms of structured deposition, therefore, is the fact that objects can potentially enter the archaeological record at any stage of their life history (Schiffer 1995, 57, 107-108).

Although a biography is linear in that an object progresses from manufacture through to use and finally discard (in whatever form this may take), each stage or phase of its life is shaped by that preceding, which in turn shapes what is to come. The choice of material(s) and the various changes in use, form, performance value, ownership, meaning and commodity value that an object may undergo during the course of its 'life' will ultimately affect its choice and deposition within the archaeological record at a certain time and place. They are thus important considerations in understanding the nature of structured deposition. Finally, it should be noted that, although beyond the scope of this book, an object's life history does not end with its 'burial' in the archaeological record. The means by which that object is retrieved from that record and its current state, location, meaning and value following that recovery are also part of its biography (Leone 1981, 5; Hurcombe 2007, 42; Watts, S. 2006a).

3.2   Querns and Object Biography

Querns are one of the oldest and longest used of all craft tools and have the potential to be immensely rewarding subjects in the study of object biography. They remained in use in parts of the British Isles into the 20th century and are still in use on a daily basis in parts of the world today providing opportunities to explore a living tradition. Far from being simple, utilitarian objects querns can be shown to be complex, multi-functional tools operating on both practical and symbolic levels. Querns can also be exceptionally long-lived artefacts. There can be few artefacts which are not only used on a daily basis but whose primary use can also span several generations. Querns may also see several phases of alternative or secondary use, although it is, of course, only their final use that is witnessed in the archaeological record. Thus, there may be many decades between the date of a quern's initial manufacture and use and the date of its final deposition in the archaeological record (Gwilt and Heslop 1995, 40; also Woodward 2000, 20).

Each quern, as indicated above, follows its own path of manufacture, use and discard, achieving a unique set of values and meanings and evoking specific memories of person, activity and place. The following object biography, therefore, although written with the prehistoric period in mind, is not intended as the life history of a particular quern at a given place and time but provides a generic overview. It draws in archaeological, historical and ethnographical data to demonstrate not only how varied those biographies can be but also to show the complexity of the biography of an artefact that is often considered to be a simple utilitarian tool. Of course, much ethnological, and indeed historical, evidence is many miles and years removed from the British prehistoric period. Habits and customs will have had many generations in which to become embedded in a particular social and ideological culture and in relationship to a particular environment (Hodder 1982, 25-27). However, although one must be wary of translating a living tradition directly into the past, using such evidence is not to say 'this is how it was' but to raise an awareness of the possibilities of what may have been. In this respect the use of ethnographic analogy can be extremely valuable particularly with regard to divisions of labour, method, dependence and related mythologies (Schiffer 1995, 95; Parker Pearson and Ramilisonina 1998; Cunningham 2003, 393-394). It should also be noted, as David (1998, 21) points out, that direct correlations between querns made of different stone types with stone or metal tools and which are used for grinding different products are not viable. Nevertheless points of commonality can be perceived which are relevant to general discussions on the object biography of querns. With the above caveats in mind, this chapter now focuses on the three key stages of a quern's life, its manufacture (birth), use (life) and discard (death). The following sections are taken partly from papers on *The Function of Querns* presented by the author at the Theoretical Archaeology Group Conference at Exeter University in 2006 and the Millstone Colloquium at The British School in Rome in 2009 (Watts, S. 2006a; Watts, S. 2011a).

3.3 Manufacture

3.3.1 Conception

The physical biography of a quernstone begins with its manufacture but prior to that is its conception, the thought that this tool is required. The reason for that requirement, as an item for sale, for example, or as a replacement rubber made by the person who intends to use it begins to set the meaning and value of that particular quernstone. Indeed it has been suggested (Sinclair 2000) that the desired end product comprises one of the four elements necessary for the manufacture of a particular tool. These four elements – desired end product, raw material, technique and implements - come together in the combination most relevant to that specific tool, a combination referred to by Sinclair as a 'constellation of knowledge'. Each element is not fixed, however, but evolves and develops in reflection and response to changes in the components of the other three elements (Sinclair 2000, 200). However, at the centre of that constellation is the world view of the society within which the manufacture takes place, which underpins and shapes those elements (Figure 3.1).

3.3.2 Desired end product

The design, the form and shape of the quern, so that it is fit for the purpose of milling, is of paramount importance. However, the technology behind that design is not static but subject to continual refinement by cultural, social, political, economic and ideological forces, leading to improvements and innovations in both product and process (Pfaffenberger 1988; Adams 1993, 331-332; Nelson and Lippmeier 1993, 286-287; Jones 2000, 133; Knappett and Leeuw forthcoming). Witness the original development of the saddle quern as a specific tool for grinding grain: with its flatter surface, the saddle quern was a more efficient grinding tool than a mortar or basin-type quern and had the added advantage of being easier to make. Using a saddle quern, however, puts great strain on the arms, back, knees and toes of the operator. Raising it up onto a platform allows the worker to stand and, if located close

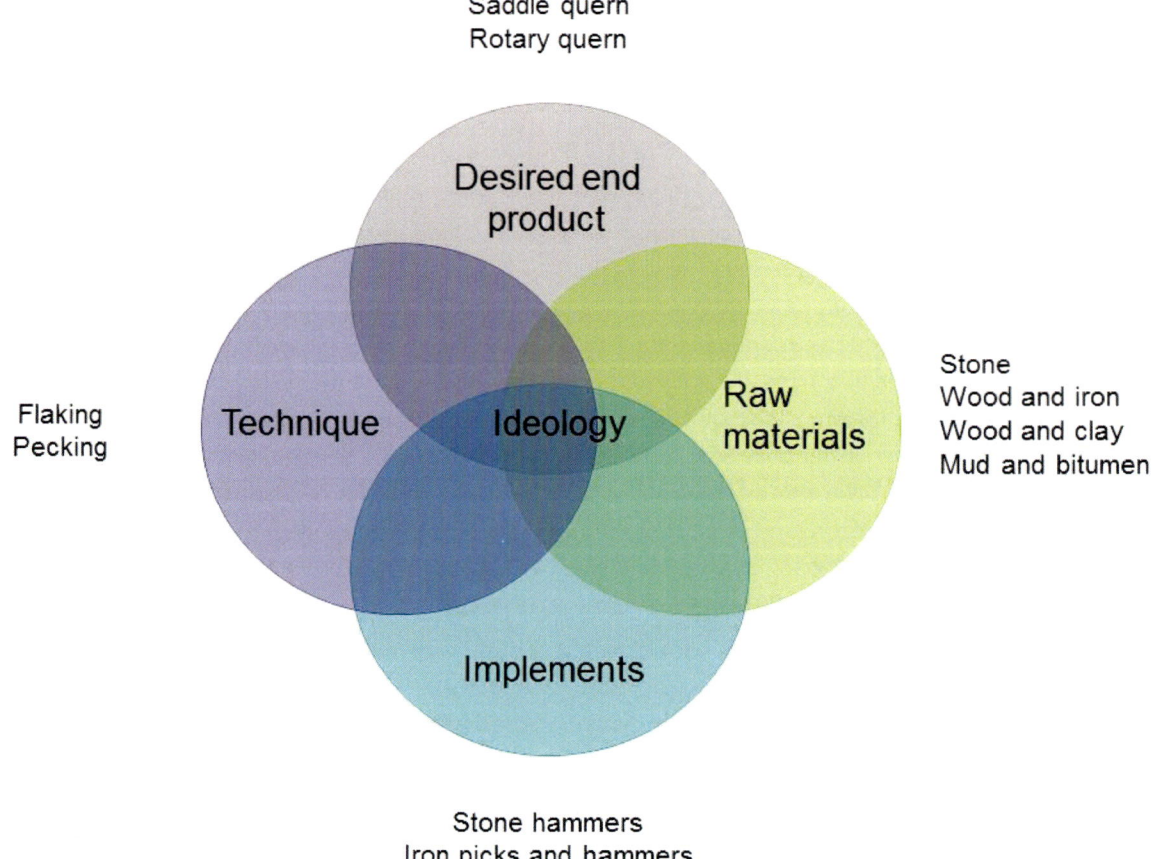

Figure 3.1: A 'constellation of knowledge' showing the key elements brought together in the manufacture of a quern (S. Watts adapted from Sinclair 2000, Figures 13.3 and 13.4).

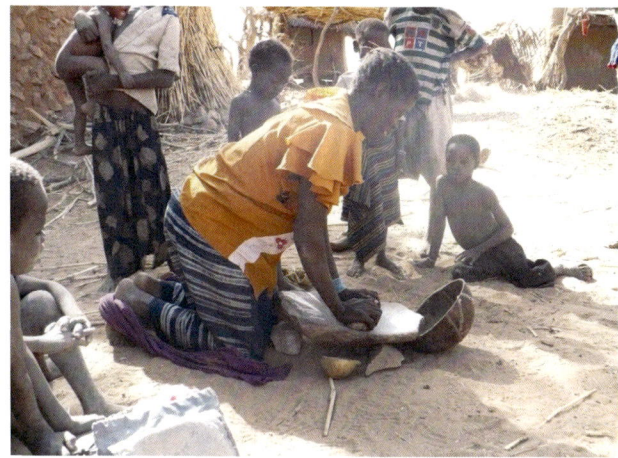 

Figure 3.2: Grinding with a saddle quern on the ground (left) and set in a raised emplacement (right) (Trough quern in Dogon country, Sogou village, Mali, photo C. Hamon and V. Le Gall, after Hamon and Le Gall 2013; replica quern emplacement based on an example found in the workmen's village, Amarna, Egypt, photo D. Samuel).

to a wall, the worker can brace his/her self against that wall thereby gaining more leverage (Figure 3.2). This makes the task of grinding both more comfortable and again more efficient (Curtis 2001, 116; Samuel 1993, 281; Samuel 2000, 563).

The development of the larger lever-operated Olynthan mill represented a further improvement on the saddle quern both in terms of output and *modus operandi* (Figure 4.1) (Curtis 2001, 286). The real breakthrough in milling technology, however, came with the introduction of the rotary quern and the fundamental change from a forward and backwards action to circular motion. The adoption of rotary motion ultimately led to the development of mills powered by animals, water and wind. It also has great implications for the application of symbolic values as related to movement. Experimental work indicates that whereas one can grind about 0.6kg of wheat per hour using a saddle quern, it is possible to grind up to 3kg or more with a rotary quern[1] (Jørgensen 2000; Samuel 2010). The gap between the upper and lower stones of a rotary quern can also be preset to grind coarser or finer as desired (a faster rate of feed and turning also produces a coarser product (Jørgensen 2000, 193)). In addition, a rotary quern can be used by two or more people working together which not only increases its efficiency but also makes the task more companionable (Figure 2.7). An article in the *Illustrated London News* in 1874, on women grinding grain in Ireland, reported that two women working together could grind about 4.5kg of meal per hour (Anon 1874, 375).

Those same cultural, political and ideological forces referred to above, however, can also inhibit, restrict or deny the development or adoption of new technology. It has been noted, for example, that despite the availability of mechanical mills, the saddle-type quern remains in daily use in parts of Africa; cost, a perceived better product and superstition outweighing the advantages of ease of use and output (Horsfall 1987, 363-368; Hamon and Gall 2013, 118). A similar initial reluctance to use powered mills for grinding maize for tortilla flour was also noted in South America, partly by the women but mainly by the men who were suspicious of the amount of free time this would give their wives (Bauer 1990, 15-16). A traditional distrust of the miller, as referred to by Chaucer in his Canterbury Tales, has also been voiced as a reason for preferring to use a quern rather than the local watermill (Cobbett 1979, 65; Anon 1901, 227).

By way of contrast, it has been suggested that the adoption of the rotary quern during the British prehistoric period was initially due to a desire to possess a new technology, as a symbol of prestige, rather than need (Heslop 2008, 18-19). As noted in the previous chapter the rotary quern did not immediately supplant the saddle quern; both types are found on the same sites in the Late Iron Age and into the Roman period. It is likely that the saddle quern continued in use for milling products other than grain but there may also have been a superstitious reluctance to use the new rotary quern or perhaps the latter was not, as implied by Heslop (2008, 18-19) available to all. However, the widespread distribution of the rotary quern by the later Middle Iron Age certainly appears to indicate that it fairly rapidly became an everyday, domestic tool. Nevertheless, the saddle quern retains the advantage over the rotary quern in that it is easier to manufacture;

---

1. This is, of course, dependent upon the size of the quern, the relative hardness and dryness of the wheat and the inclination of the miller.

one or both stones can be improvised if necessary. The rotary quern on the other hand is a manufactured tool taking considerable skill to produce.

Both saddle and rotary querns vary in size and shape. Such differences may be due to preferential changes over time, the choice of stone available for their manufacture, the crafting properties of that stone, the use for which the quern was intended, the design choices made by the manufacturer and/or the influences of the desires and needs of the consumer. The latter may be linked to ethnic choices, providing a means of expressing identity, as suggested in Chapter Two for the different forms of Iron Age beehive quern (Figure 2.9) (Hayden 1987b, 188; Adams 1993, 341; Schiffer and Skibo 1997; Adams 1999; Dant 2005, 140; Hamon 2008c, 51). Generally the larger the stone the greater the surface area for grinding and, therefore, the greater potential efficiency of the quern. There is, however, a limit to the size of stones that can be used both in terms of weight of the upper stone and reach (Adams 1993, 333-334; Maudlin 1993, 319). The optimum size for a rotary quern is rather a grey area but it is considered that stones in excess of 60cm in diameter are too large to have been turned by hand (Watts, S. 2006b). However, as Adams (1999, 479) points out, the efficiency of a quern is primarily dependent upon what it is used for and for certain products a smaller quern may be the better option. A contrast has been made, for example, between larger, two-handed manos used for grinding maize and smaller, one-handed ones used for grinding other foodstuffs and pigments (Schlanger 1991, 461-462; Walton 1974, 6). Two distinct sizes of saddle quern have also been noted on prehistoric sites in Britain (Buckley 1979, 89; Laws *et al* 1991, 396).

3.3.3 Procurement of raw material

The choice of material utilised for a quern's manufacture was especially important for a tool that was intended to be used for many years. Such a tool would have been worth the investment in time taken in acquisition of the material and in its manufacture (Nelson and Lippmeier 1993, 294). Querns can be made from a variety of rock types including sandstones, basalts, granites and limestones (Figure 3.3). The best stone is that with a well-cemented matrix of fine-medium grains that provides a naturally abrasive and hard-wearing surface such as the aptly named Millstone Grit, or a vesicular texture such as lava which produces a continuous myriad of cutting edges to shear the grain (the furrows found

Figure 3.3: Quernstones of different stone types and colours. German Mayen lava (top left); North Devon hangman grit (top right); Hertfordshire puddingstone (bottom left); Dartmoor granite (bottom right) (S. Watts).

on Roman and later querns serve to help the flow of meal to the edge of the stones and also aerate the meal (Cookson 2003, 353)). That said, querns can also be made from other materials such as wood studded with iron or coated with clay (Figure 3.4) or even bitumen-coated sun-dried mud (Gaucheron 1990; Kawakami 2005, 62; Curtis 2001, 201 n.41). These other materials tend, however, to be for specific tasks such as grinding buckwheat or hulling rice.

As far as querns made from stone are concerned both archaeological and ethnographical evidence indicates that although surface, riverine and beach boulders and cobbles can be successfully used as milling tools many querns are manufactured from freshly hewn stone. Some stone quarries have been worked over many generations imbuing the landscape with a strong sense of tradition and continuity. On the Aswan West Bank in Egypt, for example, recent fieldwork has shown that sandstone quarries there were utilised for the production of quernstones for more than 16,000 years, from the Late Paleolithic to the early Roman period (Bloxam 2011). In Europe, lava from Mayen in the Eifel Mountains of Germany was first used for the production of querns in the Neolithic period and the quarries are still in use today, although now generally making other items (Crawford and Röder 1955). In Britain, at Lodsworth in Sussex, greensand was exploited from about the 5th century BC and throughout the Roman period (Peacock 1987). In more recent times, in Arizona, it is recorded that Antelope Hill, an isolated sandstone hill in the Gila Valley floodplain, was the place where the Quechan went yearly to get grinding stones (Schneider 1996, 302-303). Such longevity of use may be due to practical reasons such as the milling properties of the quarried stone. The stone from Antelope Hill was, for example, stated to be 'the best', so much so that people were prepared to travel some 48km to obtain it (Schneider 2002, 48). However, it has also been suggested that in the prehistoric period, some quern quarries may have been deliberately located at prominent positions in the landscape in a way similar to the siting of stone axe working sites, their location determined by ideological rather than practical considerations such as ease of access (Heslop 2008, 43-44).

3.3.4 Manufacturing implements and technique

The manufacturing process is not only part of a social and economic network, it also provides a framework within which technical skills can be acquired and improvements made (Pfaffenberger 1988, 249; Jones 2000, 127). For each individual worker the process is

Figure 3.4: A buckwheat quern made of wood studded with pieces of iron (G. Clausse).

also a personal and emotional act. Working with stone is physically hard and frequently results in cuts, bruises and blisters, particularly for the inexperienced quern mason. There is also the danger of greater injury and even death from flying shards of stone and rockfalls (Hayden 1987a, 31, 34-35; Cook 1973, 1488). There may also be despair over a stone breaking at a critical point in its manufacture due to a flaw in the rock or an ill-placed blow but delight and pride in the finished product. The process can also be one charged with symbolism as the rock gives birth to the stone, as it emerges from the rough stone (after Jones 2000, 127; Fendin 2006, 161).

Ethnographic and historical evidence indicates, as might be expected, that the structure by which the manufacture of quernstones is organised is not standard but depends very much upon local tradition. That said, four levels of organisation can be discerned, with querns being manufactured by:

- The individual requiring the stone.
- Someone within the community on their behalf.
- A loose confederation of individual workers accessing the same source, the finished products usually for sale.
- A structured and managed workforce, the finished products for sale.

It is noticeable that in cases where quernstones are made for personal use, then the people making them are likely to be women (Paston 1974, 101; Schlanger 1991, 461; Graham 1994, 60; Haaland 1995, 164-166; David 1998, 25). Otherwise, quern manufacture seems to be a male preserve and it is not uncommon for the querns to be roughly shaped at source and finished at a nearby workshop or within the home (Hilton-Simpson

1922, 149-151; Cook 1970, 779; Hayden and Nelson 1981, 892; Hayden 1987a; Haaland 1995, 164-165; Schneider 1996; Hamon and Gall 2011, 21). Again, a difference in initial value and meaning can be perceived between those stones made for or by someone within the community and those made for trade or exchange. In addition, there is the transition from the potential male preserve of manufacture to the female preserve of grinding to be considered.

Amongst the Dogon and Minyanka people of Mali, for example, food preparation is a female task and a woman will peck the quern for herself before it is used for the first time. Men will not then touch the quern for fear it will sap their strength (Hamon and Gall 2013, 117; Hamon pers.comm.). Similarly, in northern Mexico the women of the Tarahumara, or Rarámuri, take over the completion of the metates before use and it is they who make the manos, rather than the men, and maintain the tools they use (Paston 1974, 101; Graham 1994, 56, 59-60). In eastern Australia, Hamilton (1980, 6) noted that the men 'handed over' the quernstones to their wives. In the American south-west, Quechan warriors collected stones to 'make metates for their wives' (Schneider 1996, 302).

Of course, it is not possible to state how the manufacturing process was structured during the prehistoric period although it has been suggested (Peacock 1987, 76; Watts, M. 2002, 27) that initially communities were responsible for sourcing and making their own saddle querns. The inherent technical difficulties in shaping rotary querns, however, suggest that their manufacture was in the hands of specialists. This is well demonstrated by the standard of prehistoric and Roman querns originating from the Lodsworth quarry in Sussex. Rotary querns from this quarry show a marked consistency of form and manufacturing technique whereas saddle querns vary considerably (Peacock 1987, 76).

The length of time taken to manufacture a quern depends on four main factors:
- The accessibility of the raw material, whether surface boulders and cobbles are utilised, for example, or if the stone has to be quarried.
- The workability of the material used for its manufacture.
- The implements used for its manufacture.
- The form of the quern.

A range of different sized stone hammers, antler or wooden picks and wedges and, where and when available, their iron/steel equivalents - crowbars, hammers, picks and chisels - are used to extract blocks of stone, and peck and flake the quern to shape (Hilton-Simpson 1922, 151; Schneider 1996, 303; Crawford and Röder 1955, 72; Cook 1973, 1487-1489; Hayden and Nelson 1981, 885-891). Hayden (1987a, 31) noted several advantages of steel over stone tools. Steel tools are not only more efficient but, being hafted, they are also safer and through changes in the sound of the 'ring' of steel on stone flaws within the stone are more quickly identified (Cook 1973, 1488). Watts, M. (2002, 29) comments on the use of iron tools to fashion Iron Age rotary querns and the implication is that it was the increasing availability of iron that made their production possible. A double-edged chisel found at Wookey Hole, Somerset 'precisely fitting the hole in one of the querns' is suggestive of use in the manner of a drill, the chisel being hammered as it was turned (Balch 1914, 94). On the other hand, the circle of small holes around the half finished eye of a broken quern found with others on Longis Beach, Alderney, Channel Islands suggests a method of fashioning the eye comprising tapping a punch round and round in a circle, a laborious version of a hole saw (Figure 3.5). The stone, which broke or was broken during manufacture, also shows that the grinding surface and hopper were shaped prior to the drilling of the eye from the underside of the stone.

Saddle querns and rubbers derived from surface boulders and cobbles that require little modification may take no more time than that needed to search out suitably sized and shaped stones, whereas a neatly shaped three-legged metate will take far longer to complete, particularly if it is also decorated (Figure 4.3). Ethnographic evidence indicates that,

Figure 3.5: Half an unfinished upper stone, Alderney Museum (centimetre scale) (S. Watts).

dependent upon the above factors, the manufacture of a saddle quern/metate takes between a half and five days including the time taken to find the material, while a rubber can take as little as a couple of hours (Aschmann 1949, 685; Cook 1970, 779; Hayden 1987a, 48; David 1998, 35; Hamon and Gall 2011). Experimental work at the site of a quern quarry near Besançon in France indicated that to extract a suitably sized block of sandstone and shape a saddle quern took 6.5 hours (Jaccottey 2009).

Rotary querns, on the other hand, are more difficult and time consuming to manufacture both in terms of shape and in the drilling of eye, spindle and handle holes. They also require a spindle, rynd or bridge and handle. It is likely, therefore, that their manufacture was the province of specialist craftsmen and that as Heslop (2008, 19) suggests, they were originally considered prestige items. Unfortunately, there is little information regarding manufacturing time at present. In his observations on the Berbers in Algeria, Hilton Simpson (1922, 151) recorded that the quarrying and rough shaping of a suitably sized piece of stone could take up to 20 days, due to the particular difficulties in extracting the stone, with a further three or four days needed for trimming and finishing. Recent experimental work at Hyllestad in Norway suggests that perhaps one to three days is more usual (Baug and Løland 2009). However, fieldwork in France has noted a change in the methods used to extract the stone between the prehistoric and Roman and later periods. Initially rough blocks of stone were hewn which were subsequently shaped as required, a technique used for both saddle and rotary querns whereas in the Roman period rotary querns were shaped in the round before being prised from the quarry face (Jaccottey 2011). In Britain evidence suggests that suitably sized boulders were used for the manufacture of beehive querns (Wright 1988; Heslop 2008, 21-23). The additional components of handle, spindle and rynd may be made of wood or iron and, as mentioned above, their attachment to a quern brings together the biographies of two or even three different materials. Iron working is generally regarded as a male preserve (Hingley 1997) and it is suggested the use of iron components in prehistoric rotary querns may have represented a male intrusion into the female sphere of milling (Heslop 2008, 75). However, Haaland's research in western Sudan and Tanzania shows that women can participate in both activities, both making querns and grinding iron ore, indicating a strong link between grinding stones and women (Haaland 1995, 378-379).

4.3.5 Two stones make a quern

It should also be borne in mind that a quern comprises two stones and that both are necessary for it to perform its prime task of milling, the absence of one rendering the quern inoperable (Seager Thomas 1999, 45; Adams 2002, 99). This is illustrated well in the Old Testament, where the laws of Moses state that 'no man shall take the nether or the upper millstone to pledge; for he taketh a man's life to pledge' (Deuteronomy 24.6). The biographies of each stone run contiguously for the use-life of the quern or until one or other is replaced for whatever reason. However, upper and lower stones are not always of the same rock types. Finds of a saddle quern with rubbers of different materials within a pit or hollow in one of the houses in the Bronze Age settlement at Trethellan Farm, Cornwall, for example, suggest that they were used together (Nowakowski 1991, 21). The different upper stones may have been intended for grinding coarse or fine or for grinding different products and may represent the utilisation of convenient beach or river cobbles for this purpose. Likewise, several complete rotary querns with upper and lower stones of different lithologies have been found in Yorkshire and an upper and lower stone of a complete rotary quern found at Rossie Quarry, Perthshire were of igneous diorite and mica-schist respectively (Figure 3.6). Analysis of the latter stones showed that they had worked together as a pair (Nowakowski 1991, 21; Heslop 2008, 60; M. Hall pers. corresp.). The use of different stones could represent a replacement of one or the other, or that a lighter upper stone makes for easier turning while a heavier lower stone will keep the quern in place. Alternatively the bringing together of two different stone types could have symbolic connotations, perhaps representing a relationship of some form (Thomson 1877, 528; Curtis 2001, 201; Heslop 2008, 60; M. Hall pers. corresp.).

Figure 3.6: Pair of rotary quernstones of different stone types from Rossie Quarry, Perthshire (M. Hall, copyright and courtesy of Perth Museum & Art Gallery, Perth and Kinross Council, Scotland).

4.3.6 Trade and procurement

Evidence suggests that although querns tend to derive from locally available sources they may also be procured over long distances. Such procurement may be direct, as in the case of Antelope Hill mentioned above (Schneider 2002, 48). It may, however, be indirect through trade and ethnographic evidence also indicates the presence of second hand markets (Hamilton 1980, 8). In a prehistoric context querns can be a good indicator of trade routes and exchange networks. The majority of the 38 hopper rubbers found amongst the cargo of a Greek merchant ship that sank off the island of Sec, Mallorca in the 4th century BC, for example, came from Pantelleria, an island close to Sicily. It is further suggested that the ship, en route from the eastern Mediterranean, had called there to pick up the querns as 'saleable ballast' (Williams-Thorpe and Thorpe 1990). In Britain, rotary querns from the Prehistoric and Roman greensand quarries at Lodsworth in West Sussex, for example, have been found in Dorset, Gloucestershire and Northamptonshire (Peacock 1987). At the other end of the exchange network, finds of querns from disparate sources on sites such as the hillforts at Hunsbury in Northamptonshire, Danebury in Hampshire and Cadbury Castle in Somerset are indicative of relationships, trade/exchange networks and the relative importance of these sites at local and regional and even national levels (Ingle 1993-1994; Roe 2000; Cunliffe 2003, 139; Moore 2007, 92).

The presence of 'one off', exotic stones, however, such as the fragments of German lava found at the Sanctuary near Avebury, Wiltshire or the fragment of puddingstone saddle quern found in a Neolithic pit at Maiden Castle, Dorset which came from Normandy, may represent the movement of and contacts between people rather than resources or be the result of particular transactions or relationships (Cunnington 1930-1932, 332; Peacock and Cutler 2010; Moore 2007, 93; Pailler and Sheridan 2009). Likewise, the querns found within a Bronze Age metalworking enclosure at Sigwells Farm, Somerset are thought to be the result of peoples from different areas coming together to share in the experience of their craft. The querns, of greensand, Old Red Sandstone and an igneous rock, derived from sources 15km to the east, 22km to the north and 40km to the west respectively (Tabor 2008, 65-67). The quartzite saddle querns found in the Neolithic causewayed enclosure at Etton, Cambridgeshire were also probably brought especially to the site by the people who gathered there, there being no stone suitable for querns in the immediate vicinity (Pryor 1998b, 63; Pryor 1998a, 259). The methods by which quernstones were transported from one place to another, given the potential weight of individual saddle querns or rotary quernstones, should also be borne in mind.

The reason for which a quern came into a community or household is also an important consideration. It may have been made by someone within the community for their own personal use or for someone else, or it could have arrived through trading networks or have been presented as a gift. It may even have been obtained from a deserted settlement (Schlanger 1991, 461; Lange and Rydberg 1972, 430). It could have been a replacement tool or part of a dowry. Although intended as a milling tool, each method and reason for arrival would have conveyed different meanings and associations. Ethnographic evidence indicates that querns comprise an essential part of the household equipment for a newly married woman and almost obligatory as part of a dowry or bridal gift (Cook 1970, 779; Thompson 1979, 318 n94; Da Re 2003, 107; Hamon and Gall 2011, 20). In this light querns can be seen as an essential part of one of the rites of passage, symbolic of women and of the married state and setting up a home and may be contrasted with the meanings conveyed by, for example, the manufacture of a replacement rubber or by a quern that has been inherited. Of course it is not possible to discern the reasons behind the presence of particular querns on prehistoric sites, although, as indicated above, the presence of exotic stones may be indicative of particular relationships. Also, as suggested by Heslop (2008, 18-19), early rotary querns may have been considered as prestigious and desirable items.

3.4 Primary Functions and Uses

3.4.1 A woman's world

Ethnographic sources, as intimated above, indicate that the task of food preparation, of which milling is an important aspect, is one appropriated to women. The following examples serve to reiterate this point. In the village of Kizalkaya in Anatolia, Ertug-Yaras (2002) found that the success of the subsistence level at which the village operated was very much dependent on 'gender-based' organisation. The manufacture, use, care and ultimate disposal of the tools used in the preparation of food were generally perceived as part of the female domain. Likewise, amongst the Bemba of Zambia housework and the preparation of meals, particularly millet porridge which comprises the main part of their diet, together with brewing millet beer are considered female activities (Richards 1939, 91-104).

However, Haaland found that, although there was a strong association between women and grinding tools, this did not prohibit the men from using querns to grind ochre and tobacco (Haaland 1997, 378-379). Similarly, in the eastern desert of Australia querns that were used to grind seeds were used solely by women but those that were used for ochre and tobacco were used by both men and women (Hamilton 1980, 5-6, 8). Nearer to home, on Shetland in the late 19th, early 20th century it was not uncommon for men to use querns, particular for grinding malted grain for home brewing (Watts, M. 2002, 43).

It seems, therefore, that although men may use a quern, it is the task of food preparation that is exclusively female. As Casalis noted (1861, 141) this appropriation appears to be one of the ways in which the distinction between male and female is maintained in traditional subsistence societies. It is consequently not surprising that the use of ethnographic analogies has led to the assumption that the task of milling, along with other food processing and cooking activities, during the prehistoric period was likewise a female domain (Hastorf 1991, 134; Wright 2000, 114). The only potential archaeological evidence, however, comes from the damage and degenerative wear observed on the spine, knees and toes of female skeletons at Abu Hureyra, Syria. Although such damage could be caused by a combination of daily activities it is particularly suggestive of long hours spent kneeling at a saddle quern (Molleson 1994, 311-316; Moore *et al* 2000). Also, the millers depicted on the models, statuettes and wall paintings of the milling, baking and brewing scenes found in ancient Egyptian tombs tend to be women (Figure 3.7) (Tooley 1995, 8; Curtis 2001, 115-116; Howard 2006). Exceptions are the statuettes representing the high priests from the Temple of Ptah at Memphis, *circa* 1570-1070BC. These priests apparently had themselves depicted as millers so they could make eternal offerings to the gods Nut and Osiris but it is probably unlikely that they undertook the grinding of offerings in reality (Tooley 1995, 8, 28-29).

There is also some ancient literature pertaining to querns being inherited by daughters from their mothers and to the employment of female workers as millers in the state and privately run mills in Mesopotamia in the 2nd and 3rd millennia BC (Englund 1991, 257; Depla 1994, 35; Wright 2000, 115; Baysal and Wright 2005, 321). In ancient Anatolia, the Hittite King, Hattusilis I (reigned *circa* 1586-1556BC) recorded that he 'took the hands of the female slaves from the millstones' (Hoffner 2000, 566). In addition, a number of references in the Old Testament imply that milling was considered lowly work, performed by women or slaves, prisoners and captives (Genesis 18:6; Exodus 11:5; Judges 16:21; Isaiah 47:1-2; Lamentations 5:13). Moving across to Europe, there are also references in classical Greek literature to women using handmills, in Homer's *The Odyssey* (20.105-112) (*circa* 7th-8th century BC) and Plutarch's *Moralia* (157e) (*circa* AD46-120), for example.

Although one cannot say that the circumstances that applied in ancient Egypt, the Near East and classical Greece also applied in prehistoric Britain, it is suggested that as the knowledge and practice of agriculture spread from the Near East to Europe so too did the principles and practices relating to the processing and preparation of cereals for consumption (Curtis 2001, 74-75). Divisions of labour, with women responsible

Figure 3.7: Model from the tomb of King Nebheptre Mentuhotep II (2055 – 2004BC) showing a line of women working in unison (© Trustees of the British Museum).

for the preparation of food, may have become the established norm, each gender-related task surrounded by its own mythology and symbology (Haaland 1997). An antidote to this is the pseudo-Virgilian poem, *Moretum*, dated to the 1st century BC which describes the preparation of a meal by Simulus, a poor farmer. In the poem it is Simulus who mills rather than his female servant (Vergiliana *Moretum* 19-30). All-male enclaves such as monasteries and armies also ground their own flour. Herodian (4.7.5), for example, keen to show that the Emperor Caracalla shared in the life of an ordinary soldier states that among other tasks, the Emperor ground his own daily ration of grain. It can also be argued that division of labour was rather more skills or class based than gender based, hence why milling was a task consigned to the lower classes, to slaves and prisoners. Diodorus (3.13.2), in his account, written in the 1st century BC, of the wretched lives of those condemned to labour in the gold mines on the Egyptian-Ethiopian border, states that the ore mills were worked by women and old men. Consequently, the circumstances in which the quern was used, whether it was used, for example, in an everyday domestic setting by the women of the household, by a slave, or was part of an army's baggage train may have had a bearing on that quern's subsequent choice as a structured deposit.

3.4.2 A social whirl

A quern can thus be seen to function as part of a particular social setting within which it plays a key role in the process that transforms a raw material into a usable product. Within that social setting the quern interacts with people and other items of material culture on both spatial and temporal levels (Hill 1995, 108; Schiffer 1999, 22-26; Watts, S. 2006a; Fendin 2000, 91). It is primarily associated with the person(s) who uses it together with a set of artefacts directly related to the task of milling, such as a container for the grain and a cloth or bowl to catch the ground meal. It is also, however, linked with the people and artefacts that comprise the other processes in the life history of the ground product such as the mortar used for de-husking the grain (although querns can also be successfully used for this part of the process) and the pot used for cooking porridge. In addition, it is indirectly associated with a totally unrelated set of artefacts and people bound up in other activities which nevertheless form part of the social setting within which the quern was used (Figure 3.8) (after Schiffer 1999, 22-26). In a domestic setting, therefore, the quern is very much associated with the home, family and the provision of food and in early 20th century rural Mexico, for example, it was one of

Figure 3.8: The quern as part of a social setting, Tille Village, Adiyaman province, Turkey (S. Blaylock).

the four items – hearth, griddle, grinding stone and pot – considered necessary for the house (Brumfield 1991, 237; Paston 1974, 100). Consequently, the location of a quern *in situ* in its primary working position on an archaeological site together with the hearth and other artefacts such as cooking pots and spindle whorls within a domestic scenario may be indicative of a female activity area (Damp 1984, 580). However, this makes the assumption that these tools were actually used close to the places in which they were found (after Schiffer 1995, 35, 48, 175-185; Jones and Taylor 2010, 66). Ethnographic evidence shows that, with the exception of those set in permanent emplacements, querns, despite their size and weight, are moveable objects and may be found inside and/or outside dwellings and subject to change due to environmental or social reasons (Casalis 1861, 143; Graham 1994, 56). Querns may also be used in one place but stored in another and furthermore, the upper and lower stones of saddle querns may also be stored in different places (Graham 1994, figure 26; Hamon and Gall 2013, 117). That said, nomadic communities tend to leave their querns at campsites convenient to sources of grain or seeds (Gould *et al* 1971, 164; Allen 1974, 315; Hamilton 1980, 8; Gast 2003, 63).

The number of querns within a household is also important as this can reflect social and familial organisation as well as being indicative of food processing strategies and, in a prehistoric context, this may have had a bearing on a quern's subsequent use as a structured deposit. In current saddle quern/metate using communities the numbers are generally, although not always, related to the number of adult women and/or daughters living in each dwelling (Paston 1974, 100; Horsfall 1987, 358; David 1998, 23). Where there are two querns, one may be used for grinding more finely than the other (they may be pecked to different finishes). Alternatively, several different rubbers of increasing smoothness are used with a single quern to achieve the same result (Graham 1994, 56; David 1998, 23). Multiple saddle quern emplacements are also known (Figure 3.9) and it is not uncommon for cereals to be dehusked or coarsely ground on the first quern and then passed onto the second quern where it is ground a little finer and so on down the line. Harlan (1995, 233-234) records watching four women working together 'expertly grind[ing] off the bran' before grinding the grain as fine as was required (Harlan 1995, 233; Adams 1999, 479).

Archaeological evidence for grinding tool kits comprising a saddle quern with two rubbers has been found on several sites in prehistoric Britain such as Mingies Ditch in Oxfordshire, Maddle Farm in Berkshire and Trethellan Farm, Cornwall (Robinson 1993, 79; Gaffney and Tingle 1989, 82, 86; Nowakowski 1991, 21). At Nornour, Isles of Scilly two hearths were found within a 'kitchen' annexe attached to an Iron Age dwelling each with a saddle quern beside it. A third saddle quern appears to have been found close by and six rubbers were found in one of the compartments in the adjoining structure (Figure 3.10). At Bodrifty, an Early Iron Age site in north Cornwall, two saddle querns were found *in situ* close to a cooking hole within one of the roundhouses (Dudley 1967, 5, 7; Dudley 1956, 6). Moreover, one or two saddle querns with two or a single rubbers respectively have also been found on Bronze Age, Chalcolithic and Neolithic sites across mainland Europe, Anatolia and the Near East such as Bylany in the Czech Republic, Güvercinkayası in Anatolia, Akrotiri on Thera, Çatalhöyük in Turkey and Abu Hureyra in Syria. Likewise pairs of mortars and pestles were found on an early Natufian site at Wadi Hammeh, dated 12,650-10,450BC (Pavlů 2008, 20-21; Curtis 2001, 265; Baysal and Wright 2005, 313; Moore *et al* 2000, 168-169; Wright 2000, 94). This suggests that grinding tool kits, that potentially enabled either one or two women to grind different qualities of meal, were found to be a practical application from earliest times and engendered widespread and long-lasting use.

The situation appears different with regard to the rotary quern with most evidence pointing towards one quern per family unit. This may be due to cost of acquisition or to the fact that the rotary quern can dehusk and grind in one operation and that the gap between the upper and lower stones can be altered to grind coarse or fine as necessary. Also, as noted above, a rotary quern can be efficiently and also companionably operated by two women working together (Figure 2.7, 3.8). Thomson (1877, 526) noted in a village in Israel 'two women… sitting before the door of their house….grinding on a hand-mill' and it was reported in *The Penny Magazine* in 1834 that 'this labour is generally performed in the early morning by the women of the household. They sit upon the ground, commonly two to a mill…' (Anon 1834).

The domestic scenario contrasts strongly with the milling rooms of the prisons and state-run and royal milling establishments of the type found in Mesopotamia, Syria and Egypt in the 2nd and 3rd millennium BC (Figure 3.7) (Curtis 2001, 202-203; Englund 1991; Judges 16:21). Although in such settings querns can still be seen to have had a primary role in the act of milling and in many respects would have been associated with a similar set of artefacts, the whole ethos would have been different as would have been the meaning and value of each quern. The person using the quern would not have been its owner but the labourer or prisoner assigned to it. The amount of time each person spent working at the mill is also likely to have been longer and there would also have been a foreman overseeing the work to ensure that orders were fulfilled and that sufficient flour was produced on time. An ancient text from Ur, in modern day Iraq, dated *circa* 2100-2000BC which contains a one year account of a group of 37 female millers at one of the state-run mills shows that over the course of the year, that is 360 days, they milled more than 280,000kg of flour of varying sorts (Englund 1991). In prisons, in particular, the task of milling would have been a lowly, demeaning, onerous chore, the quern functioning as an instrument of punishment, even torture. A similar

Figure 3.9: Pueblo multiple grinding bins (postcard from the collection of P. Hill).

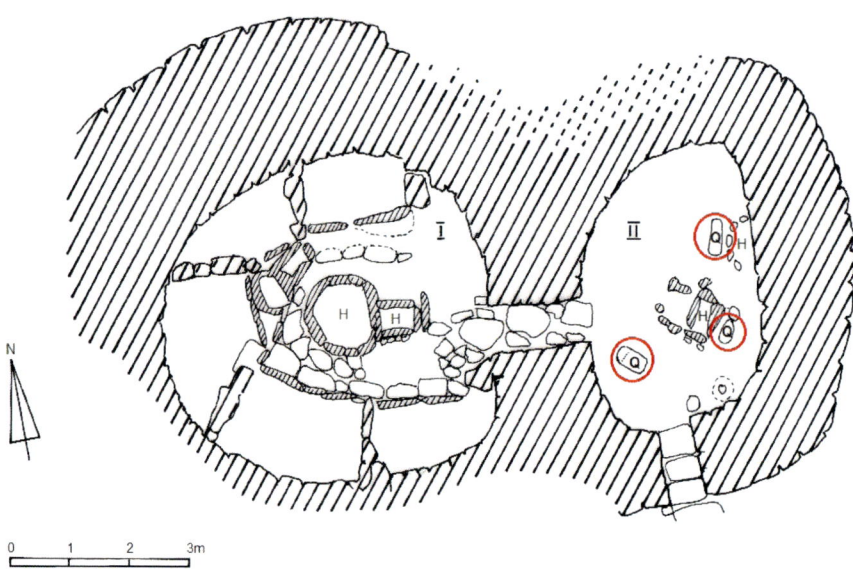

Figure 3.10: Plan of an Iron Age dwelling on Nornour, Isles of Scilly showing three saddle querns in situ in room II (M. Watts after Dudley 1967, Figure 6).

tortuous relationship between labourer and mill can be implied from Diodorus' description of the African gold mines mentioned above (Diodorus 3.13.2) and can be contrasted with that which existed between mill and overseer. Although it is not known if such establishments existed in prehistoric Britain it is perhaps worth bearing in mind the suggestion made by Van der Veen and Jones (2006) that one of the roles of hillforts was the mass storage of grain in readiness for feasting events. Teams of millers would presumably have been needed to grind the grain for baking and brewing in preparation for such feasts.

It was also mentioned above that all male enclaves such as armies would also have been responsible for grinding their own flour and here again a different relationship can be seen between quern and user. According to the Greek writer Xenophon (*circa* 481-355BC), Cyrus the Great of Persia (*circa* 580-530BC) stated that an army on the move should 'be ready provided [in unplundered country] with handmills, with which to prepare our corn; for this is the lightest of the instruments used in making bread' (compared to donkey mills or hopper-rubbers) (Xenophon *Cyropaedia* 6.2.31). Querns were important but burdensome pieces of equipment and in the Roman army there were slaves designated to carry them (Frontinus *Strategems* 4.1.6). Inscriptions found on military querns, such as that from the fort at Saalburg in Germany, inscribed 'CON[tubernium] BRITTONIS' or that from Greatchesters on Hadrian's Wall with the name of the centurion followed by '[MOLA VII]', suggests that each contubernium of 8-10 men had its own quern (Birley 1932). A single legion on the move could, therefore, be carrying some 400-500 querns in its baggage train.

The amount of time spent grinding at the quern each day depends on a number of factors including the product, the quantities required (or demanded), the form and size of the quern and the type of stone from which it is made, and the skill and inclination of the miller (Maudlin 1993, 319; Adams 1999, 485). Ethnographic and experimental evidence indicates, for example, that it takes on average 12.5 minutes to grind a kilogram of millet with a saddle quern (some 2.7kg would be required to feed the average family per day), whereas to grind a kilogram of wheat can take between 1.5 and 2.5 hours, depending upon the hardness and moisture content of the grain (Richards 1939, 103-104; Samuel 2010, 464; Menasanch *et al* 2002, 98). Consequently several hours milling would be required to furnish a family with enough meal for one day. A rotary quern worked by one or two people, on the other hand, can complete the same task in less time, taking perhaps just 12-15 minutes to grind a kilogram of grain (Anon 1874, 375; Jørgensen 2000, 191). Grinding maize with a metate is, however, in a league of its own. In Tepoztlán, Mexico, for example, Lewis (1963, 99) recorded that women regularly spent 4-5 hours a day grinding corn for tortillas.[2]

Using a quern has generally been considered to be a tiring and time-consuming operation, one to be beguiled by socialising and singing (the latter also helps effect a rhythmic movement of the upper stone, key to milling efficiently). In the 1st century BC poem *Moretum*, for example, Simulus alternates the turning of the quern between his right and left hands and consoles his task with 'rustic' songs (Vergiliana *Moretum*

[2]. To these timings, of course, must be added the time taken beforehand to ready the grain for milling and the time taken afterwards to sieve and regrind as necessary and to prepare and cook the ground product.

24-29). In 19th century South Africa, Casalis (1861, 143) recorded that Basuto women ground their corn together in unison, singing as they did so, 'to lighten their labours'. Similarly in former Northern Rhodesia Richards (1939, 92) noted that the women sang as they milled, 'the rhythmic to and fro of the grinding stone and the notes of the song falling flatter and flatter are ... common sounds in a village in the later afternoon'.

3.4.3 Products and transformation
There is no doubt, however, that the quern, in its various forms, is a practical milling tool. Although very much associated with grinding grain there is also plentiful evidence to show that querns can be put to use for grinding a wide variety of products – vegetable, mineral and animal – from cereals, lentils, salt, chocolate, spices, tofu beans and rice to snuff, medicines, dye stuffs and pigments to mineral ores and pottery temper (Anon 1895, 412; Aschmann 1949, 683; Hayden 1987b, 188; Schlanger 1991, 462; Baudais and Lundström-Baudais 2002, 173; Ertug-Yaras 2002, 216). Consequently, as Barker (1985, 12) points out querns should not be taken automatically as evidence for agriculture. It should also be noted that although some querns may be used for grinding a variety of different products, others, whether by habit or custom, tend to be used solely for milling cereals. Likewise, oily products tend to be ground on separate querns as are medicinal roots and herbs (Hayden 1987b, 188; Hamon and Gall 2013, 115.). But although the physical action of using a quern may be the same for each product the reason for that action and the meaning behind it and thus the cultural significance of the function attached to it is dependent upon what is being ground and why. The task of grinding pottery temper, for example, would carry with it a different set of meanings and values compared to that of grinding gold ore, as would milling corn for an everyday meal compared to preparing malted grain for brewing beer for a festival (Watts, S. 2006a).

However, of potentially more importance is that whatever product is being ground it is transformed by the quern from raw material into usable resource. The quern too was also gradually transformed over time as the stones wore thinner through the action of grinding. Potentially strong metaphorical links can be perceived, therefore between notions of transformation and ageing, death, regeneration and life (Hill 1995, 108; Fendin 2000, 91-92). In an archaeological context, however, the form and shape of a quern may give little indication as to its primary function. It is important, therefore, to consider the context in which it was found together with any changes to its performance characteristics and appearance such as gouging and pocking or staining on the grinding surface which may indicate, for example, that the quern had been used for grinding minerals or ochre rather than food products. In addition, starch grain or use wear analysis can be invaluable in determining the use to which a quern was put, although as Hamon (2008b, 1516) points out these will only show the last or main use. However, just as it should not be assumed that the presence of querns on archaeological sites equates with cereal cultivation so it should also not be presumed that querns found on metalworking sites were used for grinding ore (Barker 1985, 12; Craddock 1995, 162).

Nevertheless, most querns found in a domestic context are likely to have been used for grinding staple food products and their importance for this task should not be underestimated. As Richards (1939, 46) comments it is hard for the western world with its abundance and choice of foods to fully appreciate the meaning of a staple crop to subsistence communities. Crop failure due to environmental conditions, disease or war can lead easily to hardship and starvation. Cereals cannot be easily digested by humans until their hard, outer cellulose shells have been broken up or removed. Although this can be achieved by pounding in a mortar or cooking in a dish like frumenty, current milling practice together with ethnographical evidence indicates that cereals are usually ground between two stones. Historical and archaeological evidence also suggests that this was the case in the prehistoric period. Diodorus (5.21.5) comments that 'the method [the Britons] employ of harvesting their grain crops is to cut off not more than the heads and store them away in roofed granges, and then each day they pick out the ripened heads and grind them'. Carbonised wheat and rye were found remaining in upper stones at Hunsbury hillfort in Northamptonshire (Fell 1936, 99). Further afield, in Bulgaria, a mixture of wheat, barley and acorns was found on a saddle quern at a Late Bronze Age site at Raskopanitza (Renfrew 1973, 155). The acorns were perhaps to eke out a meagre grain supply, although it may have been common practice to grind a mixture of foodstuffs. The ground meal is likely to have been used for porridge or making flat bread to be cooked on hot stones, although ovens are not unknown. The remains of bread have been found on a number of sites, most particularly in ancient Egyptian tombs where loaves were included in funerary offerings (Samuel 2001, 196; Samuel 2002). In Britain bread has been found on a Neolithic site at Yarnton, Oxfordshire (3640-3350 cal.

BC) and the last meal of the Lindow II bog man (cal. 2BC-AD119) included bread thought to comprise a mixture of barley, emmer and spelt (Robinson 2000, 89; Holden 1995, 79).

It is the task of milling cereals, therefore, that is the quern's *raison d'être*. This may be a utilitarian, everyday task but it is one that is intimately connected with what for many peoples is and was the basis of life. Furthermore, it is a link that can be traced back to the Neolithic period and the beginnings of agriculture. Use-wear and residue analyses have indicated a strong link between Neolithic saddle querns and cereal cultivation and it has been suggested that an increased use of meal-based foods led to the development of and an increasing use of the saddle quern (Hamon 2008a; Adams 1999). In a domestic context, the sound of the quern turning coupled perhaps with the voices of the women singing as they worked, would have been a familiar, even comforting sound, bringing with it the knowledge that all was well, that one was going to eat that day (Thomson 1877, 526; Watts, S. 2008a, 95). As Robert Jamieson's poem states, 'The music for a hungry wame [stomach]/Is grindin' o' the quernie' (Colville 1892, 126). In this respect it is easy to understand why, in the Bible, the laws of Moses state that one should not take an upper millstone as a pledge for that is taking a man's life away, and why the absence of the sound of millstones is used as a sign of desolation, symbolic of a place that is uninhabited and forsaken (Deuteronomy 24:6; Jeremiah 25:10; Revelation 18:22). The link between querns, grain and life can be seen, therefore, to be strong and enduring, and one that functions on both physical and symbolic levels.

However, cereals are also the chief ingredient of ale and beer and it has been suggested (Dineley and Dineley 2000, 151) that it is the use of cereals for brewing rather than baking that accounts for the rapid spread of their cultivation across Europe. The basic method of brewing – soaking the grain, allowing it to germinate before drying and crushing it, then adding hot water, draining if off and letting it ferment – has remained largely unchanged. The carbonised grain found on some prehistoric sites may have been burnt, therefore, during the malting process (Dineley and Dineley 2000, 137-138). Kilns or ovens could have been used for drying the malted grain but for small amounts pots by the fire would have sufficed. As Dineley and Dineley (2000, 151) point out and as the author has found the same quern can be used for grinding both ordinary and malted grains. Malted grain is also easier and quicker to grind and the stones of a rotary quern need not be set so close together. Dineley and Dineley (2000, 142, 146) further suggest that the bread found at Yarnton, which was made from very coarse ground grain may have been a *bappir*, a part-baked malted grain loaf such as used by the ancient Mesopotamians and Egyptians for brewing. The *bappirs* were crumbled in water and the mixture left to ferment, aided by the warm climate. The brew, which was thick and cloudy, was then strained into large vats and decanted into smaller jars for use (Renfrew 2000, 197-198; Wilson 2001, 19). The part-baked cakes found at Glastonbury Lake Village, Somerset which comprised whole wheat grains mixed with a sticky substance, probably honey, may also have been *bappirs* (Bulleid, 1924, 45).

To subsistence societies ale may be an important source of nourishment but archaeological finds together with historical and ethnographic sources, as well as modern western practices, indicate the significant and timeless role of alcoholic beverages in social, religious and political events, creating and affirming relationships and obligations (Richards 1939, 76-78, 109; Goody 1982, 73-74; Graham 1994, 21; Sørensen 2000, 118; Arnold 2001). However, it should also be noted that food can be used in similar, if less intoxicating ways (Richards 1939, 109). As indicated above, querns will have played an important role in the preparation of food and drink for feasting events. Such preparation may also have been a social event in itself as women came together to work (Graham 1994, 53).

3.4.4 Maintenance
It is not surprising, therefore, to find that such important tools well cared for. Similus, the rustic farmer of the poem *Moretum* brushed his quern with a goat's tail before starting work (Vergiliana *Moretum* 22-23). In Mali, Hamon (pers. corresp.) noted that the saddle querns and rubbers were brushed down when grinding was complete. They were leant against the wall of the house (either inside or outside) or against a stone, their working surfaces facing inwards and thus protected. Their upper stones were left on their backs with their working faces turned upwards (Hamon and Gall 2013, 117). In households in the highlands and islands of Scotland the quern was brushed down with a wisp of straw on a Saturday night (no milling was done on a Sunday) (Campbell 1990, 35).

The key to a quern's successful performance as a milling tool, however, is its grinding efficiency. This efficiency decreases as the quern's performance characteristics are affected through use, as the grinding surfaces gradually wear smooth and it no longer grinds as well (after Schiffer 1999, 23). This reduction in grinding efficiency can be remedied by pecking the grinding surface to roughen it and provide a new series of cutting edges. This is generally undertaken with a suitably sized hammerstone or a special quern 'pecker' (Crawford 1909, 396; Graham 1994, 59-60). The quern pecker, as Fendin (2006, 160) points out, also forms an essential part of the milling tool kit but is not an implement generally looked for or recognised on archaeological sites. Ideally such repecking should be done as infrequently as possible for this is more likely to break the stone and will cause more wear than the actual act of milling itself (Schlanger 1991, 462; Watts, M. pers. comm.). The speed with which a quern wears, however, depends upon three main factors; firstly, the characteristics and composition of the rock from which the quern is made, secondly the amount of use it receives and thirdly the material(s) it grinds (David 1998, 21; Adams *et al* 2009). Consequently, data on the frequency with which a stone is repecked varies considerably, from between every five days or so to every four-five months (Horsfall 1987, 341; Schlanger 1991, 341; Tewolde 1993, 223; Hamon pers. corresp.).

Using both sides of a saddle quern or rubber, however, can extend their working lives (Adams 2002, 25). Likewise the provision of additional handle holes can potentially prolong the working life of a rotary quern. An upper stone found at a Romano British site at Penryn, Cornwall, for example, had two handle holes in its side, one set higher than the other, and a handle slot across the top, all of which could have potentially extended its use-life (Figure 3.11). Similarly, an upper stone from Glastonbury Lake Village, Somerset with a broken out handle hole in its side had a replacement slot across the top of the stone in order to prolong its working life. Examples have also been found of repairs to rotary querns such as the two halves of an upper stone from Glastonbury, Somerset which had been pegged back together with a new handle hole drilled at right angles to the first (Bulleid 1917, 613, 614). These repairs suggest that the querns were valued items, perhaps not easily replaced. Spindles and handles also wear over time and may need replacing, although as Crawford (1909, 394) records a piece of rag wrapped around a worn spindle can effect a simple cure by raising the upper stone and enabling it to turn freely again.

3.5 Secondary Functions and Reuse

Ethnographic evidence indicates that quernstones that have broken or become too worn for their primary milling function are often used for grinding other products such as salt, sugar, coffee, medicines, clay or minerals for temper or colours (Walton 1974, 7; Hayden 1987b, 191; Schlanger 1991, 463). For some querns, of course, grinding products such as these is their primary function and, as mentioned above, querns may be used for grinding more than one product (Hayden 1987b, 191; Horsfall 1987, 336). Quernstones may also be recycled, that is reused in the manufacture

Figure 3.11: Upper stone from Penryn, Cornwall with two off-set handle holes in the side and a handle slot across the top (S. Watts).

of another artefact. At Thorpe Thewles, Cleveland and Culduthel Farm near Inverness, Scotland, for example, rotary quernstones had been reused as mouldstones (Figure 3.12) (Heslop 2008, 65-66; Pitts 2007, 6). These differing secondary uses will all have impacted upon the particular quern's meaning and value.

There is also plentiful archaeological evidence demonstrating the reuse of querns as building stones, paving slabs and pivot stones and they were also reused as work surfaces and more particularly as hearthstones (Gray and Bulleid 1953, 180, 183; Alcock 1960, 99-10; Beresford 1971, 61; Frere 1972, 78, 158; Buckley and Major 1988, 36; Neal *et al* 1990, 167; Bellamy 2000, 313). These may represent pragmatic reuses of useful pieces of stone but it can also be argued that they are structured deposits and to this end it is worth noting that many querns thus reused, although worn are not worn out. If a quern can be utilised as a foundation stone or incorporated in an abandonment deposit then a fragment in a wall, floor or hearth can also be seen as socially significant (Watts, S. 2006a). Hearths in particular symbolise the home but there is also a link between querns and the provision of food (Nowakowski 2001, 141; O'Sullivan and Kenny 2008, 10-11). Fragments reused in walls or floors may denote a particular point or event in the life history of the structure or of its occupants or to provide a continuity or link from/to the past (Brück 1999b, 154; Robinson 2007; O'Sullivan and Kenny 2008, 9). In this light it is also worth bearing in mind that quernstones thus reused can potentially have seen more that one phase of reuse (after Woodward 2000, 20). The incorporation of a pair of millstones at the bottom of the church tower at Hope Bagot, Shropshire, however, has a different story to tell. The stones were apparently a deodand, forfeited to the crown for pious use, having caused the death of the miller (information from the Church of St. John the Baptist, Hope Bagot). Quernstones have also been found reused in the fabric the parish churches of Takeley and Great Chesterford in Essex (Major 1987, 114-115).

The reuse of querns as gravestones or in the construction of burial cists may also represent more than a pragmatic exercise. A potent link between life and death can be seen in such a reuse but the possibility of a direct link between a quernstone and the person buried should also be borne in mind (Bennett and Elton 1898, 144-145; Henshall 1955-1956, 262, 282-283). Today querns and millstones are often found reused as decorative features in gardens or buildings (Figure 3.13). Each form of reuse represents a different category or level of structured deposit, each placed with a particular reason or meaning. Such reuse may be purely aesthetic but something of the stones' original function or from whence it came may also have been indirectly in mind.

The physical parameters of a quern, however, its affordances, can also lead not only to such reuse as a hearthstone or building stone but also to its use as a weapon. Abimelech, an Israelite ruler *circa* 1250-

Figure 3.12: Rotary quernstone reused as a mouldstone from an Iron Age settlement at Culduthel Farm (© Headland Archaeology).

Figure 3.13: Lower stone of an Iron Age rotary quern reused as a decorative stone in the wall of a building near Bristol (S. Watts).

1030BC, was struck down by a quernstone thrown from the fortified tower he was besieging in the centre of Thebes. Not wishing history to record that he had been killed by a woman he asked his sword bearer to run him through (Judges 9:50-55). Did he see the woman throw the quernstone or was this an assumption on his part? As a murder weapon the quern also finds its way into fiction in Agatha Christie's *Murder in Mesopotamia*.

3.6 Discard and Deposition in the Archaeological Record

The working life of a quernstone is determined by the lasting qualities of the stone used for its manufacture coupled with the amount of use it receives and what it is used for. Consequently it is difficult to generalise on its life span. A report on Irish querns in 1850 remarked on the difficulties in determining the age of those still in use as they had been handed down from mother to daughter over many generations (Anon 1850, 395). American metates on the other hand appear to have a use-life of 15-30 years, although some have been reported to be up to 100 years old (Paston 1974, 101; Horsfall 1987, 342; Hayden 1987b, 193).

Eventually, however, a quernstone will wear too thin or, in the case of a saddle quern too concave, to be comfortably used. At this point the quernstone(s) may be discarded, which in some communities literally means throwing them out of the house (Paston 1974, 101). Quernstones may also become surplus to requirements and consequently no longer used. This may be due to additional querns coming into the household on the occasion of a marriage or through inheritance or to the increasing use of powered mills. In Mali disused saddle querns may be reused as benches or steps, or simply left in a corner of the courtyard (Hamon and Gall 2013, 118). These factors have potentially great bearing on the meanings of querns interpreted as unstratified surface finds or found reused in buildings.

Querns, however, can enter the archaeological record at any point in their life history and the nature of their deposition is also part of their biographies, just as they become part of the biography of the feature within which they are deposited. This also includes their manufacturing stage. Quern rough-outs and blanks have been found at a number of quarry sites and it has been suggested (Heslop 2008, 45) that potentially usable rough-outs found on prehistoric quarry sites may have been deliberately left as some form of offering. Such 'depositions' may be related not to the quern's intended function as a milling tool but the quern-mason's craft, a thank-offering for the safe working of the quarry or the stone it provides. Other collections of unfinished and broken stones have different tales to tell. The 14 or so broken or unfinished rotary quernstones of sandstone recovered from Longis Beach, Alderney, for example, are presumed to represent sailing ship ballast or to have come from a nearby quern-finishing workshop, probably of Roman date (Watts, S. 2003). The mass of late Saxon lava quern fragments found on the Thames waterfront in London are also thought to be debris from a workshop (Freshwater 1996).

Archaeological evidence also shows that it was not uncommon in the prehistoric period and later to place querns in pits, ditches and postholes in the ground. As indicated in Chapter One, much of the material found in such features was originally interpreted as rubbish but it is now considered that many objects, including querns, were purposefully placed in the positions in which they are found with more meaning and intent than the mere disposal of refuse. Hodder (2005, 13) refers to the 'aura' generated by the removal of objects from the everyday visible world. Furthermore, although the upper and lower stones of querns may be found together evidence, as shown in the literature review, suggests that most tend to be deposited separately. This signifies a separation of the two stones at some time prior to deposition at which point their biographies also separate into divergent paths. Likewise, some quernstones are found in a complete and apparently reusable state, while others are broken. The breakage of quernstones may be accidental due to post-depositional processes such as ploughing. However, this is unlikely in the case of fragments found in pits, postholes and ditches and it is thought that many of these represent quernstones that were deliberately broken prior to deposition. This would have been a difficult task unless the stone was worn very thin or flawed. Querns by their very nature are not objects that break easily. Burning, however, can help and burnt quern fragments have been found on a number of sites (Curwen 1931, 145; Nowakowski 1991, 73). Several reasons have been put forward to account for the fragmentation of querns. Chapman (2000b) for example suggests that quernstones and other objects were broken and pieces shared, perhaps taken off site for deposition elsewhere, thus linking people and places, a practice he refers to as 'enchainment'. Alternatively the breaking of a quernstone may signify the ending of a relationship or place, or release or destroy its powers (Brück 2006, 297-299; Moore 2007, 94; Grinsell 1961, 476-477). As with the splitting of upper from lower stone, once a quernstone is broken into pieces, each fragment has its own biography. Finally, as noted earlier in this chapter, a quernstone's life does not necessarily end with its deposition in the archaeological record but continues as and when it is retrieved from that record. The method of retrieval, its current state and location are all part of its continuing life history.

3.7 Object Biography and the Structured Deposition of Querns

An exploration of the object biography of querns raises a number of issues that have a direct bearing on their use as meaningful, structured deposits at the end of their use-lives. Each quern has its own unique biography determined by the cultural context(s) within which it is manufactured, used and discarded. Contrasts can be seen, for example, between querns used on an everyday basis for grinding staple foods and those used on a particular occasion or for another product, and between those used in a domestic context and those used in a factory, prison or by an army in the field. Consequently each quern has its own set of meanings and values which may be related to the stone itself, the rock from which it is made, the product(s) it was used to grind or the social context in which it was used and which may ultimately determine its place in the archaeological record.

Querns, however, also share points of commonality. They are first and foremost grinding tools. Consequently, in their different forms and modes of operation they are well-suited to the task of milling and play a key role in transforming a raw material into a usable product. The choice of a particular quernstone as a structured deposit may have drawn, therefore, upon one or more unique or common values. It is also possible, however, that everyday objects such as quernstones were transferred from domestic to ritual use which may also have resulted in their incorporation in structured deposits, thereby acquiring more import through such formal placement (Bradley 2005a, 35; Walker and Lucero 2000, 133; Osborne 2004, 2). This latter scenario has a bearing on the composition of structured deposits and the relationship between the deposition of a quernstone and the artefacts found with it. It was noted that at each stage of its 'life' a quern is associated with a particular set of people, artefacts and social settings. Are the artefacts found in contiguity with a quern in the archaeological record reflective, therefore, of a particular social setting? Can the use of querns for grinding products be implied from certain combinations of artefacts or is that combination so unusual that it can only be construed as relating to a special event?

Also important is the treatment of quernstones prior to deposition. The deposition of a single stone, for example, marks the splitting up of a pair. This potentially renders the quern inoperable although saddle querns may be worked with several different rubbers and this may be important in the choice of rubbers in structured deposits. The latter are also comparatively easy to replace. Quernstones may also be in a complete or fragmentary state. Depending upon the nature of the context in which they are found, some complete stones may be interpreted as caches, buried with the intention of retrieval and reuse but others appear to be permanent structured deposits of some form. This is an important distinction as the latter will have been taken from their primary task as milling stones for use in a depositional event prior to the end of their use-life. It was also mentioned above that many of the fragmentary quernstones, as found in the archaeological record, appear to have been deliberately rather than accidently broken. This implies that complete and fragmentary stones were deposited with different levels of meaning and intent and that the presence of such stones in the archaeological record can be used to signify different categories of deposit.

The importance of querns in the lives of subsistence communities, for grinding grain for everyday consumption, is well-demonstrated. However, it is considered (Thomas 1999, 16; Richmond 1999, 42; Pollard 2002, 10) that grain did not become a subsistence crop until the Middle Bronze Age in Britain. This is an important consideration in the use and deposition of querns in the Neolithic period. In theory, one would expect an increase in the numbers of querns in the Bronze Age, although it has been suggested (Watts 2008a, 100) that the use of querns in depositional events in the Neolithic period was a pre-established norm introduced as part of the overall Neolithic cultural package.

The task of milling is a vital socially meaningful act through which practical and symbolic links can be seen between querns and the home, women, grain, the provision of food and the transformation of raw materials. Through these links one can begin to appreciate why querns were chosen for use as structured deposits in the prehistoric period. To further that understanding, the symbolic properties are now investigated in more detail.

4

THE SYMBOLIC PROPERTIES OF QUERNS

4.1 Introduction

The exploration of the object biography of querns demonstrated that querns are:
- A key part of the process that transforms raw products into usable materials.
- Of vital importance at a daily subsistence level.
- Connected with women and the grinding of foodstuffs.
- Indicative of social structures and relationships.

These four important facets of querns can be traced back from living tradition into history and each, therefore, is enough perhaps to explain the presence of querns as structured deposits on prehistoric sites. Through these different aspects one can begin to see a duality of practical and symbolic functions linked to gender, the agricultural cycle and the transformation of natural things. These assumptions are compelling and appear to confirm, therefore, the theories put forward in much of the published literature that querns are to be symbolically associated with lifecycles, agriculture and fertility, and also with gender, family and reproduction. As such it is easy to understand why in Biblical times the taking of a quernstone as a pledge was tantamount to taking a person's life and why the absence of the sound of millstones is used as a symbol for an uninhabited, forsaken land (Deuteronomy 24:6; Jeremiah 25:10). At first glance the meaning behind the structured deposition of querns seems clear. Querns were tools used for grinding cereals, a staple, life-giving food and consequently broken/disused querns are to be associated with death and abandonment (Campbell 1987, 112; Brück 1999b, 154; O'Sullivan and Kenny 2008, 11; Graefe *et al* 2009, 93). This has some resonance in the ethnographic record. Amongst the aboriginal peoples of the Western Desert of Australia, for example, a woman's quern may be broken on the occasion of her death (Cane 1989, 113). On the other hand it has also been suggested that the deposition of querns signifies continuity and regeneration and that their fragmentation denotes the making rather than the breaking of relationships (Chapman 2000b, 94; O'Sullivan and Kenny 2008, 94; Moore 2007).

The meaning of an object is not necessarily fixed, however, but dependent upon particular social, ideological and contextual circumstances and subject to spatial and temporal change and adaptation. Artefacts can function as symbols, metaphors, metonyms or mnemonic devices, the meanings of which can be associated with what they were used for, who used them, where they were used or even how they operated. The physical properties of the artefact can also be important. As Parker Pearson and Ramilisonina (1998, 310) point out 'the physical properties of materials such as stone, wood, water and fire are such that they resist certain interpretations and invite others'. A quernstone is a durable item, harder than the material it grinds. This 'invites' such metaphors as 'his heart is ... as hard as a piece of the nether millstone' (Job 41:24). Size and weight can also be important characteristics. A number of saints, for example, were martyred by being crushed under a millstone or drowned with one tied around their neck (see front cover) (see also Matthew 18:6; Revelation 18:21).

Artefacts, however, can also mean different things to different people and they can carry several different meanings at the same time. Everyday objects may acquire esoteric properties through the timing or nature of their manufacture or acquisition or through the symbolism attached to them (Drennan 1976, 357). Each artefact not only has its own biography, evoking particular meanings, relationships and memories and producing a unique set of reactions but its placement in contiguity with other artefacts may tell a different narrative. How that placement was enacted may also be of import (Garwood *et al* 1991, ix; Pollard 2001, 317, 330-331; Jones 2004-2005, 124-125). As Gerrard (2003, 224) comments, 'the symbolic meaning of object[s] can change according to the context in which [they are] found', embodying, for example, a specific place, person, event or task. Furthermore, such meanings may also be peculiar to particular communities and impossible to understand by those who do not have the same world view (Tilley 1999, 9).

Nevertheless, despite the problems inherent in interpreting the meaning behind particular deposits, living tradition, history and mythology indicate that objects both acquire and maintain a specific set of meanings. This chapter, therefore, explores the symbolic and metaphoric meanings appropriated to querns. In doing so it provides further insight into the importance of querns to the communities who used them and how they may have acted as one of the mediums through which prehistoric society's world view was manifested and which is witnessed in their structured deposition in the archaeological record.

4.2 Querns as Symbols of Gender

Chapter Three showed that, although men may use querns in particular circumstances or on particular occasions or for grinding particular products, querns as tools for preparing food are very much the province of women. In modern, traditional societies it is through such gender-related tasks that the distinctiveness of being female is maintained (Casalis 1861, 141; Lidström Holmberg 2004, 227). Thus tools used in a domestic context for the preparation of food can be seen as symbolic of women, home and family. The association between querns and women is further strengthened in some societies by lengthy grinding sessions held as part of the rituals to celebrate female rites of passage. These sessions may be communal as with the Lala of Nigeria where all the women of the village come together to grind corn to mark the onset of puberty of a young girl (Kirk-Greene 1957). Saddle querns are placed within a specially erected shelter in the centre of the village and the women grind all day, keeping time to the beat of drums and singing. Within the Hopi of north-east Arizona, however, it is the young girl only who performs the grinding ritual, grinding corn within a darkened room over a period of four days. A similar grinding ritual is also performed by a Hopi bride before her wedding (Bradfield 1973, 34-37). In both Lala and Hopi societies the use of a quern in such contexts can be seen as an affirmation of womanhood. The transition from girl to woman is expressed symbolically through the action of grinding and the transformation of grain to meal, from one state to another as the girl becomes the provider of food (Lidström Holmberg 2004, 227).

However, although a clear link can be seen between querns and women, this is but one way in which gender is enacted through querns. Querns comprise two stones which are brought together for the act of grinding and are seen, therefore, as an ideal metaphor for the expression of gender relations. The movement of the upper stone of a saddle quern forward and back across the lower stone may be seen to have an overtly sexual meaning, with the lower stone as female and the upper stone as male (Lidström Holmberg 2004, 225-228). In this respect, it is perhaps worth bearing in mind that the word for donkey (*ovos*) was used in Greek literature from at least the 5th to 3rd centuries BC to denote the upper stone of a saddle quern (Moritz 1958, 10). This could, as Moritz suggests, stem from the fact that donkeys were work animals and that it was the upper stone that did all the work but perhaps more likely, however, as Moritz also subsequently suggests, the connection lies in the similarity in size and shape of a certain donkey attribute, as shown clearly in the literary scene depicted on a decorated Megarian bowl from Thebes dated to the 3rd or 2nd century BC (Figure 4.1) (Rostovtzeff 1937, 90; Moritz 1958, 11, 16).

The playing out of the male/female sexual relationship can also be seen in the rotary quern, the lower stone this time taking the male role, its fixed upright spindle penetrating the eye of the upper stone (after Heslop 2008, 75). The personification of the quern is continued in a Gaelic riddle. 'An old woman in the corner, spokes through her two eyes, and she grumbling' is thought to refer to a two-handled quern (Curwen 1941, 31). Millstones are still described in feminine terms in modern traditional milling. The central hole in the stone is called the eye, the mid section of the grinding surface the breast (or chest) and the outer section the skirt. Likewise, the fitting on top of the spindle that knocks against the shoe (which hangs below the hopper) to feed the grain into the eye of the stone is called a damsel (it is often stated that the name is due to the fact that it chatters (clatters) as it turns!) (Watts, M. pers.comm.). In terms of genuine symbolism rather than lewd thought, the role reversal from lower-female to upper-female represents a tremendous shift in mind set, particularly in communities where saddle querns and rotary querns were used concurrently. This may suggest that such a change did not occur until later, perhaps not until the development of the water-powered mill, traditionally a male preserve.

In some communities, however, such as the Minyanka in Mali, the upper stones of saddle querns also represent children (Hamon pers. comm.). This may be because women were often responsible for making their own upper stones and it is the upper stone that a woman has most contact with as she works, or simply through the different sizes of upper and lower stones. In both male/female and mother/child relationships, therefore,

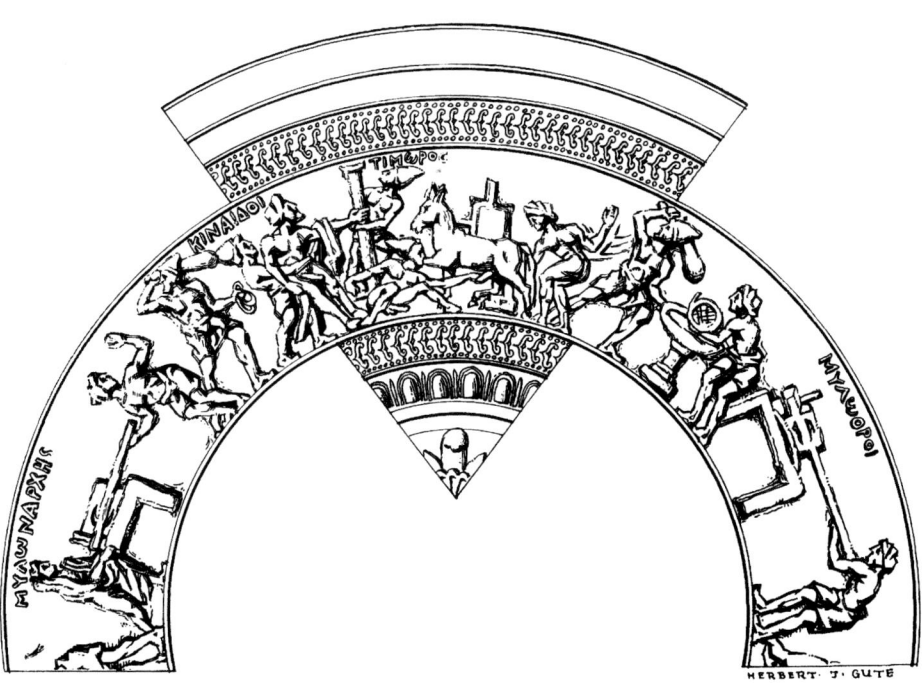

Figure 4.1: Milling scene on a Megarian bowl showing a donkey in a prominent positon. The upper stones of the Olynthan mills depicted left and right are on plan. The words from left to right read 'Master of the mill', 'Catamite', 'Avenger' and 'Millers' (Rostovtzeff 1937, Figure 1. Courtesy Archaeological Institute of America and American Journal of Archaeology).

the lower stone of a saddle quern appears to represent the woman. Of course, the picture is not always that simple. In Indian non-vedic birth rituals, for example, the upper stone represents both child and mother goddess. Painted and dressed, it is passed around the cradle by the most senior woman in attendance before being laid beside the new born in a ceremony intended to bestow blessings on the child (Kosambi 1965, 46).

Lidstrom Holmberg (2004, 229-230) also makes an interesting association between the deposition of upper stones in adult graves and lower stones in the graves of children at the respective early Neolithic sites at Fågelbacken and Östra Vrå in Sweden. Hamon (pers. comm.) has also noticed that in western European Linearbandkeramik and post-Linearbandkeramik cemeteries querns tend to be found in the graves of women and children. On the other hand, at Khirokitia, a Neolithic settlement on Cyprus, Brun (2001, 116) comments on the preference for querns with male rather than female burials while Gimbutas (1991, 133) noted that in central Europe querns are found with both female and male Neolithic burials. Unfortunately, it is not clear whether these are upper and/or lower stones. In addition, not all burials contain querns and to compound the problem, in Britain and northern Europe Neolithic burial chambers which have been found to utilise querns within their construction contained multiple, disarticulated burials.

There are, however, a number of other reasons that could account for the presence of querns with human burials. Where they are in direct association with a burial, for example, they may have been placed as grave goods, perhaps intended to provide sustenance in the after life. Querns may also have been used for preparing a funerary meal or even for grinding human bone in preparation for burial (Brück 2001, 155). Alternatively, it has been suggested (Hill 1995, 108; Bradley 2005a, 107) that their presence is linked to the cycle of life, death and regeneration as witnessed in the agricultural year (see below). This theory seems especially pertinent with regard to the deposition of querns in Iron Age storage pits that were also used for human or animal burials.

4.3 Querns as Symbols of the Harvest, Fertility and Feasting

There are, however, other potential meanings behind the deposition of querns in pits. According to Gimbutas (1987, 20), large flat stones, dedicated to or representing Ops Consiua, a Roman goddess of earth fertility, were stored in pits and covered with straw. They were taken out once a year during the harvest season; in the Roman world her festival was celebrated on 25th August (Scullard 1981, 181). Unfortunately, Gimbutas does not explain what the stones were used for, although she does imply that they represented the goddess. However, it is tempting to link this practice to finds of complete saddle querns placed upside down in Neolithic pits at Etton, Cambridgeshire and Milsoms Corner, Somerset. That from Etton appeared to have been packed in leaves and twigs while that from Milsoms Corner was laid upon a bed of carbonised material (Figure 6.3) (Pryor 1998a, 22; Tabor pers. corresp.). These querns were perhaps curated and stored safely underground, which raises the possibility that, like the stones mentioned by Gimbutas above, they were taken out for use following the harvest. This use may have been at once both practical and symbolic (after Bradley 1987, 351).

With the introduction of agriculture in the Neolithic period the harvest took on a new meaning, although autumn would always have been a time of plenty in terms of wild fruits, nuts and seeds. Indeed there is evidence in some areas to suggest that wild woodland was 'managed' by Mesolithic peoples (Zvelebil 1994, 35). However, with the cultivation of crops came a new regime of preparing the ground, sowing the seed and harvesting and storing the grain both for consumption and as seed corn for the following year. It has been suggested (Gimbutas 1987, 12) that the belief system of the European Neolithic derived from the natural order of birth, growth, death and regeneration. This was manifested in the cultured nature of agriculture, particularly in the cultivation of cereals. As the adoption of agriculture spread across Europe so it is thought that the practices and principles associated with the cultivation and processing of grain were also adopted, albeit perhaps in changed and altered states as the new techniques and technologies were adapted to local needs and environments (Curtis 2001, 74-75). It is also likely that beliefs and symbolism associated with grain were also adopted and adapted.

To subsistence based communities the success of the harvest is paramount. A poor harvest leads to hardship, even starvation and death. It is important, therefore, that the ground is prepared and crops sown at the most auspicious and propitious times. To this end, in the prehistoric period and later, the gods were consulted and appropriate gifts and offerings made (Green 1997, 37). As Green (1997, 37) points out there has always been a strong link between religious and farming calendars. The first fruits of the harvest are seen as of particular importance. In the Old Testament, for example, we read that 'Cain brought of the fruit of the ground an offering unto the Lord' who was not pleased with his gift but that he was with Abel who 'brought of the *firstlings* of his flock' (italics mine) (Genesis 4:3-7). It has been suggested that the story of Cain and Abel may have been devised to explain and justify the tensions that lay between sedentary farmers and nomadic pasturalists in the region of the Meiden valley in Iran *circa* 5500BC (Rohl 1999, 407-408). However, it is also of note that Cain did not bring the *first* fruits of the harvest as a gift, hence why God was displeased, rather than the fact that God preferred an offering of lambs. This fact appears to be confirmed when God says to Moses, 'When ye be come into the land which I give unto you, and shall reap the harvest thereof, then ye shall bring a sheaf of the *first-fruits* of your harvest unto the priest: And he shall wave the sheaf before the Lord, to be accepted for you' (italics mine) (Leviticus 23:10-11).

Customs prevailing in Ireland and western Scotland in more recent times hark back to pre-Christian origins. In Ireland, on the morning of Lammas, 1st August, some of the grain was harvested in the morning and turned into bread or porridge before evening (Ross 1986, 165). Similarly in the Western Isles of Scotland, Macleod Banks (1941, 63) records that a bannock, the *moilean moire*, prepared from freshly gathered grain, was shared around the family on the feast day of St. Mary, 15th August. These dates coincide with the Celtic religious festival of Lughnasadh that was celebrated over the four-week period surrounding 1st August (Green 1997, 36).

The tools associated with the cultivation, processing and consumption of grain may also, therefore, have been considered important and worthy of special treatment. In addition, the possibility that the deposition of querns in storage pits was linked to feasts celebrating the harvest must also be considered. In these respects, querns may have been thank offerings for the harvest, or for the safe storage of the grain, or to promote the growth of the new crop. At this point it is also interesting to note that the Roman god Consus is thought to have been a guardian of underground stored grain. Festivals in his honour were held on 21st August after the harvest during which time a burnt offering of first fruits was proffered and also on 15th December following the successful completion of sowing the crops (Scullard 1981, 163, 177, 205). However, as Hill (1995, 100) comments storage pits on British Iron Age sites were not infilled on a regular, yearly basis. Alternatively, therefore, querns may have been propitiatory offerings for soured pits, whose contents had gone mouldy (Cunliffe 1992; Watts, S. 1999).

4.4 Querns as Symbols of Death

During the milling process raw, unusable and inedible materials are ground into usable and edible products. This is a particularly important symbolical process in relation to grain, which is itself a powerful symbol of life, death and resurrection (John 12.24). As the grain is ground so it is effectively killed, it cannot be sown and grown. This is shown well in the Hopi language, for whom the lifecycle of the corn plant is metaphorically linked to that of humans. The word *tuqyakni* means 'others killed' and derives from *tuu-+qöya* (the plural form of to kill) and *–kna* (pounded corn kernals) (Black 1984, 282).

The killing of the grain is the subject of *John Barleycorn*, an English folksong thought to be the survival of a myth relating to the slaying of a corn god (Vaughan Williams and Lloyd 1959, 56-57, 116). John Barleycorn rises up green and living after being buried in the ground and presumed dead, only to be cut down in the prime of life. In the tortuous treatment he subsequently receives, the miller, we are told, plays his part by grinding John Barleycorn between two stones.

The story of John Barleycorn echoes the fate of Mot, an ancient Canaanite god. Mot, a god of death and drought, traps Baal, a god of rain, vegetation and fertility, in the underworld. Anat, a goddess of fertility and war, and wife and sister of Baal, travels to the underworld and attacks Mot. She cleaves and winnows him and burns him in a fire before grinding him in a mill and scattering him over the fields. Her actions release Baal and in due course Mot is also restored to life (Jordan 2002, 167; Anon 2010). The bones of Tammuz, a Sumerian god, are similarly ground in a mill and scattered to the wind (Santillana and Dechend 1969, 92).

The story of Mot is recorded on tablets dated to *circa* 1200BC from Tell Ugarit, a Late Bronze Age metropolis in what is now northern Syria, while the legend of Tammuz originates from a Nabataean text *circa* 300BC-AD100. However, these stories could be far more ancient in origin. As Graves (1959, v, viii) comments, myths were not only a way through which peoples sought to understand the natural world around them such as the annual death and regrowth of vegetation but also, in a fantastical way, explained and justified earthly events including migrations and the introduction and adoption of new or foreign ideas and cultures. The stories of Mot and Tammuz potentially, therefore, have their origins in the Neolithic period and the beginnings of agriculture in the Near East.

Humans must kill plants (and animals) so that they might live and it is suggested (Jacob 2007, 57) that ancient peoples honoured and made retribution to the natural world which they personified in the form of gods and goddesses. The quern, instrumental in the death of the grain, may have been a suitable offering of atonement. Again its placement in a disused grain storage pit can be seen as particularly symbolic.

4.5 Querns as Symbols of Transformation

Through its death in the mill, however, the grain is transformed from an indigestible material into a potentially life-giving product (Jacob 2007, 57; Watts, S. 2008a, 100). The act of milling can be seen, therefore, as both destructive and creative (Stone 2008). As such it echoes the natural order referred to above. As Gimbutas (1987, 12) states, 'life on earth is in eternal transformation, in constant and rhythmic change between creation and destruction, between birth and death'. The quern, a familiar everyday object, is an ideal medium through which changes in the human state can be explained (Brück 2001, 155). The transformation through grinding from raw material to refined product, from one state to another, provides the perfect metaphor for the transition from girl to woman, from life to death and from death to rebirth.

It is further suggested (Fendin 2000, 92-93; 2006, 161) that the metaphorical link between querns and changes in the human state is not only manifest in the transformation of the raw material into refined product that occurs during the grinding process but also within the lifecycle of the quern itself. Thus the manufacture of a quern symbolises birth, its use and gradual wearing of the grinding surface the passage of human life and finally its discard represents death. Fendin further suggests that the passage of time is also made manifest through the repetitive action of grinding and the wearing of the stone (Fendin 2000, 92). Brück (1999b, 155) in her analysis of Bronze Age settlements in southern England comments that querns were, like their owners, 'burnt, broken, and buried upon death'. The fragmentation of the quern both enabled and symbolised the transition of settlements and people from one stage of their lives to the next (Brück 2006).

However, not all querns in the archaeological record are worn and broken through use and age. Many are found complete and apparently still in a usable condition. As mentioned previously, this suggests that some querns were deliberately removed from circulation for depositional purposes. As symbols of human life and death, however, such querns could represent those who died before their time, before they reached old age.

The transformation metaphor becomes particularly potent when considered in the light of the invisible grinding process that takes place between the two stones of a rotary quern (Figure 2.3). As Heslop

(2008, 18) points out, when the rotary quern was first introduced this would have been a 'startling magical innovation' after the very visible crushing of the grain on a saddle quern. Even today, amazement is expressed by those unfamiliar with the process. In the prehistoric period the novelty would have worn off as the rotary quern became a more familiar, everyday tool but the idea of an invisible, magical transformation may have lingered in metaphorical form. It is this unseen transformation that may lie at the root of tales of magical querns that grind either prosperity or adversity. In Norse mythology, for example, the *Grotta-Söngr* tells of a large quern called Grótti that belonged to King Frodi. Grótti was turned by two giant-maidens, Fenia and Menia, who ground wealth and happiness for Frodi. In his greed Frodi allowed Fenia and Menia little rest and in revenge they ground an army to attack him. In one version of the tale, their frenzied grinding pulls the frame on which the quern stands to pieces and the stones are broken. In another, the leader of the attacking army is a sea-king called Mysing who takes Fenia and Menia on board his ship and bids them grind salt. This they did until the ship sank and they are grinding still which explains why the sea is salt (Johnston 1910; Magnússon 1910; Mackenzie 1912, 246-249). Subsequent Scandinavian folk tales pick up on the theme of a magic quern that will grind anything that is asked of it and generally ending with the quern grinding salt (Mackenzie 1912, 249-253). As Stone (2008) points out, the quern does this magically, requiring no input. He suggests that the quern is a symbol of the earth and the riches it provides (Stone 2008). However, there is also a warning here that if the quern/earth is misused or mistreated it will grind harm and ruin instead. Thus the quern, a symbol of plenty, may also have been used as a gift or offering in times of famine and hardship.

The unseen, magical or mystical transformation from grain to flour also finds expression in medieval Christian allegory. The mystic or eucharistic mill is typically depicted as a hand mill. Although other meanings may be read into the mystic mill, it is usually taken to represent the transformation of the laws of the Old Testament (grain) through Christ (the mill) into the teachings of the New Testament (flour) (Moffett 2003, 215; Roberts 2005; Ambrose 2006; Worthen 2006, 264-265, 269-271).

4.6   The Cosmic Mill
The introduction of the rotary quern in the Iron Age is seen as an innovation in milling technology with the transference of the forward and backwards motive operation of the saddle quern to the circular motion of the rotary quern. It was also a revelation in efficiency and comparative ease of use. The introduction of the rotary quern would not only have led to the renegotiation of the meaning and moral value of the saddle quern, which had been in use since the Neolithic period, but it also enabled the development of new mythologies and meanings based on rotary motion.

The turning of the upper stone thus came to symbolise the turning of the heavens with its revolving constellations, the lower stone the apparently stationary earth. Although Santillana and Dechend (1969) and also Kelly (2002) attempt to push the origins of the cosmic mill back to the Bronze Age or earlier, the application of the movement of the upper stone to the movement of the sky cannot predate the origin of the rotary quern in the Iron Age. It should also be noted, as mentioned in Chapter Two that many Iron Age rotary querns are considered to have been worked with an oscillatory motion rather than being fully rotated. Roman rotary querns, however, appear to have been generally turned anticlockwise, as evidenced by the pattern of furrow dressing found on many stones and also by feel; the grinding surface is smoother in the direction of turn. Later querns were usually turned clockwise, that is with the sun and in the Northern and Western Isles it was considered unlucky to turn them anticlockwise (Firth 1974, 27; Macleod Banks 1946, 85).

The earliest reference to the cosmic mill, however, appears to be a comment made by the character Trimalchio in the *Satyricon* written by Petronius, a courtier of the Emperor Nero, in the 1st century AD. Following a description of the zodiac Trimalchio declares 'so the world turns like a mill[stone], and always brings some evil to pass, causing the birth of men or their death' (Petronius *Satyricon* 39). According to Norse mythology the cosmos was turned by Mundilfoeri, 'the one who turns the mill' and through whom the timing of the seasons was ordered. The 9th century Arab astronomer, al-Farghani likewise described the revolving of the sky around the Pole Star as 'like the turning of a mill' (Stone 2008; Worthen 2006, 260). In Aelfric's homilies, written in the 10th century there is a reference to a quernstone that turns continually but accomplishes no journey, which appears to symbolise the world (Thorpe 1844, 515). On a different slant, as mentioned above, a link can also be made between querns and the passage of time seen both through the time-consuming operation of milling and the gradual wearing of the quern itself (Fendin 2000, 92).

4.7 The Colour of Querns

The symbology attached to querns may also derive from their physical attributes. Querns are made from a variety of different rock types and consequently vary greatly from red or yellow sandstones, to black/white/pink speckled granite, to pebbly puddingstone to garnet-studded schist to grey-black lava (Figure 3.3). Where querns within a community are derived from locally available sources, the stone from which they are made may not occasion particular comment. The presence of exotic stones, on the other hand, gives pause for thought as does the deposition of upper and lower stones from disparate sources together. These could be representative of relationships and/or the movement of people but other factors such as the texture or the colour of the quernstones may also have influenced their choice for particular depositions.

The use of different coloured stones, in particular red, white and grey has been noted in the construction of some Scottish stone circles and, of course, the blue stones from the Preseli Mountains are a feature of Stonehenge. White quartz is also a feature of many prehistoric ceremonial or ritual sites and is often found in the kerbs of Cornish Bronze Age barrows (Darvill 2002; Bradley 2005b, 106-108; Jones and Taylor 2004, 110). On a smaller scale, a 'nest' of blue-grey quartzite stones, broadly dated to the Bronze Age, was found beneath the pebble mound at Jacob's Well on Woodbury Common in East Devon (Tilley 2009, 27). The items found in later Neolithic pits also often appear to have been chosen for their shape, texture and/or colour and within the Middle Bronze Age metalworking enclosure at Sigwells, Somerset a preference for red-coloured items was noted in the abandonment deposits placed in postholes (Pollard 2001, 325; Tabor 2008, 69).

A number of archaeologists have also commented on the colour of querns found in prehistoric contexts. At Winnall near Winchester, Hampshire, for example, Chadwick Hawkes noted that, although the upper and lower stones of the complete saddle quern deposited in a Bronze Age pit were a pair, they were of a dark brown coarse grained sandstone and a white medium to fine grained sandstone respectively (Chadwick Hawkes 1969, 6). This contrasts with a saddle quern fragment and rubber placed as a pair in the centre of a ditch segment within the Neolithic causewayed enclosure at Etton, Cambridgeshire. Here the different colours and surface textures of the two stones were taken to indicate a simulation rather than actual pairing (Pryor 1998a, 260). Likewise, the deposition of two saddle querns together in the ditch of a Bronze Age metalworking enclosure at Sigwells in Somerset, one of greensand, the other of a red igneous rock are similarly taken to signify a relationship; the stones deriving from sources 15km to the east and 40km to the west respectively (Tabor 2008, 65, 68). However, the contrasting colours of the two stones, one of greensand, the other a red igneous rock is particularly noticeable (Figure 4.2) and it is suggested, therefore, it is this that prompted their choice, although it does not necessarily preclude their also representing an alliance (Watts, S. 2008b).

The meaning of colour is difficult to quantify. Colours can be both metonyms and symbols and there is no core universal meaning; the meanings of colours can change depending upon the contexts in which they are used. Red is a particularly significant colour with many different meanings (Gage *et al* 1999; Jones and MacGregor 2002). In our own society a red traffic light indicates stop. Red roses are a token of love but we see red when we are angry. A red letter day is a good day but to be in the red (financially) is not good. Other colours have meanings too. We go green with envy, feel blue when we are depressed, fall into a brown study and clouds have silver linings. Black is associated with mourning, white with weddings

Regarding the colour of stone, in the Roman world white pebbles symbolised happiness (Evans 1897, 468). In Mesoamerica green stones are associated with health (Horsfall 1987, 346-347). However, as Scarre (2002, 238) points out the significance of the colour may not lie so much in its visual aspect but in the fact that it denotes the origin of the object. Thus the fragment of puddingstone saddle quern placed in a Neolithic pit at Maiden Castle, Dorset or the fragments of lava found at the Sanctuary near Avebury, Wiltshire would not only have stood out by virtue of their colour but that colour would also have denoted their origins, from France and Germany respectively (Peacock and Cutler 2010; Cunnington 1930-1932, 332). A deposition of two or more different coloured stones may indeed, therefore, represent a relationship, the different colours symbolising the different parties involved. Alternatively, they could also represent in coloured form a particular myth or story or symbolise a transformation from one state to another (after Young

Figure 4.2: Two contrasting coloured querns from the ditch of a Bronze Age metalworking enclosure at Sigwells. (R. Tabor; S. Watts).

2006, 179). Is it more than coincidence, therefore, that, within a metalworking context, the red and green quernstones from Sigwells are reminiscent of copper ore or molten metal and its mould or verdigris; the raw material or molten metal/metal object and its mould which was burnt in the process and broken or decayed metal; birth, life and death (Watts, S. 2008b). Once again, the meaning behind the deposition may only be read by the understanding eye (Tilley 1999, 9). Nevertheless it is clear even to the uninitiated that depositions such as these were made with purpose and intent and that they have a story to tell.

4.8 Decoration

Some prehistoric and later querns are notable for their decoration. Decoration is an adornment, an additional element that communicates social information enabling a quern to function in other ways[1]. It may have been added at the time of manufacture or later in the quern's life. It may act as a talisman, to lighten the load of milling, thus moving the stone beyond its practical milling function and increasing its qualitative rather than its quantitative output, or it may indicate that the quern was to be used for a specific purpose. Alternatively, decoration performs more esoteric functions discernible only to the initiated eye. A number of Iron Age querns, for example, from Ireland, Wales and north-west England are carved with lines or swirls (Figure 4.3) (Griffith 1951, plates 6-8; Raftery 1984, 244-245; Ingle 1987, 13, figure 1). The latter form of decoration is similar to that found on high status metalwork, bringing, as Bradley (2005a, 101) points out, the work of highly skilled craftsmen into the domestic sphere. Although we may not understand the meaning behind such decoration it is clear that it raised the respective quern out of the everyday. The meaning behind the phallus found carved upon several fragments of Roman querns is perhaps more explicit. The phallus was an often used image in the Roman world, functioning as both a fertility symbol and a sign against evil (Frere *et al.* 1983:302; Henig 1984, 167, 185-6). The sign of the cross carved on some medieval quernstones may also have been intended to ward off evil or to have been a blessing, or to denote that the stones were for grinding a particular product.

Another form of decoration takes the form of a human head carved around the spout of a medieval pot quern (Figure 4.3). They may well represent those of real people; visible examples of medieval humour as the ground meal is spewed through the carving's mouth (Hall 2011). The heads may also carry a Christian message, however. Jesus states (Matthew:15.11) that it is not that which goes into a man's mouth that defiles him but what comes out. Such pot querns, which are not uncommon finds on medieval monastic sites, can thus be seen to amuse and teach at the same time.

Anthropomorphic or zoomorphic figures are also a feature of the ornately decorated metates dated *circa* AD500-1500 found in Central America, particularly in Costa Rica, Nicaragua and also Panama (Figure 4.3). The side panels and legs may be carved with abstract geometric designs, human figures or animals, and occasionally a carved head of a bird or jaguar is added to the lower end. These elaborate carvings are thought to be related to the function of the metate for grinding corn and to have been used in ceremonies and rituals concerned with agricultural fertility and the harvest (Precolumbian Stone 2011).

There is also presumably a meaning behind the carvings of curled-up, sleeping foxes that are occasionally found on the upper stones of a particular type of post-

---

[1]. In this sense the inscriptions on some Roman military querns which identify the stone as the property of a particular *contubernium* cannot be considered as decorations.

Figure 4.3: Top: Decorated Iron Age rotary querns from Blochty and Rhydd Gaer, Anglesey (M. Watts after Wheeler 1925, Figure 83; Barnwell 1881, Figure 3). Middle: Medieval pot quern with a face mask carved around the spout, Forteviot (left); Post-medieval sleeping fox quern, Merano, Italy (right) (M. Hall, with owner's permission; G. Clausse). Bottom: Decorated metate from Costa Rica (Birmingham Museum of Art, Alabama, USA; Museum purchase, photo S. Pathasema).

medieval/early modern rotary quern that was apparently used for grinding salt (Figure 4.3). Examples are known from northern Italy and the Auvergne, France. There is also one on display in Anglesey Abbey, Cambridgeshire, which probably originated on the continent and several examples have also recently come to light in London on which the fox looks more like a hound (Clausse, pers. comm., Cruse, pers. comm.; Watts 2011, 342). At the time of writing the meaning of the fox/hound is unclear but could perhaps derive from a folk tale or relate to the maker's name.

4.9   Querns as Part of the Body of the House

It is now a recognised fact that the majority of Bronze Age and Iron Age roundhouses have entrances that face east or south-east. This phenomenon led to the theory that prehistoric roundhouses were oriented with particular cosmological references to light and dark as representing life and death in the northern and southern halves of the house respectively. It is this, it is suggested, that ordered the easterly/south-easterly setting of the doorway and the activities carried out within rather than utilitarian considerations (Parker Pearson 1996, 119-120; Oswald 1997; Fitzpatrick 1997, 77-78; Williams 2003, 239-240). However, more recent research suggests that the orientation of doorways was governed more by the practical need for light, coupled with shelter (Pope 2007; Pope 2008, 19). As reconstructed roundhouses show the maximum light falls in a band across the centre of the house from the door towards the back of the structure, gradually decreasing on either side; the darkest area is either side of the doorway, particularly if the house has a porch. The light recedes gradually throughout the day (Figure 4.4) (Pope 2007, 216). Pope's (2007, 215) research in central and northern Britain indicates a preference for hearths located in the centre of roundhouses, the focus of daily life, while in southern England, Webley (2007) has shown that the position of cooking pits in Bronze Age and Early Iron Age houses appears to run counter to the 'sun-wise' theory. Webley (2007) argues that the location of most artefacts within roundhouses is related to formalised abandonment procedures rather than to the location of particular activities. This suggests that activities, features and deposits associated with the life and occupation of the house followed different, although related cosmological orders compared to those associated with its death and abandonment. Thus querns found *in situ* in their primary working locations were placed according to the particular needs and requirements of the life of the household. This is well demonstrated at Nornour on the Isles of Scilly (Figure 3.10) where a saddle quern was found beside each of two hearths in the 'kitchen' annexe attached to an Iron Age dwelling (Dudley 1967, 5, 7).

However, ethnographic evidence suggests that metaphorical interpretations should also perhaps be considered. The Roman writer, Seneca, quoting Posidonius, described the tasks of milling and baking as imitating the actions of the teeth and stomach (Seneca *Ad Lucilium Epistulae Morales* 90.22-23). Today, for the Betamaliba of West Africa, the analogy between teeth and querns is a key part of their world view. Their houses are metaphors for the human body and so are constructed of flesh, bone and blood or to the non-initiated, earth, stone and water. The door is the mouth and the granaries the stomach. It is perhaps not surprising, therefore, that just inside the door are the teeth, that is the quern which is used for grinding (chewing) grain (Tilley 1999, 44-45).

4.10   Wholes, Parts and Orientation

The state of a quern as found in the archaeological record is also an important consideration in furthering our understanding of the meaning or reason for its deposition. As has been mentioned, it is noticeable that querns may be deposited as paired or single stones, in a whole or fragmentary condition. Upper and lower stones deposited together, for example, may denote an intention to preserve the working partnership of the stones whereas single stones may have been chosen for a particular purpose (Graefe *et al* 2009, 93). The separation of upper and lower stones renders that quern inoperable. This is symbolised in 10th century Welsh law, where in the event of a divorce the man took the upper stone and the wife the lower (Bennett and Elton 1898, 162). As suggested above, the deposition of separate or pairs of stones may represent, therefore, the breaking or making of a relationship (the division of the stones also reflects the female/male role of the respective upper and lower stones). Alternatively, one stone may have been representative of the whole, be that of the quern itself or person, family or community of which it was part.

Whole quernstones are, however, potentially reusable and their deposition within relatively shallow pits, for example, may have been for practical rather than symbolic reasons, for safe storage. On the other hand, a complete quernstone found at the bottom of a deep Iron Age storage pit is unlikely to have been in storage and must, therefore, represent an offering or a meaningful placement of some form.

Figure 4.4:
The interior of a reconstructed roundhouse at the Peat Moors Visitor Centre, Somerset showing the light falling in a band from the doorway across the centre of the building (S. Watts).

Likewise many quern fragments may also have been deposited with purpose and meaning. Querns, by their very nature, are large, durable items and unless there is an unseen flaw in the piece of stone used for their manufacture, they are not easy to break. Very worn and thin stones may eventually crack but many quernstones appear to have been still usable when they were broken suggesting that this breakage was deliberate. Curwen (1929, 63; 1931, 145), for example, suggested that the small size of the fragments of Iron Age querns found at The Trundle, Sussex was due to them having been broken up intentionally, and that they may have been burnt in order for this to have been achieved. Such fragmentation may also have signified the ending of a relationship, a life, event or place; the breaking of the object both symbolizing and enpowering the transition from one state to another (Brück 1999b, 155; Brück 2006, 297-299; Moore 2007, 94).

Alternatively, these particular objects may have become 'polluted' in some way so that they could no longer be used (Thomas 1999, 66). Such items may have had to be carefully disposed of, with appropriate rituals, including their fragmentation, to render them 'safe'. Items belonging to a deceased person, particularly one who had died from a virulent disease, or objects that were used within funerary rituals and feasts may have fallen into this category (Grinsell 1961, 476-477). Artefacts for use in the after-life may also have been broken to release the spirit of the object. Alternatively, it may have been considered inappropriate to reuse artefacts appropriated for funerary rituals within the domestic sphere thereafter and they were thus broken to remove them from circulation. Breaking an object effectively removed it from the earthly realm (Grinsell 1961, 476-477; Chapman 2000b, 23-26). Fragmentation could also render an object powerless or conversely release its power. It may also have enabled it to become an acceptable offering.

However, as Chapman comments these explanations do not fully explain why, in many instances, the object in its fragmentary state is nevertheless incomplete. He suggests, therefore, that artefacts were deliberately broken and the pieces distributed as a form of contract or bond, an 'enchainment' denoting a specific relationship, transaction or event (Chapman 2000b). The specific meaning of the object thus lies in the relationship that its fragmentation represents. Each piece could be separately curated perhaps for reunification or deposition at a subsequent date or even further fragmented and shared amongst third parties. Such processes of enchainment, the linking of people and place, the living and the dead through the sharing of an object is seen as one of the ways in which social relationships were created and maintained (Chapman 2000b).

But there are other explanations to account for the dispersal of fragments such as the wanton destruction of property during the course of an attack. Pieces from the same object may be buried or reused in separate contexts in the resultant clear-up and rebuilding operations, whether by the aggressors or the victims. The appropriate disposal of polluted objects referred to above may also have entailed the burial of each fragment separately. Alternatively, part(s) of an object may have represented the whole; the fate of the other pieces may have been immaterial.

The orientation of the quern within its depositional context may also be important, a fact that has been, unfortunately, rarely recorded, particularly with fragmentary querns. A complete quernstone laid on its side or in an inverted position for example may have been placed in a position of protection, to cushion and protect the grinding surface. On the other hand, as Pryor (1998b, 61) suggests, the inversion of a saddle quern and/or alternatively its placement on top of its rubber represents 'the world turned upside down' (Figure 1.7). The stones would not and could not have been used in these positions. They may, therefore, represent offerings or items removed from the domestic sphere for use in the spirit world. However, the inverted position of stones may also be seen as a gesture of closure. At Trethellan Farm, Cornwall, for example a saddle quern was placed over a collection of rubbers in a pit during the formal demolition and abandonment of the site (Figure 1.6) (Nowakowski 1991, 25). The picture is more complicated with regard to fragments as these have already been rendered inoperable by their very fragmentation. However, they could have similar signification particularly if, indeed, one part represents the whole.

4.11 The Spirit of the Quern

It is also important to bear in mind that not all querns or fragments thereof were necessarily deposited with reference to a particular symbolic or metaphorical meaning. Mention has already been made of complete quernstones stored away for future use, or to contaminated objects that had to be carefully disposed of. Depositions may also have been made to mark a particular occasion or in memory of a person/ancestor or in relation to what the quern was used for. Alternatively, the deposition may have been in reverence to the quern itself. In Japan, for example, querns and other tools were once collected and built into monuments to give thanks to the spirits of the tools (Figure 4.5) (Kawakami 2005, 26). Finally, the possibility that some depositions were indeed of unwanted material should also be considered. The fact that in Mali querns surplus to requirement may be left in the corner of a room or courtyard may be relevant here (Hamon and Gall 2013, 118).

4.12 Symbolism and the Structured Deposition of Querns

In Chapter One it was established that there is a reason for the position of all artefacts as found in the archaeological record, including querns. Although the locations of some items may be due to chance loss, casual discard or to post-depositional processes many appear to have been structured deposits, that is they were placed in the positions in which they were found for reasons that had meaning to the person(s) who deposited them. It was also suggested that such depositions were made with varying levels of intent and meaning. The meanings behind particular depositions are, as Pollard (2001, 317) points out, potentially many and varied, dependent upon the circumstances in which the depositions were made. However, certain objects, whether through their personal associations or their materiality, evoke certain responses resulting in specific and enduring meanings. The symbolic links between querns and women, the provision of food and the agricultural cycle, for example, appear strong and persistent. Yet, the above exploration of the mythology and traditions relating to querns and their colour, movement and decoration all indicate that there may have been other motives behind the deposition of querns in the prehistoric period and that the subject is in fact far more complex than at perhaps first thought.

Querns can be seen as:
- the embodiment of gender relations
- metaphors for the turning of the heavens
- symbols of misfortune or well-being
- symbols of death and regeneration
- symbols of the harvest and fertility
- symbols of feasting and plenty
- symbols of relationships
- symbols of transformation
- simply querns

These analogies, of course, derive from different times and places and the myths and traditions behind them will have developed in response to specific cultural situations. Nevertheless, it is likely that some later mythology and symbology will have derived from earlier traditions even though the connections linking them back to the prehistoric period are now broken (Green 1999).

However, the purpose of this chapter is not to say that these are the specific meanings that underpinned the structured deposition of querns in the prehistoric period. As Garwood et al (1991, ix) state 'the hope of identifying single unconditional "meanings"...must at best be doubtful'. Rather the intention has been to raise an awareness of the possible meanings that may lie behind that deposition. Compelling as it may be, the use of querns in depositional events should not be automatically linked with the agricultural cycle and

*Figure 4.5.
Japanese quern monument
(Kenjiro Kawakami).*

the production of food. Indeed, not all depositions may have had a symbolic meaning; querns were also placed in the ground as a means of safe storage. To misquote Freud, 'although oftentimes it is a great deal more, sometimes a quern is just a quern' (after Worthen 2006, 278).

Nevertheless the type of context and the state of the quern within that context may invite the suggestion of certain symbolic associations. The deposition of a quernstone in a boundary ditch, for example, may have drawn upon the transforming qualities of the quern, the crossing from one side to the other symbolised in the grinding of grain to flour. On the other hand a quernstone at the bottom of a storage pit may have been an offering related to the harvest while another, manufactured from a non-local rock may represent a relationship of some form. First and foremost, however, the quern is a milling tool. It is this prime function that ultimately lies at the core of its meaning and significance, both practical and symbolic. It is through the use of familiar everyday objects such as querns that difficult concepts such as the different roles of men and women or the cycle of life and death can be both explained and controlled (after Brück 2006, 305). With these thoughts in mind the evidence for the structured deposition of querns within the south-west of England is assessed over the course of the next four chapters.

5

AN OVERVIEW OF THE QUERNS FOUND IN STRUCTURED CONTEXTS WITHIN THE STUDY AREA

5.1 The Dataset

The analysis presented in the following chapters is based on a dataset of 990 querns found in structured contexts on 104 sites across the south-west of England (Figure 5.1; Appendix 1). Although unprovenanced and chance finds and site finds from unstratified and unknown contexts, topsoil deposits and general surface finds were not included in the analysis, it is nevertheless of interest to note that the addition of these 'unstructured' finds brings the number of prehistoric querns currently known in the south-west to in excess of 1200 (Figure 5.2). Of the 990 querns, 33, 324 and 633 derive from the Neolithic, Bronze and Iron Age periods respectively (Figure 5.3). Given the general increase in the evidence for cereal cultivation throughout the course of the prehistoric period these figures are perhaps not surprising. However, such figures can be deceptive, owing more to archaeological causation than the true state of prehistoric agricultural affairs. The number of querns recorded for the Iron Age, for example, is much enhanced by sites such as the Meare Lake Villages and Cadbury Castle in Somerset, large sites which have seen extensive excavation and for which 199 and 129 querns are recorded respectively. However, other sites have also yielded large numbers of querns. Fifty six querns for example are included from the Bronze Age settlement at Trethellan Farm, Newquay, Cornwall and a further 47 from another Bronze Age site at Gwithian also in North Cornwall. By way of contrast other sites such as Holworthy Farm in north Devon produced just one quernstone but in terms of structured deposition it is none the less valuable.

5.2 The Sites

Of the 104 sites, 12, 47 and 64 are dated to the Neolithic, Bronze and Iron Ages respectively[1]. These increases are discussed further in the ensuing chapters but can be broadly ascribed to both the increase in settlement and cultivation over the course of the prehistoric period. As Figure 5.1 shows these sites are

1. The higher total is due to the fact that some sites are multi-period.

not evenly distributed across the south-west but show a distinct bias towards western Cornwall, Dartmoor and north-east Somerset with smaller groupings apparent in east and south Devon and a solitary find in north Devon. The picture is slightly improved with the inclusion of unstructured findspots (Figure 5.4) which add a sprinkling of sites across Exmoor and the Vale of Taunton and in the valley of the River Taw and in north Devon. Mostly, however, these additional sites simply enhance the general pattern of distribution.

The lack of querns in certain areas may be due to the underlying geology of the region. Much of north-east Cornwall, west and mid Devon, for example, comprises Culm Measures, an area of clays, sandstones and shales. The Culm Measures produce heavy, wet soils that are hard to work and the area, therefore, has been traditionally used for pasture rather than arable (Welldon Finn 1967, 292; Hesketh 2008, 8). In east Devon and south-west Somerset, the ridges and plateaus of the Blackdown Hills are formed of gault clay, greensand and chalk and have thin soils. Welldon Finn and Wheatley (1967, 216) noted that at the time of the Domesday Survey in 1086 this area was one of the 'least productive parts of the country'. Also, in the east of the region, between the Quantocks and the Mendips lie the Somerset Levels, a low lying marshy area subject to periodic inundation where settlement has focused upon islands of higher land (Welldon Finn and Wheatley 1967-217; Natural England 2009).

The pattern of distribution, however, may be more apparent than real. It is noticeable, for example, that 'Red Devon', a band of Permian sandstones and breccias which stretches from the eastern side of Exmoor to the valley of the River Teign and Torbay with a tongue midway extending westwards towards Crediton and Hatherleigh, is also largely devoid of querns. This is an area of fertile, productive soil where it is to be expected that agricultural settlements growing grain and using querns would develop. Some

Querns found in structured contexts

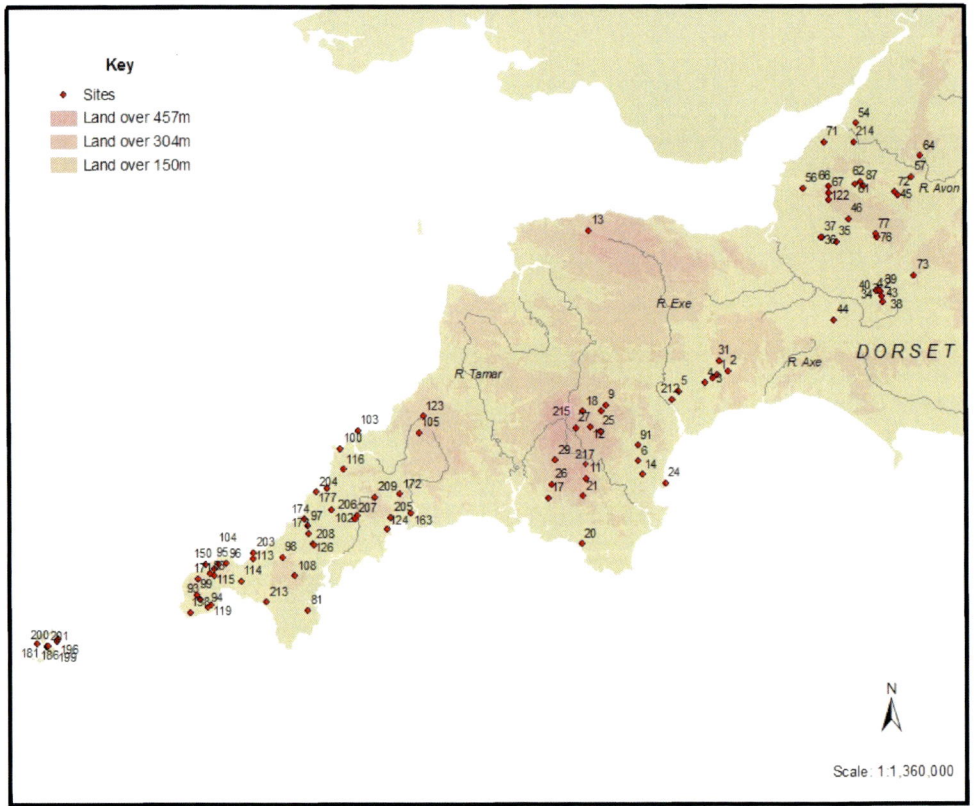

Figure 5.1: Map showing the location of sites included in the analysis where querns have been found in structured contexts (site details are given in Appendix One).

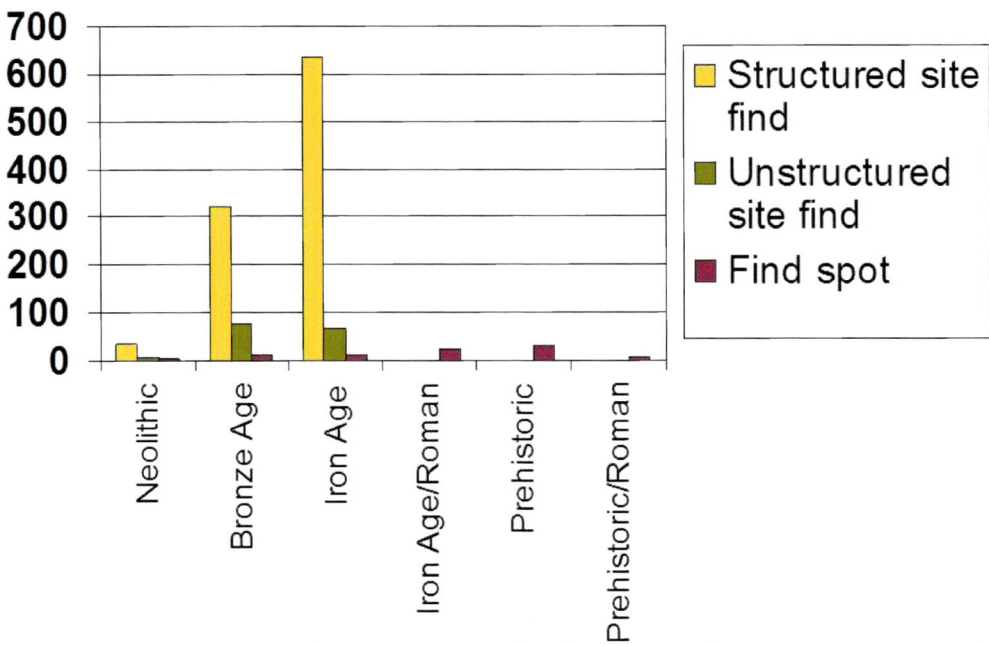

Figure 5.2: Graph showing the numbers of prehistoric querns found in structured contexts, as unstructured site finds and find spots (unstructured finds from multi-period sites extending into the Roman period are not included).

of the bias is probably due, therefore to a lack of excavation in certain areas such as east Cornwall and west, mid and north Devon. This theory is perhaps confirmed by the neat line of sites producing querns in east Devon (Sites 1-5) which correspond with excavations along the route of the new A30 in the 1990s and the cluster around Cadbury Castle, the result of the Cadbury Castle Environs Project (Sites 38-43) in the late 1990s and early 2000s (Fitzpatrick *et al* 1999a; Tabor 2008). In addition recent finds of

Quern Type	Complete			Fragment			Unknown			Sub Totals			Total	Totals
	Neo	BA	IA	Neo	BA	IA	Neo	BA	IA	Neo	BA	IA		
Saddle Quern	6	42	63 (111)	6	61	119 (186)	0	3	11 (14)	12	106	193	311	Saddle Querns & Rubbers (incl. unknown) 716
Rubber	4	102	81 (187)	6	56	77 (139)	3	15	8 (26)	13	173	166	352	Unknown (Saddle/Rubber/Rotary)
Quern Type Uknown	-	-	-	7	41	114 (162)	1	4	20 (25)	8	43	134	187	187
Rotary Upper	-	-	14	-	-	63	-	-	1	-	-	78	78	Rotary Querns
Rotary Lower	-	-	21	-	-	23	-	-	0	-	-	44	44	140
Rotary Type Unknown	-	-	-	-	-	17	-	-	1	-	-	18	18	
Totals	10	144	179 (333)	19	158	413 (590)	4	22	41 (67)	33	324	633	990	

Figure 5.3: Table showing the numbers of querns from structured contexts included in the analysis for the Neolithic (Neo), Bronze Age (BA) and Iron Age (IA) periods (the dashed line indicates that no figure was expected for that particular category).

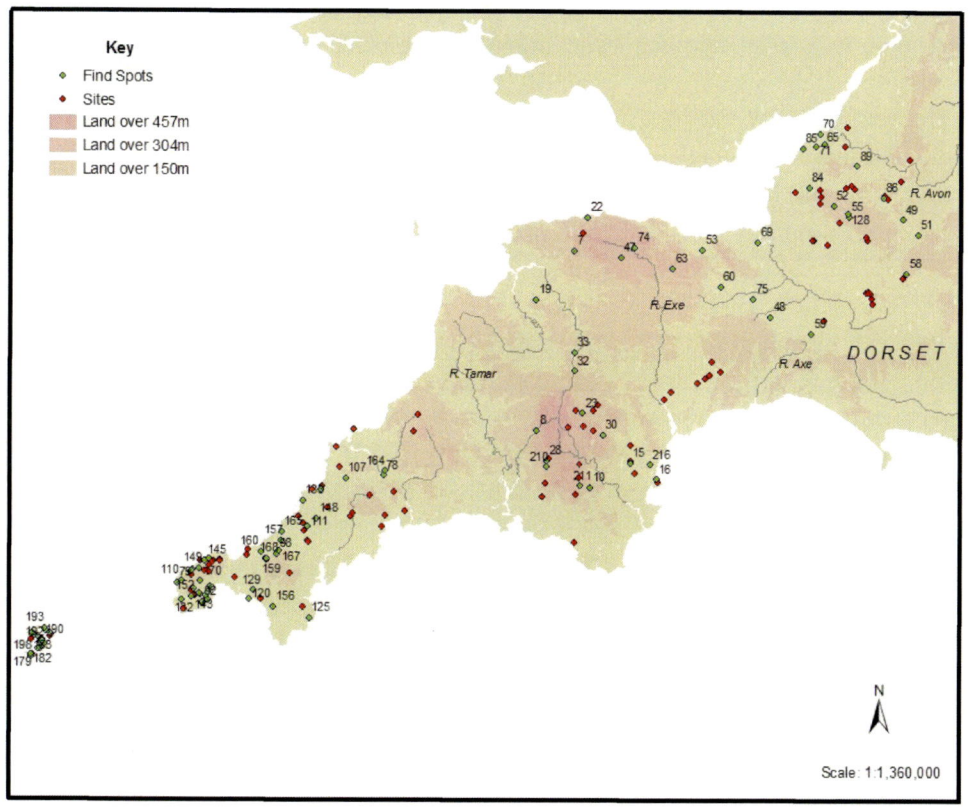

Figure 5.4: Map showing sites and find spots (details of find spots are given in Appendix Two).

quernstones at Holworthy in north Devon and Rydon Lane on the outskirts of Exeter also demonstrate how well gaps in the archaeological record can be filled (Green 2009; John Moore Heritage Services 2010).

Dartmoor, on the other hand, has been extensively investigated and yet comparatively few sites have produced querns. None, for example, were found during excavations at Grimspound (Baring-Gould *et al* 1894, 118; Burnard 1897, 385). However, much of the investigation was undertaken by the Dartmoor Exploration Committee in the late 19th and early 20th century and the lack may be due to the standard of their excavations compared to that of modern excavations. This is implied by the rapidity of their explorations; 43 hut circles at Standon Down, Peter Tavy, for example, were investigated by four men in just eight days (Baring-Gould 1902). Nevertheless evidence from Dean Moor, excavated in the 1950s, continues the theory that the absence is genuine. The enclosure at Dean Moor contained some twelve roundhouses of which nine were excavated but only one saddle quern and one rubber were found (Fox 1957, 70). Environmental analysis also indicates that the increase in land clearance activity on Dartmoor in the Bronze Age was to make way for pasture rather than crops and it has been suggested that the upland areas were used for transhumance (Beckett 1981, 262; Quinnell 1994, 76, 80). It is, of course, also possible that querns were brought to such sites for use in the summer months and then removed. As indicated in Chapter Three, querns, despite their weight, are portable objects. The implication is that these sites were generally not used as depositional locations.

The lack, however, is belied by the enclosure at Shaugh Moor where the remains of some 42 quernstones were found during excavations in the late 1970s[2] (Wainwright and Smith 1980; Shaugh Moor Archive). However, it is of import that half that number were utilised in the construction of the five stone-built roundhouses within the enclosure representing building events over a period of some 500 years from *circa* 1500-1000BC (Wainwright and Smith 1980, 104, 110). Quernstones have also been found in the wall tumble of other roundhouses on Dartmoor at Kestor, Scadbrook, Holne Moor and Heatree for example (Fox 1954, 56; Masson Phillips 1982, 57; Fleming 1988, 77; Quinnell 1991, 18) suggesting that querns so utilised have been missed in the past and that there are yet more to be found. However, it is also noticeable that those sites producing querns, including Shaugh Moor, tend towards the more sheltered eastern and southern sides of the moor which were perhaps more suitable for cultivation. These sites are also predominantly Bronze Age in date supporting the broadly held theory that occupation of these areas decreased in the Iron Age perhaps as a result of climatic deterioration (Fitzpatrick 2008, 125). However, evidence from Kestor indicates occupation in the Early Iron Age and at Cranbrook Castle overlooking the moor the lower stone of a rotary quern was found in one of the roundhouses excavated at the turn of the 19th/20th century (Quinnell 1998; Baring-Gould 1901, 132).

Nevertheless, despite the bias shown on the distribution map towards certain areas, querns have been recovered from structured contexts on a wide variety of sites.

2. Only 24 of these were included on the database, the remainder were unstratified or had been subject to post-depositional movement.

These range from Neolithic fortified enclosures and occupation/activity sites to Bronze Age settlements and barrows to Iron Age hillforts and rounds. The south-west also has some unusual settlement and occupation sites. These are predominantly Iron Age in date, such as the Lake Villages of Glastonbury and Meare in Somerset and rock shelters and cave dwellings such as Kent's Cavern, Devon and Wookey Hole Cave, Somerset. Querns have been found at each of these sites. The variety of site types and the fact that some are non-domestic in nature demonstrates well the important part that querns played in the lives (and deaths) of prehistoric peoples. In addition several quern roughouts have been found at quarries which may represent a particular form of structured deposit as suggested by Heslop (2008, 45-46).

5.3 The Querns

The quernstones included on the main database comprise 311 saddle querns of which 111 are in a complete or near complete state, 352 rubbers including 187 complete or almost complete examples and 140 rotary quernstones of which 35 are complete or nearly so (Figure 5.3). In addition the database also includes 187 indeterminate fragments; those dated to the Neolithic or Bronze Age being saddle querns or rubbers while those from the Iron Age could potentially have derived from saddle querns, rubbers or rotary querns. Generally, therefore, more broken quernstones were found in structured contexts than complete (joining fragments found in the same context were counted as one on the database). It is also of note that, in accordance with the published literature, most quernstones were deposited separately and that although fragments from more than one quernstone may be found in the same context very few paired upper and lower stones were found together.

The higher numbers of saddle querns and rubbers compared to rotary querns does not occasion surprise given the 4000 years or so of their existence in the British prehistoric period compared to the mere 400 years or so of the rotary quern. All the rotary querns derive from Iron Age contexts as expected but of interest is the fact that many more rotary upper stones are recorded than lower stones (78 compared to 44). Yet, conversely, almost 50% (21) of lower stones are complete or nearly so compared to just 22% (14) upper stones. Also of note is the increase in the number of saddle querns found in structured contexts in the Iron Age which may be

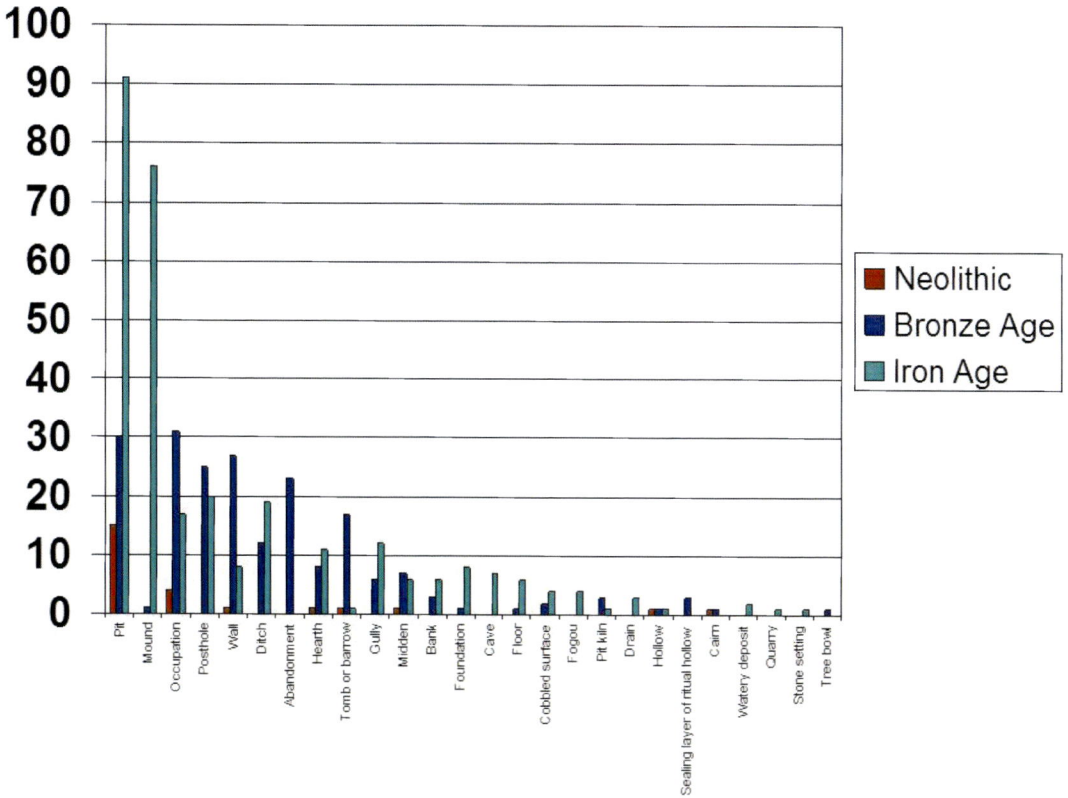

Figure 5.5: Graph showing the numbers of broad context forms by period.

related to the introduction of the rotary quern. The majority of prehistoric querns in the south-west were sourced comparatively locally and consequently a gradual shift in stone type can be seen from Old Red Sandstone and greensand in the east to Permian lava, quartz porphyry and granite in the west. There are exceptions, of course; a fragment of rhyolite saddle quern found in the terminal of a ring ditch at Sheep Slait in Dorset originated either from north Dartmoor or north Cornwall (Figure 7.4) (Tabor 2008, 98). At Ben Bridge a saddle quern and rubber from two different sources and hence two different colours was found; the lower stone was of local Old Red Sandstone but the upper stone, of Corallian sandstone, came from a source in Wiltshire some 32km distant (Rahtz and Greenfield 1977, 202). No querns of exotic, imported stone, however, have been identified to date.

5.4 Contexts of Deposition

A total of 530 individual contexts were recorded which can be grouped into 26 context or feature types ranging from ditches, pits and gullies to occupation layers and abandonment deposits to barrows, fogous, clearance cairns and quarries (Figure 5.5). These context types can be divided almost equally into below ground, liminal deposits such as pits and postholes and above ground, positive deposits such as walls and occupation layers. The contexts can be further divided into domestic and non-domestic and within and external to roundhouses with some features such as pits being found in all. These divisions indicate that deposition was indeed a complex process with many levels and layers of meaning with each context selected for a particular reason at a particular time.

Although some forms of depositional context such as pits, hollows, middens, occupation layers and hearths are found throughout the prehistoric period others appear exclusive to one period. Abandonment deposits, for example, are only recorded for the Bronze Age and fogous are Iron Age features. Pits are the most common form of context, of which the majority can be dated to the Iron Age. This is probably due to the sustainable nature of their subterranean location; they are less susceptible to post-depositional environmental processes and human activity. However, the individual mounds of the Iron Age Lake Villages of Glastonbury and Meare also account for a large number of contexts, 76 in all, by virtue of the extensive excavations undertaken in the late 19th and 20th centuries. Most of the querns found in these mounds are probably structural rather than occupational, the querns being reused in the construction and rebuilding of mounds. However, those querns stated in the excavation reports to have derived from hearths or from the foundations of specific mounds are recorded in the database as such. Finally, in this overview, it appears that the artefacts found in contiguity with querns throughout the prehistoric period are broadly domestic in nature although there are several depositions related to various craft activities, particularly in the Bronze Age.

There are also a number of unusual combinations of artefacts with querns and animal skulls being a particular feature of deposit found in Iron Age storage pits. In addition there are also lone deposits of querns and also lower stones found *in situ* in their working positions, all pointing to different categories of deposit. The following three chapters now consider the data in more detail.

6

THE NEOLITHIC PERIOD

6.1 Setting the Scene: Activity Locales and Subsistence

The nature of the onset of the Neolithic in the south-west of England, as across Britain in general, is still open to debate with recent research moving away from acculturation by indigenous Mesolithic peoples to the small scale migration of communities from Normandy and Brittany. In the south-west the passage tomb at Broadsands near Torquay, for example, is seen as similar to those found in north-western France while outside the study area a saddle quern of Normandy puddingstone found in a Neolithic pit at Maiden Castle, Dorset is also indicative of continental contact (Pailler and Sheridan 2009; Collard *et al* 2010; Peacock and Cutler 2010; Sheridan 2011). However, late Mesolithic flint scatters from the vicinity of Bolster Long Barrow and the Devils Bed in Somerset and, further afield, beneath the chambered cairn at Hazleton North, Gloucestershire may indicate a continuity of local presence (Webster 2008, 76). The truth probably lies somewhere in between but whatever the modes and methods of introduction, adoption and adaptation it seems that the basic tenets of Neolithic culture – monumental construction, the use of pottery, the raising of livestock and cereal cultivation – were all being undertaken to a greater or lesser extent within a generation or so of *circa* 4000BC.

The south-west contains some of the earliest dated Neolithic monuments and structures in the country. The passage tomb at Broadsands, for example, appears to have been in use by 3845-3726 cal. BC while the Post Track, the precursor of the Sweet Track, across the Somerset Levels is dated by dendrochronology to 3838BC (Sheridan 2011, 24, 28-29). Some differences in monumental architecture are apparent across the study area. Causewayed enclosures are found in Devon at Membury, Hembury and Raddon, for example, while fortified hilltop enclosures such as at Helman Tor and Carn Brea appear exclusive to Cornwall. Chambered tombs are concentrated on the northern edge of Dartmoor and in West Penwith, where they are known as quoits but long barrows or long mounds are scattered across the area. The caves of the Mendips and south Devon were also exploited for funerary use in the Neolithic period. In the later Neolithic period, as in other areas of Britain, new monuments appeared including stone circles on the moors of Exmoor, Dartmoor, Bodmin and West Penwith. Several henge monuments are also known such as Priddy and Gorsey Bigbury in Somerset and Bow near Crediton, Devon and a cursus has been identified at Nether Exe. A change in funerary rites also occurred in the Late Neolithic period with a shift from communal, often disarticulated burial in tombs to complete single inhumations in barrows (Griffith and Quinnell 1999a and b; Webster and Mayberry 2007, 25-28; Sheridan *et al* 2008; Webster 2008, 77-78, 97).

In common with much of the British Isles there is little evidence for Neolithic domestic settlement in the south-west although lithic and pottery scatters and clusters of pits are indicative of widespread occupation and activity. Hearths and stake or postholes have been found, however, on earlier Neolithic sites at Milsoms Corner and Maperton Ridge in Somerset and Hazard Hill near Totnes, Devon and also within the causewayed enclosure at Hembury with evidence for more substantial post-built structures at Haldon in Devon, and Chew Park, Somerset. The exact nature of the latter is unknown but it is thought unlikely that they were for domestic use (Fox 1973, 34-36; Griffith and Quinnell 1999b, 51-2; Webster and Mayberry 2007, 25; Webster 2008, 82; Rahtz and Greenfield 1977, 25-27). There is less evidence for later Neolithic activity although sites bearing Peterborough Ware have been found at Topsham and Castle Hill, Devon. The number of sites with Late Neolithic grooved ware pottery is also gradually increasing as evidenced at Doulting Abbey Quarry, Somerset, Hemsford and Harberton, Devon and Tremough, Cornwall (Hollinrake 2003, 137; Jarvis and Maxfield 1975, 246-258; Fitzpatrick *et al* 1999a, 23-26; Cotswold Archaeology 2010, 45, 55; Gossip and Jones 2007, 29-30; Quinnell 2011b, 46).

It has been suggested that Neolithic communities were largely nomadic and that although some aspects of Neolithic culture such as monumental architecture and pottery were rapidly assimilated, the change from an economy based on hunter-gathering to one based on subsistence farming was far more gradual with cereals not becoming a staple food until the Middle Bronze Age, *circa* 1700BC (Thomas 1999, 16; Pollard 2002, 10; Schulting 2004; Bayliss *et al* 2008; Thomas 2008a, 72; Cummings and Harris 2011). It is further suggested that they practiced 'swidden' cultivation, that is areas were cleared, farmed and then abandoned as communities moved onto a new area (Pollard 2002, 10). Ethnographic evidence demonstrates that the sowing, harvesting and storage of crops can fit well within the annual cycle of a nomadic or semi-nomadic community (Fairbairn 1999, 139; Graham 1994, 10-14, 18-20; Thomas 1999, 25; Pessolana 2007). The Neolithic landscape is thought, therefore, to have comprised a patchwork of small clearances, predominantly for pasture but also for the small-scale cultivation of crops, deserted clearings reverting to scrub and areas of mature woodland (Clapham and Stevens 1999, 196; Pollard 2002, 10; Wilkinson and Straker 2008, 73).

In accordance with the general view of Neolithic agriculture, only small quantities of cereal remains have been recovered from sites within the study area. Nevertheless, evidence from a gradually increasing number of earlier Neolithic sites such as Portscatho and Penhale Round in Cornwall and Hembury, Haldon Hill, Langland Lane, Castle Hill and Membury in Devon indicates that emmer (*Triticum dicoccum*), hulled barley (*Hordeum vulgare*) and also possibly einkorn (*Triticum monococcum*) were grown (Jones 2006, 14-15; Clapham and Stevens 1999, 197; Carruthers 2006). (The Neolithic date originally attributed to the sample of spelt (*Triticum spelta*) from Hembury is doubtful (McLaren 2000, 92)). Such crops may have been utilised as both a social and symbolic resource, perhaps as a status symbol or to supplement the range of naturally available food resources. They may have been consumed in the form of flat bread (emmer, the main wheat species grown in the British Neolithic, is best suited to this type of bread as it is low in gluten) or as porridge or gruel, added to stews or most especially as an alcoholic beverage (Fairbairn 1999, 156; Jones and Rowley-Conwy 2007, 408; Dineley and Dineley 2000; Renfrew 2000, 195, 197).

Cereal cultivation appears to have declined in the later Neolithic period. No cereal remains were recovered from the six late Neolithic pits at Hemsford, for example (Carruthers 2010, 207). It is suggested (Brown 2007; Dark and Gent 2001) that small cultivation in woodland clearings initially produced a good harvest but that pests and diseases then developed which together with other environmental and cultural factors impacted significantly on yields. However, the low concentration of cereal remains from many Neolithic sites could also be explained, however, by different processing and/or consumption regimes that may have prevailed at that time compared to the later prehistoric period (Jones and Rowley-Conwy 2007; Stevens 2007; Brown 2007). The winnowing and threshing of crops in the field, for example and the storage of clean grain, or its consumption soon after the harvest and/or the short-term occupation of sites could all result in the under-representation of grain in the archaeological record (Stevens 2007). More evidence is needed, therefore, to confirm or refute the theory. By way of contrast, the greater evidence for the collection of hazelnuts in the form of burnt shells can be explained by the fact that these are a waste product and, therefore, more likely to be burnt than grain (Jones and Rowley-Conwy 2007, 400). Hazelnuts can be ground into flour but simply roasting them in a shallow pit produces a nutritious and tasty food that keeps well (Mears and Hillman 2007, 26). Such practice could well account for the quantities of burnt shells and nuts found on such sites as Milsoms Corner, where a basin shaped hearth was found within an occupation hollow (Tabor 2008, 44). However, other plant material such as acorns or seeds and also pottery temper and ochre may all have been ground using saddle querns.

6.2 Querns from the Study Area

Thirty three quernstones from structured Neolithic contexts are included on the database. These comprise 12 saddle querns, 13 rubbers and eight indeterminate fragments that could have derived from either saddle querns or rubbers (Figure 5.3). They were recovered from a total of just 12 sites (Figure 6.1) comprising both hilltop and lowland occupation sites including causewayed enclosures, tor enclosures, isolated activity areas and also a chambered tomb. The majority of the quernstones are dated to the earlier Neolithic period with only one being deposited in a certain later Neolithic context. Those from Camerton and Ben Bridge, Somerset, however, can only be broadly dated to the Neolithic period and could, therefore, be later in date. A pit containing grooved ware was found near the latter (Rahtz and Greenfield 1977, 85). Likewise that from Sperris Quoit, a chambered tomb in West Penwith, may be Bronze Age in date (see below).

The 33 querns generally appear to be of stone local to the sites where they were found. Several rubbers from the Bunter pebble beds were found at Hembury, Devon and a quern fragment of Pennant Sandstone was found in a pit at Chew Park, Somerset but again these would have been obtainable fairly locally to the sites. However, there are several querns which were found some distance from their

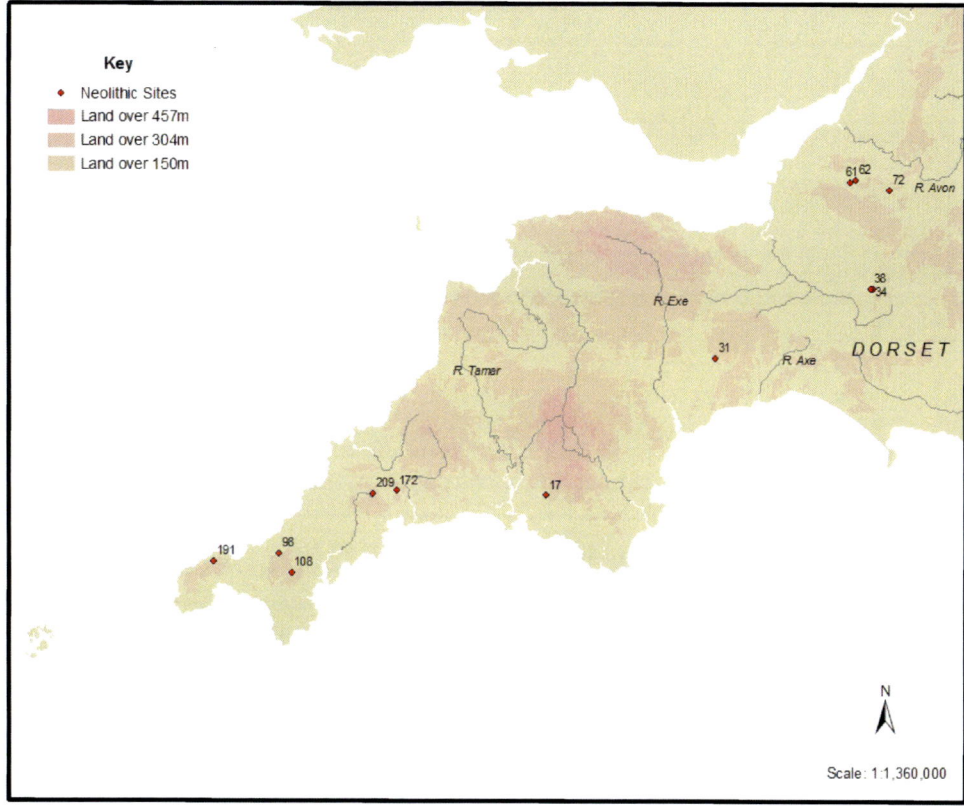

Figure 6.1: Map showing the location of Neolithic sites where querns have been found in structured contexts (site details are given in Appendix One).

original source. Saddle querns and rubbers of Mendip Old Red Sandstone, for example, were found at Milsoms Corner, Somerset, about 24km distant and a rubber of Corallian sandstone from the Westbury area of Wiltshire, some 32km away was found with a saddle quern of Old Red Sandstone at Ben Bridge, mentioned above (Tabor 2008, 45; Rahtz and Greenfield 1977, 202).

Most of the 33 querns were single deposits and ten appear to have been found in a complete or near complete condition. However, a complete upper and lower stone were found together at Ben Bridge (Rahtz and Greenfield 1977, 85) and multiple deposits are also known. Five fragments probably from more than one quernstone were found in a pit at Milsoms Corner (F737) and a rubber and fragments from another were found in a pit on Hazard Hill (Watts, S. 2008b; Houlder 1963, 26). At Cadbury Castle, Somerset two fragments, possibly from the same stone were found in one pit (T260) and a further four fragments were found in another pit or hollow (G180) (Cadbury Castle Archive). The differing states of the querns together with the contexts in which they were found are suggestive of different types of deposit.

6.3 Contexts of Deposition

Within the 12 sites the 33 querns were recovered from 8 main types of depositional context (Figure 6.2). These include a hearth, a clearance cairn, walls and a midden although it is notable that more than half the querns came from pits or hollows indicating perhaps the enduring nature of these subterranean features.

6.3.1 Pits

Twenty querns were recovered from a total of 17 pits or hollows (Table 6.1). These pits and hollows were either within the confines of more permanent hilltop sites or part of a cluster of features denoting more ephemeral occupation. The pits vary greatly in shape from circular pits 0.5m in diameter to oval pits more than 2.0m long. All the pits, however, are rather shallow being less than 1m deep with most being less than 0.5m deep (the shallowness of some, however, such as at Tregarrick Farm, Cornwall, is due to modern topsoil stripping (Cole and Jones 2002-2003, 111)). All but one appear to date to the earlier Neolithic period. The accompanying artefacts are generally domestic in nature comprising mainly pottery, flints, animal bone and plant remains, although the pits at Cadbury Castle were also found to contain arrowheads and slingstones. The latter though are perhaps not out of place in a domestic hunting scenario.

6.3.1.1 Earlier Neolithic pits circa 4000-3000BC

Most Neolithic pits are now presumed to have fulfilled non-utilitarian functions, that is they were dug especially for the purpose of placing artefacts within them (Thomas 1999, 64; Richmond 1999, 45-46; Pollard 2001, 323-325). Earlier Neolithic pits are seen as containing a mixture of a charcoal-rich soil, animal bone, pottery sherds, flints and

The Neolithic period

	Early Neolithic	Neolithic	Late Neolithic	Total
Cairn	1			1
Chambered tomb		1		1
Hearth	1			1
Midden	1			1

Figure 6.2: Table showing the numbers of querns found within each type of Neolithic depositional context.

debitage (Pollard 2001, 323). These pits are interpreted as being an integral part of clearing up operations that took place on leaving, or even during, the occupation of a site. Although the nature of their fills may show little or no signs of formality, their excavation and filling is nevertheless thought to have been part of a formalised procedure (Jones and Reed 2006, 21; Gossip and Jones 2007, 29; Pollard 2001, 323; Leverett and Quinnell 2010, 10).

It has also been suggested (Thomas 1999, 87) that the function of pits was to forge a link between people and place. In this respect it may be relevant that the pits at Milsoms Corner and Tregarrick Farm appear to be visually aligned with Cadbury Castle and Roche Rock respectively (Tabor 2008, 44; Cole and Jones 2002-2003, 136-137). The contents of the pits may be seen, therefore, as a fusion of domestic and ritual, directly related to the occupation of the site, or to a particular event within that occupation but also, perhaps offerings to the gods or ancestors of the place or returned to the earth from which everything came (Thomas 1999, 70; Alcock 1972, 110; Cole and Jones 2002-2003, 136-137, 140; Jones and Reed 2006, 22; Tabor 2008, 45). Such pit fills can be seen, therefore, as closed deposits, their contents intended to be a permanent buried memorial.

Two of the pits at Milsoms Corner and the isolated pits at Chew Park and Camerton, Somerset admirably fit the above description of early Neolithic pits (Houlder 1963; R. Tabor pers. corresp.; Rahtz and Greenfield 1977, 27; Wedlake 1958, 19). That at Camerton, for example, was described as a small pit filled with black earth containing flint, charcoal, pottery, two pounders or rubbing stones and a saddle quern (Wedlake 1958, 19). The pit at Chew Park was similarly filled with a dark soil flecked with charcoal containing pottery, flint and stone including a possible fragment of quern (Rahtz and Greenfield 1977, 11). However, although a lack of silting in the pits at Milsoms Corner demonstrated that they were filled fairly promptly, at Hazard Hill a number of pits are thought to have been used as storage or cooking pits and had, therefore, lain open for sometime before filling (Tabor 2008, 45; Houlder 1963, 16). Likewise, at Tregarrick Farm, two pits showed evidence for *in situ* burning signifying that they were used as hearths and that, therefore, they too were not dug solely for the purpose of filling (Cole and Jones 2002-2003, 135). Nevertheless, such longer term use did not preclude them from ultimately being filled in a similar manner.

However, there are exceptions to the characteristic charcoal-rich fill which suggest that not all pits were filled with the same intent and meaning. The Neolithic pits at Cadbury Castle for example, were rendered distinctive by their clean red clay earth fill and at Hazard Hill, pit 8 was filled with clean earth, from which the stones had been removed (Alcock 1972, 110; Houlder 1963, 16). Although the latter was described as 'sterile', it contained a rubber, the presence of which suggests it was a deliberate deposit, suitable recompense perhaps for taking the stones from the soil.

Querns, however, are not universal finds within Early Neolithic pit groups in the south-west. None were found, for example, at Tremough or Portscatho in Cornwall or at Hayes Farm or Membury in Devon (Gossip and Jones 2007; Jones and Reed 2006; Barber 2000; Tingle 2006). The lack of querns in these circumstances may be due to the nature or timing of the activities carried out at the respective sites, or that querns were not always considered appropriate for deposition within such pits or that grain was indeed not widely grown and/or ground using querns. Similarly at Tregarrick Farm, Cornwall only one small saddle quern was recovered from a series of ten pits that potentially represented some 400 years of activity between *circa* 3790 and 3370 cal. BC. Likewise, at Hembury one quern was found in a group of five pits in area N (Cole and Jones 2002-2003, 112, 140; Liddell 1933-1936, 150-151). These sites can, however, be contrasted with Milsoms Corner where a large fragment of a rubber, five fragments from two or more saddle querns or rubbers, and a complete saddle quern were recovered from three of the four pits excavated there (Watts, S. 2008b).

Where saddle querns and rubbers are found in pits they may be in a complete or fragmentary condition, although it is noticeable that more than twice as many were in a fragmentary state (13 compared to 6). Each form and state potentially carries with it a different meaning indicative of a different category of structured deposit. The fragments, as suggested in Chapter Four, may be tokens, one part representing the whole which suggests that, despite the random appearance of the fill, the contents of the pits were chosen with due deliberation. Again this indicates that this is more than the casual disposal of rubbish. It also, however, raises the question as to what happened to the other fragments? Although at Milsoms Corner, for example, two of the five fragments found in pit F737 were found to join, no further joining fragments were found in the adjacent pits or working hollow. The missing pieces were either placed in pits which have yet to be discovered or, alternatively, were removed from site altogether. It should also be noted that some of these fragments derive from quite large stones that are unlikely to have broken accidently implying that these quernstones were deliberately broken prior to deposition. Chapman (2000b) has suggested that artefacts were broken up and pieces distributed in an enchainment process that linked peoples and places. This further suggests that people from different communities were coming together to partake in the events and activities that took place at these particular sites. The deposition of broken querns and other artefacts in pits certainly seems to betoken, therefore, more than a mere cleaning up exercise.

Six pits were found to contain complete stones. These could potentially have been retrieved for reuse, although the grinding surface of that from Tregarrick Farm had worn through by virtue of being used on both sides (Quinnell 2002-2003, 121). However, the nature of the deposition of this particular stone and also those at Camerton and Hazard Hill within a soil matrix suggests, as indicated above, that they were permanent or closed deposits. Similarly, the large portion of a rubber found in one of the pits (F619) at Milsoms Corner, although potentially still in a usable condition was probably also intended as a permanent deposit.

The particular placement of a complete saddle quern in another pit (F726) at Milsoms Corner, on the other hand, appears significantly different in nature (Figure 6.3). The pit in which it was found was offset from and smaller than the other three in the group and was possibly dug especially for the quern. The quern was laid upside down on a bed of carbonised material with similar material laid upon it. The remaining fills are thought to have formed quite quickly and contained few artefacts (Tabor 2008, 44; Tabor pers. corresp.). Although whole saddle querns deposited in pits have been found on several Neolithic sites outside the study area, such as Husbands Bosworth, Leicestershire and Barford, Warwickshire, the placement of the Milsoms Corner quern, as mentioned in Chapter Four, is most similar to the quern found packed within organic material in the causewayed enclosure at Etton, Cambridgeshire (ULAS 2007; Beamish pers. corresp.; Buckley 1993, 3; Pryor 1998a, 21-22).

The different treatment accorded these querns suggests that they were special deposits of some form, perhaps a particular offering. Alternatively, they were open deposits, that is, they were curated, stored safely in the ground for reuse during seasonal visits to the site. Ethnographic evidence indicates that nomadic or semi-nomadic communities do not regularly carry querns with them but leave them at convenient locations (Gould *et al* 1971; Graham 1993, 32; Hamilton 1980, 8). The inverted position not only protected the working surface but may also have been to stop unfriendly spirits using the quern. On Shetland, in more recent times, the upper stone of a rotary quern was removed during Yule to stop the fairies turning it anticlockwise, an unlucky direction (Macleod Banks 1946, 85). The covering of organic material may have been intended to both conceal and protect the quern. Such careful burials, however, also bear comparison with the earth goddess stones mentioned by Gimbutas (1987, 20) that were packed in straw in holes in the ground and taken out each year during harvest celebrations.

The question may be asked of the saddle quern from Milsoms Corner (and also Etton) as to the fate of their respective rubbing stones. Ethnographic evidence shows, however, that the upper and lower stones of saddle querns are not necessarily always stored together. Graham's mapping of a Rarámuri warm weather residence in Rejogochi, north-western Mexico during the period that its owners were occupying their cold weather rock shelter showed two manos left quite separately from the metates (Graham 1994, figure 26). To return to Milsoms Corner, it is possible that the upper stone was left as a closed deposit in one of the other pits, or that being a smaller and, therefore, a more portable object it was taken when the community using the site moved on, perhaps even for

The Neolithic period

 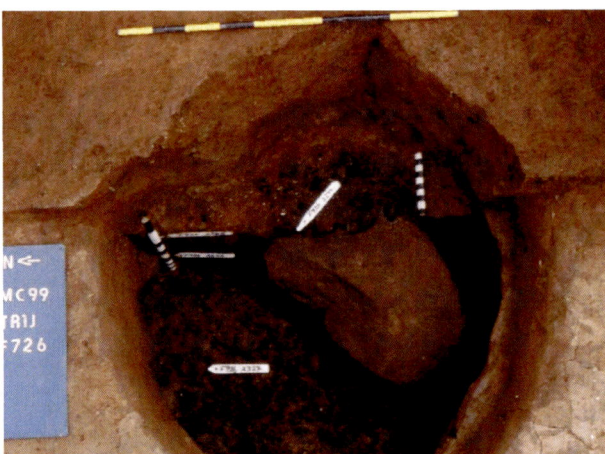

Figure 6.3: Saddle quern from Milsoms Corner, Somerset (centimetre scale) (left) and as found on a bed of carbonised material (right) (S. Watts; R. Tabor).

use with another saddle quern elsewhere. However, in this respect it should perhaps be noted that the saddle quern itself was brought to site from a source some 24km away (Tabor 2008, 45), although, of course, such transportation could have been undertaken in stages. Whatever the meaning behind the deposition it is nevertheless clear that the saddle quern was placed in the pit and covered with due care and attention. Again this signifies more than the disposal of waste material.

As mentioned above artefacts found in the same pits as querns are generally not out of context in a domestic scenario. Objects representative of more than domestic occupation are found in some pits, however, such as part of a human jawbone found in a pit at Cadbury Castle and a polished Cornish axe recovered from one of a line of three pits at Milsoms Corner, while at Tregarrick Farm sherds from a vessel were so placed that the lower edges faced each other (Alcock 1972, 110; Tabor 2008, plate 3; Cole and Jones 2002-2003, 111, 136). The fact that no querns were found in association with these more esoteric/exotic items suggests that the placing and combination of artefacts was undertaken with reference to prescribed formulae. There are, of course, exceptions to the rules. The contents of Pit 5 at Hazard Hill, for example, in addition to a rubber, also included a flake from a polished greenstone axe and a pink flint pebble. Outside the study area a fragment of saddle quern that had been reused as a sharpening stone was found in a pit at Maiden Castle, Dorset together with pottery, scallop shells and an unusual chalk figurine (Houlder 1963, 26-27, 29; Wheeler 1943, 85). These may well be personal items and, like the deposition of complete quernstones, their presence also indicates that deposition in pits was more than mere rubbish disposal.

6.3.1.2 Later Neolithic pits circa 3000-2000BC

Although querns are by no means universal finds in early Neolithic pit groups in the south-west they appear to be even more infrequent finds in later Neolithic pits. Indeed only one pit out of *circa* 33 later Neolithic pits or tree throws has been found to contain a quern compared to 17 out of *circa* 60 dated to the earlier Neolithic. None are recorded from the group of six Late Neolithc pits near Hemsford, the three at Moore Farm, Harberton or the five at Doulting Abbey Quarry nor were any recovered from the five mid-late Neolithic pits at Topsham (Quinnell 2007, 83; Watts, S. 2008a, 100; Cotswold Archaeology 2010, 55; Hollinrake 2003, 137; Jarvis and Maxfield 1975, 246-258) To date, therefore, the only definitively dated later Neolithic find in the south-west is the small saddle quern from one of a group of eight or so pits at Tremough in Cornwall dated 2570-2290 cal. BC (Gossip and Jones 2007, 29-30). The lack could, in addition to the circumstances suggested for their lack in early Neolithic pits, indicate that querns were not considered appropriate for inclusion with certain elements of material culture or locales (after Bradley 1984, 125). Recent research, however, as mentioned above, also suggests a reduction in cereal cultivation in the period after *circa* 3000BC (Brown 2007, 91; Pollard and Healy 2008). The lack of querns on later Neolithic sites coincides with this drop. Whatever the circumstances, the saddle quern from Tremough can, on current evidence be considered unusual.

Later Neolithic pits are thought to show a greater degree of 'crafting' in both their excavation and infilling compared to those of the earlier Neolithic period. They frequently comprise neatly shaped pits with a selection of artefacts chosen for their shape, colour and/or texture rather than their utilitarian function which are buried within a charcoal-rich soil or midden material (Pollard 2001, 323, 325). At Tremough, Gossip and Jones (2007, 30) commented on the selection of decorated pieces of Grooved Ware pottery, a glossy decorative pebble and finely worked flints for inclusion in the loose group of eight pits there. It was also noted that joining sherds from a vessel that had been broken for some time prior to deposition were found in different pits (Gossip and Jones 2007, 30). These items, not out of place in a domestic situation, suggest that again we are witnessing more than the simple disposal of rubbish. In this respect it is interesting to note that although the pottery associated with the saddle quern in pit 494 was undecorated it did include a complete inverted base. Also within the pit were several fine flints, one of which is described as being 'distinctively milky-grey' in colour (Quinnell 2007, 57; Lawson-Jones 2007, 95). The quern itself, however, was a small slab of fine-grained granite and generally unremarkable. Nevertheless, its presence suggests that it had a particular value and meaning that warranted its inclusion within a form of context in which querns at this period are otherwise rarely found (Quinnell 2007, 83; after Gossip and Jones 2007, 30).

6.3.2 Other depositional contexts

Although comparatively few querns derived from contexts other than pits are included on the database these nevertheless indicate that querns were being deposited or left within a wide range of different locales. They form, therefore, a small but diverse and thus significant group (Table 6.2). Most are dated to the first half of the Neolithic period with the exception of the complete quern from Ben Bridge which is undated and the fragment from Sperris Quoit which could potentially be Bronze Age rather than Neolithic in date.

6.3.2.1 Occupation spreads and in situ querns

Seven querns were recovered from what appear to be general occupation surfaces or layers at Hembury a causewayed enclosure in East Devon, Helman Tor, a defended settlement in Cornwall and a site of unknown character at Ben Bridge, Somerset. With regard to the querns from Hembury and Helman Tor there is little additional information regarding the form of the contexts in which these querns were found, other than that they signify areas of activity presumably of a domestic nature. Consequently, it is difficult to gainsay anything about the nature of their deposition in the archaeological record. However, it seems that they were left in the positions in which they were found when the occupants of the sites moved on. As will be shown in the following chapters this appears to be a recurring theme.

The complete saddle quern which was found together with its rubber embedded in marl during excavations at the Ben Bridge site at Chew Valley Lake is, however, worthy of further comment (Rahtz and Greenfield 1977, 85). Consequently, despite the fact that no trace of a pit or any other evidence of occupation or activity was found in association with the stones and they are, in essence, unstructured finds they were included on the main database. They show that upper and lower stones may be deposited together and as such provide an interesting contrast to the deposition of the lone saddle querns at Milsoms Corner and Carn Brea. It is also of import that the saddle quern was found lying on its side. Similar depositions have been found at other Neolithic sites in Britain. At Etton, Cambridgeshire, for example, a saddle quern was found placed on its side in a small pit with its rubber beneath it (Figure 1.7). One of the two saddle querns found in pits at Husbands Bosworth, Leicestershire was also on its side as was that at Thirlings, Northumberland, unusually of late Neolithic date (Pryor 1998a, 103; Beamish pers. corresp.; Miket 1976, 117, 119). In each case, like the inverted stones in pits mentioned above, these saddle querns were also placed in protective positions. In present day Mali, Minyanka women tend to stand their saddle querns upright or on their sides with the grinding surface against the wall of the house or a stone when not in use in order to keep the grinding surface clean (Hamon and Gall 2013, 117). The quern at Ben Bridge may, therefore, have been left at a campsite, the lower stone turned on its side in a similar fashion, in a position of protection but signifying that it was ready to use.

It is also worth noting, as mentioned above, that although considered a pair, the two stones are of different geological origins. The saddle quern, probably a riverine boulder, is of Old Red Sandstone and local in origin while the rubber is of Corallian sandstone and is thought to have come from the Westbury district in Wiltshire, some 32 kilometres away (Rahtz and Greenfield 1977, 202). There are several potential reasons to account for the bringing together of two separate materials. They could, for example, be indicative of a relationship or that the upper stone derived from some form of trade/exchange or that both the Chew Valley Lake and Westbury areas formed part of the territory of the community to which the stones belonged and that the choice of stones was either aesthetic, or that used in combination to grind a particular material - the saddle quern was stained with ochre - or that they were just found to work together well. The combination of the dark sandy colour of the Corallian sandstone and the red of the Old Red Sandstone would also have been quite striking.

6.3.2.2 Hearths

A number of saddle querns and rubbers have been found at Hazard Hill, an early Neolithic hilltop settlement comprising several structures and domestic working areas with sheltered hearths, cooking holes and pits (Houlder 1963). At least one saddle quern was collected as a surface find and mention was made above of several rubbers found in pits during excavations in 1951-2. In addition, another saddle quern was also found in the centre of a hearth (Houlder 1963, 13, 28). The quernstone showed no signs of burning and had, therefore, been placed there after the hearth had become disused. Although it was suggested that it may have been dragged there by ploughing in more recent times, the fact that it was in the centre of the hearth is perhaps more than coincidental and it may have been placed there as a closure deposit. A small saddle quern was recently found face down in a hearth within a late Neolithic settlement at Green, Isle of Eday, Orkney, with its rubbing stone beside it. Like the saddle quern from Hazard Hill, it was unburnt (Coles 2009; Coles pers. corresp.).

6.3.2.3 Middens

Just one rubber is recorded as being part of a midden deposit, at Helman Tor (Roe 1997, 53-54), although it is possible that some of the querns found within the occupation layers mentioned above also derived from midden debris. A midden exposed in a cliff face at Halangy Porth, St. Marys, Isles of Scilly originally interpreted as Neolithic (Hencken 1932, 30) is now considered to be Bronze Age in date (Pearce 1981, 54, 69). The two saddle querns recovered from it are included in the next chapter, therefore. Middens are known from the Mesolithic period and are a feature of a number of Neolithic sites in Britain including Noltland and Skara Brae on Orkney and Grimes Graves in Norfolk but they reached their zenith in the deep and extensive spreads at sites such as East Chisenbury and Potterne, Wiltshire in the Late Bronze Age (Clarke and Maguire 1989, 16; McOmish 1996). Far from being mere piles of waste material, middens are seen as fulfilling a number of different functions. It is suggested, for example, that they may have functioned as territorial markers, as stock piles, as symbolic structures or as conspicuous monuments of feasting and, as the settlement at Skara Brae shows midden can also be utilised as a construction material (Pryor 2003, 101; McOmish 1996; Needham and Spence 1997; Mulville 2008, 238-239; Clarke and Maguire 1989, 14). As such middens are open deposits and contrast markedly with the almost covert secretion of selected material remains in pits.

6.3.2.4 Clearance cairns

Amongst the several querns recovered during excavations of Carn Brea, a defended hilltop settlement near Redruth, Cornwall, 3885-3505 cal. BC, was a complete saddle quern found within a clearance cairn (Mercer 1981, 63, 79, 159; Healy 2009). The clearance cairn was one of a number found at fairly regular intervals on the gentler, southern slope of the hilltop site and their presence amongst an area of disturbed soil is suggestive of small scale cultivation (Mercer 1981, 77-81). The saddle quern may have been stored within the cairn which as Mercer (1981, 81) suggests, raises the compelling possibility that crops were processed in the field rather than being taken back to the settlement area. It is also reminiscent of the harvest stones mentioned above, stored in this instance above rather than below ground. Its rubber, as suggested above, may have been kept elsewhere. The practice of processing crops in this way not only accounts for the lack of cereal remains from Neolithic contexts (Stevens 2007, 378-379) but also for unexpected stray finds of querns such as that from Ben Bridge. However, experiential exercises indicate that grain both mills and bakes better if it is left to 'rest' for a week or so after harvest (Watts, M. pers. comm.), although this might not have been appreciated at that time. However, it was also noticed at Carn Brea that the cairns included stones from different geological sources (Mercer 1981, 79). Although all the stones derived from the vicinity of Carn Brea they must have been brought especially up on to the hilltop suggesting that the cairns were used for more than simple field clearance. In this scenario the location of the saddle quern, which was of local granite, within the cairn may have been intended as a special form of stone deposit rather than being curated.

6.3.2.5 Enclosure walls

Fragments of a saddle quern and rubber were also found in the wall tumble of a section of the enclosure wall at Carn Brea (Mercer 1981, 63, 79, 159). As will be seen, the reuse of quernstones as building stones is a recurring theme throughout the prehistoric period and one that will be discussed in more detail below. Suffice it to say here that such reuse raises the question as to whether this denotes the use of convenient pieces of stone or if their placing within structures also had a symbolic role. At Carn Brea their reuse in this way also potentially points to occupation of the hilltop prior to the construction of the enclosure wall.

6.3.2.6 Funerary monuments

To date only one fragment of saddle quern has been recorded from a Neolithic funerary monument in the south-west. This is from Sperris Quoit, a chambered tomb in West Penwith which was originally constructed 3600-3500 cal. BC (Thomas and Wailes 1967; Jones and Quinnell 2011, 204). (The entrance graves on the Isles of Scilly are now considered, on the basis of the pottery found within them, to be Bronze Age in date (Pearce 1981, 54; Johns 2011)). The West Penwith chambered tombs had a long currency of use, originating in the late Neolithic and continuing in use into the Early Bronze Age (Pearce 1981, 54). Unfortunately, the exact location of the quern within the tomb is unknown and it could, therefore, be Bronze Age rather than Neolithic in date. That querns were utilised in the construction of Neolithic chambered tombs and entrance graves is shown by evidence from sites outside the study area such as Waylands Smithy in Oxfordshire, Burn Ground, Hampnett in Gloucestershire and Gwernvale in South Wales (Whittle 1991, 87; Grimes 1960, 75; Britnell and Savory 1984, 134). The south-west has its share of Neolithic chambered tombs and long barrows and although many no longer survive intact the possibility that quernstones are still to be found within their constructive material remains.

6.3.3 Associated artefacts

As far as associated artefacts are concerned, these are mainly from pit deposits and appear to be generally domestic in nature such as animal bone, flint, charcoal, pottery, rubbing stones and pounders. Two pits at Milsoms Corner contained baked clay, thought to be the remains of ovens. Again these are not out of place in a domestic context (Tabor 2008, 45). However, the pink flint pebble and fragment of greenstone axe from a pit at Hazard Hill, Devon, and the arrowhead and slingstones from pit B410 at Cadbury Castle perhaps have more significant connotations (Houlder 1963, 26, 27; Cadbury Castle Archive). A sandstone axe fragment was also found within an occupation layer at Helman Tor although here the finds can only be said to be loosely associated (Roe 1997, 53).

6.4 Discussion

Thirty three querns from twelve sites must be considered a low number for the 2000 years or so of the Neolithic period although the number can be increased slightly by the addition of those currently known from unstructured contexts such as the saddle quern and rubbers found on the occupation site on Tower Hill, St. Cuthbert Out, Somerset (Hack 1982, 72). Nevertheless, the low number is consistent with the theory that grain was not a staple food at this time. The lone example of a saddle quern dated to the later Neolithic from Tremough also appears to follow the wider pattern with querns rarely found in association with grooved ware deposits (Quinnell 2007, 83; Watts, S. 2008a, 100). This also appears to coincide with the decrease suggested in cereal cultivation and lends further support to the primary use of querns for grinding grain. However, although a dual use is possible, the fact that the saddle quern from Ben Bridge was stained with ochre demonstrates that querns were also put to grinding other materials.

Ten of the 33 querns were found in a complete or near complete condition. Although worn, the majority of these appear to have been in a still usable state. The complete saddle querns found at Milsoms Corner and Ben Bridge may have been open deposits, placed with the intention of retrieval at some future date. That found in a cairn at Carn Brea may also have been a cache but the inclusion of stones of different geological origin points to a special deposit of some form. Likewise, the complete saddle quern in the centre of a hearth at Hazard Hill may also have been a symbolic gesture. The double-sided saddle quern from Tregarrick Farm, Cornwall, which had broken through where its two opposing grinding surfaces had worn the stone to a mere 3mm thick, appears to have been in a closed deposit. Other complete quernstones, mostly rubbers, were also in closed, permanent deposits. This suggests that the latter were deliberately taken out of use before reaching the end of their use-lives.

The inclusion of fragments of quernstone in both pits and other contexts can be contrasted with the deposition of complete stones. This introduces the notion of deliberate fragmentation and that pieces were retained, perhaps for deposition elsewhere (Chapman 2000b). It is also notable that, in keeping with the conclusions drawn from the published literature, the majority of Neolithic quern deposits are either of single upper or of lower stones. The separation of upper from lower stone may represent an ending of some form but single stones, whether complete or fragmentary, could also be representative of the complete quern, a case of *pars en toto*. Exceptions are those represented in pits at Milsoms Corner and the upper and lower stone found together at Ben Bridge, Somerset. The two stones derived from different sources and their pairing also potentially represents a relationship of some form.

The majority of Neolithic querns in the south-west derive from pits and the general nature of the deposits in both earlier and later Neolithic pits appears to conform to those excavated elsewhere in the country (Thomas 1999; Pollard 2001). This suggests that they are localised versions of a much wider practice. Not all pits were dug with the same sense of meaning and purpose and several categories of deposition can also be found within the same type of feature. Although most pits appear to comprise closed, permanent deposits related to the occupation or the leaving of a site, different levels of meaning and intent can also be envisaged between the depositions of fragmentary or complete quernstones within a charcoal-rich fill and those in a clean soil fill. Different again appears to be the placement of a complete saddle quern in one of the pits at Milsoms Corner. This, as mentioned above, is best interpreted as an open deposit, carefully buried with the intention of recovery.

Although pits may be the most common form of depositional context, the small number of querns recovered from other contexts indicates that a variety of depositional features were utilised from a date early in the Neolithic. The fragment of saddle quern from Sperris Quoit also indicates that they were selected for deposition on non-domestic sites. Although this may be a pragmatic reuse of stone it is also possible that its deposition was symbolic related to the quern's transforming properties. The range of sites and features in which querns are found has correlations elsewhere in Britain and comparisons can also be drawn with depositional practices on the European mainland (Watts, S. 2008a, 100; Graefe *et al* 2009). This suggests that communities were embracing both the practical and symbolic aspects of their new material culture and lends credence to the suggestion that, whether as a result of migration or acculturation or through a mixture of the two, new ideologies were adopted and adapted together with new modes of living, building and material culture (Watts, S. 2008a, 110).

6.5   Conclusions

The nature of the evidence for the structured deposition of querns in the Neolithic south-west appears to fit that from other sites in Britain and indicates that the structured deposition of querns was a widespread practice established early in the period. The contexts in which querns are found and their condition as found, together with the accompanying artefacts or lack thereof clearly suggests that they were deposited with different levels of meaning and intent. Contrasts can be seen, for example, between the complete pair of stones left at Ben Bridge, the complete saddle quern in a cairn at Carn Brea and the fragment of saddle quern in a chambered tomb at Sperris Quoit, the latter showing that querns were taken for deposition, whether for practical or symbolic reasons, on non-domestic sites (Rahtz and Greenfield 1977, 85; Mercer 1981, 81; Thomas and Wailes 1967, 18). Twenty of the 33 querns were recovered from pits and hollows and the different composition of the fills found in these features demonstrates that different categories of deposit can also be found within the same type of context. The deposition of a complete saddle quern in a pit at Milsoms Corner which appears to have been curated can be compared with the quern fragment found together with pottery and flint, burnt bone and hazelnut shells in a charcoal rich soil in a pit at Chew Valley Lake which has all the appearance of a clearing-up exercise (Watts S. 2008b; Rahtz and Greenfield 1977, 27). Although the querns from Ben Bridge and Sperris Quoit could potentially date to the later Neolithic period only one securely dated Late Neolithic quern has been found in the south-west to which appears to fit the theory that querns are rarely found in contiguity with depositions of grooved ware.

A variety of potential reasons can be advanced, therefore, to account for the structured deposition of querns in the Neolithic period. These include:

- Offerings or deposits representative of a site's occupation; the quernstones may be complete or fragmentary.
  - Depositions made with no obvious structure or formality, in essence the result of clearing up operations, although this may in itself have been a formalised process.
  - Deposits showing apparent choice in the selection of artefacts, forging a link between people and place.
- Safe storage of complete quernstones with the intention of reuse, such reuse is potentially both practical and symbolic.
- Reuse of fragmentary stones as construction material.

The sites and contexts within which querns are found on Neolithic sites in the south-west of England thus begin to set the agenda for discussions on patterns of deposition and subsequent changes in practice in the area in the Bronze Age. The Bronze Age witnessed the transition from nomadic to settled communities and the establishment of permanent farmsteads. This gave rise to additional and more archaeologically visible contexts of deposition based primarily on the home and the domestic environment. At the same time, although the saddle quern remained the prime tool for milling grain and other substances, a new, smaller and neater version came into play which was perhaps related to a specific use.

7

THE BRONZE AGE

7.1 Setting the Scene: Activity Locales and Subsistence

The earlier part of the Bronze Age, *circa* 2200-1500BC, in the south-west witnessed a gradual but inexorable shift from mobile communities who cultivated crops on a small scale within the precincts of their nomadic lifestyle to permanent farming settlements both open and enclosed with associated field systems in which grain was grown as a staple food. Such settlements, found in both lowland and upland areas, include Gwithian, Trethellan Farm, Bodrifty and Stannon Down in Cornwall, Dean Moor, Shaugh Moor and Hayne Lane in Devon and Brean Down, Somerset. A number of field systems and associated groups of roundhouses have also been identified on Exmoor which may be of Bronze Age date while on Dartmoor, which has a wealth of Bronze Age roundhouses, settlements and field systems, long linear boundaries or reaves perhaps associated with land-holdings and transhumance were laid out *circa* 1700/1600BC (Sturgess 2007; Nowakowski 1991; Dudley 1956; Mercer 1970; Fox 1957; Fitzpatrick *et al* 1999a; Riley and Wilson-North 2001, 20; Fleming 1988, 105; Fitzpatrick 2008). Dictated by geology and topography, those settlements in the east of the region and in lowland areas tend to comprise timber-framed roundhouses while those in upland and granite areas are predominantly stone-walled.

Other, fundamental, changes were also taking place. Metalworking in copper, gold and bronze was introduced and new forms and styles of weaponry appeared. Monumental building ceased and communal burials in chambered tombs gave way to individual inhumations and cremations in round barrows, a process that had begun in the later Neolithic period (Pollard and Healy 2008; Quinnell 1988, 8; Fitzpatrick 2008, 120). Barrows and cairns are well distributed across the south-west although not all appear to be the recipients of burials. In the Late Bronze Age, *circa* 1100-700BC, however, there appears to have been a move away from inhumation and cremation burials towards the interment of partial human remains (Fitzpatrick 2008, 126). The upland areas of Devon and Cornwall were largely abandoned at the beginning of the 1st millennium BC, perhaps due to climatic deterioration, although it is likely that they continued to be used for summer grazing (Quinnell 1994, 76; Fitzpatrick 2008, 125).

A particular feature of the Bronze Age in the south-west is the procedure by which many settlements and structures were formally decommissioned at the end of their use lives. Although a general, logical pattern of demolition, infilling and levelling can be discerned, each site appears to have had its own course of actions by which it was closed down. This suggests communities performed personalised versions of a wider practice (Jones 1998-1999; Jones and Taylor 2004, 31). Indeed, as evidence from Trethellan Farm and Scarcewater, Cornwall shows, even within the same site no two buildings followed the exact same process of abandonment. In addition, evidence from sites such as Callestick, Cornwall, and Sigwells, Somerset, demonstrates that the phenomenon was not peculiar to settlements but was also followed on sites with specific, non-domestic functions and, furthermore, that sites with short-term occupation could also be subject to the same processes (Nowakowski 1991; Jones and Taylor 2010; Jones 1998-1999; Tabor 2008, 61-69).

The demolition of timber-framed structures such as at Sigwells is unlikely to have left any lasting mark on the landscape. However, demolished and infilled stone-walled or stone-kerbed roundhouses would have been left as low mounds reminiscent of barrows. It is suggested (Jones and Taylor 2010, 78-79) that this was deliberate, that houses of the living were transformed into houses of the dead. Moreover, earlier barrows may have been considered as the transformed houses of the ancestors. This allusion was taken further at sites such as Scarcewater and Callestick with the addition of stone kerbs to some of the roundhouses (Jones 1998-1999, 15, 50; Jones and Taylor 2010, 78-79). Likewise at Dainton, Devon, the sites of several former roundhouses or activity areas were covered over with stone cairns (Silvester 1980, 44).

The principal crops grown in the south-west during the Bronze Age were emmer, spelt, bread wheat (*Triticum aestivum*) and barley (both naked and hulled varieties). Peas (*Pisum sativum*), Celtic bean (*Vicia faba*) and flax (*Linum usitatissimum*) were also grown (Straker 1991, 161-179; Clapham and Stevens 1999, 197; Jones and Taylor 2004, 30; Carruthers 2007, 103-104). Flax may have been grown for its fibres or for its seeds. The seeds and unripe capsules can be roasted (Bremness 1988, 277), although Pliny mentions that flax seed was added to barley and ground into flour. He also notes that bean pottage was a sacrificial food (Pliny *Natural History* 18.14.73; 18.30.118). In addition, the quantity of hedge mustard seeds (*Sisymbrium officinale*) recovered from a pit at Trethellan Farm, Cornwall has led to the suggestion that the plant was deliberately cultivated (Straker 1991, 169). Likewise, the quantities of brassica seeds including black mustard (*Brassica nigra*) from Tremough and Truro College, Cornwall are also suggestive of a cultivated crop (Carruthers 2007, 104; Carruthers forthcoming). Mustard seed can be ground or crushed for medicinal or culinary uses (Bremness 1988, 60).

The seeds of Fat Hen (*Chenopodium album*) and black bindweed (*Convolvulus arvensis*), often identified as weeds, may also have been collected and ground (Reynolds 1979, 67-69). Indeed Reynolds (1979, 68-69) has suggested that Fat Hen could have been used as a crop in its own right, sown in an emergency if a grain crop failed early in the year. Carbonised hazelnut shell fragments from sites such as Castle Hill and Hayne Lane in east Devon, Scarcewater in Cornwall and, just beyond the study area, acorns from an early Bronze Age pit at Bestwall Quarry Dorset, indicate that wild resources also continued to form part of the diet (Clapham 1999, 59, 112; Jones and Taylor 2010, 23; Ladle 1998, 110). The increased dependency on cultivated crops in the Bronze Age, as they became vital rather than special or supplementary foodstuffs, would presumably have affected the meaning and values attached to those crops and thus, by extension, to the tools used to process them. If one accepts the theory that the symbolic meanings attached to querns were adopted with the introduction of agriculture from the continent (Watts, S. 2008a, 110) then the move to permanent farming settlements will have given added nuance to that symbolism.

In addition to plant foods, saddle querns may also have been used for grinding copper and tin ore. Beyond the study area saddle querns have been found in association with copper mines in central Europe and with a mineral processing workshop on Minoan Crete and at the tin working sites at Eskragh, Co. Tyrone and nearer to home at Bestwall Quarry, Dorset (Much 1893, 263; Procopiou 2011; Williams 1978, 47; Ladle 1998, 110). However, as mentioned in Chapter Two, it was probably not necessary to crush fine alluvial tin ore prior to smelting (Newman 1998, 30, 40). Unfortunately little direct evidence for prehistoric tin working has been found in the south-west due in part to later mineral extraction. Querns reused as anvils were found in an enclosure on Shaugh Moor, Dartmoor and some of the quern fragments found within the metalworking enclosure at Sigwells near Cadbury Castle in Somerset may have derived from querns that had been put to similar use (Shaugh Moor Archive; Tabor 2008, 64). In addition to the use of querns for metalworking there is also evidence from Gwithian, Cornwall to indicate that saddle querns were used in the production of pottery (Sturgess 2007, 31).

7.2   Querns from the Study Area

A total of 324 complete and fragmentary querns broadly dated to the Bronze Age are included on the database from 47 sites. The distribution (Figure 7.1), as indicated in Chapter Five, shows a bias towards western Cornwall and Dartmoor with a cluster of sites around Cadbury Castle, Somerset, which are the result of the Cadbury Castle Environs Project. The scatter of sites on Bodmin Moor, Cornwall, in east Devon, north Somerset and the solitary quern from Holworthy in north Devon, however, suggest that the use of querns in the Bronze Age was more widespread than the current data indicates. The sites where querns have been found in structured contexts range in date from the Late Neolithic/Early Bronze Age through to the Late Bronze Age/Early Iron Age (Figure 7.2) although there is a notable contrast between the number of querns from secure Early Bronze Age contexts (9) and those dated to Middle (152) and Middle-Late Bronze Age (124). However, some sites such as Gwithian and Shaugh Moor have produced evidence for lengthy, although not necessarily continuous, occupation from 1800-900 cal. BC and 1500-600 cal. BC respectively (Sturgess 2007; Wainwright and Smith 1980). Other settlements, such as Trethellan Farm and Scarcewater, Cornwall and Hayne Lane, Devon also show evidence for the rebuilding of roundhouses and for occupation lasting several generations (Nowakowski 1991; Jones and Taylor 2010; Fitzpatrick *et al* 1999a). These can be compared with the short-life spans of contemporary

The Life and Death of Querns

Figure 7.1: Map showing the location of Bronze Age sites where querns have been found in structured contexts (see Appendix One for site details).

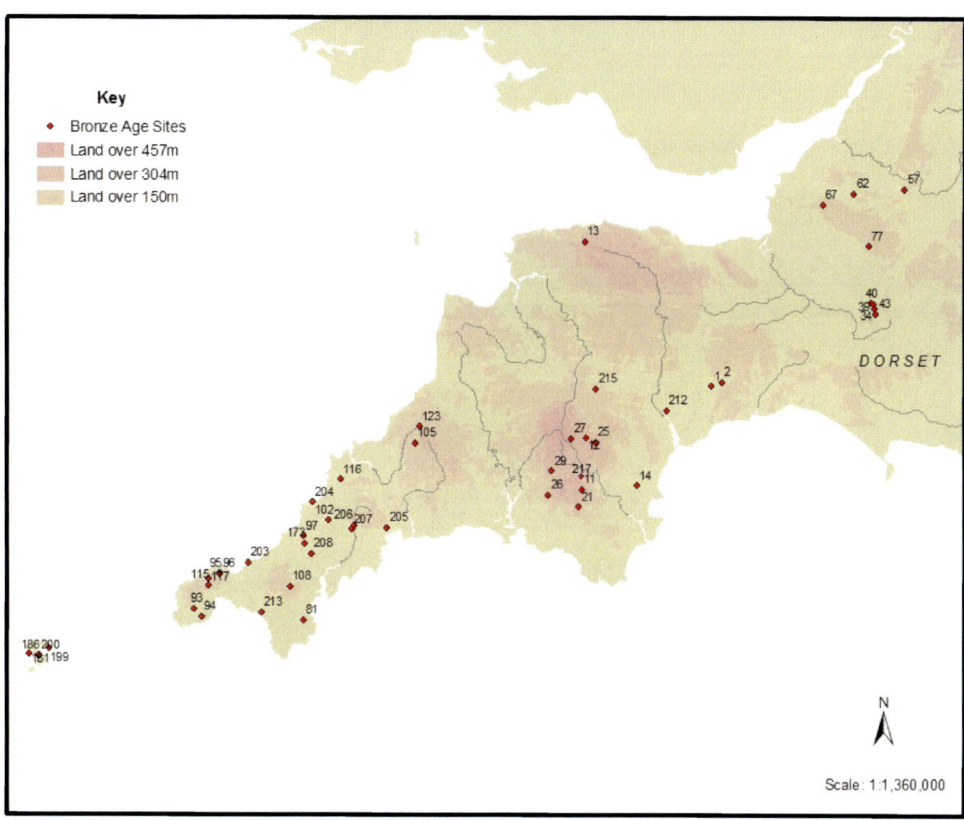

Figure 7.2: Table showing the numbers of querns found within each Bronze Age depositional context. Rh: Round house

	Early Bronze Age		Bronze Age		Middle Bronze Age		Middle-Late Bronze Age		Late Bronze Age		Total
	Rh	exRh	Rh	exRh	Rh	exRh	Rh	exRh	Rh	exRh	
Abandonment layer				1		24		3		12	40
Bank								1		2	3
Barrow/grave		1		19		1				1	22
Cairn										5	5
Cobbled surface						1	1				2
Ditch		3		2		5		1		3	14
Floor					1						1
Foundation				1							1
Gully	2				1	1		1	1		6
Hearth/cooking pit				1	6	1			1		9
Hollow						1					1
Midden				2	1	3		4			10
Mound						1					1
Occupation layer	1		6		18		24	1	1	2	53
Pit		1			23	20		2	3	13	62
Pit kiln				1	1					1	3
Posthole	1			1	23			3	6	2	36
Ring ditch wall						8					8
Sealing layer						3					3
Tree bowl				1							1
Wall				4	4	5	19	3	8		41
Total	4	5	12	27	102	50	52	11	32	29	324

settlements in southern England which appear to have been occupied for perhaps a single generation only (Brück 1999b). Such continuity of occupation provides more and different opportunities for depositional events related to both present and past, linking one to the other. By way of contrast it is suggested that a metalworking enclosure at Sigwells, Somerset was occupied for a few months only (Tabor 2008, 66).

The majority of Bronze Age querns on the database, however, derive from Middle Bronze Age settlements and include several large assemblages from Trethellan Farm, Scarcewater and Gwithian from which 55, 51 and 46 querns were recorded from structured contexts

Figure 7.3: Collections of rubbers and saddle quern fragments from Pit 5027, Truro College, Cornwall (left) and Pit 1610, Scarcewater, Cornwall (right) (© Historic Environment, Cornwall Council).

respectively[1]. In addition, 23 querns are also included from the enclosure on Shaugh Moor, 20 from the combined sites of Higher Besore and Truro College, Cornwall, 14 from a metalworking enclosure at Sigwells and 12 from an enigmatic Late Bronze Age structure at Callestick. The querns comprise 173 rubbers of which 102 are in a complete or near complete state, 106 saddle querns including 42 complete or near complete examples and 45 indeterminate fragments (Figure 5.3).

As in the Neolithic, depositions of single quernstones or fragments predominate but it is also of note that some contexts contained several querns. Each of the roundhouses at Shaugh Moor utilised a number of quernstones within their construction, while at Dainton in south Devon several different quern fragments were found within the same cairn. *In situ* deposits of querns in what appear to be their primary working positions have also been found on Bronze Age sites in the southwest including Trethellan Farm and Gwithian. Also amongst the saddle querns are a number of small, neatly made examples, which as suggested earlier may have been for a specific use[2]. Of particular import, however, are the hoards of quernstones, mostly rubbers, that have been found in pits on several Cornish Bronze Age sites (Figure 1.6; 7.3). These, together with other depositions of complete saddle querns, for example, are suggestive of different categories of structured deposit.

All the querns appear to be of stone local to the south-west including Cornish and Dartmoor granite, Permian lava from the Exeter area, a red quartz porphyry from south Devon and Old Red Sandstone from the Mendips. River and beach cobbles were frequently used for rubbers. The nearest available sources of stone were generally utilised, the raw material acquired by the individual or community rather than being the result of exchange mechanisms (Watts, M. 2002, 27). However, there is also evidence showing that, as in the Neolithic period, communities occasionally obtained stones from sources 10km or more away. Several beach cobble rubbers were found at Scarcewater where the nearest beaches are some 11km to the east. Such cobbles probably represent the fruits of gathering expeditions. At Truro College the acquisition of a beach cobble for use as a rubber from the Lizard, 23km to the south-west, is likely to have coincided with that of gabbroic clay for pottery manufacture (Quinnell 2010, 113; Quinnell and Taylor forthcoming). On non-domestic sites there is evidence for the transportation of querns over even greater distances. A rubber from the 'ritual' structure at Callestick near Truro came from Mounts Bay some 25km away (the other querns from the site came from the Cligga Head, St. Agnes and Carnmenellis granites, 4km, 6km and 12km away respectively) (Quinnell and Taylor 1998-1999, 27-28). Querns of greensand, Old Red Sandstone and a red igneous rock found at Sigwells, Somerset originated from sources 15km east, 22km north and 40km west of the site respectively while the fragment of rhyolite quern found in a ring ditch at Sheep Slait, Dorset (Figure 7.4) came from Dartmoor or possibly north Cornwall (Tabor 2008, 65-66, 98). The incorporation of querns from distant sources in structured deposits is surely significant, perhaps indicative of a relationship of some form; at Sigwells it is suggested that people came together to share in the experience of metalworking and other craft activities.

---

1. These totals do not include unstratified querns and those recovered from top or plough soil or which were subject to post-depositional movement.
2. Another small saddle quern was also found recently in a Bronze Age ditch at Ham Hill, Somerset (not included on database) (N. Sharples 2012, 38). By way of contrast several very large rubbers have recently been found during excavations on St. Agnes, Isles of Scilly (not included on database) (information from H. Quinnell).

7.3 Contexts of Deposition

Within the 47 sites, analysis of the database indicates that 21 main types of depositional context can be discerned (Figure 7.2). Pits continue to be an important feature with 61 querns being recovered from various pit deposits. Occupation spreads, however, account for 53 querns, 43 were found reused within stone-built walls and a further 36 came from postholes. Although just nine quernstones have been found in Early Bronze Age contexts it is of note that they derive from six different contexts suggesting that the variety of depositional locations evidenced in the Neolithic period continued into the Bronze Age. An intriguing aspect of the period in the south-west, as mentioned above, is the process by which some Middle and Late Bronze Age settlements and structures were demolished and abandoned at the end of their use-lives. It is of particular note, therefore, that at least 40 querns from the dataset were incorporated within various demolition and levelling deposits indicating that querns played a part not only in the life of settlements and structures but also in their death.

Some two thirds of the querns derived from contexts directly related to roundhouses and other structures. However, other features such as ditches and funerary sites were also utilised as depositional locations, the latter demonstrating the deposition of querns outside the domestic arena, a phenomenon first observed in the Neolithic. Although the dataset is dominated by Cornwall (225 querns from 21 sites, excluding the Isles of Scilly) some regionality is apparent, partly dictated by topography and geology. The majority of ditch deposits come from Somerset with one from Devon whereas all the querns reused in stone walls derive from sites in Cornwall or on Dartmoor. All the midden deposits containing querns come from Cornwall or the Isles of Scilly. The deliberate demolition and abandonment of sites and structures and the use of querns within that process also appears to be a particular feature of the Cornish Bronze Age but evidence from Holworthy in North Devon, Sigwells in Somerset and also potentially from Hayne Lane in East Devon and, outside the study area, Rowden in Dorset indicates that the practice occurred across a wider area (Watts, S. 2009; Tabor 2008, 68; Fitzpatrick *et al* 1999a, 95; Woodward 1991, 45, 46).

7.3.1 Structural contexts

Just over 62% of the total dataset for the Bronze Age was recovered from roundhouses and other structures ranging in date from possibly as early as 1890-1610 cal. BC for structure 1642 at Gwithian to *circa* 1100-700 cal. BC for the ritual structure at Callestick (Sturgess 2007, 26; Jones 1998-1999, 5). These dates suggest that the deposition of querns in these locales was probably a natural continuation of the deposition of querns on occupation and activity sites in the Neolithic period and that it became a well-established and long-lasting practice. As shown below, analysis of the particular contexts in which the querns were found indicates that they were deposited in association with all aspects of these buildings' construction, occupation and abandonment. The nature of the various depositions, however, varies considerably and suggests local variations and adaptations of practice. Not all roundhouses contain querns and it seems that different roundhouses were chosen to receive particular depositions which may have been related to their occupants or to the activities that were carried out within. At Trethellan Farm (15th to 13th centuries cal. BC) querns were found in each of the main structures with the exception of roundhouse H3021 which appears to have gone out of use fairly early in the site's occupation. Roundhouse H2001 produced the greatest number of querns, a reflection perhaps of its role as a major domestic structure throughout the life of the settlement (Nowakowski 1991; Trethellan Farm Archive). At Scarcewater (*circa* 1500-1100 cal. BC) the largest and most complex of the three roundhouses produced the most querns and the smallest roundhouse the least (Jones and Taylor 2010). Similarly, at Shaugh Moor the number of querns per structure appears related to both the size of the respective roundhouse and its length of occupation. Six were recovered from the wall of H67 the largest and most frequently rebuilt of the five roundhouses, five from H15, the earliest roundhouse, four from H18, three from H66 and only two from H19 the final roundhouse to be built on the site (Wainwright

Figure 7.4: Fragment of rhyolite quern and other finds from a ring ditch at Sheep Slait, Dorset (R. Tabor).

and Smith 1980; Shaugh Moor Archive). By way of contrast quern fragments were only recovered from the smaller of the two roundhouses in an Middle-Late Bronze Age enclosure at Hayne Lane, Devon (1520-800 cal. BC) (Laidlaw 1999a, 108). A possible reason for this is discussed further below.

7.3.1.1 Walls and floors

At least 40 querns derived from the extant walls or tumble of stone-built roundhouses and a further two appear to have been reused as paving material[3]. As indicated above 20 saddle querns and rubbers are recorded from the walls and porches of the five stone-built roundhouses within the enclosure at Shaugh Moor. Eight querns were found in association with structural walls at Gwithian. At Stannon Down on Bodmin Moor two saddle querns and a number of rubbers were built into the roundhouse walls of a settlement there and querns were also incorporated into the walls of roundhouses at Heatree, Scadbrook and Holne Moor on Dartmoor. A further five were found in the wall of a circular structure at Callestick. In addition, the quern fragments found in the infill of structures at Callestick and Trevilison, Cornwall and Nornour, Isles of Scilly may have also have derived from their respective walls (Wainwright and Smith 1980; Shaugh Moor Archive; Sturgess and Lawson-Jones 2006; Mercer 1970, 32; Quinnell 1991, 18; Masson Phillips 1982, 57; Fleming 1988, 77; Dudley 1967, 18; Jones and Taylor 2004, 108; Quinnell and Taylor 1998-1999; Butcher 1978, 94-95).

Although it is difficult to say with certainty that the inclusion of a quern within the construction of a building denotes anything more than simple reuse of a convenient piece of stone its incorporation nevertheless denotes a phase of rebuilding. This may in turn be associated with changes in occupation or status of the building. Most of the roundhouses at Shaugh Moor, for example, showed evidence for rebuilding and reconstruction. Unfortunately, particularly with older excavations, the exact location of a quern within a roundhouse wall has rarely been recorded, although in many instances the quern was found within tumble from the wall and its original location is, therefore, lost. However, regardless of this, the quern's placement and location are clearly related to the construction and life of the roundhouse.

At Bussow in West Penwith a saddle quern was found inverted at the foot of the wall of one of the roundhouses of the former settlement there which is suggestive of a foundation deposit (Noall 1971, 30). Its placement is reminiscent of the half saddle quern found inverted in the wall core of a house at Ness of Gruting, Shetland (Calder 1955-1956, 353). The latter, found adjacent to a pile of carbonised barley, also appears to be a foundation deposit. If one accepts the principle of using querns as foundation stones and also of their use in abandonment deposits then the possibility of their symbolic reuse within other phases of a structure's life must also exist. At Holne Moor Fleming (1988, 77) noted that one of the two quern fragments reused in the wall of the small roundhouse that was constructed within a larger hut circle lay at the entrance.

Brück (1999a, 334; 1999b, 154; 2006, 298-299) has suggested that special deposits were made at key points in the life of a roundhouse or, alternatively, those of its occupants which may account for such 'odd deposits'. A sherd of decorated pottery found deep in a crevice within the wall of roundhouse at Dean Moor, Devon, for example, is unlikely to have found its way there by accident and so must represent a deliberate placement (Fox 1957, 41). The presence of querns within walls, porches and floors may also, therefore, be deliberate. There is some ethnographic evidence for the reuse of querns in buildings. In the American South-West Schlanger (1991, 463) noted the use of complete and still usable metates as building stone even though ordinary building material was readily available. In Britain it is not uncommon to find pieces of millstone reused in the walls and floors of watermills[4]. This may simply be a case of 'waste not, want not' but it is also possible that such redeployment was at once both practical and symbolic. As Robinson (2007, 97) comments, it creates a link, a continuity between the past and the present. It evokes ancestral memory and a sense of community and belonging. These are particularly important concepts for sites such as Shaugh Moor which is seen as being occupied on a seasonal basis only (Wainwright and Smith 1980, 115).

Both complete or near complete and fragments of saddle querns and rubbers were reused as building material. It is possible that some stones, particularly saddle querns were broken before being reused and the fact that potentially usable quernstones were utilised in this way suggests that a decision was made to remove them from everyday use. This may have been a premeditated action,

---

3. The actual number of querns found in walls is unknown but higher than this total. At some sites such as Nornour, Isles of Scilly, it was simply recorded in the published literature that worn saddle querns were built into the walls but not exactly how many (Dudley 1967, 18).

4. Querns and millstones are also reused as decorative features on modern buildings. This particular aspect of reuse, however, does not seem to have occurred in the Bronze Age.

based upon their previous life history. A difference in meaning can be envisaged, therefore, between the reuse of complete quernstones versus fragments. It was suggested in Chapter Four that the breaking of an object can render it powerless or conversely enable the release of its powers. Alternatively, one part of an object may have represented the whole. Thus the placement of both complete and fragmentary querns in walls may have enabled the transference of their powers and properties to the building or to the occupants (Cassel 2005). These powers and properties may be related to the role of querns as transformers of raw material, in particular of staple, life-giving crops or to the women (ancestors) who used them. Artefacts may have been added during construction in the same way. It has been suggested (McOmish 1996, 75) that middens were enhanced with choice deposits. A wall, however, is a liminal structure, a boundary separating the inside from the outside both practically and symbolically. In this light the placement of quernstones within walls can be seen as both protective, drawing upon the ancestors to safeguard the present occupants, and as links to the past thus justifying the present.

These theories fit well with the reuse of five quern fragments within the walling of a single phase Late Bronze Age circular structure at Callestick. The generally 'clean' nature of the building, the lack of evidence for occupation together with its long entrance way led the excavators to conclude that the building was non-domestic in nature. It was suggested, therefore, that the structure may have been a mortuary building or a special building within which rites of passage were performed (Jones 1998-1999, 52). In either case it is clear that the quern fragments used in the building's construction were brought to site for reuse.

7.3.1.2 Postholes
Thirty six querns found in a total of 25 postholes are recorded on the database, the majority of which are dated to the Middle Bronze Age. They comprise ten fragmentary and two complete or near complete saddle querns, nine complete and seven fragmentary rubbers and eight indeterminate fragments (Table 7.1). The two complete saddle querns came from Scadbrook on Dartmoor and Scarcewater. The former was only 25.4cm long, sufficiently small enough to fit a structural posthole, while that from Scarcewater had been broken in two (Masson Phillips 1982, 61; Quinnell 2010, 121). Of the 25 postholes, 20 were in roundhouses or similar structures and most were structural; a further two, from Higher Besore, formed part of a Late Bronze Age structural windbreak (*circa* 1210-970 cal. BC) (Gossip forthcoming). The total number of structures bearing querns in postholes was 13 from nine sites (excluding the windbreak). This number is but a small proportion of the total number of excavated roundhouse postholes but it is noticeable that several structures contained quern fragments in more than one posthole. At Sigwells three postholes out of at least seven associated with a metalworking structure were found to contain querns while at Hayne Lane quern fragments derived from two out of about 29 postholes associated with roundhouse 439 (Watts 2008b; Fitzpatrick *et al* 1999a, 95). At Scarcewater quern fragments were recovered from postholes in two of a group of three or more roundhouses; two from the main phase of occupation of house 1250, out of 21 postholes, and two also from house 1500 out of the 17 postholes associated with the phase 2 structure (Jones and Taylor 2010, 13, 16). Elsewhere, only one posthole out of 65 in a group of four Middle Bronze Age structures at Tremough, Cornwall (1500-1100 cal. BC) was found to contain a quern fragment (Gossip and Jones 2007, 14-20). At Trethellan Farm quern fragments were recovered from just five postholes in four of the seven roundhouses out of some 94 excavated postholes (Nowakowski 1991; Trethellan Farm Archive). These figures could be taken to indicate that the presence of quern fragments in postholes is mere happenstance but the fact that they are found in so few postholes is more indicative of deliberate meaningful deposition.

There are, however, three main reasons to account for the presence of querns and other artefacts within postholes. Firstly, they may be part of the post-packing: secondly they may have been inserted to block the hole when the post was removed and thirdly, perhaps the least likely in the case of quern fragments, unless they were very small, they were somehow included within the fill by accident, perhaps when the post was removed for replacement or when the building was demolished (after Brück 1999b, 151). Whatever the reason behind the deposition, all the deposits are closed, that is they were intended to be permanent. Unfortunately, it is not always clear if a quern fragment recovered from a posthole was part of the post-packing or fill. Each type of use clearly carries with it a different meaning; the former is related to the life of the structure, the second to the ongoing occupation or abandonment of the building. Posthole 111 in roundhouse H142/3022 at Trethellan Farm is a case in point. The posthole, situated in the south-west quadrant of the roundhouse, contained two joining quern fragments and some pottery. The closeness of this posthole to the adjacent posthole (112) suggests that one was the replacement of the other. As such the quern fragments may have been post-packing, related either to the construction or to the repair of the roundhouse during its occupation or were placed in the old posthole when it was in-filled. The roundhouse was subsequently demolished, at which time all the posts were removed, the postholes and pits were covered over and the site became an open air activity area (Nowakowski 1991, 51, 54). If posthole 111 was the replacement, that is the latter of the two postholes, then the quern fragments could potentially be posthole fill rather than post-packing. If this was the case the quern fragments represent a closure deposit, related to the demise of the building.

A similar ambiguity can also be seen at Scarcewater where saddle quern fragments were found within three postholes in two of the three roundhouses. The closeness of posthole 1300 to its neighbour (1305) in the south-west quadrant of roundhouse 1250 indicates that again one replaced the other. The few plant remains found scattered throughout the fill of 1300 suggest that the quern fragment also found within it belongs either to a rebuilding episode or to the demolition and abandonment of the roundhouse (Jones and Taylor 2010, 13; Jones forthcoming). On balance, Jones (Jones and Taylor 2010, 76; Jones forthcoming) sees this deposition, and also that in posthole 1319, within the same quadrant as abandonment deposits. The saddle quern fragments found in posthole 1160 in the north-west quadrant of house 1500, on the other hand, are interpreted as a closure rather than an abandonment deposit made when the house was demolished and the site leveled prior to the construction of a completely new roundhouse (Jones and Taylor 2010, 74; Jones forthcoming). This is potentially similar to that in H142/3022 at Trethellan Farm, mentioned above.

At Hayne Lane, six small fragments, probably all from the same quernstone, were recovered from two postholes within the entranceway to ancilliary structure 459. Both postholes are thought to relate to rebuilding episodes and the presence of small finds such as plant remains and charcoal lend support to this (Fitzpatrick *et al* 1999a, 95, 123; Laidlaw 1999a, 108). However, the fact that at least one of the other postholes appeared to be capped (Fitzpatrick *et al* 1999a, 95) suggests that the roundhouse may have ultimately been demolished and, again, the possibility that the quern fragments are abandonment deposits must be considered.

The half rubber capping a posthole in a Middle-Late Bronze Age structure 1134 at Gwithian is also likely to have been an abandonment deposit, as is the complete rubber found together with a pounding stone in the mouth of a non-structural posthole (a.11) at Trevisker, Cornwall (Sturgess and Lawson-Jones 2006, 110; ApSimon and Greenfield 1972, 345). The fragments recovered from a posthole on a Late Bronze Age site at Porthleven, Cornwall are also interpreted as abandonment deposits, although the posthole does not appear to have been structural (Watts, S. 2011b). Likewise, at Sigwells evidence suggests that the quern fragments and other artefacts found in the postholes of the structure within the metalworking enclosure were abandonment deposits, placed after the posts had been removed (Tabor 2008, 68). On the other hand several of the postholes forming part of the structural windbreak at Higher Besore still contained their stone packing. The rubbers and fragmentary saddle quern recovered from postholes 6583 and 6585 are likely, therefore, to be part of this packing (Gossip forthcoming).

At Tremough a large broken rubber and a pottery sherd were recovered from posthole 485 on the northern side of the entrance to structure 392 (Gossip and Jones 2007, 20). The fact that the posthole was subsequently cut through by another posthole suggests that the artefacts were placed as post-packing earlier in the life of the roundhouse, potentially as foundation deposits. It is also tempting to regard the placement of a rubber in posthole 2634 on the south side of the entrance to roundhouse H2222 at Trethellan Farm as a foundation deposit. The house had one main structural phase and, in contrast to other roundhouses within the settlement, was not subject to the same abandonment and demolition processes, having ended its life as a midden (Nowakowski 1991, 47, 101).

The saddle quern found in the central posthole of one of the 11 roundhouses in an enclosure close to the Scadbrook near Owley Gate in the parish of Ugborough, Devon was interpreted as a post-footing and, therefore, also a possible foundation deposit (Masson Phillips 1982, 61). Particularly interesting, however, is the fact that it was inverted. The placement of a quern upside down, in a position in which it could not have been used, is considered to have especial symbolic meaning. It may, therefore, have represented an ending rather than a beginning and the possibility that this was also a closure deposit, made on withdrawal of the post, must also be considered (given that its more uneven underside would have been uppermost). But whether the quern was intended as an abandonment deposit or was utilised as a post footing its presence in the posthole represents deliberate choice and placement, even if, in the latter scenario, it was only chosen by virtue of its size and shape.

The majority of postholes with quern fragments contained few if any other artefacts. However some accompanying finds such as the mussel shells found in an entrance posthole (1527) of structure 1642 at Gwithian, the stone spindle whorl in posthole 58 forming part of the porch of structure 459 at Hayne Lane and the bone tool, hammerstone and decorated pottery in the centre posthole (F036) of the metalworking structure at Sigwells all point to deliberate selection and deposition. The pieces of burnt human skull from posthole F021 midway along the entrance corridor of the same structure are also unlikely to have entered the posthole accidently. It is also of note that the quern fragment found in this latter posthole is from a different source in the Mendips to the others found in the structure (Sturgess and Lawson-Jones 2006, 388; Fitzpatrick *et al* 1999a, 126; Tabor 2008, 68-69; Watts, S. 2008b). Several postholes at Sigwells also contained more than one quern fragment; four came from F036 and a further 12, from at least two saddle querns, and a small rubbing stone were found in posthole F043 on the western side of the structure (Figure 7.5). One of the fragments from F036 was later found to join the remains of a saddle quern in F043. The deposition of pieces from the same quern in different postholes again points to choice rather than happenstance, particularly as the deposits were made on the termination of the enclosure (Watts, S. 2008b). The four rubbers and saddle quern in postholes 6585 and 6583 of the windbreak at Higher Besore, Truro and the three in posthole 2249 in H2222 at Trethellan on the other hand are considered to be part of the post-packing and, therefore, belong to the life of the respective structures (Quinnell and Taylor forthcoming; Nowakowski 1991, 38, 40). Their use as post-packing material can also, however, be seen as the result of choice. It is possible that these tools were deemed to have reached the end of their use lives; two of the rubbers at Higher Besore had been used on both sides. It may also have been considered normal practice to 'dispose' of certain items that belonged to a previous state of occupation by placing them in the postholes of new or rebuilt structures. Such depositions also created and maintained links with the past and may have been made in ways similar to that suggested for the reuse of querns as building material, enabling the transference of their powers to the building and occupants. Whatever the reasoning behind the inclusion of quernstones in postholes, it is clear that it represents a decision to remove them from daily use.

Of the 18 structural postholes that formed part of roundhouses nine were located in the western half of structures, five being in the south-west quadrant; six formed part of entranceways and a further two the centre posthole. The location of the other posthole is unknown (Figure 7.6). An apparent preference for postholes in the southern halves of structures with particular emphasis placed on entranceways suggests a significance can be attached to their choice for quern deposits. It is also noticeable that four of the six entrance postholes are on the southern or western side of a porch or doorway and that two other postholes, 2249 in H2222 at Trethellan Farm and 1585 in H1500 at Scarcewater, are located directly opposite the entrance.

Although the choice of entrance postholes is seen as important (Cleary 2006, 20) very few in fact contain

Figure 7.5: Querns fragments from posthole F043 at Sigwells, Somerset (R. Tabor; S. Watts).

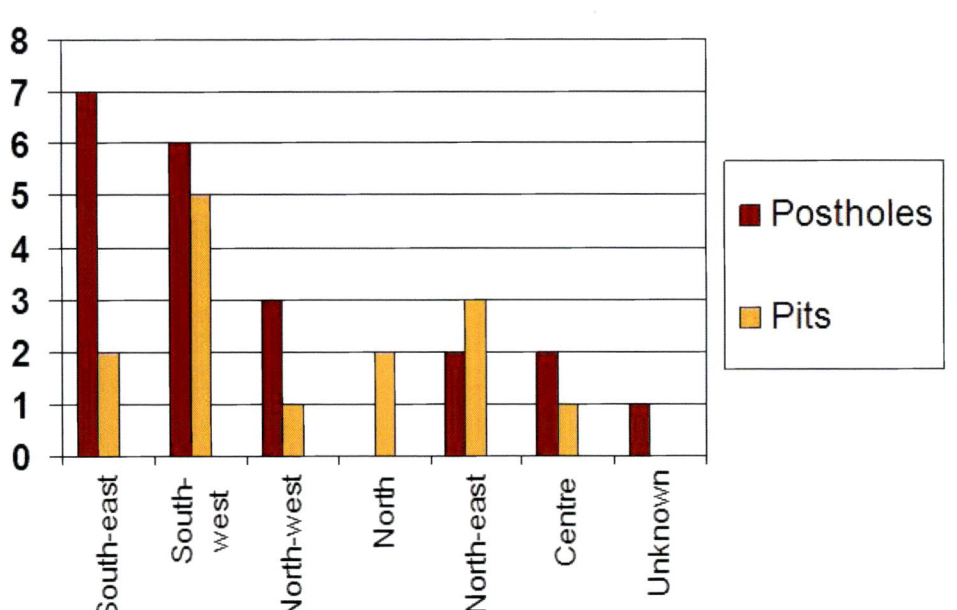

Figure 7.6: Graph showing the cardinal locations of querns in postholes and pits in Bronze Age roundhouses.

querns. Of the seven roundhouses at Trethellan Farm only roundhouse H2222 produced a quernstone (a rubber) from an entrance posthole.[5] Similarly, depositions of quernstones in entrance postholes were recorded from only one of the four roundhouses at Tremough and from just one of the two at Hayne Lane. None were recorded from the three roundhouses at Scarcewater or the two at Trevisker but the sole roundhouse representing Early Bronze Age occupation at Gwithian and the Middle Bronze Age metalworking structure at Sigwells both contained quern fragments in entrance postholes. Every roundhouse, of course, has its own unique life history but nevertheless each of the five roundhouses with querns in entrance postholes can be shown to be special within the site or settlement in which it stood. The most obvious are the structures at Gwithian (1642) and Sigwells which stood alone within their respective enclosures. Structure 392 at Tremough and H2222 at Trethellan Farm were major domestic structures, while house 459 at Hayne Lane appears to have been an ancilliary structure devoted to traditional feminine tasks of spinning, weaving and food preparation. There is also tentative evidence to suggest that it was the earlier of the two roundhouses (Sturgess 2007, 25-26; Tabor 2008, 64; Gossip and Jones 2007, 17; Nowakowski 1991, 39-47; Fitzpatrick *et al* 1999a, 124, 127).

It appears, therefore, that in each case we are looking at a localised enactment of a wider practice. The predominance of querns in postholes in the western and southern half of structures and in entranceways suggests that their deposition was a prescribed rather than random action, perhaps related to an underlying cosmology. Bradley (1998, 149; 2005b, 106) comments upon the importance of the south-west horizon in the alignment of circular henge monuments and stone circles and notes the continuity in shape not only to round barrows but also to roundhouses. This continuity may also be reflected in the location of particular 'depositional access points' (Lionái 2010). The preference across the country for doorways within the south-east quadrant of both Bronze and Iron Age roundhouses is now well-established, although whether this is due to practical or symbolic considerations is still open to debate with some authors returning to the original theory that the orientation was to gain maximum light and shelter (Hamond 1979, 150; Parker Pearson 1996, 119; Oswald 1997; Bradley 1998, 149; Pope 2007; Pope 2008, 19-20). However, there is no reason why the orientation of roundhouses should not have fulfilled both criteria. An underlying cosmology based on an east/sunrise – west/sunset orientation fits the evidence presented by the deposition of querns in roundhouse postholes. In addition, thresholds and boundaries may be considered as liminal, transitional areas over which care must be taken in crossing (Fitzpatrick *et al* 1999a, 125-127; Cleary 2006, 20). The transforming powers of the quern in converting materials from raw to usable, from one state to another, may have been seen as protective in this area with particular respect to certain roundhouses, both during the life of the structures and in their closing.

---

5. As a caveat to this it should be noted that not all the 7 roundhouses were completely excavated and it is possible, although not provable, that H2010 and H648 may have had quern deposits in their entrance postholes.

Although the possibility that some quern fragments were selected simply because they were handy sized pieces of stone must be considered, certain deposits such as those at Sigwells indicate premeditated choice, breakage and placement. Just as the orientation of a roundhouse may have been at once both practical and symbolic so too may the utilisation and deposition of quern fragments. This potential dual use of quern fragments as post-packing or posthole fill and as metaphors for a stage in the life of the structure or household begins to demonstrate the importance and function of querns to Bronze Age peoples on these two levels. The fact that quern fragments are found in postholes in relation to the construction, occupation and abandonment of roundhouses also illustrates that different levels or categories of deposit can be found within one form of context. As will be shown further below, the burying or leaving of artefacts in redundant features is a theme that runs throughout the life history of a roundhouse.

7.3.1.3 Gullies
Just as entrance postholes were used for the deposition of querns fragments, so too were adjacent construction slots and gullies. A broken saddle quern and two other quern fragments were found in the two curved construction trenches on the east and west sides respectively of the entrance to structure 1642 at Gwithian. No other finds were recorded in the eastern gully but the western gully contained a perforated whelk shell, a pottery ring and a bronze awl. The quern fragments together with some pieces of slate and flat stones formed a partial lining. Structure 1642 was initially interpreted as a two phase building, the construction gullies belonging to the second phase, but it is now seen as a single phase structure (Megaw 1976, 53; Sturgess 2007, 25-26). As such the gullies are to be associated with the initial construction of the building. The two quern fragments found at the northern end of the eastern gully may well, therefore, be foundation deposits and likewise the shell, ring and awl in the western gully. Although the saddle quern seems to have had a more practical application, the fact remains that it was broken into a dozen fragments at some point prior to its reuse as a lining for the gully and on this basis it can also be seen as a form of foundation deposit.

7.3.2 Occupation layers and hearths
Sixty three querns, including both fragmentary and complete saddle querns and rubbers, are recorded in the database from occupation layers, hearths and the general interior of roundhouses. There are a number of explanations for the presence of querns and fragments in occupation layers, each representing a different class or category of structured deposit. They may, for example, have been left close to where they were last used. Even fragments may still have had a use-life grinding such materials as medicines and minerals, while those found in close association with hearths, such as a burnt fragment of granite quern found next to a slate-lined hearth (2371) in H2010 at Trethellan Farm (Nowakowski 1991, 31) may have been reused as pot boilers, heat stones or even as pot stands. Querns may also have been placed within hearths as closure or abandonment deposits, a phenomenon first seen in the Neolithic period at Hazard Hill, Devon (Houlder 1963, 13, 28). This is certainly considered to be the case at Scarcewater where a rubber placed in the central hearth of the second house on the site of 1500 is one of the few actions associated with the demise of the building (Jones and Taylor 2010, 76). A fragment of rubber found within a fire pit (2715) at Trethellan Farm may have been placed or left within it as a form of closure deposit when the floor of the working hollow in which it lay was covered over prior to the construction of roundhouse H2010 (Nowakowski 1991, 29, 30). Querns, like hearths, are an important part of the household. Both play a key role in the preparation of food and both have transformative qualities, changing grain to meal, and raw to cooked food respectively. As mentioned in Chapter Three, in early 20th century Mexico the quern, hearth, griddle and pot formed the heart of the house (Brumfield 1991, 237). At Trethellan Farm it was noted that the hearths were not scattered when the settlement was abandoned but simply covered over. It was suggested (Nowakowski 1991, 208) that this signified that the abandonment was not intended to be permanent. However, the scattering of a hearth, central to the life of the household, may have carried a different meaning, symbolising the breaking up of a household rather than the abandonment of the dwelling (after Auel 2002, 703).

Several complete saddle querns were found *in situ*, on or close to their primary working positions in five roundhouses or similar structures, all broadly dated to the Middle Bronze Age. One example was found on the floor in the north-east quadrant of Roundhouse 1 at Stannon Down on Bodmin Moor while at Halangy Porth, Isles of Scilly a sea-worn quern found on the beach is also considered to be *in situ* in the centre of the remains of a roundhouse, most of which has now been destroyed by the sea (Mercer 1970, 32; Ashbee 1983, 11). At Trethellan Farm, a saddle quern was found at the edge of a stone-lined pit (38) in the north-west quadrant of H142/3022 while in H2001 it is suggested that the saddle quern and rubbers found in a shallow pit (2527) in the south-west quadrant may have been used in this location (see below) (Nowakowski 1991, 41, 57).

A remarkable collection of querns and other stone tools was found *in situ* on the floor of one of the Middle to Late Bronze Age structures (725) at Gwithian. Here, along the north-east side of the building a saddle quern was found together with two wooden bowls and stone tools, including rubbers, pebbles and rubbing stones, some of which were stored in a shallow pit (see below) (Sturgess and Lawson-Jones 2006, 168). As a caveat to the above, however, it should be borne in mind that saddle querns, despite their size and weight, are mobile objects and their location in the archaeological record does not necessarily reflect the location of past activities (Graham 1994, figure 26; after Schiffer 1995, 35, 48, 175-185; Jones and Taylor 2010, 66). That said the contiguity of the associated tools and raw materials within structure 725 at Gwithian certainly gives the impression that they were all used close to where they were found.

Following the recognition of a preference for east to south facing entranceways in prehistoric roundhouses it was suggested that activities within followed a 'sunwise' pattern with the southern and northern halves being symbolic of daytime, light and life and night-time, darkness and death respectively (Parker Pearson 1996, 119; Fitzpatrick 1997, 77-78). It has also been suggested (Webley 2007; Jones and Quinnell 2011, 218-219) that the location of the majority of artefacts found in roundhouses such as those in the postholes described above is the result of specific depositions mostly related to the abandonment of the structure within which they are found. Consequently, finds of querns in their working positions must be considered important in terms of the location of occupational activities even though their leaving *in situ* may have been a deposition in itself. The location of the *in situ* querns at Stannon Down and Gwithian run counter to the sunwise theory (H142/3022 at Trethellen Farm was an open working area at the time pit 38 was dug). In addition, the cooking pits, hearths and kilns bearing querns fragments were all sited, not surprisingly, away from the doorway in the centre or northern part of their respective roundhouses. Their location follows Webley's (2007) argument that the archaeological evidence for the location of daily activities in southern England in the Late Bronze Age and Early Iron Age is contrary to the sunwise proposal. This suggests that practical factors such as light and the position of hearths govern the location of querns within Bronze Age roundhouses for everyday usage rather than cosmological considerations.

The exact nature of the presence of many of the querns found within occupation layers and deposits cannot, however, be determined. Nevertheless a difference in meaning and value can be distinguished between complete and fragmentary stones. This difference lies in the fact that each was at a different stage in its life history, including those that were apparently broken immediately prior to deposition. It is of import, therefore, that regardless of their state, all these querns were left when a new floor was laid or when a building was abandoned. At this stage both complete stones and fragments were treated the same, being transformed from open to closed deposits. The leaving of old, broken stones is understandable both in practical and symbolic terms but why were potentially still usable querns not recovered? It is possible there was a taboo against the retrieval and reuse of these artefacts and that the leaving of an older occupation layer *in toto* was a prescribed action within the social context in which the new floor was laid. In this respect all the querns, both complete and fragmentary, those *in situ* and those apparently not, can be seen as part of the closure deposits relating perhaps to a change in status or occupation of the building or to its formal closure and abandonment.

The totality of such closure is evidenced well at Gwithian where the tools and wooden bowls on the floor of structure 725 were sealed with clay spreads and the whole covered by the floor of a new building (724) (Sturgess and Lawson-Jones 2006, 19; Sturgess 2007, 31). Similarly, at Scarcewater a 15cm thick layer of silty clay completely filled and covered all features associated with the first phase of occupation of roundhouse 1500. The house was completely demolished, the posts removed and the site levelled at some time prior to the construction of a new and larger roundhouse (Jones and Taylor 2010, 167). The artefacts recovered from this sealing layer included several fragments of rubber, a slate pot lid and four plain sherds of pottery which may have been inserted as closure deposits. As will become clear below the demolition and levelling of a site prior to rebuilding drew upon the same set of principles and practices as would be employed in its final abandonment.

7.3.3 Pits

Twenty eight querns on the database were recovered from 14 different Bronze Age pits within 10 roundhouses on five sites. This is less than the number of structures with postholes containing quern fragments (Table 7.2). Most of the querns are rubbers, 18 in all including 14 complete or near complete examples. Only two complete saddle querns were found. The majority of roundhouse pits bearing querns are from Trethellan Farm. This does give a bias to the results but allows comparison on an inter-site basis. Interestingly only two of the three roundhouses at Trethellan Farm with querns in postholes also contain pits bearing querns. As with postholes there is some ambiguity as to the causation of the deposit. Nevertheless several different categories of deposition can be recognised within the one form of context, although most deposits are probably ultimately related to the closure or abandonment of the respective structure.

Five of the seven roundhouses at Trethellan Farm contained pits with querns. Two similar pit deposits comprising pottery and a quern fragment were found in H142/3022 and H2222 respectively. However, whereas the pot in pit 2289 in the south-west quadrant of H2222 was complete, although broken, that in pit 3140 in the north-east quadrant of H142/3022 was incomplete (Nowakowski 1991, 52). Given the different states of the pottery it is tempting to conclude that these two deposits were placed with different intents. The different lifecycles of the two houses and the place of the pits within those lifecycles lends support to this conclusion. H142/3022 started life as a house but subsequently the site was turned into an open working area at which time the existing pits, postholes and other features within the house, including pit 3140, were covered over. Pit 3140 was, incidentally, the only feature from the initial phase of occupation to contain any artefacts (Nowakowski 1991, 54), suggesting that it may have been a closure deposit.

H2222 on the other hand, as mentioned above, did not undergo any major structural changes although the building witnessed several phases of occupation during which various pits were dug and subsequently covered over (Nowakowski 1991, 39). Pit 2289 in the south-west quadrant of the house dates from the early part of the building's occupation and the pot and indeed the quern fragment may have been stored there or, alternatively, placed in the pit when it was eventually covered over. Another pit (2267) situated in the northern part of the house, which contained several rubbers and sherds of decorated pottery, also dates to the earlier phase of occupation. It was subsequently covered with a stone slab effectively sealing the artefacts within, again suggesting that they were purposefully left or placed there (Nowakowski 1991, 43). The implication is that these artefacts had personal associations.

Several pit deposits were also found within H2001 at Trethellan Farm including a saddle quern and two rubbers in pit 2527 in the south-west quadrant (Nowakowski 1991, 21, 41). It was suggested (Nowakowski 1991, 41) that the pit was large enough for the saddle quern to have been used within it and that the stone, which was rather heavy, had, therefore, been left *in situ*. Stepping down into the 0.48m deep pit, however, would have been quite an awkward exercise. Moreover, its location at the edge of the house on the south-west side of the doorway would have been in one of the darker areas of the roundhouse. The possibility remains, therefore, that the saddle quern was not *in situ* but was placed in the pit when the floor was covered over. Nevertheless, it seems likely that the saddle quern and rubbers comprised a milling kit; the use of different handstones for grinding coarse or fine was commented upon in Chapter Three. Another two rubbers in pit 2541 close by may have been part of another milling kit.

Both pits 2527 and 2541 and the saddle quern and rubbers within them appear to have been covered over when a new floor was laid, marking the start of the third phase of occupation of the roundhouse (Nowakowski 1991, 21, 23). Complete and still usable tools were thus taken out of circulation. The querns can be seen, therefore, as closure deposits relating perhaps to a change in status or occupation of the houses. No depositions of querns, however, were found in association with the first phase of occupation of H2001, despite the presence of cereal grains indicating that food preparation was one of the structure's main activities. On this basis it can be tentatively suggested that the occupants of the first two phases of H2001 were one and the same but that there was a change in the nature of the occupancy between phase 2 and phase 3 that necessitated the leaving of querns in pits as the new floor was laid. The leaving and burial of complete querns on floors and in pits appears to be a prescribed practice and demonstrates well the important role that querns played in the lives of Bronze Age people. In these scenarios querns can be envisaged as symbols of both people and place.

This importance of querns is shown further in the course of actions by which H2001 was formally abandoned. As one of the final acts, six rubbers together with another fragment of rubber or saddle quern were thrown into a pit (2027) in the north-west quadrant and a saddle quern placed on top of them (Figure 1.6) (Nowakowski 1991, 25). The meaning behind this deposit is potentially very complex. The placement of the saddle quern over the rubbers is suggestive of a position of protection and it was proposed that the deposit was a sign, like the hearths which were not scattered but simply covered over, that the abandonment was not intended to be permanent (Nowakowski 1991, 208). However, the fact that the site of the house was then covered with soil suggests that this was intended as a closed rather than an open deposit.

The leaving of hearths and tools has parallels in more recent times. When the inhabitants of St. Kilda left the island in 1930, fires were lit in the hearths and open Bibles laid upon tables together with piles of oatmeal. These symbolic acts were not in anticipation of a return but to create a sense of place and belonging. The people left something of themselves in the place they were leaving, not wishing to leave their homes totally deserted and bereft (Britain's Lost World, BBC 1, 7.30pm, 27th June 2008).

The positioning of the querns with the saddle quern over the rubbers at Trethellan Farm is one in which the stones could not have been used implying their removal from the earthly world (Pryor 1998b, 61). Such a position implies a gesture of closure and may have drawn upon the same cosmological principles as the breaking of querns seen, for example, in the scattering of fragments through the demolition layers of another structure at Trethellan Farm (see below). Brück (2001, 152-153; 2006) suggests that human lifecycles were understood and explained through the lifecycles of houses and artefacts such as pots, metalwork and querns. Querns, symbolic of the household and of transformation, can be seen as particularly powerful metaphors for life, death and regeneration. Brück (1999b, 155; 2001, 152) further suggests that like humans querns were removed from the earthly world through burial or cremation.

The number of rubbers and fragments in the pit, seven in all, and which were incidentally of a variety of materials – mica, elvan, sandstone and granite – may also be significant. One of the rubbers in particular, of greisenised granite, was unusual to the site having come originally from a source some 10km to the south (Nowakowski 1991, 141). While they could constitute an extensive milling kit, they could also have a more symbolic meaning. They could, for example, represent each of the seven roundhouses that stood within the settlement at one time or another during the course of its existence, the saddle quern representative of the settlement as a whole. Alternatively, they could be representative of people, perhaps of the adult women leaving the settlement. The deposition of different types of stone appears also to be a recurring theme, first witnessed in the Neolithic period, at Carn Brea.

Moving away from Trethellan Farm, at Scarcewater, the nature of the finds, including some unusual pottery sherds, a quartz crystal, pestles and rubbers within pit 1901 (1410-1250 cal. BC) in the south-west quadrant of roundhouse 1500 led to the conclusion that this was a special deposit. It is not clear if this was linked to the construction or demolition of the building, which was subsequently levelled and a new roundhouse built. However, the location of the pit within the post-ring of the initial roundhouse is perhaps rather more suggestive of a foundation deposit containing personal items (Jones and Taylor 2010, 19, 73). It bears comparison with pit 6581 at Higher Besore which was similarly placed within the post-ring of a structural windbreak (see below) (Gossip forthcoming). On the other hand the rubbers, pebbles, scallop shell and antler found in a shallow pit (425) in the north-east quadrant of structure 725 at Gwithian appear to have been broadly *in situ* (Sturgess and Lawson-Jones 2006, 188). The pit and tools were covered over when the building was rebuilt.

Pits bearing querns are found within all quadrants of roundhouses but show a bias towards the south-west, although conversely several deposits were also found in the north-east quadrant (Figure 7.6). Fourteen pits, however, is rather a low number on which to base any definitive conclusion. Consequently it is difficult to relate their location to a particular cosmology, although pit 2027 in H2001 at Trethellan Farm which contained an abandonment deposit comprising a saddle quern and rubbers was coincidentally on the western (sunset/death) side of the roundhouse.

7.3.4 Demolition and abandonment deposits
As mentioned at the beginning of this chapter, the actions by which sites and settlements were demolished and abandoned is a feature of the Middle-Late Bronze Age in the south-west. In excess of 60 querns were found in features and layers associated with the final

demolition of roundhouses and other structures. The particular state of a number of these querns suggests that they had an important part to play in this operation. This again appears to elevate their function above that of purely utilitarian and domestic. It is suggested (Jones and Taylor 2010, 78-79) that through the processes of demolition roundhouses took on the appearance of barrows, being transformed from houses of the living to houses of the dead. Querns as transformers of materials from one state to another can be seen, therefore, as particularly apt choices of artefacts for deposition as part of the procedure.

The placement of querns in pits, postholes and gullies as part of the abandonment process has been commented upon above. In addition, a further 40 querns lay within the layers of material with which the roundhouses were infilled and levelled. At Gwithian where evidence suggests that two of the three roundhouses associated with the Middle-Late Bronze Age settlement were burnt down on abandonment, a burnt layer overlying the floor of house 724 contained a rubber together with a variety of other artefacts including an anvil, hone, slickstone and rubbing stones (Sturgess and Lawson-Jones 2006, 172; Sturgess 2007, 31). The abandonment layers of a Bronze Age roundhouse at Penhale Farm near Indian Queens, Cornwall contained pottery, flint, a stone mould and a quern fragment while those of another Middle Bronze Age roundhouse at Trevilson comprised a mixture of earth, pottery, charcoal, briquetage, stone and included in the upper fills fragments of a rubber and saddle quern (Nowakowski 2001, 145; Jones and Taylor 2004, 31, 63, 118). Fragments of saddle quern were found throughout the levelling layers of H648 and a fragment of rubber was also included within the rubble backfill of a ritual structure at Trethellan Farm. At Scracewater, eight quern fragments were incorporated in the construction of a ring ditch wall on the site of roundhouse 1500 (Nowakowski 1991, 73; Trethellan Farm Archive; Jones and Taylor 2010, 23).

Much of the material which was used to infill roundhouses and other structures probably derived from re-spread occupation layers or middens. It has been suggested (Robinson 2007, 95) that the importation of midden material to infill a house represents a reversal of the activities and actions associated with the life of the house. Middens were stores of useful waste material (see below) and consequently, although representative of both activities and people, the occurrence of quern fragments and other assorted artefacts within a levelling layer is probably generally coincidental. However, the occasional presence of more unusual or exotic items such as the copper alloy spearhead in the larger of the two roundhouses at Penhale Moor, Cornwall and the briquetage at Trevilson point to a more personalised and deliberate deposition (Nowakowski 2001, 145; Jones and Taylor 2004, 108, 111). Into this category must also fall the fragments from the single, burnt quern strewn throughout the levelling layers in H648 at Trethellan Farm (Nowakowski 1991, 73). The quern, symbolic of life and productivity, was burnt and broken, its remains scattered and buried on the death of the settlement (Brück 1999b, 155).

It was also not uncommon for stone walling to be partly demolished and stones pushed into the interior of the roundhouse. In this way querns that had been placed within the wall may have become incorporated within abandonment layers and deposits. Again their presence may be no more than happenstance. This may account for the querns found within the rubble fills of houses and structures at Nornour, Isles of Scilly, Higher Boden and Callestick, Cornwall and also possibly that within the rubble fill of the ritual structure at Trethellan Farm (Butcher 1978, 94-95; Quinnell in press a; Quinnell and Taylor 1998-1999, 35; Nowakowski 1991, 100). Of particular note, however, is a fragment of granite saddle quern that was found inverted in the centre of the infill of the structure at Callestick and which had been used in its fragmental state prior to its deposition (Jones 1998-1999, 15; Quinnell and Taylor 1998-1999, 28, 30). Its placement, in a position of protection, is surely more than coincidence. Rendered safe but unusable, the placing of an overturned quern as part of the demolition procedures may be interpreted as a gesture of closure. The location and orientation of the quern suggests that it did not derive from the wall but was used within the structure. Given the potential esoteric nature of the building it had perhaps been used to grind hallucinogenic substances or special pigments for use in the rituals and ceremonies that had been carried out within.

The placement of a small but complete saddle quern (Figure 7.7) in an inverted position within a hillslope enclosure at Holworthy, Devon can also be seen as deliberate. Just 25.8cm long, and comparatively light-weight, the quernstone was an eminently portable artefact and yet it was found lying just outside the post-ring of a roundhouse adjacent to the bowl-shaped end of a 'fire-trench' which passed through the post-ring into the interior of the roundhouse. The relationship between the fire-trench and roundhouse is unclear

The Bronze Age

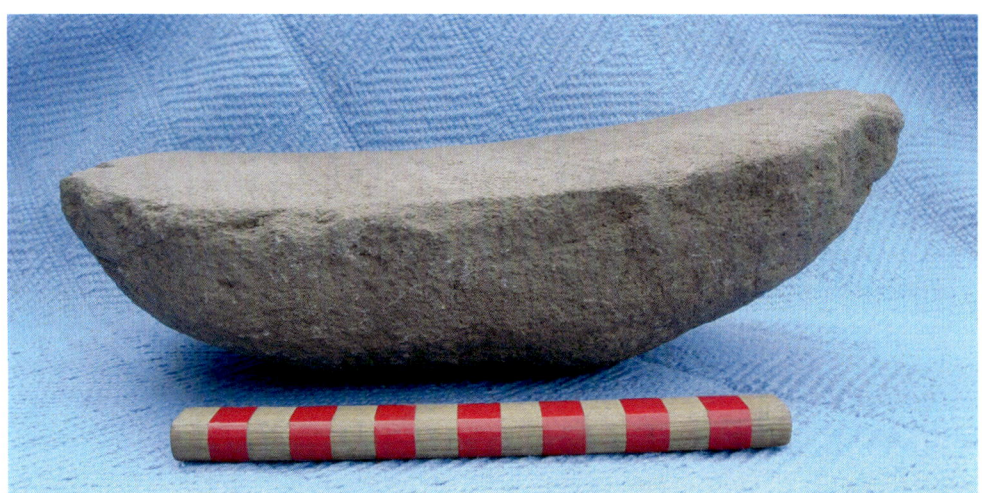

Figure 7.7: Small saddle quern from Holworthy Devon (centimetre scale) and plan of roundhouse showing where it was found (S. Watts; T. Green/North Devon Archaeological Society).

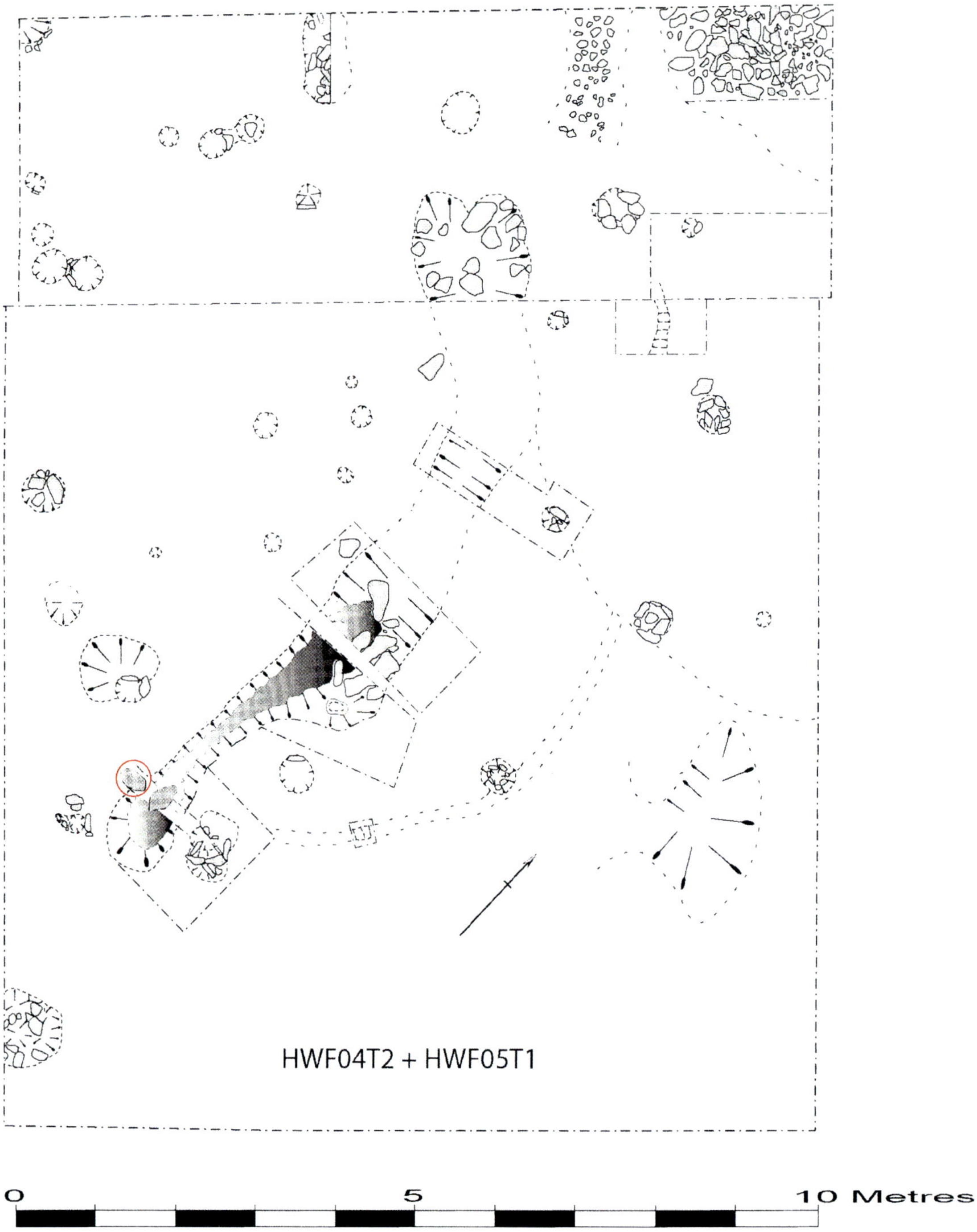

HWF04T2 + HWF05T1

although radiocarbon dates indicate that the two features are broadly contemporary; the roundhouse is dated 1430-1260/1460-1310 cal. BC while the fire-trench is dated 1400-1020/1240-1210 cal. BC (Watts, S. 2009; Green 2009).

The leaving of the quern appears to be associated with the actions that took place when the site was vacated. Several posts of the roundhouse were removed and the holes covered with stones, a pottery vessel was left standing in the centre of the floor and a shallow hollow close to the quern was found to contain pottery, a broken loomweight and a broken hammerstone, all indicative perhaps of the activities that took place in the roundhouse and by association with the people who performed them.

As mentioned above, it is suggested (Jones and Taylor 2010, 78-79) that the structured process of demolition and infilling transformed the sites of roundhouses both visually and symbolically, into barrows. This process was taken further at some sites such as Callestick or Scarcewater with the addition of stone rings or kerbs to some of the roundhouses (Jones 1998-1999, 15, 50; Jones and Taylor 2010, 78-79). On the site of roundhouse 1500 at Scarcewater this took the form of a ring ditch containing a low wall which was found to contain two fragmentary and one unfinished saddle quern and five rubbers all thought to have derived from the occupational phases of the settlement (Jones and Taylor 2010, 76). The inclusion of quernstones within the ring ditch wall suggests that its construction was a premeditated action and that the querns were kept to one side when the roundhouse was demolished.

7.3.5 Other pits

In addition to the 28 querns found in pits within roundhouses a further 34 querns were recovered from pits ostensibly external to roundhouses (Table 7.3). The context form is dominated by pits at Scarcewater and Truro dated to the Middle and Late Bronze Ages respectively, some of which may in fact have originally formed part of structures or working areas (Jones and Taylor 2010; Gossip forthcoming). Again, different categories of deposit are recognisable. Within a group of Late Bronze Age pits and postholes at Truro College, pit 5027 (1050-890 cal. BC) was found to contain six beach cobble rubbers and a broken granite saddle quern (Figure 7.3). The rubbers, which appeared to have been stacked together, are double sided suggesting they were well-used. They are also of a variety of materials - granite, sandstone and elvan - that could effect a coarse or finer milling finish as required. Two other beach cobble rubbers of different granites were found in a shallow pit or hollow close by and in a separate and probably slightly later group two more pits (5035 and 5033) contained a fragment and a broken saddle quern respectively (Gossip forthcoming; Quinnell and Taylor forthcoming).

Similar collections of saddle querns and rubbers were also found at Scarcewater where there were several groups of pits and postholes of Middle Bronze Age date. In one group (1600) six rubbers, again of different materials, were found in one pit (1610) (Figure 7.3) and in an adjacent stone-lined pit (1601) was a saddle quern split in two together with a rubber and several fragments. In another pit group (1650) three rubbers were found in pit 1018 (Jones and Taylor 2010). These collections may be caches but the fact that at both Truro College and Scarcewater the saddle querns are broken suggests they are abandonment deposits, bearing comparison to the saddle quern and rubbers left in pit 2027 within H2001 at Trethellan Farm (Nowakowski 1991, 25). The latter may also have been intended as a cache but the placement of the saddle quern in an inverted position over the rubbers appears to have been symbolic, signifying its removal from practical usage. The breaking of a saddle quern may have effected a similar message. The choice of different materials may also be significant beyond their milling attributes.

A different interpretation can be placed on the contents of pit 6581 at Higher Besore, namely a complete saddle quern and a cluster of quartz crystals. The pit produced a radiocarbon date of 2140-1940 cal. BC but it is suggested that this may be from residual material and that the pit is in fact later in date, contemporary with other pits and postholes associated with Structure 1 (Gossip forthcoming; Quinnell and Taylor forthcoming). Regardless of date, the deposit appears to be that of especially chosen personal items, reminiscent of the foundation deposit at Scarcewater mentioned above or the rubbers and sherds of decorated pottery in a covered pit within H2222 at Trethellan Farm (Jones and Taylor 2010, 19, 73; Nowakowski 1991, 43).

The contents of a pit (531) dated 1260-1010 cal. BC near Meacombe Farm, Chagford, Devon not only appear to have been especially chosen but also to have been placed in the pit in some order (Figure 7.8). Sherds from a large (incomplete) pottery vessel together with pieces from two others were found beneath a large fragment of saddle quern which was accompanied by

Figure 7.8: Pit 531 near Meacombe, Devon under excavation showing the saddle quern near the top of the pit (left) and arranged pottery sherds beneath (right) (© Exeter Archaeology).

a whetstone. It was noted that the pottery sherds were arranged; a group of body sherds were packed together and the base sherds lay inverted (Dyer and Salvatore 2011, 4; Quinnell 2011a, 6-7). The pit, which cut through an earlier pit (535), is likely to be related to the roundhouses situated to the south (Devon Historic Environment Record No. 16536) and may have been dug with reference to the Neolithic chambered tomb situated about 50m to the north-west. The contents of pit 531 may have been a special deposit, therefore, perhaps an offering to the ancestors.

A different interpretation can be placed on the fragment of rubber, stone blocks and animal bone from a pit or posthole situated just to the east of the centre of a causeway between two ditch sections at Field Farm near Shepton Mallet, Somerset. Interestingly, no apparent special deposits were found in either of the adjacent ditch terminals which, from the evidence cited below, were perhaps to be expected. The pit's location, however, appears to be significant and it is suggested that it was a posthole for a marker post (Leach 2008, 18). In such a situation, the rubber may also be fulfilling a dual function of post-packing and boundary deposit, symbolising the crossing from one side to the other, from the outside to the inside.

A further five querns were found in association with external cooking pits and kilns. At Sigwells, the incorporation of a fragment of saddle quern, possibly burnt, within the upper fill of a cooking pit in the south-western quadrant of the metalworking enclosure is seen as a closure deposit. Also within the pit were animal bones, fragments of globular urn and burnt stone (Tabor pers. corresp.). The complete lower stone of a saddle quern found lying vertically near the top of a pit within a Late Bronze Age occupation site at Combe Hay, Somerset may also have been part of a closure deposit. The fill of the pit, which included clay, charcoal, burnt and unburnt stone and a burnishing or polishing stone, led to the interpretation of the pit as a kiln. It is likely, therefore, that the saddle quern, which was described as being 'small and possibly of specialised use' (Price and Watts 1980, 13, Microfiche 6) was for grinding pottery temper rather than grain. The pit, therefore, appears to have been filled with the tools and accoutrements of the trade.

Pits such as these demonstrate that the practice of structured abandonment was not just reserved for the demolition of buildings but was observed across a wide spectrum of Bronze Age structures and features. The pit at Meacombe potentially moves the role of querns within Bronze Age society beyond the domestic arena while that Combe Hay, serves as a reminder that querns were not solely used for grinding grain.

7.3.6 Ditches

Fourteen querns included on the database were recovered from linear and enclosure ditches dating from the Early through to the Late Bronze Age (Table 7.4). The structured deposition of objects in ditches is a practice that was first established in the Neolithic period with the placement of querns and other artefacts in the ditch segments of causewayed enclosures. The particular locations and combinations of artefacts within these ditches suggest that their presence was more than the result of the casual disposal of waste material or simply backfilling of the ditches (Whittle 1996, 272-274; Whittle *et al* 1999; Pryor 1998a; Watts, S. 2008a, 97). In the

Bronze Age the fact that ditches were often filled quite quickly together with the apparent meaningful placement of artefacts within them, particularly in the entrance or end terminals, suggests that their function was not so much to define a boundary physically but rather to represent that boundary in a symbolic sense. Indeed the act of digging the ditch may have been more important than the ditch itself (Hill 1995, 76, 102; Fitzpatrick 1997, 78-79).

It is often difficult, however, to say if the incorporation of quern fragments within the fill of a ditch construes a specific, purposeful deposit or was just chance. The artefacts found at the southern end of the Middle Bronze Age enclosure ditch at Castle Hill, east Devon, for example, which included quern fragments together with flints, pottery, carbonised plant remains, charcoal, pieces of quartzite and a whetstone could have derived from midden material (Fitzpatrick *et al* 1999a, 32-34). At Field Farm, Somerset, several of the sections within a series of Middle and Late Bronze Age ditch systems also appeared to have been filled with a mixture of upcast and midden material, the latter again including a number of quern fragments (Leach 2008, 18, 25, 28). The presence of quern fragments in the fill of such ditches may well, therefore, be coincidence. Similarly, at Sigwells, a fragment of quern was included within the rubble fill of a section of linear ditch (F009), on top of which lay a single bovine mandible. Bovine mandibles are considered to be major features of other 'ritual' deposits in the Cadbury Castle area (also at Field Farm below) and the placement of one in the ditch is, therefore, seen as deliberate (Tabor 2008, 68, 178). Is the quern fragment in the ditch fill to be viewed, therefore, as simply part of the fill, with no particular meaning intended in its inclusion, or should it not also be seen as having a significance (after Buckley 1993, 4)?

The same question can be asked of the quern fragments found in the southern terminal of a Late Bronze Age Ditch section (F23/F5) at Field Farm. The collection of two cow mandibles, a horse skull and a concentration of pottery found in the southern terminal of another of the Late Bronze Age ditch sections (F30) was, not surprisingly interpreted as a meaningful structured deposit as was the large quantity of pottery, charcoal, burnt stone and bone recovered from the northern terminal of section F23/F5. Yet the quern fragments from the same ditch section were not given the same level of recognition despite being the only finds in the southern terminal, although the placement of a saddle quern fragment in the northern terminal of another section (F7) of broadly similar date was viewed as 'more certainly deliberate' (Leach 2008, 30, 31). It seems that some depositions of quern fragments do not have that 'alerting quality' referred to by Hill (1995, 96) which, to modern eyes, raises the deposit above the rank of mere occupational debris. Lionái (2010) refers to 'depositional access points' that is 'points within [a] ditch deemed appropriate for concentrated single-event deposition or repeated depositional episodes, rather than just an accumulation of occupation debris'. But this does not necessarily mean that the latter was not placed in the ground in structured, meaningful ways. Indeed the general deposition of midden material in a ditch or any other feature may not have been simply a means of disposing of unwanted material (McOmish 1996). Brück (1995, 256) comments on the use of rubbish to delimit the edge of a settlement and Graham (1994, 71) noted than amongst the Rarámuri the ring of swept debris that accumulated around the exterior of the maintained activity area marked the threshold of a residence and that it was courteous to ask permission to cross it (Figure 1.1)

The deposition of a pebble macehead, large sherds of pottery and a quern fragment in a ditch terminal of an enclosure off Old Rydon Lane, Exeter, on the other hand, construes an unusual enough combination of artefacts to draw the attention (John Moore Heritage Services 2010, 7, 55). Similarly the fragment of rhyolite quern and quartz crystal found together with decorated pot sherds in the north terminal of a Late Bronze Age ring ditch at Sheep Slait, Dorset, also signal something more than the disposal of waste material (Figure 7.4). Both quern and crystal originated from Dartmoor or North Cornwall and are indicative of contacts or relationships between disparate peoples (Tabor 2008, 98).

The depositions of complete quernstones can also be much more easily seen as meaningful deposits. The placement of two saddle querns in the western enclosure ditch at Sigwells, Somerset seems to be particularly redolent with symbolism. Located upside down and adjacent to one another, the two querns, the smaller of red igneous rock and the larger quern of greensand presented a striking appearance in the ditch (Tabor 2008, 68) (Figure 4.2). The complete state of the quernstones, unlike the others found in the enclosure which were in a fragmentary condition, is surely significant as is their inverted position. The latter in the context of the rapid rubble fill of the ditch suggests that they were closure deposits. The enclosure at Sigwells is rather unusual being interpreted as a site where itinerant metalworkers came together for a short period of time to practice their craft. The two querns, which originated 40km to the west and 15km to the east of the site respectively, may have been placed in the ditch as part of the 'official' closure of the craft fair to create and maintain a bond between the peoples who had met there and in doing so reinforced social identity and kinships (Tabor 2008, 65-68). In this respect it is worth noting that the predominant source of the querns found within the enclosure, Old Red Sandstone from the Mendips 22km to the north, was not represented in the ditch.

However, as suggested in Chapter Four, the use of these two particular querns as structured deposits may have been determined more by their colour rather than by their point of origin. In the context of a metalworking site it is surely significant that their complimentary red and green colours are those of molten metal and its mould or possibly verdigris (after Jones 2002, 163; Keates 2002, 111). Elsewhere within the enclosure a choice of red artefacts, including quern fragments of Old Red Sandstone, was noted for the filling of some of the metalworking structure's postholes while in the north-west corner of the enclosure ditch were several pieces of limestone transformed to a bluish hue by burning (Tabor 2008-69). The two colours and their associated meanings are brought together in the two querns which may have been used as a metaphor for the active life and death of the enclosure and the metalworking craft carried out within it, symbolising the transformation from one state to another.

Once again, different categories of quern deposit can be seen within the same broad form of context ranging from quern fragments mixed with midden material to the placement of a fragment with more auspicious artefacts to the deposition of complete quernstones as individual items. Like roundhouse walls, ditches are liminal places forming boundaries between one side and another, between one territory and another, between the outside and the inside. Querns in their role of transformers of material from one state to another may have been seen as potent, protective symbols in these areas, particularly at the crossing points over the boundary. Of the 14 querns found in ditches, four were located in ditch terminals and another was placed just to the south of an entranceway. As domestic tools in a non-domestic space querns may also have represented the life of the household and by extension the community itself.

7.3.7 Middens

The accumulation of midden material was of prime importance to Bronze Age peoples as witnessed in the particularly large spreads at Potterne and East Chisenbury in Wiltshire (Clarke and Maguire 1989, 16; McOmish 1996). Middens potentially performed a number of functions such as stock piles or as conspicuous mounds of 'waste' material symbolising the wealth of the community or as stores of fertility (McOmish 1996; Needham and Spence 1997; Mulville 2008, 238-239). As the former, items may have been placed in the midden with the intention of retrieval for reuse at a future date. As the latter, it may have been considered politic to enhance the midden with choice deposits (McOmish 1996, 75).

The use of midden material to infill ditches, structures and other features on termination or abandonment has been mentioned above and the probability that the presence of quern fragments within such spreads is coincidental was also considered. In addition, eight quern fragments were also found within extant middens at Trethellan Farm, Nornour and Gwithian, dated to the Middle-Late Bronze Ages. These fragments mostly derive from rubbers and it seems likely that they were thrown on the respective middens when they broke or wore too thin at the end of their primary use lives.

The presence of two possibly complete saddle querns in a midden exposed in a cliff at Halangy Porth, St. Marys, Isles of Scilly (Hencken 1932, 30), on the other hand, point to more deliberate deposition. As symbols of provision they may have been placed in the midden to enhance its fertility value. However, as indicated above, the querns may also have been put on the midden with the intention of future reuse. Graham (1994, 71-72), for example, noted that the 'concentrated refuse area' of Raramuri residences in north-west Mexico contained not only the bulk of the refuse produced by the household but was also used to 'store' items that had a potential reuse value (Figure 1.1).

Middens are generally external features but roundhouse H2222 at Trethellan Farm became a midden at some point prior to the settlement's abandonment. The fate of H2222 as a midden may have been due to the presence of a human burial under the central hearth which dates from the latter period of the house's occupation (Nowakowski 1991, 44, 209). The use of a house as a midden is reminiscent of the Biblical story of the decree that Darius, King of Syria made concerning the building of the temple in Jerusalem *circa*

515BC. The decree stated that should anyone alter it, 'let timber be pulled down from his house, and being set up, let him be hanged thereon: and let his house be made a dunghill for this' (Ezra 6:11). While not suggesting that this is the reason for H2222 becoming a midden, indeed the hearth was reused after the burial, it does allow for the possibility that the house was defiled. The use of houses as middens has been noted on other sites such as Amberley Mount, West Sussex (Brück 1999b, 151).

7.3.8 Funerary contexts

Clear evidence for the deposition of querns in non-domestic contexts is shown in the use of querns in the construction of funerary monuments (Table 7.5). Twenty two saddle querns and rubbers on the database were found within the construction material of ten barrows and a rubber was also found amongst the artefacts in an Early Bronze Age cremation burial at Chew Park, Somerset (Figure 7.9). In addition, a rubber was reused as a paving slab in the entrance grave on North Hill, Samson, Isles of Scilly and another rubber was recovered together with some Bronze Age pottery from the entrance passage of Bants Carn on St. Marys, Isles of Scilly (Figure 7.10). Two of the 13 sites are in Somerset, the rest in Cornwall and the Isles of Scilly[6]. This is a very small proportion of the numbers of known Bronze Age barrows and cairns in the south-west which totals in excess of 2000 (information derived from English Heritage Pastscape). The lack is in part due to the fact that comparatively few barrows have been completely excavated; most of the querns derived from the construction and makeup of barrows. However, it is also clear that querns are not to be found in all barrows. At Stannon Down on Bodmin Moor, where excavations took place in advance of china clay waste tipping in 1976-1977 and 1998-1999, quern fragments were found in four out of eight barrows (Harris *et al.* 1984; Jones 2004-2005). On Davidstow Moor, Cornwall a single rubber was found in just one of the 28 cairns examined prior to the construction of the airfield in 1941-1942 (Christie 1988).

The saddle querns and rubbers that have been found in tombs and barrow cairns are unlikely to simply represent the reuse of convenient pieces of stone but will have been specially brought to the site from nearby settlements. At North Hill on Samson, Hencken (1933, 27) suggested that it was the smoothness of the grinding surface that 'recommended [the quern] to the

6. Several fragments of saddle quern have also been found recently in a cairn at Hemerdon near Plymouth (not included in the database) (Information from J. Valentin, AC Archaeology).

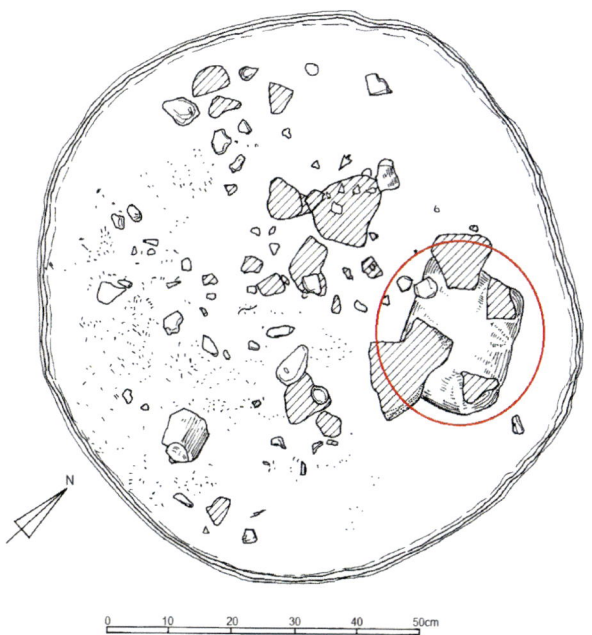

Figure 7.9: Cremation burial at Chew Park, Somerset with a rubber (ringed in red) amongst the grave goods (M. Watts after Rahtz and Greenfield 1977, Figure 15).

builders as a paving stone'. A number of other reasons, however, have been put forward to account for the presence of querns in funerary contexts, as recounted in Chapter Four. They may, for example, have a connection with one of the dead or have been intended to provide sustenance in the after life or have been used for grinding food for attendant feasts prior to or during the construction of the tomb or barrow and as a consequence, incorporated within them. Alternatively, querns were so placed because of their symbolic values as related to transformation and regeneration (Bradley 2005a, 107). This later theory becomes more pertinent if one considers the possibility that one function of querns was the grinding of human bone, although there is no definitive evidence for this (Brück 2001, 155). In their role as providers of nourishment, however, querns are also symbolic of the living community and their placement could thus reinforce the link and continuity between the living and the dead.

Differences in meaning can also be perceived between the utilisation of querns as cairn material and their direct or indirect placement within a grave. The rubber and pottery in the entrance passage of Bants Carn may, for example, represent choice deposits of midden material. Ashbee (1976, 21-23) describes Scillonian entrance graves as *fana*, sanctuaries or repositories for midden and occupation material and it is suggested (Thomas 1985, 140-142) that this material was placed in the tomb at a time of stress brought about by

Figure 7.10: Bant's Carn, St. Mary's, Isles of Scilly (S. Watts).

agricultural infertility. The tombs are seen as foci for ancestral power and the midden material, itself a source of fertility, was an offering. Bradley (1984, 14) refers to this material as 'symbolic manure'.

On the other hand, the combination of artefacts found in the grave at Chew Park, which included pottery sherds from at least eight vessels including bell beakers, flint tools, a beach pebble, a rubber and two fragments of stone axe, one of local manufacture, the other from Great Langdale in the Lake District, are not out of place as personal possessions of the deceased (Figure 7.9) (Rahtz and Greenfield 1977, 29). The various fragmentary items can be seen as exchange gifts or tokens symbolising particular relationships and the rubber as a tool used by the deceased for grinding substances other than grain such as pigments. However, as indicated above there are alternative explanations. The artefacts may not be grave goods *per se* but associated with the mourning and funerary rituals on a practical and/or symbolic basis (Jones 2004-2005, 124). We may never know the exact meaning of the rubber but it was clearly placed with meaning and intent. The fact that querns are rarely found as grave goods gives this particular artefact an added significance.

Although the number of querns found in barrows is too few to reach any definitive conclusions, it may also be of import that the querns are predominantly found in the north-east or south-west quadrants of the barrows. This includes, for example, the large piece of saddle quern found within a barrow at Boscawen-un, Cornwall (Figure 7.11) (Borlase 1872, 220-221). Similarly, the rubber in the grave at Chew Park is also in the north-east quadrant while the entrances to the tombs at Bants Carn and North Hill coincidentally face just north of east and just south of east respectively. This pattern of placement bears broad comparison with the location of pits containing querns and *in-situ* querns found in roundhouses and suggests that the analogy between roundhouses and barrows seen in the transformation of the former into the appearance of the latter on abandonment is also evinced in the corresponding placement of artefacts in barrows (Jones and Taylor 2010, 78-79; Bradley 1998, 155).

The location of the rubber at North Hill virtually in the centre of the main part of the burial chamber also appears deliberate as does the fact that it was placed with its grinding surface uppermost, other than simply providing a flat surface. Not only is this a position in which the rubber would not have been used, but it may have been believed that the exposed surface enabled the release of its transforming properties to the spiritual world or that conversely it enabled the transfer of beneficent powers of life and fertility from the ancestors to the living (after Thomas 1985, 142). Whatever the reason for its presence it is nevertheless clear that a still usable rubber was especially chosen and placed in the monument.

However, just as querns are found in non-domestic contexts so human bones are found in association with querns in non-funerary contexts. Several human baby long bones were found with the tools and other artefacts on the floor of structure 725 at Gwithian (Sturgess and Lawson-Jones 2006, 173-174; Sturgess 2007, 31). Were these bones also tools, or were they used in esoteric rituals connected with pottery production or were they placed on the floor when pottery making ceased? It may be of relevance that a complete neo-natal skeleton was also found in the north-west quadrant of the structure.

Similarly, the artefacts recovered from the Middle Bronze Age enclosure at Sigwells are generally consistent with the function of the site as a metalworking and craft fair. However, as mentioned above, pieces of burnt human skull were found in a posthole on the western side of the entrance corridor together with a fragment of saddle quern. Although, as Tabor (2008, 69) comments we can only 'speculate' on the origins and inclusion of the skull fragments, it is worth considering the possibility that the roundhouse was more esoteric than utilitarian in function. The 4m long entrance passage and interior dividing screen would have restricted both light and access to the western side of the structure. In this respect the building is similar to the later Bronze Age ritualistic structure at Callestick which had an entranceway of similar length (Jones 1998-1999).

7.3.9 Miscellaneous features

Finally some 13 querns in the database derive from a variety of miscellaneous postholes, gullies, external walls, field banks and other features on settlement and occupation sites. For the most part there is little to be gainsaid regarding the presence of quern fragments in such features. Nevertheless, they should not be entirely dismissed for they add to the spectrum of contexts in which querns were deposited, whether by accident through the utilisation of midden or occupation material or through design. As in other depositional contexts, each placement will have been made with varying degrees of intent and meaning. The presence of querns in enclosure walls or field banks, for example, can be related to a building episode, that is the active life of the feature, and presumably derived from a nearby settlement. There are, however, two particular features worthy of further comment.

Five quern fragments were found within a cairn (S2) broadly dated to the Late Bronze Age on Dainton Common, Ipplepen in south Devon, the site of a once extensive prehistoric field system (Silvester 1980). The exact purpose of the cairn is unclear. Most of the cairns within the field system appear to be clearance cairns and it is possible that S2 falls into this category. However, the presence of the quern fragments plus pottery and bone suggest that it could be a burial cairn or was possibly built over a roundhouse or activity site, evidence for which has been found elsewhere on the common (Silvester 1980, 44). It seems that trouble was taken on the abandonment of occupation sites to transform them into cairns, thus rendering them indistinguishable from the other cairns on the common, in a way similar to the transformation of roundhouses into the appearance of barrows.

At Trethellen Farm there were at least two hollows within the settlement which appeared to be the foci for specific depositional events. No quern fragments were recovered from the various pits that were dug in the hollows but several fragments of rubber were incorporated within the layers of material that were spread on occasion across these 'ritual' hollows (Nowakowski 1991, 87-96, 205-

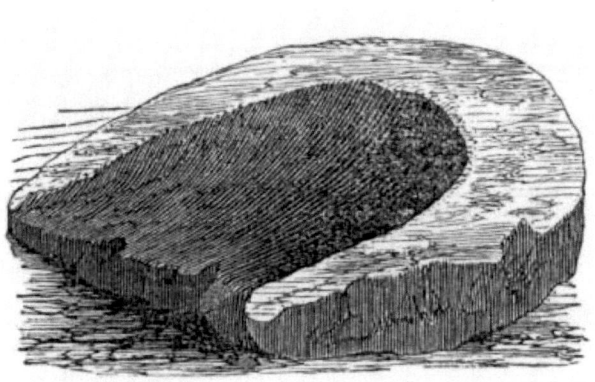
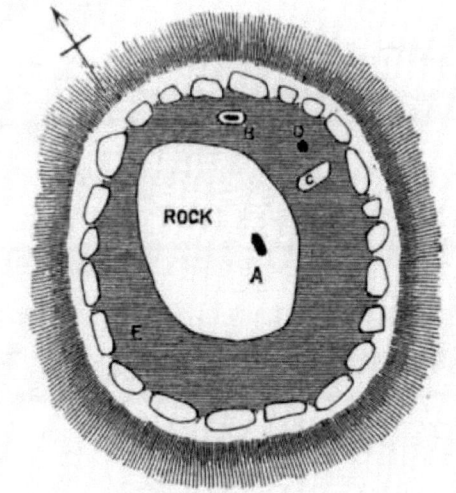

Figure 7.11: Saddle quern from a barrow at Boscawen-un (left) and plan of the barrow (right) showing the location of the quern (B) (Borlase 1872, 220-221).

206). Although not abandonment spreads, these layers nevertheless appear to be a deliberate attempt to conceal earlier pits and features, rather in the same way that earlier occupation levels within roundhouses were covered by the laying of a new floor. The covering layers also appear to be derived from midden material and so, again, the rubber fragments must be seen as coincidental. It is the lack of quern fragments in the pit deposits, however, that is of real import here as clearly they were not considered appropriate for deposition in these contexts.

A similar 'ritual' hollow of Middle Bronze Age date has also been excavated at Trenowah, St. Austell, in advance of road construction. The lack of structural remains and the quality of artefactual remains led to the conclusion that the hollow fulfilled a special rather than domestic or industrial function. One of the two pits dug within the hollow contained 24 fragments of white quartz, a material which seems to have been of some import to Bronze Age peoples, together with one sherd of pottery. As at Trethellan Farm, no quern fragments were found in the pits but a broken rubber was found in the charcoal-rich infill of the hollow (Johns forthcoming).

7.3.10 Associated artefacts
Most of the artefacts found in association with quern deposits are, as in the Neolithic period, broadly domestic in nature. However, it is also notable that at sites such as Gwithian, Sigwells and Combe Hay the artefacts lean towards those that would not be out of place in craft-working scenarios such as bone tools, flints, utilised and burnt stones, hammerstones, clay and burnishing stones. Also of interest are the caches of rubbers and saddle querns. Very few associated artefacts can be flagged as unusual or exotic. The presence of burnt human bone in a posthole at Sigwells is, however, worthy of further comment as are the human baby long bones found in association with an occupation surface at Gwithian (Sturgess and Lawson-Jones 2006, 19, 187-188; Tabor 2008, 64, 69; Price and Watts 1980, 13, microfiche 6.2). Also of note is a quartz crystal from either Dartmoor or North Cornwall found in the terminal of a ring ditch at Sheep Slait, in Dorset (Figure 7.4) (Tabor 2008, 98). Quartz crystals were also found in pits with quernstones at Higher Besore and Scarcewater (Gossip forthcoming; Jones and Taylor 2010, 16). Four broad categories of artefactual deposition can be distinguished, therefore.

1. Quern hoards
Several caches of rubbers and saddle querns have been found in pits at sites such as Truro College, Scarcewater and Trethellan Farm (Gossip forthcoming, 21, 25; Jones and Taylor 2010; Nowakowski 1991). As mentioned above, those from Truro College and Scarcewater (Figure 7.3) may be hoards, collections of stone tools, buried with the intention of reclamation but the fact that the saddle querns are broken suggests that they are closure or abandonment deposits. It is possible, however, that the stones were left *in situ*. In other words what may have originally been open deposits were closed when the site was left. This may also have been the case at Trethellan Farm where a saddle quern and two rubbers were found in a large shallow pit within roundhouse H2001 with two further rubbers in another pit near by. These appear to have been left, perhaps *in situ*, when a new floor surface was laid. When the house was finally abandoned another saddle quern was placed over a collection of seven rubbers that had been thrown in a pit (Figure 1.6) (Nowakowski 1991, 21, 25). At Gwithian, a saddle quern and associated caches of stone tools including rubbers, pebbles and rubbing stones were sealed *in situ* beneath the floor of a later building (Sturgess and Lawson-Jones 2006, 173-188).

2. Domestic depositions.
Many of the artefacts found with quern depositions would not be out of place in a domestic situation. These include pottery, whetstones, hammerstones, flint tools, bone tools, animal bone and charcoal. Some of the fills and layers from which this material came derived from occupation layers or from reused midden material and the combinations of artefacts may be only coincidental. It is of note, therefore, that few querns are found in direct association with the other traditionally female objects, namely loomweights and spindle whorls. Such finds tend to be loosely associated within occupation spreads, although interestingly at Tynings Farm, Somerset a spindle whorl and saddle quern were found together with Late Bronze Age pottery in a recut barrow ditch (Taylor 1949-1950, 161). At Hayne Lane five small fragments of quern were found in the same posthole as a spindle whorl, together with pottery, charcoal and carbonised plant remains. Loomweights were found in another posthole close by. The nature of the artefacts led to the suggestion that the house may have been a female activity area or residence (Fitzpatrick *et al* 1999a, 95, 126-127).

3. Craftworking deposits
A particular feature of Bronze Age quern deposits is the association of artefacts related to craft activities. At Combe Hay a small saddle quern was found in the top of a pit, the contents of which also included burnt clay,

pottery, a pebble burnisher, burnt stone and charcoal. These artefacts are all in keeping with the interpretation of the pit as a kiln for pottery manufacture (Price and Watts 1980, 107). Similarly at Gwithian the general character of the features and artefacts found on the floor of structure 725 suggests that the building was a pottery workshop. In the north-east quadrant of the building were two wooden bowls filled with clay, a saddle quern and stone tools while along the south-east side of the building were two clay-lined pits (Sturgess and Lawson-Jones 2006, 19, 167-168, 187-188). At both Combe Hay and Gwithian it is likely that the saddle querns were used for grinding pottery temper rather than grain.

At Sigwells the bone tools, pottery and hammerstone placed with the quern fragments in two of the postholes in the main body of the roundhouse are consistent with the function of the enclosure as the site of a metalworking and craft fair (fragments of mould were found in scoops near the structure) (Tabor 2008, 67, 68). The possibility that querns were used for grinding ore or were reused as anvils for metalworking must, therefore, be considered. However, a general 'red' theme was also noted with the deposition of burnt red stones in many of the postholes; a red stone loom weight was also found in one of the postholes and the quern fragments were of Old Red Sandstone (Tabor 2008, 69). This suggests that many of the items in the postholes were also chosen for their aesthetic qualities, their red colour picking up perhaps on the colour of molten metal (Keates 2002, 111). The burnt pieces of human bone found in the post settings of the entrance corridor perhaps also follow this general theme.

4. Exotic deposits
The association of querns with more unusual and exotic artefacts points definitively to deliberate choice and purposeful deposition. At Scarcewater, for example, the rubber fragments, pestles and a broken slate slab in a pit might not have warranted particular attention. However, the presence of a quartz crystal in the pit, and pottery sherds bearing unusual styles of decoration (which had been clearly kept for some time) coupled with the location of the pit under the wall of a roundhouse (1500) together with its was clay-lining, raise the deposit out of the ordinary. These artefacts are seen as heirlooms buried as a foundation deposit or perhaps for safekeeping (Jones and Taylor 2010, 16, 19, 73, 78; Jones forthcoming). Similar meanings may lie behind the complete saddle quern placed in a shallow pit at Higher Besore together with a cluster of quartz crystals (Gossip forthcoming).

The combination of pebble macehead, quern fragment and large sherds from an urn in a ditch terminal of an enclosure at Old Rydon Lane near Exeter also appears unusual (John Moore Heritage Services 2010, 7, 55). These are probably also a foundation deposit perhaps related to a particular person(s). More exotic still are the fragment of rhyolite saddle quern and quartz crystal from Dartmoor or Cornwall found in a ring ditch at Sheep Slait (Figure 7.4) (Tabor 2008, 98). Placed at the bottom of the rubble fill of the north terminal these again construe a special deposit signifying a particular person or relationship.

7.4 Discussion

The general increase in the number of querns found in Bronze Age contexts compared to those of the Neolithic period and the greater numbers from Middle and Later Bronze Age contexts can best be explained by the increase in grain as a staple food and also by the development of permanent farming settlements during the course of the Bronze Age. As cereals became a staple rather than occasional food so querns will have acquired an increased but perhaps rather different importance as necessary, everyday tools for grinding grain, an importance reflected not only in their incorporation in depositional events on primarily domestic sites but also their placement on non-domestic sites. However, depositions of querns within the metalworking enclosure at Sigwells, dated to the earlier part of the Middle Bronze Age and Callestick, a Late Bronze Age non-domestic structure, together with finds of querns in association with pottery making tools, and features at Gwithian and Combe Hay, serve as timely reminders that querns were also used for grinding products such as mineral ore and pottery temper and perhaps also more esoteric substances (Tabor 2008, 65, 68; Quinnell and Taylor 1998-1999; Sturgess and Lawson-Jones 2006, 19; Price and Watts 1980, 13).

Although just a small number of querns derive from Early Bronze Age contexts a continuity can nevertheless be seen from the Neolithic period in the deposition of querns in pits and ditches. By far the majority of Bronze Age querns, however, are from Middle-Late Bronze Age sites with the greater proportion being found in association with roundhouses in contexts related to their construction, occupation and abandonment. This demonstrates well the importance of querns at both practical and symbolic levels to the life of the household, whatever the nature of that 'household' may have been. If the radiocarbon date of 1890-1610 cal. BC for structure 1642 at Gwithian is correct (a later radiocarbon date was also obtained) (Sturgess 2007, 26), this is an association that can be dated back to the first establishment of settlements in the Early Bronze Age.

Twenty one context types can be identified across 47 sites which are biased particularly towards western Cornwall but also to Dartmoor and Somerset. Depositions of querns in occupation contexts and pits predominate but querns are also found in postholes and within the walls of stone-built roundhouses or included in deposits relating to the demolition of structures. Stone walls provide opportunities for depositional events that are not possible in timber roundhouses and on sites such as Shaugh Moor on Dartmoor perhaps also an alternative to pits in an area where the digging of the latter is difficult. A number of quernstones have also been found *in situ* in their working locations but even these were covered over upon the laying of a new floor or when the site was leveled on abandonment. Ironically, it is the utilisation of querns in abandonment deposits that highlights the important role that querns played in the life of the community.

The laying of new floors over old, the demolition and infilling of structures on abandonment and the covering over of pits and deposits of apparent ritual purpose are all variations on a theme. As part of the passage from one stage of life, use or occupation to the next it was clearly deemed appropriate to cover over, to bury that which belonged to the stage before. In many instances the covering material was drawn from midden deposits. The presence of quern fragments within such covering layers was probably, therefore, coincidental. However, certain deposits such as the burnt and scattered fragments of quern in H648 at Trethellan Farm and the upturned saddle quern in the centre of the structure at Callestick point to choice and meaningful intent (Nowakowski 1991, 73; Jones 1998-1999, 15). It has been suggested (Brück 1999b, 154) that special deposits were made to mark significant moments in a building's lifecycle, perhaps simply to denote a rebuilding exercise but which may have coincided with a change in use or status or occupancy or to mark its closure. As tools for grinding grain querns had an important role to play in the life of the household. It is not surprising, therefore, that broken, sometimes burnt, and buried querns should be seen as appropriate deposits signifying the end of that household (Brück 2001, 152; Robinson 2007, 98). This theory works well with the breaking of querns for closure and abandonment deposits but quern fragments were also utilised as post-packing and in the construction of walls and are thus part of the life of the structure rather than its demise. The converse is also true with the placement of complete saddle querns and rubbers in abandonment deposits. There is clearly a difference in meaning between those depositions made during the construction and occupation of a structure and those made at the time of its demolition and abandonment, and between the deposition of complete versus fragmentary querns although all may have drawn on the same symbolic references. As in the Neolithic period it is clear that within each context form there are several levels or categories of deposition. This is evidenced not only by the location or phase of the context itself but also by the state of the quern upon deposition and the artefacts with which it is associated.

Querns are not found in all pits or postholes, however, nor in all roundhouses. It could be argued, therefore, that their presence in such features is happenstance, merely representing the reuse of useful pieces of stone. This could be said to be a form of structured deposit in itself as there is a meaning and purpose behind such reuse. However, if one accepts the principle of querns as foundation deposits then one must also accept that their presence in a wall or posthole may have an equally significant meaning. This is well illustrated at Callestick where the querns used in the construction of the building must have been brought to site. Also at Scarcewater, the quern fragments incorporated in the ring ditch wall that was constructed on the former site of a roundhouse must have been retained for such reuse (Jones 1998-1999, 12; Jones and Taylor 2010, 23). In addition, deposition above or below ground may also be a distinction. Deposition above ground, in the walls of structures, clearly relates to the life of the building. Below ground deposits in pits and postholes, on the other hand, are more liminal in nature and while some are related to the life of a roundhouse the majority appear to be associated with the latter's closure or abandonment. An apparent preference for the deposition of querns in postholes and pits in the south-west quadrant of roundhouses can also be seen which may follow an underlying cosmology. On the other hand, some roundhouses are marked by deposits of querns in entrance postholes, perhaps linked to a desire to protect the entranceway. Thresholds are seen as liminal places over which care must be taken in crossing. The transforming nature from one state to another embodied in the quern may have been seen as protective in crossing a boundary or threshold. The same is also possible with the locating of querns in walls. The presence of querns in enclosure ditches, again a liminal point, marking the edge of a site or settlement, also potentially draws upon the same transformative qualities.

Where querns are not found is as important in some respects as where they are found. There are areas of life represented in other structured deposits such as hoards of metalwork in which querns are not involved. Likewise, there are many Early-Middle Bronze Age barrows in the south-west but very few contain querns. The fact that querns are not regularly placed in barrows, compared to their deposition in roundhouses, implies that they were not important in this aspect of Bronze Age life, or rather death. Those that have been found can be considered exceptional, therefore, particularly as where they are found there appears to be a preference for deposition in the north-east or south-west quadrants of the barrow. This reflects the location of quern deposits and *in situ* querns in roundhouses and suggests a relationship between houses of the living and houses of the dead. The rubber found with a cremation burial at Chew Park was also placed within the north-east quadrant of the grave (Rahtz and Greenfield 1977, 29). This is also a most unusual deposit as querns are rarely found as grave goods. There are several potential meanings to explain its presence; it may have been a personal possession or be representative of the deceased or have been used at a funerary feast or even for grinding cremated bone.

Almost half (48.8%) of the querns are in a fragmentary state but it is notable that at least 57% of saddle querns are broken compared to just 32% of rubbers. This can be compared to the Neolithic period where the number of fragmentary versus complete querns is more even. However, whether this difference is significant is difficult to determine given the much lower number of Neolithic querns. Suffice it to say that in the Bronze Age saddle querns were more likely to have been broken prior to deposition than rubbers. This may well be due to the relative size of the stones. Some querns may have been used in their fragmented state but it is suggested that many saddle querns in particular were deliberately broken prior to deposition. On the other hand, the small size of the fragments of Permian lava quern found at Hayne Lane is probably due to the friable nature of the stone (Laidlaw 1999, 108). At Scarcewater, however, it was noted that no clear evidence of breakage was visible and it was suggested (Quinnell 2010, 113, 115) that, with one possible exception, the querns may have broken along weak points while in use. The means by which a quern may be broken and the evidence this leaves needs empiral testing but it is probably unlikely that all the querns were flawed.

The act of breaking a quernstone would not have been an easy task unless the stone was indeed naturally flawed or had worn very thin. Such an act was potentially practical, in order to obtain small pieces of stone to fit a posthole, for example, or symbolic, releasing the power of the stone or conversely rendering it powerless. Such fragmentation may also have signified the end of a relationship, event or place (Brück 1999b, 155; Moore 2007, 94). It is also of import that many of the quernstones are incomplete. This raises the question as to what happened to the missing pieces. Chapman (2000b, 94) has suggested that, rather than signifying an ending, artefacts such as querns were broken and shared in order to create relationships, binding people and places together. It is possible, therefore, that some fragments were keepsakes or tokens in memory of a particular person, place or event or even that they are the remains of quernstones that were broken to provide such momentos. This theory works well at a site such as Sigwells which evidence suggests was the site of a craft fair where metalworkers and other craftspeople came together to practice their art and ply their trade (Tabor 2008, 61-69, 70). As Tabor (2008, 67) comments this would also have provided an occasion for creating and reaffirming relationships and alliances. Fragments from the same saddle quern were found in two different postholes, placed when the structure was dismantled, and it is possible that other fragments were taken by people returning to their homes. However, as a caveat to this it should be noted that the enclosure was not fully excavated and it is possible that the missing fragments are still to be found within the unexcavated areas of the enclosure.

Similarly, just under half (44.7%) of the Bronze Age dataset comprised possible complete or near complete quernstones. However, in comparison with fragmentary stones the situation is reversed with saddle querns only accounting for 29% (42). As mentioned above, this may be due to the generally smaller size of rubbers. However, hoards of rubbers appear to be a feature of Middle Bronze Age sites in Cornwall with collections of two or more being found in pits at Truro College, Scarcewater and Trethellan Farm, while at Gwithian a collection of stone tools including rubbers was found on the floor of a Middle-Late Iron Age pottery workshop (Gossip forthcoming; Jones and

Taylor 2010; Nowakowski 1991; Sturgess and Lawson-Jones 2006, 268). These deposits generally appear to be caches and while some may have been left with the intention of retrieval others appear to have been closure or abandonment deposits.

The artefacts generally found in association with querns tend to be domestic in nature or those utilised in craft activities. It appears, therefore, that the contiguity of the artefacts as found in the archaeological record is related to that of their use lives. Several depositions appear to have personal associations. The combination of pottery sherds and querns in several pits within the roundhouses at Trethellan Farm or the foundation deposit at Scarcewater appear to be specially chosen objects (Nowakowski 1991, 43, 52, 54; Jones and Taylor 2010, 19, 73). Unusual or more exotic combinations of artefacts also occur ex-roundhouse which again raises the respective deposit above the everyday and mundane. These include the fragment of rhyolite quern and quartz crystal from Dartmoor or Cornwall found at Sheep Slait (Tabor 2008, 98).

The rhyolite quern and crystal are also indicative of long distance contacts and relationships. Similarly the two complete saddle querns found together in the enclosure ditch at Sigwells and from sources 40km to the west and 15km to the east respectively also mark the coming together of disparate peoples (Tabor 2008, 65). The contrasting red and green colours of the two querns may have served to further highlight this relationship. However, it may also be more than coincidence that these are also the colours of molten metal and its mould, or possibly verdigris. As such they may have been seen as symbolic of a transformation from one state to another, marking a beginning and an end, a particularly potent deposition within a short-lived metalworking site. Although worn, the stones were not worn out. This together with their arrangement suggests that they were removed from their primary use lives and placed in the ditch with particular intent and meaning.

7.5 Conclusions

From domestic settlements to funerary monuments, from roundhouse walls, pits and postholes to ditches and cairns, from long term settlements to short-lived specialist sites, the locations and contexts in which querns are found across the south-west throughout the Bronze Age show that they pervaded all aspects of life and death, functioning on both practical and symbolic levels. As in the Neolithic period, the state of the querns and the contexts in which they are found illustrate well the theory that artefacts were deposited in the archaeological record with different levels of structure and intent, even within the same type of context. These vary from quern fragments simply left within an occupation deposit or midden to complete quernstones placed in an ordered manner in a pit or ditch. The reasons and meanings advanced for the deposition of querns in the Neolithic period can be expanded upon for the Bronze Age to include:

- Offerings or depositions of complete or fragmentary querns made or left during the occupation, rebuilding or demolition of a structure, symbolising the life or death of the household.
- Complete querns *in situ* in their working positions but left either as part of an act of closure or with the intention of reuse.
- Depositions in pits as a means of safe storage or as a foundation or closure deposit, the former probably more likely to contain complete quernstones, the latter may be complete or fragmentary.
- Depositions of complete or fragmentary querns in pits and ditches forging a link between people and place, making and breaking relationships.
- Depositions of complete or fragmentary querns with direct personal meanings or related to a particular trade or craft.
- Depositions of complete or fragmentary querns drawing upon the transforming qualities of querns, symbolising changes in state of both humans and buildings or, where placed at a boundary crossing, the transition from one side to another.
- Complete or fragmentary querns utilised as construction material, creating links between the past and the present.

The Bronze Age saw a movement away from communal monuments and, with the growth of a settled rather than nomadic lifestyle, the rise of domestic farmsteads and settlements. In the ensuing Iron Age agricultural production intensified and greater importance and emphasis was placed on territories and land divisions. Great changes were also to take place in milling technology with the introduction of the rotary quern.

8

THE IRON AGE

8.1 Setting the Scene: Activity Locales and Subsistence

The 1st millennium BC is a tale of two halves. The first half of the millennium to *circa* 600BC, covering the period from the Late Bronze Age to the Early Iron Age, was a time of great social and economic change brought about by a number of factors including wetter climatic conditions, a decline in the population and the spread of iron working across Europe which undermined established bronze trading relationships. The basis for political power appears, therefore, to have shifted during this time from control over the exchange and consumption of bronze to control over land and agricultural resources and products. In the second half of the millennium, from *circa* 600BC the average rainfall decreased and the climate warmed slightly, the use of iron became more widespread, agricultural production increased; the use of iron plough shares enabled heavier soils to be cultivated, and whether by cause or effect the population rose. New settlement and monument types appeared with hillforts a particular feature of the landscape (Cunliffe 1984a, 30-31; Sharples 1991, 84; Pryor 1998b, 148; Straker *et al* 2008, 108-109, 112-113).

As Fitzpatrick (2008, 129) points out there is much regional diversity in monument and settlement type in the south-west, although basically small settlements, both open and enclosed are found across the region. Hillforts, particularly the more developed, multivallate sites, are more common in the east of the region including Ham Hill, the largest hillfort in the country, Brent Knoll and Cadbury Castle in Somerset and Berrywood and Hembury in Devon. However, smaller Devonian and Cornish examples are known such as Blackbury Camp and Killibury and around the rugged coastlines of Devon and more particularly Cornwall are a series of promontory forts. In the western part of the region there is a prevalance of hillside enclosures and, in the Late Iron Age, smaller enclosed sites known as rounds developed and which continued in use into the Roman period (courtyard settlements such as Chysauster in West Penwith are now considered to be Roman in date). Somerset is remarkable for its two Lake Villages of Glastonbury and Meare and for its cave dwellings such as Wookey Hole. Barrow cemeteries had largely ceased to be used in the Late Bronze Age and instead those dead that were given burials were either placed in flat inhumation cemeteries, isolated graves, ditches or disused storage pits. The latter, however, are only found in the east of the region, in Somerset (Fitzpatrick 2008; Cornwall Council Historic Environment Service 2009).

In the south-west the general range of crops established during the Bronze Age continued to be cultivated throughout the Iron Age with sites such as Killibury in Cornwall, Langland Lane and Blackhorse in east Devon, and Ham Hill, Glastonbury and Meare in Somerset producing evidence for emmer, bread wheat, spelt, barley, beans and peas (Hillman 1977, 110; Clapham 1999, 155, 188; Ede 1990, 39-43; Ede 1999, 120; Minnitt and Coles 1996, 56). There appears, however, generally to have been an increase in the cultivation of hulled barley and spelt, a particularly hardy variety of wheat, perhaps as a result of poorer climatic conditions (Fitzpatrick 2008, 139). Other crops included black mustard seed of which quantities were recovered from storage pits at Ham Hill (Leivers *et al* 2007, 42, 44).

The burnt remains of small bun-shaped loaves were discovered at both Glastonbury and Meare. The grains appeared whole or only partially ground and mixed with honey (Gray and Cotton 1966, 383; Bulleid 1924, 45). It seems unlikely that grain was routinely so coarsely ground as both saddle and rotary querns are capable of producing a fine meal. Indeed the state of the fragments of wheat and barley found in the stomach of Lindow II bog man from Cheshire showed the grain to have been finely milled (Holden 1995, 79). The fragments from Glastonbury and Meare presumably, therefore, derived from a particular sort of 'bread' perhaps a *bappir*, a malted bread or cake, intended for use in brewing (after Dineley and Dineley 2000, 142).

The Iron Age

The introduction of the rotary quern to Britain *circa* 400BC is considered to be a major advance in milling technology (Watts, M. 2008, 11). Less tiring to operate than the saddle quern, the rotary quern could also be worked by two people thus lightening the load still further and making the chore a more companionable task. It is suggested (Heslop 2008, 19) that the rotary quern was initially a prestige item but its widespread appearance across southern England during the Middle Iron Age implies that it quickly found its niche as an everyday milling implement. Although the rotary quern did not entirely replace the saddle quern it is likely its advent will have affected the perceived value of the saddle quern. The latter was probably gradually used less and less for grinding grain as the rotary quern became more universally adopted. It is also likely that the rotary quern brought with it new meanings, based perhaps on its circular motion compared to the forward and back action of the saddle quern, as well as its function as a milling tool.

8.2 Querns from the Study Area

The database includes 633 querns from the south-west broadly dated to the Iron Age comprising 193 saddle querns of which 63 are complete or nearly so, 166 rubbers of which 81 are complete and 140 rotary querns including 78 upper stones and 44 lower stones of which 14 and 21 are complete or nearly so respectively. There are also 133 indeterminate fragments, of which at least 48 are probably saddle querns or rubbers (Figure 5.3).

The querns derive from 64 sites (Figure 8.1). As with the Bronze Age data, there is a bias towards western Cornwall and also a clustering around Cadbury Castle, Somerset. However, more sites are apparent in north Somerset which contrasts with the disappearance of sites from Dartmoor. Again there are large areas of east Cornwall, north and mid Devon and east Somerset which are devoid of querns from structured contexts although comparison with the location of find spots (Figure 5.4) suggests that this is largely due to archaeological causation. Of the 633 querns included on the database, however, 328 come from just two sites, with the Somerset Lake Village of Meare West and the hillfort at Cadbury Castle accounting for 199 and 129 querns respectively. A further 80 querns come from Meare Village East, 55 from Glastonbury Lake Village and 17 from the large hillfort of Ham Hill, also in Somerset.

A high majority of the querns are dated to the Mid-Late Iron Age (Figure 8.2) but the number (406) is enhanced, as indicated above, by finds from the Lake Villages of Meare and Glastonbury which were founded *circa* 350BC and 250BC respectively with occupation at both sites ceasing *circa* 50BC. Twenty nine querns were found in Early Iron Age contexts and as was to be expected none were rotary querns; the rotary quern fragments from Shaugh Moor, Devon originally dated to the earlier Iron Age are now considered to be later in date[1]. It generally appears that rotary querns were coming into use in the east of the region in the 4th century BC in common with evidence from sites elsewhere in southern Britain, as shown in Chapter Two. At Cadbury Castle, although there is some slight evidence to suggest the presence of rotary querns in the 5th century BC the majority of the rotary querns were not deposited before *circa* 350-300BC (Cadbury Castle Archive; Bellamy 2000, 211). Of the nine rotary quernstones recovered from pits at Ham Hill, one came from a pit dated *circa* 400-200BC, the others from pits dated post *circa* 200BC (Adkins and Adkins 1991; McKinley 1999; Leivers *et al* 2007). At Glastonbury Lake Village the lower stone of a rotary quern was found beneath Mound 74, one of the earliest mounds to be constructed *circa* 250BC (Coles and Minnitt 2000, 85, 112). Further west and most particularly in Cornwall rotary querns do not seem to have been used until later in the Iron Age. In Devon rotary querns have been found at Berrywood[2] and Cranbrook Castle, both hillforts dated to the Middle-Late Iron Age while in Cornwall examples from Trevisker, The Rumps and Castle Gotha are all probably post *circa* 200BC in date (Saunders and Harris 1982, 150; Gallant and Silvester 1985, 47; Baring-Gould 1901, 132; ApSimon and Greenfield 1972, 347; Brooks 1974; Quinnell 1998, 16).

The general form of Iron Age rotary querns in the south-west is broadly comparable to Curwen's (1937) Wessex style beehive quern with a rounded shape, a wide central eye and a concave grinding surface (Figure 2.3, 2.9). The handle hole is usually in the side of the stone, although there are several examples from the east of the region with a handle slot cut across the top of the stone more in the style of Curwen's Sussex type quern.

---

1. The two fragments, from a large, flatter lower stone were originally dated by association with a sherd of decorated pottery to the 5th-4th century BC, an early date for a rotary quern (Quinnell 1994, 78). However, the association is tenuous at best and the quern probably relates to a later use of the enclosure. I am grateful to Henrietta Quinnell for discussions on the dating of this and other querns and sites in the south-west.
2. None of the rotary querns from Berrywood are included in the database as their location, within and outside the ramparts, is presumed to be the result of site clearance for a fair in the 19th century (Gallant and Silvester 1985, 39, 47).

Figure 8.1:
Map showing the location of Iron Age sites where querns have been found in structured contexts (see Appendix One for site details).

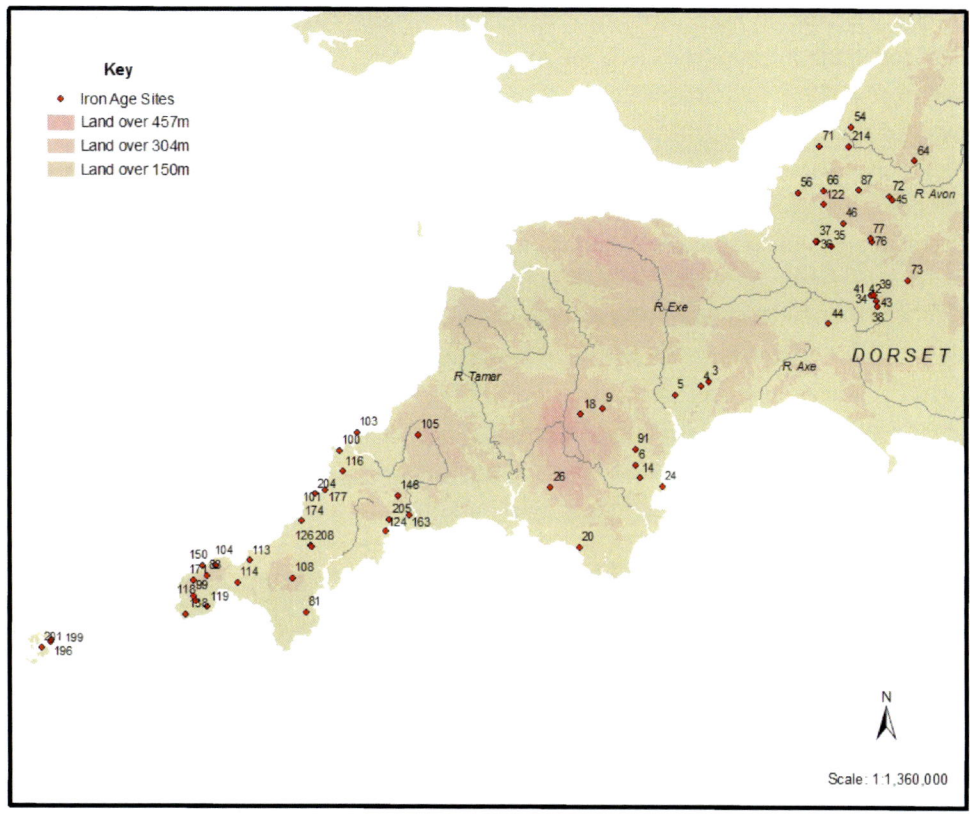

Figure 8.2:
Table showing the numbers of querns found within each form of Iron Age depositional context (S = Saddle quern, Ru = Rubber, Q = Quern, Ro = Rotary quern).

	Early Iron Age			Early-Mid Iron Age			Middle Iron Age			Mid-Late Iron Age			Late Iron Age			Iron Age			Total
	S	Ru.Q	Ro	S	Ru.Q	Ro	S	Ru.Q	Ro	S	Ru.Q	Ro	S	Ru.Q	Ro	S	Ru.Q	Ro	
Bank				2			2						1			2	2		9
Barrow/grave																1	1		2
Cave													5			3	2		10
Cobbled surface							4	4								3			11
Ditch	5	1					1			2	1	1	2	1		3	3	2	22
Drain							2										2		4
Floor										1			1			2	2		6
Fogou	1															7			8
Foundation										2						9			11
Gully							1	2		3	2		1	1	2	1			13
Hearth				1			1			3				1		5			11
Midden										2	1		4	2		1			10
Mound										242	11	62				1			316
Occupation layer	14			7								1				5	1		28
Pit	2			1	1	2	4	3	1	18	17	15	10	4	13	9	7	11	118
Pit kiln										1	4	10							15
Posthole	2			1	1		6	1		1	2	2				4			20
Quarry																	2		2
Stone setting	2																		2
Wall	2			1												9	1		13
Watery deposit											2								2
Total	28	1	0	12	2	3	20	10	2	275	38	93	23	8	17	62	15	24	633

As in the preceding Neolithic and Bronze Age periods the sources of stone from which Iron Age querns are manufactured tend to be fairly local to the south-west with granites and sandstones predominating. However, the range is extended by the use of limestone, breccia and an Old Red Sandstone conglomerate which were used mainly for the manufacture of rotary querns. Most sites sourced or acquired stone within a 25km radius, although querns of Devonian or Cornish granite are recorded at Cadbury Castle and Meare and a complete saddle quern and rubber of an igneous rock were found at Glastonbury, indicative of more long distance contacts and relationships (Roe 2000, 264; Gray and Cotton 1966, 385; Bulleid 1917, 617). As commented upon in the previous chapter, the use of querns from distant sources as structured deposits appears to be an unusual occurrence indicative of a particular significance and meaning. Such querns may relate to particular relationships, be part of a dowry or signify trading contacts. A wide range of sources is also evident at both Cadbury Castle and Meare demonstrating the importance of the sites at both local and regional levels and reflecting their functions as meeting places. Indeed, the presence of some querns at Meare may also be explained by the fact that they were intended for trade or exchange, as there were several that appeared unused (Gray and Cotton 1966, 385-406).

Secondary use is evident in querns from a number of sites. Quern fragments utilised as whetstones were found at Meare and several saddle querns from Early to Middle Iron Age contexts at Trenowah, Cornwall appear to have been reused as mortars for grinding metal ore (Gray and Cotton 1966, 393, 395; Quinnell forthcoming). At Glastonbury, a large heavy upper stone found in the southern part of the site in association with floor 1 of Mound 5 showed evidence of burning. The earlier levels of Mound 5 were associated with metalworking and it is likely that the stone was used as a work surface. One and a half unfinished lower stones were also found in Mound 5, the half stone described as having fractured in the making and a partly made upper stone was also recovered from floor 1 of Mound 4. This floor has been interpreted as an open clay spread which replaced an earlier house (Bulleid 1917, 616; Coles and Minnitt 2000, 34, 36). The presence of these querns suggests that this area of Glastonbury was used at various times for different craft activities such as metalworking and quern finishing.

In contrast to this, several upper stones from rotary querns at Glastonbury show evidence of efforts made to increase their working lives. Three upper stones had handle slots cut across their upper surfaces to replace handle holes in the side that had broken through to the grinding surface. On another upper stone, which had broken in two through the handle hole, an attempt had been made to mend the stone by dowelling the two halves together; a new handle hole was drilled at right angles to the first. Several saddle querns from Meare West and also Trenowah also showed evidence for use on both sides (Bulleid 1917, 613-614; Gray and Cotton 1966, 389, 391, 392, 399; Quinnell forthcoming).

More than half (65%) of Iron Age querns included on the database are broken and, as in the preceding Neolithic and Bronze Ages, the greater proportion of all the quernstones, whether fragmentary or complete, are found as single stones. Although stones from different querns may be found in the same context only seven pairs of stones are known, all but one of which are matching saddle querns and rubbers. There also appears to be a drop in the numbers of saddle querns and rubbers in the later Iron Age which may be due to the introduction of the rotary quern. The finds of complete quernstones, whether as pairs or single stones, can be compared to those of fragmentary stones and are suggestive of depositions made with differing levels and layers of meaning and intent.

8.3   Contexts of Deposition

Analysis of the database shows that 21 broad forms of depositional context can be distinguished (Figure 8.2). As in the Bronze Age the majority of querns derive from structural and occupational contexts. Of these, however, 332 come from the clay spreads, the sites of former dwellings, workshops and activity areas within the Lake Villages at Glastonbury and Meare. In addition 133 querns were recovered from pits, of which 92 came from pits within Cadbury Castle, including 15 from the same pit kiln. Querns, however, also continue to be deposited in postholes, gullies, middens, enclosure banks and ditches and occupation layers as well as in some rather more unusual contexts such as cave dwellings and fogous, the enigmatic underground passages found in Cornwall. Two quernstones were also potentially recovered from watery deposits and another two fragments were found in association with a Bronze Age barrow and an Iron Age grave. The former appears to represent continued veneration and use of an ancient site. The latter, however, is probably coincidental.

8.3.1 Structural contexts
8.3.1.1 Clay spreads at Glastonbury and Meare
Despite their lack of stratigraphic and contextual detail, the large assemblages of querns from the Lake Villages of Glastonbury and Meare are of particular interest. Strictly speaking, of course, they are not lake villages. The site at Glastonbury was established on a patch of fen carr in a swamp and is, in essence, a large crannog built upon spreads of clay on a foundation of trees, brushwood, bracken, rubble and clay. The 'villages' at Meare on the other hand developed on the edge of a large raised bog. Occupation was initially directly on the surface of the bog, clay floors being laid when the ground surface became too wet (Minnitt and Coles 1996). Deliberately sited in marginal land and broadly contemporary in date, the two sites have a similar material culture with occupation ceasing at both when rising water levels made activity no longer tenable. However, whereas Glastonbury is thought to have been permanently occupied, the lack of structural evidence at Meare, coupled with the plentiful evidence for on-site production and the fact that the site was probably prone

to seasonal flooding, has led to the suggestion that Meare was the site of an annual meeting place and craft fair (Bulleid and Gray 1948, 10-11; Coles 1987; Cunliffe 1991, 242; Minnitt and Coles 1996). This difference in function is reflected in the querns found at each. It is likely, however, that many of the 310 quernstones and fragments recovered were incorporated into the foundations or make-up of floors at both sites. They may have been used close to where they were found (Coles 1987, 143). Alternatively, it is possible that a number of the querns found were brought to the sites together with other rubble stone specifically for reuse. Patterns, however, can be perceived in the distribution of querns within each site suggesting that the former scenario is more likely. Not all mounds produced querns.

At Glastonbury, although querns were found in all areas of the site, more saddle querns were apparent in the southern part (Figure 8.3) (Coles and Minnitt 2000, 194). It is also noticeable that the querns were mostly located in connection with working areas rather than houses. There are also discrete concentrations associated with Mounds 3-6, 37-38 and 44 and in addition there are several depositions of multiple fragments in the north-west corner of the site in relation to Mounds 71 and 74. Nine burnt fragments of an upper stone and 30 fragments from another were found to the south-east of Mound 71 and a lower stone broken in four and five fragments of another upper stone came from the east side of Mound 74. The four fragments of lower stone were found underneath the mound and although the others were unassigned such groupings of fragmentary stones appear to represent a particular form of deposit, perhaps related to the laying of new floors or to the particular function or status of this part of the site.

Possibly the two most important stones from Glastonbury, however, are the complete upper and lower stones of a saddle quern which were found in the foundation of Mound 38, close to the centre of the site (Bulleid 1917, 617). Also found near the centre of the site were six 1m long posts each with a ring of stakes around it. These post and stake settings may have supported raised objects such as beehives but their location has led to the suggestion that they were 'consecrating elements' (Coles and Minnitt 2000, 59, 113, 199). The location of the saddle quern and rubber, may therefore, be significant and it is suggested that they were a primary foundation deposit. The fact that both upper and lower stone were deposited together, one of the few paired examples, and that furthermore they are of a non-local igneous rock from Devon or Cornwall, the only two stones from this source found on the site, lends support to this theory.

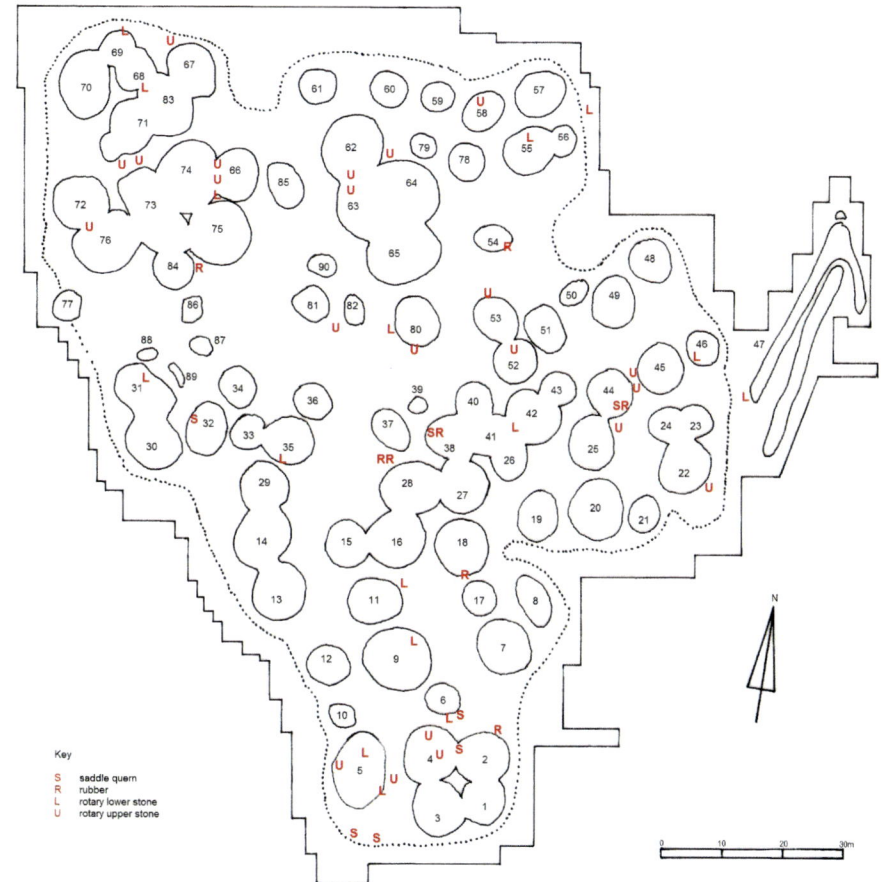

Figure 8.3: Plan of Glastonbury Lake Village, Somerset showing the location of querns found (M. Watts derived from Coles 1986, Figure 38; Bulleid 1917).

At Meare East the querns found in association with Mounds 13/14 and 17 account for almost half the total number of quernstones recovered. The mounds generally produced abundant quantities of finds suggesting they were major activity areas possibly dating from early in the site's occupation (Coles 1987, 143, 243). Likewise at Meare West Bulleid (1936, 216) noted that only 18 of the 40 mounds produced milling stones. Concentrations of querns were found in Mounds 7, 9, 22 and 34 with lesser numbers from Mounds 24 and 33; Mounds 7, 9 and 34 also produced an above average quantity of artefacts. Mounds 34 and 22 contained several series of hearths as did Mound 13/14 at Meare East suggesting that they were food preparation areas, possibly on a communal basis; ovens were also found in Mounds 34 and 22 (Bulleid 1936, 216; Coles 1987; Gray and Cotton 1966).

At Meare West a complete lower stone of a saddle quern lay in the foundation of Mound 34. This was the largest clay spread within the site and was associated with several series of hearths indicative of a communal cooking area (Gray and Bulleid 1953, 175-190; Gray and Cotton 1966, 399). In contrast to the foundation deposit at Glastonbury, the saddle quern beneath Mound 34 was a single stone of fairly local Old Red Sandstone. It is tempting to see its location as related to the function of the mound as a food producing area. In Mound 33, also at Meare West, a rubber and half a saddle quern are recorded from the foundations (Gray and Cotton 1966, 400). Situated at the north-east edge of the site, Mound 33 was one of the smaller mounds but contained a comparatively high number of artefacts including 15 quernstones or fragments. Part of an infant skeleton and that of a large dog were also recovered from the mound and a crushed human skull was found off the edge of the mound clay (Gray and Cotton 1966, 407-408). The dog skeleton was the only one found at Meare West which together with the fact that the human remains account for almost a quarter of those found on the site suggests that Mound 33 was the site of some particular and perhaps esoteric activities.

8.3.1.2 Walls and floors
Thirteen querns included on the database were found reused within the walls of stone-built roundhouses. These are predominantly saddle querns. Three joining fragments of saddle quern were found in different parts of the low wall of a Middle Iron Age roundhouse on Dainton Common, Devon (Willis and Rogers 1951, 87; Smith 1987). Although much worn the saddle quern, which was incomplete, was still some 7.5cm thick suggesting that it was purposefully broken for reuse as building stone. As mentioned in the previous chapter such reuse marks, whether by accident or design, a (re)building event. The stones may have been deliberately chosen to create a link with previous occupation and people. Similarly at Bodrifty in Cornwall and Kestor on Dartmoor fragments of saddle quern were reused in roundhouse walls (Dudley 1956, 18; Fox 1954, 56). Both settlements had a long, although not necessarily continuous, period of occupation, from the Middle Bronze Age into the Iron Age (Quinnell 1998; Anon 2011, 15; Quinnell 2011b, 233). The querns reused in the walls are likely, therefore, to have derived from earlier occupation. Again a dual function of practical building stone and a symbolic link with the past can be seen.

In addition to their reuse as walling material quern fragments were also utilised as paving stones in roundhouses at Homeground, Somerset and Sheep Slait Dorset and at Carn Euny in Cornwall (Tabor pers. corresp.; Christie 1978, 346, 388). A fragment of saddle quern was also found in a stony deposit on the floor on the north side of Structure 2 within the settlement enclosure at Twinyeo Farm, Kingsteignton, Devon (Valentin pers. corresp.). As with the inclusion of quern fragments within walls, their utilisation in floors and surfaces may be no more than the simple reuse of conveniently shaped pieces of stone but again such reuse creates a link with the past. At Chun Castle, Cornwall a rubber found beneath the floor of a roundhouse may have been a foundation deposit (Leeds 1926-1927, 222) but it is difficult to apply anything other than a practical application to the reuse of quern fragments in various cobbled tracks at Cadbury Castle.

It has been suggested (Alcock 1960, 99-100) that the incorporation of saddle querns within the floors and walls of Iron Age structures is a result of their becoming redundant as milling tools due to the introduction of the rotary quern. While it is tempting to say that this may have been part of the reasoning behind the reuse of saddle querns at later Iron Age sites it cannot have been so at Dainton Common or Twinyeo as both sites are dated to the Earlier Iron Age, prior to the introduction of the rotary quern. At these sites the utilisation of saddle querns in constructional events can be seen as a continuation of the practice witnessed in the Bronze Age. In addition, the fact that saddle querns continued to be used throughout the Iron Age and were still being deposited in the archaeological record in the Late Iron

Age suggests that they continued to be used and to have some meaning and value.

8.3.1.3 Postholes

Twenty querns are recorded as coming from a total of 18 postholes on eight sites (Table 8.1). However, whereas the majority of postholes containing querns on Bronze Age sites in the south-west were located within roundhouses, seven of the Iron Age postholes form part of four- or six-post structures dated from the Early through to the Late Iron Age. Six of the structures are within the hillfort at Cadbury Castle and interestingly all the querns are found in postholes in the northern halves of the structures. Similarly at Long Range in east Devon (*circa* 400-100 cal. BC) a quern fragment was found in the posthole at the northern apex of a three-post structure (Barrett *et al* 2000, 354-355; Laidlaw 1999a, 148). By way of contrast, at Blackhorse, also in east Devon (cal. 370BC-AD90), the posthole (34) was on the east side of a posthole group forming potentially the south-east corner of one of a line of three four-post structures (Fitzpatrick *et al* 1999a, 166). These sturdy structures are generally interpreted as raised granaries providing a clear link between querns and grain. However, it has also been proposed that these structures could, in certain circumstances, be excarnation platforms (Gillard *et al* 2010, 28) and again, an association can be seen between the transformation of the dead body and the quern as a transformer of materials.

Querns also continued to be deposited in roundhouse postholes with examples being found at Milsoms Corner and Cadbury Castle in Somerset, Blackhorse and Twinyeo in Devon and Trevisker in Cornwall. At the latter two sites the querns, a fragment of saddle quern and a rubber respectively, were from entrance postholes demonstrating the continued association of querns with thresholds. The presence of a burnt post in posthole F.37 at Trevisker suggests that the rubber was part of the post-packing and not an abandonment deposit (Valentin pers. corresp.; ApSimon and Greenfield 1972, 319, 347). It is also of note that both postholes are on the northern side of the entrance, suggesting perhaps a common depositional code with four post structures. In line with this, postholes 654 at Blackhorse and T348 at Cadbury Castle were in the north-west and north-east quadrants of roundhouse gullies respectively (Laidlaw 1999a, 178; Cadbury Castle Archive).

8.3.1.4 Gullies and drains

Thirteen querns on the database were recovered from 12 gullies and a further four came from three drains (Table 8.2). All but two of the querns retrieved from gullies were in a fragmentary state. Nine of the gullies were penannular, associated with roundhouses and it is noticeable that querns were found in the southern halves of five of these. Indeed it was noted at Blackhorse (Fitzpatrick *et al* 1999a, 221) that most of the finds from gully 203 derived from its southern half as did those in the enclosure ditch (see below). The posthole containing a quern fragment at Blackhorse mentioned above was also potentially on the south-east side of a four post structure. The prevalence of querns in the southern half of roundhouse gullies points to deliberate rather than random location. It also suggests that the associated artefacts which were mainly domestic in nature were likewise purposefully placed in the gullies. The artefacts found in the gully of House 6 at Higher Besore on the other hand are associated with metalworking and it was noted that the rubber also found in the gully, one of the two complete quernstones, was abraded at both ends suggesting that it had been utilised as a pounding tool (Gossip forthcoming; Quinnell and Taylor forthcoming).

The other complete quernstone was a saddle quern found in a short linear gully (N954/E724) at Cadbury Castle. The gully, 0.75-1.00m wide with three postholes along its northern side, appears to have formed the northern edge of a clay floor associated with a series of hearths (Barrett *et al* 2000, 166, figure 84). The artefacts which include bronze and iron fragments, charcoal, bone and antler tools, a whetstone and burnt stone reflect the industrial and craftworking nature of the area. The saddle quern rests naturally so that one end of the grinding surface is higher than the other; the slope to one side was probably countered by a wedge. Although worn, the saddle quern, which is a maximum of 11.5cm thick, still has plenty of life in it and it is probably unlikely that it was just randomly discarded in the gully. It may even have been used in the gully and left *in situ*.

It may also be more than coincidence that three of the four querns from drains also derived from the southern halves of roundhouses. At Stannon Down on Bodmin Moor two fragments of saddle quern had been utilised in the construction of a drain (214) that ran north-south across a roundhouse. Impact marks on one of the pieces suggest that the saddle quern from which it came had been purposefully smashed (Quinnell 2004-2005, 97). It is further suggested that the quern fragments may have derived from the earlier Bronze Age occupation of the site, reused perhaps with the objective of linking the past to the present or simply because they were useful flat pieces of stone (Quinnell 2004-2005, 97). At Trevisker complete upper and lower rotary quernstones, possibly a pair, were found in the top of drain fills (M29 and M25) in the north and south of roundhouse 2 respectively (ApSimon and Greenfield 1972, 347). The upper stone appears to have been taken out of use for grinding by virtue of the fact that the stone had broken out where its grinding surface had worn too close to the handle socket. Its potential reuse as a drain cover appears rather practical as its central eye could have been used for tipping liquids away. The lower stone on the other hand had a spindle socket and cannot, therefore, have been used in this way. However, the socket could have been used to hold a stick or stake in place or, if it were placed in an inverted position, its underside would have provided a good flat paving stone or working surface. The locating of rotary quernstones over drains continued to be an occasional feature of Roman and later stone-built houses in the south-west. A lower stone, for example, was reused as a drain cover in a courtyard house at Halangy Down and on Beacon Hill, Lundy an upper stone was placed on top of a stone over a drainage gully in a roundhouse of 3rd-4th century date. A lower stone was also found covering a drain outside the entrance to a rectangular living cell within the small medieval monastery on St. Helen's, Isles of Scilly (Gray 1972, 24; Thomas 1991, 45; O'Neil 1964, 53).

8.3.2 Occupation layers and in situ querns
Thirty eight querns were found within occupation layers at 15 sites including four cave dwellings. In addition many of those found within the mounds at Glastonbury and Meare and for which there is no stratigraphic information also derived from occupation layers. At some sites such as Cranbrook Castle, Devon (Baring-Gould 1901, 132) it is simply reported that the quern was found within the interior of a roundhouse and in these cases it is not really possible to comment on the nature of the deposition save for the fact that the quern was left, presumably on or near to its last place of use when the building ceased to be occupied. The situation is similar with occupation deposits within caves.

Ten quern fragments have been recovered from occupation layers and deposits in cave dwellings in Somerset and Devon. Kent's Cavern, Torquay, for example, is most well-known for its Palaeolithic deposits but it also saw periods of use in the later prehistoric period. It appears to have been used for burial in the earlier Bronze Age and subsequently as a seasonal occupation site (Silvester 1986). The artefacts, which all derive from 19th century excavations of the black 'mould' on top of the deposits, include a collection of Mid to Late Iron Age South-West Decorated Ware (Quinnell 1998). Also amongst the artefacts was a fragment of saddle quern reused as a polishing stone, which perhaps accords with the interpretation of the site as seasonal (Silvester 1986, 16). Evidence has also been found for occupation in a number of caves in the Mendips in Somerset including Read's Cavern where a rubber was found; again occupation here may have been intermittent (Fitzpatrick 2008, 133; Palmer 1919-1920, 12-13). The fragments from several saddle querns and some five rubbers found in Gough's Old Cave are perhaps suggestive of more permanent or longer-term occupation. For the most part there is little to gainsay regarding the nature of the querns' depositions in these caves although two of the rubbers found in Gough's Old Cave were associated with a hearth dated *circa* 200BC (Tratman 1959-1960, 13). A saddle quern and rubber were also found in the Iron Age occupation levels at Wookey Hole and the implication from the text is that they were found together (Balch 1914, 101). It seems, therefore, that these tools were generally found close to where they were last used. Again these querns seem to have been left when the occupants vacated the caves.

However, a number of querns are recorded elsewhere as being found *in situ* in their primary working positions. At Nornour, on the Isles of Scilly, for example, two saddle querns were found each located beside a hearth within a 'kitchen' room added to House 1 in the early Iron Age. There was a third saddle quern close by and in one of the compartments within the adjoining structure were six rubbers (Figure 3.10) (Dudley 1967, 5, 7). At Bodrifty in Cornwall two saddle querns, one of which appeared little used, were found on the floor of Hut G. They were set about 15.0cm apart close to one of the five cooking pits in the south-west quadrant of the roundhouse (Dudley 1956, 12). The location of these saddle querns seems, as suggested for the Bronze Age, determined more by the location of hearths and cooking pits than by any cosmological influence. Given the increase in the Iron Age in the cultivation of hulled barley and spelt, a hulled wheat, it is likely that one quern was used for dehusking or coarse grinding and the other(s) for finer grinding. Slightly different is the nature of the leaving of the lower stone of a rotary quern at Trevisker which was found inverted over the emplacement where it was formerly situated (ApSimon and Greenfield 1972, 323). This suggests that it was left in a 'safe' position when the roundhouse was deserted.

A number of quernstones recovered from the Lake Villages at Glastonbury and Meare may also have been found on or close to their working positions. These include two saddle querns, one from Meare East associated with Mound 5 and the other from Meare West, Mound 24, which were both found with their rubbing stones (Coles 1987, 143, 145; Gray and Cotton 1966, 395). At Glastonbury the lower stone of a saddle quern found on floor 4 of Mound 4, and one of the few querns found in association with a roundhouse, also appears to have been *in situ*. The floor of the roundhouse was repaired several times before the house was replaced by an open clay spread and the area where the saddle quern lay was subsequently covered by part of another clay spread and a stone path (Coles and Minnitt 2000, 34-35). The description of the saddle quern suggests that, although worn, it was not worn out (Bulleid 1917, 616). Other complete lower stones of rotary and saddle querns which are dated to the late and final phases of the site's occupation may likewise have been left *in situ* as activity on the site decreased (Coles and Minnitt 2000, 38, 61-63, 66, 68, 71, 80). In addition, the heavy rotary upper stone that had been used for metalworking and the unfinished stones found in Mounds 4 and 5 may all have been left broadly where they were last used or worked upon (Bulleid 1917, 615, 616).

Once again it appears, therefore, that apparently still serviceable quernstones were not 'rescued' when restructuring and rebuilding took place or when sites were abandoned, a phenomenon first noticed in regard to Bronze Age structures and sites. As suggested in Chapter Seven there may have been a taboo against retrieving and reusing these stones. They, together with other artefacts, may have been left or placed in position when new floors and spreads were laid, signifying building events and changes in a specific area's status, use or occupation. Those from the final phases of occupation may also have been deliberately left. This may have been simply because they were considered too heavy to carry at the time. Alternatively, they were left for the same reasons that complete stones were covered over during rebuilding or as a purposeful abandonment deposit. The act of leaving artefacts both maintains a sense of place and creates a memory. The similarity to the modern day abandonment of St. Kilda was noted in the previous chapter.

8.3.3 Hearths, ovens and kilns

Twenty six querns on the data base were found in association with hearths, ovens and kilns. The majority of these appear to have been structural such as one of the two hearths in roundhouse X (G) at Bodrifty which had been built upon a saddle quern (Crofts 1952-1953, 19). However, at Higher Besore in Cornwall a complete rubber and fragments of saddle quern found in hearth pits within one of the Iron Age roundhouses were probably utilised in one of the craft activities that appear to have taken place within the structure and left when the structure was abandoned (Gossip forthcoming). Fifteen quern fragments were recovered from a stone and clay-lined pit kiln or oven (E982) at Cadbury Castle. They were probably all part of the lining, although it is possible that some/all may have derived from the mixture of burnt stone, charcoal and soil with which the pit was filled when it went out of use (Cadbury Castle Archive; Barrett *et al* 2000, 167).

On Mound 12 at Meare West several fragments of rotary quern were incorporated into the paving of the upper hearth (Gray and Bulleid 1953, 130). In the southern quadrant of Mound 34, also at Meare West, there were two series of hearths, one containing 12 superimposed hearths (Series B), the other 11 (Series C), below which was a small circular oven of baked clay. Embedded in hearth d of Series B were several pieces of broken saddle quern. In the same mound, in Series D, the middle hearth (ii) consisted of a circular area of baked clay, at the centre of which was a broken saddle quern (Gray and Bulleid 1953, 179-180, 183). Several fragments of quern also appear to have been incorporated into the make up of hearths at Meare East while at Cadbury Castle a rotary lower stone was found reused in an oven or furness N451 (Figure 8.4) (Coles 1987, 143-145; Bellamy 2000, 313-314).

The incorporation of querns in hearths, ovens and kilns, like their reuse as building stone in walls and floors, may just have been a convenient use of suitably sized and shaped pieces of stone. The use of quern fragments to line or infill a pit kiln, such as E982 at Cadbury Castle certainly seems a practical reuse of disused and unwanted pieces of stone. However, if this was the case, why are so many different querns represented and why are they all incomplete? Why were not all the pieces used? The implication is that there is more happening here than meets the eye, although of course the fragments could have derived from a stockpile of stone, their former function no longer of import. There is, however, no reason why such reuse

The Iron Age

Figure 8.4: Lower stone reused in an oven or kiln, N451, at Cadbury Castle (centimetre scale). Museum of Somerset (S. Watts).

should not have fulfilled dual practical and symbolic functions. Querns and millstones continued to be used in the construction in grain drying or malting kilns and ovens in the Roman, medieval and post-medieval periods, providing an ongoing symbolic link between grain, milling and the provision of food (Van der Veen 1989, 315; Curwen 1950; O'Sullivan and Kenny 2008, 10-11; Beresford 1971, 61, 71; Fitzpatrick *et al* 1999b, 258, 265).

8.3.4 Pits
8.3.4.1 Generally
Iron Age pits vary considerably in size and shape with the larger, cylindrical, barrel or beehive shaped grain storage pits that are characteristic of Iron Age sites in southern England only being found in the east of the study area at sites such as Cadbury Castle, Ham Hill, Sigwells and Dibbles Farm in Somerset. Pits, however, particularly those that are comparatively small, shallow or irregularly shaped may have served a variety of functions such as cooking or the storage of products other than grain. They may also have been used in dyeing or tanning or other craft processes or served as kilns (Reynolds 1979, 78-79; Barrett *et al* 2000, 167).

At Ham Hill three basic types of pit were identified depending on size, number of layers and the presence of 'special deposits' (McKinley 1999, 86-89; Leivers *et al* 2007, 42-44, 58-59). At Dibbles Farm, although generally no patterning could be seen in the combination and treatment of finds within the group of 68-70 pits, nevertheless two pits contained larger quantities of certain artefacts (Morris 1988, 75). Similarly at Cadbury Castle differences were noted not only in the size and shape of the excavated pits but also in the character of their fills, with particular classes of artefacts being grouped together (Alcock 1972, 136-137; Bellavia *et al* 2000). To Alcock (1972, 136, 153) the placement of horse and cattle skulls in pits within the vicinity of a later shrine at Cadbury Castle 'gave every impression of having been deliberately buried as part of some ritual'. Likewise the deposition of complete pots and quernstones he believed also pointed to a 'ritual' use of those pits. Commenting on the complete upper and lower rotary quernstones, a near complete pot and 528 slingstones in a pit (108) at Ham Hill, Leivers *et al* (2007, 59) remarked that 'none of this material can be regarded as rubbish'. Likewise the two wheel nave bands and a currency bar in the bottom of another pit (73) at Ham Hill can also be construed as 'special deposits' (McKinley 1999, 88, 128). Outside the study area, groupings of artefacts were also noticed at Danebury Hillfort, Hampshire with quernstones, both complete and fragmentary, being highlighted as special deposits (Cunliffe and Poole 1995, 83). This theory is echoed in Hill's (1995) study of Iron Age Wessex which showed that the material recovered from pits associated with human or animal remains was significantly different from that found in pits without such remains. Hill likewise concluded, therefore, that some pits had been used for special deposits. He also suggested that the placement of such deposits had less to do with grain storage and more to do with the wider practice of depositing artefacts below ground (Hill 1995, 110-111). This runs contrary to Cunliffe's suggestion that special depositions were made as part of a pit belief system linked to agricultural fertility which was based on the premise that the prime function of pits was for grain storage (Cunliffe 1992).

That grain was stored in pits is confirmed by Pliny who stated that the best method of storing grain is 'in holes, called *siri*….to make them in dry soil and then to floor them with chaff' (Pliny *Natural History* 18.73.306). Experimental work has shown that grain, both for sowing and consumption, can be successfully stored in pits in this country (Bowen and Wood 1968; Reynolds 1967; 1969; 1974). The underground storage of grain relies on three essential requirements: a watertight pit, an impermeable lid and low temperature. In a well-sealed pit, the grain touching the sides germinates and in doing so uses up the available oxygen in the pit, replacing it with carbon dioxide which stops further growth. Provided that an anaerobic atmosphere is maintained together with a constant moisture level and temperature low enough to prevent the growth of microflora, grain can be safely stored for some considerable time (Reynolds 1974, 119; Reynolds 1979,

74-76). As Varro wrote in the 1st century BC, 'the weevil does not breed where air does not reach. Wheat stored in this way keeps as long as fifty years' (Varro *On Agriculture* 1.57.2).

It has been proposed (Van der Veen and Jones 2006, 223-225) that storage pits were for the storage of surplus grain rather than seed corn. This surplus they suggest was consumed during feasting events, particularly at hillforts. Such visible consumption of grain was one of the ways in which the elite acquired, demonstrated and maintained their power and prestige (Van der Veen and Jones 2006, 225-226; Hamilakis 1999, 40). This raises the possibility that, on occasion, grain, whether for consumption as bread and/or ale, would have been ground on a large scale necessitating the organisation of teams of millers. Van der Veen and Jones's argument is based on three main facts. Firstly, ethnographic evidence indicates that seed corn was stored above rather than below ground. Secondly, spelt, the cultivation of which increased in the Iron Age period, is considered to be an autumn-sown crop. Thus the short period of time between harvesting and sowing would have negated the need for long-term storage. Thirdly, by the Late Iron Age the surplus was being exported rather than consumed which accounts for the general decline in storage pits at this time[3]. Strabo, writing in the 1st century BC, lists grain as one of the exports from Britain (Strabo *Geography* 4.5.2) (Van der Veen and Jones 2006-226; Cunliffe 1988, 147; Jones 1923, 255; Watts, S. 1999, 18).

However, grain stored in pits has the advantage of being safe from not only insect infestation but also raiding (Varro *On Agriculture* 1.57.2-3; Tacitus *Germania* 16). In addition it is thought to have a germination rate twice as high as that stored above ground (Fitzpatrick 1997, 80). Varro makes no distinctions in his description of the various means of grain storage in the Roman world (Varro *On Agriculture* 1.57). As Cunliffe (2003, 114-115) comments there is no reason why all grain should not have been initially stored underground and the entire contents of a pit decanted to a granary as and when necessary. The surrendering of grain to the protection of the gods in the hope of ensuring a good harvest the following year may have outweighed any practical considerations.

With annual cleansing pits can be used time and time again[4]; burning was recorded around the sides of several pits at Cadbury Castle. However, as Reynolds (1979, 76) points out, should a pit fail due to water ingress then the lurid colours and smell of the rotting grain may have been sufficient reason for the pit to be abandoned and a new one dug. Alcock (1972, 136) suggested that grain storage pits that had become sour were infilled with a mixture of midden material and earth dug from new pits but surely this is also sufficient reason for the placement of propitiatory gifts (Watts, S. 1999, 17). The failure of the harvest may also have necessitated appropriate rituals and offerings for which a grain storage pit seems a suitable receptacle.

However, although some pits were infilled as a single event many of the larger storage pits have multiple layered fills with up to seven layers being recorded for some pits. A pit once chosen for whatever reason for use as a 'depositional access point' (Lionái 2010) but only partly filled may have remained open for subsequent depositions to be made. Each layer, therefore, constitutes a separate 'depositional event' (after Leivers *et al* 2007, 58). This returns again to Hill's (1995, 110-111) theory that the infilling of storage pits had little to do with their original function, although this must surely be a distinct possibility for the initial deposit at the base of the pit. It also follows that subsequent events may have referred back to the original deposit, drawing upon the perceived power invested in that deposition to enhance their own value. Thus, although each layer was intended as a permanent, and to our eyes a closed, deposit, it in fact remained open for future reference by the community.

As Hill (1995, 100) points out pits were not infilled frequently enough for them to be part of a site maintenance routine, that is they were not reused as rubbish pits. His research suggested that offerings were only made once or twice a decade on ordinary settlement sites and once or twice a year on large, communal sites such as Danebury Hillfort (Hill 1995, 100). In the south-west an average figure of three pits a year can be suggested for Cadbury Castle by scaling up the number of pits (*circa* 360) from the size of the area excavated; both aerial photography and geophysical survey indicate that the interior of the hillfort was well-furnished with pits (Bellavia *et al* 2000, 203; Alcock 1972, plate 4, 5; Barrett *et al* 2000, figure 73).

---

3. Gussage All Saints, Dorset, where the number of storage pits increased rather than decreased in the Late Iron Age, is an interesting exception to the rule and possibly related to the function of the site (Jefferies 1979, 15; Watts, S. 1999, 19).

4. Although beyond the scope of this book, the functional life of a storage pit has a bearing on the potential storage capacity of a site and is an important consideration in understanding the economy of that site (Watts, S. 1999, 8).

8.3.4.2 Querns in pits

A total of 118 querns and fragments were recovered from 91 pits on 16 sites with a further 15 being recovered from a pit kiln at Cadbury Castle mentioned above (Table 8.3). The majority of pits are located external to roundhouses supporting the theory that, in terms of quern deposition, the Iron Age saw a move away from roundhouses to the wider settlement and community. The number of pits containing querns, however, is but a fraction of the total number of excavated Iron Age pits in the region. As mentioned above some 360 Iron Age pits were excavated within the hillfort at Cadbury Castle but less than 60 contained querns. At Ham Hill, during excavations conducted in the south-western area of the hillfort between 1991 and 2002 querns were recovered from just 11 out of 61 pits. The picture appears more varied on settlement sites. At Dibbles Farm only one saddle quern was found in 68-70 pits while at Sigwells querns were found in four out of some 26 or more excavated pits (Bellavia *et al* 2000; Cadbury Castle Archive; Adkins and Adkins 1991; McKinley 1999; Leivers *et al* 2007; Morris 1988; Tabor 2008, 121, 130-142). This suggests (following Hill 1995, 110-111) that different pits where filled for different reasons. The context form is dominated by Cadbury Castle but other sites such as Ham Hill and Sigwells, Somerset and Trenowah, Cornwall have also produced interesting combinations of artefacts.

A number of the pits can only be broadly dated to the Iron Age. Consequently, just one pit, at Trenowah, is securely dated to the Early Iron Age (600-520 cal. BC) (Johns forthcoming). A large number of the pits from Cadbury Castle are Middle-Late Iron Age in date and there are also a number of Late Iron Age storage pits from sites in the east of the region. There is also slight evidence to suggest that the pits containing both querns and animal skulls tend to be later in date.

As mentioned above, pits may contain single or multiple layered fills. The latter are generally within the larger storage pits and are only found in the east of the region. Within layered pits quernstones may be found in any one or more of the layers although there is a bias towards their deposition in the bottom or the top layer (Figure 8.5). The most common form of fill in pits or layers containing querns appears to comprise general occupation and midden type material and includes animal bone, tools and bone or iron handles, pottery and slingstones. Consequently, as mentioned in previous chapters, the presence of quern fragments may be no more than happenstance. It should not be presumed, however, that this was unwanted debris. Rather, middens are in themselves stores of fertility and the use of such material to infill grain storage pits in particular can be seen as potently symbolic. In addition objects such as tweezers, an ammonite fossil and a brooch in pits at Cadbury Castle and Sigwells point to more personal choice and by implication other objects such as spindle whorls and quern fragments may also have personal connections. They further suggest that the different pits were filled for different reasons, the contents found within them a response to a particular circumstance or event. The metalworking bias of the crucible fragments, hearth lining and slag found in Pit F303 at Cadbury Castle also appears indicative of a particular depositional event. The saddle quern fragment found in the same pit may have been utilised in the metalworking process (Cadbury Castle Archive; Barrett *et al* 2000, 298). It is also noticeable that whereas some pits have a great variety of artefacts within them others do not. Again this is suggestive of different reasons and meanings for their infilling.

One combination of artefacts that stands out in particular, however, is that of quernstones and animal skulls in storage pits dating to the mid to late Iron Age. At Cadbury Castle, Pit EB8 contained a single fill with a fragment of rubber and a dog skull. Pit C202 also contained a single fill with a fragment from the upper

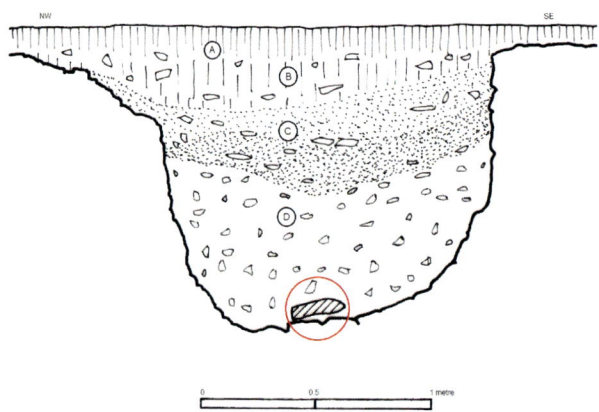

Figure 8.5: Pit A at Blaise Castle Hill, Bristol showing the location of the saddle quern at the bottom of the pit (M. Watts after Rahtz and Clevedon Brown 1958-1959, Figure 35).

stone of a rotary quern and an ox skull, and pit C655 had two layers with a saddle quern and four ox skulls at the bottom (Cadbury Castle Archive). At Ham Hill, Pit 136 was filled in a single episode and contained amongst other artefacts a near complete lower stone of a rotary quern and a fragment of another together with a quantity of animal bone including seven horse skulls. Pit 211 contained a rotary lower stone and four horse skulls and in Pit 149 a quern and horse skull were found in the same layer (Leivers *et al* 2007, 42-44). It is suggested (Leivers *et al* 2007, 58) that the horse skulls may have been spoils of war, Ham Hill being on the border between Dumnonia and Durotrigia. Are the quernstones to be similarly interpreted? On the other hand such animal skulls may represent sacrificial events; both horses and dogs were of particular import to Celtic peoples both in practical and symbolic terms; dogs were associated with healing and death and horses appear to have been representative of certain deities such as Rudiobus or Epona, the latter also a fertility goddess. As tools for grinding grain querns are also symbolically linked with death and fertility, and their deposition fits better into this latter scenario. Querns, however, are not invariably found in pits containing animal skulls and the combination must, therefore, tell a particular story, in response to a specific circumstance or event.

A symbolic link can also be seen between the burial of a raven and a fragment from the upper stone of a rotary quern at the base of a storage pit (F014) at Sigwells (Figure 8.6). They had been covered with stones including another quern fragment (Tabor 2008, 139; Watts, S. 2008b). Ravens were an important part of Celtic mythology, associated with Morrigan, a goddess of war, death and fertility (Green 1997, 90; Jordan 2002, 166). Outside the study area, the high number of ravens found in pits at Danebury compared to other species of bird was commented upon and it was suggested that they had been specially selected for deposition (Cunliffe 2003, 123-124, 147-148) The colours of the artefacts in the pit at Sigwells may also have been important, however; the black raven contrasting with the pink-red colouring of the quernstone, symbolic perhaps of death (black) and life or blood (red). Or is the meaning more prosaic; was the raven killed with the quern fragment? The meaning behind the combination of raven and quern may elude us now but it is nevertheless clear they tell a story.

On present evidence, however, the occurrence of articulated human remains and querns in the same pit seems to be an unusual combination in the south-west of England. No querns, for example, were found in association with the pit burials discovered at Dibbles Farm or Worle Hillfort, Somerset (Morris 1988; Warre 1851). At the time of writing, the only human burial and quern combination known from the study area is from Pit F011 at Sigwells (Tabor 2008, 135) and is

Figure 8.6: Raven burial (F014) at Sigwells, Somerset (R. Tabor).

discussed further below.

Other groupings of artefacts are also apparent again suggesting different reasons and meanings behind both the digging and filling of pits. This is more evident on sites in Devon and Cornwall where storage pits are not a feature but also occurs in Somerset. At Sigwells, for example, a burnt fragment of rubber was found in the lower fill of a small pit (F040), together with part of a large storage jar, a bag of cremated sheep bone, a burnt ammonite and charcoal. The pit appears to have been especially dug to receive the contents found within it demonstrating well the fact that not all pits were dug for storage purposes (Tabor 2008, 133; Tabor pers. corresp.). The pit, dated to the late 3rd to mid 2nd century BC, appears to be contemporary with the earliest surrounding enclosure ditches and the artefacts may, therefore, have been a foundation or dedicatory deposit.

Different again are the contents of a small Early Iron Age pit (345) at Trenowah, St. Austell, Cornwall which appear to be a cache or special deposit of stone tools and other curated artefacts (Figure 8.7) (Johns forthcoming). The contents bear comparison to those of Bronze Age pits at Scarcewater and Truro College, also in Cornwall (Figure 7.3). Quinnell (forthcoming) noted that the complete saddle quern found in the pit at Trenowah was a beach boulder weighing 55kg and that great effort must have been expended in transporting it the kilometre or so to the site from somewhere around the coast in St. Austell Bay. It was probably used, therefore, not far away. Both the saddle quern and another fragment found in the same pit showed evidence of pitting on their grinding surfaces indicative of reuse as mortars, perhaps for grinding mineral ores. It is tempting to suggest that this collection of artefacts, some of which appear to have been deliberately broken, represents the tools and possessions of a craftsperson which were buried perhaps for safekeeping or in response to a specific event or as an offering or in memoriam. It is suggested (Johns forthcoming) that the pit which was dug in the same vicinity as a Bronze Age ritual hollow represents a continuation of depositional activity. Their location at a point where St. Austell Bay and the sea are just visible is seen as a key factor in the location of the site. The location at, or in relation to key points in the landscape was also a feature noted in the siting of Neolithic pits particularly at Milsoms Corner, overlooking Cadbury Castle in Somerset, and Tregarrick Farm, Cornwall with its view of Roche Rock (Tabor 2008, 44; Cole and Jones 2002-2003, 136-137).

The quernstones found in a pit close to a midden in Newquay, Cornwall together with hammerstones and pottery also appear to be a specific deposition as do the two joining fragments from the upper stone of a rotary quern from a pit at Mount Folly Farm overlooking Bigbury Bay in south Devon (Cornwall Historic Environment Record No. 4653; Watts, S. 2007a). The two fragments from Mount Folly Farm were found in the fill of a stone-lined pit (Figure 8.8) (a fragment of lower stone, possibly from its partner, was found in another pit close by). The upper stone had a groove around the side, the closeness of which to the lower edge of the stone may suggest that it was no longer suitable for use. The subsequent use of the quern as pit fill does not at first glance appear surprising. If this were the case, however, why was not the whole stone thrown into the pit? The two fragments only make up about half the stone. Furthermore, the pieces were found at different levels both on the east side of the pit. This suggests that the stone was not only deliberately broken prior to deposition but that some care was taken over the placement of the fragments. The pit also contained a broken whetstone and a number of stone slabs that might have been a lining. The implication is that this was a ritual deposit of deliberately broken stone items, made in a manner reminiscent to the pit deposits of the Neolithic period.

It is noticeable that the majority of the quernstones found in pits are in a fragmentary condition and that most pits generally contain one or perhaps two fragments, although Pits C766, T254 and P758 at Cadbury Castle contained three, four and four querns respectively. It may be of import that animal skulls and/or human bone deposits were also found in these pits (Cadbury Castle Archive). In addition, Pit P758 also contained one of the few complete quernstones found. As commented upon in earlier chapters, fragmentary objects may also have been deposited with purpose and meaning. The breaking of an artefact may, for example, release or conversely deny its powers. It may have represented the making or breaking of a relationship or one piece may have represented the whole (Grinsell 1961, 476-477; Chapman 2000b, 23-26; Brück 2006, 279-299). At

Figure 8.7: Saddle quern, rubbing stones and other stone tools and pottery from Pit 345, Trenowah, St. Austell, Cornwall (© Historic Environment, Cornwall Council).

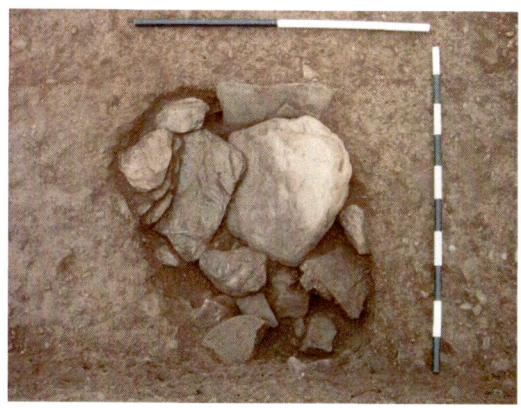

Figure 8.8: Joining fragments of upper stone (ringed in red) in a pit at Mount Folly Farm, Bigbury, South Devon (E. Wilkes, Bournemouth University).

Cadbury Castle the upper stone of a rotary quern found in pit W035 was broken into four pieces. The size of the stone, 33.5cm diameter and 9.1cm thick, suggests that it was deliberately broken, an action requiring some force and yet, unusually, the pieces were kept together. Staying at Cadbury Castle, three fragments from another rotary quernstone were found in two different pits (L002 and S207) with a fourth fragment being recovered from the so-called 'gunge feature' (Cadbury Castle Archive). Likewise at Ham Hill fragments from the same rotary quernstone were also found in two different pits (126 and 133). Although the pits are dated to the same phase of occupation in the 4th to 3rd centuries BC the fact that they are located in different pit groups may be significant (Laidlaw 1999b, 109; McKinley 1999, figure 3). The placement of joining fragments in different contexts implies that not only were the stones purposefully broken prior to deposition but that each fragment was utilised for a specific and different, although potentially related, structured deposit. It is also possible that these events took place at different times with the remaining pieces being curated in between.

Only 17 quernstones on the database were found in pits in a complete or near complete condition. Their deposition contrasts with that of fragments and points to a different, perhaps more significant form of deposit. Their complete state suggests they were taken out of circulation during their working lives. This together with the fact that several were placed on or near the bottom of storage pits confirms the theory that pits were used for more than the disposal of unwanted material. They can also be contrasted with the deposition of complete but fragmented querns such as that found in Pit W035 at Cadbury Castle mentioned above. The latter was also removed from circulation but was broken prior to or upon deposition. Again this suggests a difference in meaning. No directly paired upper and lower stones of rotary querns, such as those found together, for example, in a pit within the large hillfort of Danebury or in the oppidum of Pandours à Saverne, France have been recovered (Figures 1.5; 1.8) (Cunliffe 2003, figure 77; Jodry and Féliu 2009, 70-72). However, a saddle quern and rubbing stone from a pit at Tyning Quarry, Radstock in Somerset may have been worked as a pair and likewise one or both rubbers from Pit D838 at Cadbury Castle may have been used with the complete saddle quern found in the same pit. The same may also have been so of the rubbers and saddle quern from Pit A at Blaise Castle Hill, Bristol which were found in different layers (McMurtrie 1899, 115; Cadbury Castle Archive; Rahtz and Clevedon Brown 1958-1959, 156-157). The latter saddle quern was found upside down at the base of the pit (Figure 8.5). Its inverted position suggests that it was purposefully placed in a gesture of closure at the bottom of the 1.32m deep pit.

A complete upper rotary quernstone was also found near the base of another pit at Tyning Quarry (McMurtrie 1899, 110). Its concave grinding surface was worn, with evidence of concentric rings of wear but the stone is still some 13-15 cm thick and, with a handle slot across the top rather than in the side of the stone, apparently still usable. The state of the quern together with its location at the bottom of the pit again indicates that it was meaningfully and purposefully deposited with the intention of removing it permanently from its working life. Several complete or near complete rotary quernstones were also found at Ham Hill including an upper and a lower stone found together in the lowest fill of pit 108. The two stones were, however, from different querns and, like the saddle quern from Pit A at

Blaise Castle, both were placed in an inverted position (Leivers *et al* 2007, 44). The two stones were not only, therefore, rendered practically inoperable by separation from their respective partners but also symbolically so by being placed upside down. The deposition of these two quernstones is clearly of particular significance. It is also of note that comparatively few complete or near complete quernstones have been recovered from pits at Cadbury Castle again suggesting that their deposition was in response to or the result of a particular circumstance. Exceptions are a lower stone of a rotary quern from pit P758 and saddle querns from pits D838 and C655. The latter also incidentally contained horse and ox skulls (Cadbury Castle Archive).

Contrasts in meaning can be seen, therefore, in the deposition of whole versus fragmentary querns in pits. In addition, the fact that not all pits contain querns suggests that there were also particular reasons for depositing querns within certain pits. The low rate of deposition also indicates that this was not an everyday random event but one that had purpose and meaning, although the reasons and thus the specific meaning for the deposition will have varied. It is also clear that not all pits were dug as storage pits. Some pits may have been used as part of craft processes such as tanning, pottery or metalworking and the fill of such pits may reflect those crafts. Other pits appear to have been dug specifically for the curation of certain artefacts or for the safe and/or ritualistic disposal of material or for the deposition of foundation or abandonment deposits. Different categories of fill can also be discerned in storage pits, as commented upon by Hill, Alcock and others. Some storage pits were filled in a single episode, others contain distinct layers, some contain apparent special deposits, others do not. These variations indicate that different storage pits were used for different depositional events and returns to Hill's (1995, 110-111) suggestion that the filling of pits was not necessarily related to their original function. Indeed some may never have been used as storage pits. Nevertheless, the link between querns, grain and the symbolic transformation from life to death or death to life seems too strong for there not to have been a connection. This must be seen as especially so on those occasions where a quernstone is deposited at the bottom of a storage pit, forming part of the first deposit within that feature.

8.3.5 Fogous
At least eight quern fragments have been found in association with fogous, artificially constructed underground passages found in the West Penwith area of Cornwall. The fragments were either utilised within the construction of the fogous or found amongst the occupation deposits. Fragments from a rubber and a saddle quern, the latter apparently deliberately broken, were also found incorporated within one of the two lines of stones leading towards the Early Iron Age fogou at Boden Vean. These are possibly the remains of a timber roofed section of the fogou or an unfinished extension (Gossip and Johns in press; Quinnell in press a). The querns probably derived from earlier, Bronze Age activity on the site. At Carn Euny, an Iron Age and Roman settlement site, a broken saddle quern was reused as a paving stone on the north-west side of a round underground chamber attached to the west side of the fogou by a short passage. The 4.6m diameter chamber was constructed within a large pit and would have been roofed originally. The roof would have projected above the ground, perhaps looking rather like a small barrow. Sherds of decorated pottery found under the paving date the chamber's construction to the 5th century BC, prior to the building of the earliest timber structures on the site and the fogou passage (Christie 1965, 28; Anon 1974; Christie 1978, 321, 385). If the round chamber does indeed predate the foundation of the settlement then the saddle quern fragment will have been specially brought to the site for inclusion in the paving.

A different form of, but nevertheless still deliberate, deposition can be seen at Boden Vean. In addition to the quern fragments found within the line of stones mentioned above, a rubber fragment was also found in the silty deposits on the floor of the fogou along with pottery, a whetstone, a polished pebble and two ceramic beads. The nature of the finds and the manner of their placement together with the fact that the fogou was infilled shortly afterwards suggests that these were special deposits. The polished pebble, for example, was propped against one of the stone uprights while the rubber, a beach cobble of a hard Tregonning greisen is unlikely to have broken accidentally. The deposition of the ceramic beads, rare in themselves on Iron Age sites in southern England, is reminiscent of the two carnelian beads left on the floor of one of the roundhouses at Dean Moor when the latter was abandoned (Gossip and Johns in press; Quinnell in press a and b; Fox 1957, 42).

Different again is the deposition of a granite saddle quern at Treveneague fogou, St. Hilary, which was found amongst occupation debris together with a granite mortar, iron objects, human and animal bone and sherds of south-western decorated pottery[5] (Anon 1868-1870, 69; Hencken 1932, 143). As noted previously, the filling of spaces with occupation or midden material is not without meaning above that of the mere disposal of unwanted material, a fact reinforced by the presence of human bone at Treveneague. Midden material, a source and symbol of fertility, may, therefore, have been shoveled into fogous with the same intent with which, it is suggested, it was used for the infilling of Scillonian entrance graves; as an offering to the ancestors or gods to increase the fertility of the land (Ashbee 1976, 21-23; Thomas 1985, 140-142). The presence of quern fragments in such deposits is probably largely coincidental but the possibility of the deliberate salting of midden material must be considered, given the querns' symbolic association with grain and fertility (after McOmish 1996, 75). A saddle quern, three quern fragments and a number of rubbers were also apparently found in association with the alleged fogou at Vyneck near Boscawen-un. The exact location and context of the querns within the structure is unfortunately unknown. The fogou was destroyed pre 1867 and the site has not been subsequently located (Anon 1868-1870, 71; Cornwall Historic Environment Record Monument No. 28808).

Three distinct forms of deposition can be seen, therefore, in the presence of querns in fogous: the use of querns as construction material, the placement of a quern as a distinct gift or offering and its inclusion within a deposition of midden or occupation material. All would have been intended as permanent closed deposits. The function of fogous is still unclear, however, although several theories have been advanced to account for their presence including storage spaces, hiding places and places for esoteric ritual activities (Clark 1961, 136-138; Quinnell 1986, 118-119; Wood 2000, 102). However, as Quinnell (1986, 119) comments, it is the modern western mind that tends to compartmentalise activities and fogous may have fulfilled both secular and religious functions. Hill's (1995, 110-111) suggestion that the location of a site below ground may have been more relevant than its function may also be pertinent here.

8.3.6 Middens
In addition to the querns found within the occupation and midden material used to infill fogous, ten querns on the database were also found in general midden layers. Of these, nine came from the 'rubbish layer' at Cadbury Castle which contained many artefacts and animal bones. The tenth, a fragment of rotary quern, was found in a midden at Harlyn Bay in north Cornwall together with animal bone, hammerstones, spindle whorls, pottery, slate and shell implements and pottery (Barrett *et al* 2000-168; Cadbury Castle Archive; Bullen 1930, 81, plate 10). As mentioned previously middens were probably not considered as rubbish layers but rather as stores of useful material with potentially both practical and symbolic uses (McOmish 1996; Needham and Spence 1997). It follows, therefore, that the quern fragments found in middens were likewise put there with similar intents. The 'rubbish layer' at Cadbury Castle, however, was generally only a few centimetres deep and broadly overlay a cobbled surface and an area of hearths and ovens (Barrett *et al* 2000, 167-168). It is quite likely therefore that some of the quern fragments derived from these latter features.

8.3.7 Enclosure walls, banks and ramparts
Nine querns are recorded from enclosure banks and walls and from the ramparts of hillforts. Two saddle quern fragments were found in the stone-built bank around a Middle Iron Age enclosure at Trenowah, a rubber was incorporated within the construction of the bank on the eastern side of Trevarnon Round, Gwithian and a broken upper stone of a rotary quern was apparently also found in the wall of Castallack Round, Paul in West Penwith (Quinnell forthcoming; Thomas 1964, 38; Blight 1864-1867, 502). On hillforts, two rubbers were found in association with a rampart at Solisbury Hill Camp near Bath, while at Cadbury Castle part of a worn lower stone of a rotary quern was found in a layer within rampart C (Falconer and Adams 1935, 189; Cadbury Castle Archive).

Banks, walls and ramparts present a positive, above ground boundary separating one side from another, the outside from the inside. They are thus likely to have served both practical and symbolic functions. The ramparts of hillforts, although in their final state would have presented a formidable obstacle to would-be attackers, can also be seen as impressive status symbols, restricting and directing access into the interior of the fort. Likewise the function of enclosure walls and banks was probably more symbolic, in terms of delineation than defensive, although they may have also served the practical purpose of keeping animals out/in. The use of querns in the construction of such features may once again represent the functional reuse of convenient pieces of stone. At Trenowah,

---
5. The fogou at Carn Euny was also infilled with occupation or midden material containing a fragment of rotary quern. However, Samian pottery from the fill suggests that this infilling did not take place until the Roman period or later (Hencken 1932, 141).

for example, both fragments of saddle quern showed evidence of percussive use. This suggests that they had ceased to be used as milling stones at the time of their deposition in the enclosure wall and that they were perhaps considered to have reached the end of their use lives (Quinnell forthcoming). However, such utilisation also denotes the deposition of querns in contexts apart from the purely domestic scenario of the roundhouse. The strengthening of a bank or rampart also served to strengthen the cohesion of the community within. The practical use of querns in that work may also have indirectly symbolised that community through the people and households they represented.

8.3.8 Ditches

Twenty two querns included on the database came from the fills of ditches (Table 8.4). All but two of the querns were in a fragmentary condition and only three fragments were recognisable as being from rotary querns. The two complete quernstones were rubbers. Consequently, it is easy to understand why finds of querns and other artefacts in ditches have been viewed in the past as detritus (Winbolt 1929-1930, 162). However, as evidence from the Neolithic and Bronze Age periods demonstrates, ditches provided opportunities for depositional events. The presence of querns in Iron Age ditches should also be seen, therefore, as significant. They may, for example, have been placed as symbols representative of a particular household, community or territory or as symbols of the transformation that occurs when crossing from one side to another. The material for banks and ramparts usually derived from corresponding ditches. Ditches are thus the inverse of banks and ramparts. They likewise delineate a boundary but in penetrating the ground they create a liminal, potentially powerful space.

The ditches serve various functions including enclosure, field, linear and rampart ditches. Each type of ditch potentially tells a different depositional story. Of the nine querns found in enclosure ditches, for example, six came from the southern or south-eastern side of the respective ditch and another was found on the eastern side. At Blackhorse it was also noted that not only did the quern fragments and indeed the majority of artefacts found in the enclosure ditch come from its southern half but also the finds from the roundhouse gully (203) within the enclosure likewise came from its southern side (Fitzpatrick et al 1999a, 221). This suggests that the deposition of quern fragments and other artefacts within the enclosure ditch were part of a planned process and not merely the disposal of unwanted material. Apart from the southern terminal the enclosure ditch showed little evidence for re-cutting and appears to have silted up naturally suggesting that its function was the symbolic rather than physical demarcation of a boundary (Fitzpatrick et al 1999a, 172-173, 193).

At Trenowah near St. Austell two fragments of saddle quern and a rubber were found in a linear ditch (65) extending on a north-west to south-east axis for at least 94.0m while at Langland Lane, east Devon three quern fragments were found in a ditch (167) running north-east to south-west across the site (Johns forthcoming, 134; Mepham 1999). Ditch 65 at Trenowah, dated to the Early Iron Age, was subsequently replaced and it is suggested that it represents a major land boundary, perhaps cutting across earlier land divisions (Johns forthcoming). Ditch 167 at Langland Lane is likewise at a different angle to the other ditches on the site and may have also been a boundary ditch (Fitzpatrick et al 1999a, 131). Johns (forthcoming) noted that ditch 65 at Trenowah, like the enclosure ditch at Blackhorse, had filled gradually. Ditch 65, however, was then replaced by a new ditch suggesting that although the ditch was a depositional access point, its function as a visible boundary marker was also clearly of import.

At The Moor, near Cadbury Castle, an earlier ditch was also found to have been recut and extended in the Middle Iron Age (F001). However, the later ditch had been rapidly filled with rubble. A quern fragment was associated with this rubble (Tabor pers. corresp.). This once again raises the question as to whether the quern fragment was a handy piece of stone with which to help fill the ditch or if the rubble was 'salted' with the quern. The fact that the ditch at The Moor also contained human bone perhaps implies that the quern should also be viewed as a special deposit, as suggested in the previous chapter for the Bronze Age ditches at Sigwells.

Likewise at Ham Hill two pieces from the upper stone of a rotary quern and a fragment from another quernstone were found in broad association with a skeleton found in the rampart ditch on the east side of the spur (Gray 1925, 65). Gray presumed that the man had died as a result of being injured in battle and that the body lay where it came to rest in the ditch (Gray 1925, 65-66). However, the crouched position of the body lying on its side suggests that this is a formal burial (Whimster 1977, 318). Taking Hill's (1995, 100) suggestion on board, if one accepts that the body in the ditch represents a proper burial then

8.3.9 Human burials

Fourteen querns have been found in association with human burials and depositions of human bone from eight different contexts on as many sites (Table 8.5). Although a low number compared with the number of known Iron Age burials in the south-west it nevertheless demonstrates that the association continued to be an important one to make. The association varies, however, from one context to the next. Two rubbers and a saddle quern came from the fill of the fogou at Treveneague within which human bone was also apparently found. The deposits at Read's Cavern and within a ditch at The Moor also included pieces of human bone but these finds can, on present evidence, only be loosely associated (Hencken 1932, 143-144; Palmer 1919-1920, 9-20; Tabor pers. corresp.). The complete lower stones and fragment of human cranium found in the same layer of Pit P758 at Cadbury Castle on the other hand must have been placed as part of the same depositional event (Cadbury Castle Archive). A different form of association can be seen at Crig-a-Mennis near Perranporth in north Cornwall where a fragment of granite rotary quern together with two greenstone rubbers or pounding stones were found in the ditch fill on the west side of a Bronze Age barrow (Christie 1960, 86). These particular fragments are to be associated with Iron Age activity at the site suggesting that the site continued to be venerated after it had ceased to be used for burials. The rubber fragments found in association with an Iron Age grave at Trethellan Farm, Newquay, Cornwall, on the other hand, are probably unintentional, derived from the Bronze Age settlement that underlay part of the cemetery (Nowakowski 1991; Trethellan Farm Archive).

At Ham Hill, as mentioned above, an articulated adult burial was found in one of the rampart ditches on the east side of the north spur (Gray 1925, 65). As a deliberate act of burial, it raises the possibility that artefacts also found in the ditch were similarly the result of purposeful depositions (Hill 1995, 100). These included an ox skull and boar tusk at the bottom of the ditch and at a depth of 1.37m, perhaps about 1m above the skeleton, half the upper stone of a rotary quern. There does not appear to be a direct relationship between the quern and skeleton, however, and they probably belong to separate depositional events. The combination of finds is similar to that found in storage pits and it is also possible, therefore, that the later deposits were placed with reference to the burial.

The lack of human burials in pits containing querns was commented upon above. This appears to contradict Hill's statement that 'putting quernstone fragments and human remains in the same pits seems to have been a particularly important association to make' (Hill 1995, 55). However, Hill goes on to suggest that this association is with infant rather than adult burials. In keeping with this theory, a quern fragment was found in the upper fill of a pit (F011) at Sigwells which also contained a neonatal infant and a young lamb. Stones and sherds from two broken pots were placed over the bodies, in a similar way to the raven burial mentioned above, and over these the quern fragment was placed (Tabor 2008, 135; SCEP Archive). As currently the only example of an articulated human burial and related quern deposition within the study area, pit F011 must be considered unusual.

8.3.10 Cave deposits

As mentioned above, ten saddle querns and rubbers have been recovered from the occupation deposits of various cave dwellings in the south-west. A different inflection, however, can be put on the complete upper and lower stones of a rotary quern that were used, with other stones, to block off the entrance to a small cavity on the west side of the Great Cave at Wookey Hole (Balch 1914, 181). Nothing was apparently found in the cavity but it could have contained an organic 'offering' which has long since decayed. The stones were subsequently shown to be still in working order (Balch 1914, 102; Long 1931, 24). Once again complete and usable stones had been taken out of everyday use, their secondary use for blocking the cavity clearly taking priority over their primary use as grinding stones. This is also one of the few examples of an upper and lower stone deposited together.

8.3.11 Watery deposits

Two complete lower stones were found outside the encircling palisade at Glastonbury, essentially a large crannog, in what would have been swamp. One was found to the east of Mound 57 and the other at the southern end of the causeway (M47), also off the eastern side (Figure 8.3) (Bulleid 1917, 612, 615). There are a number of reasons to potentially account for their location such as post-depositional movement due to flooding or contemporary accidental loss during the loading or unloading of a boat. A number of other items of interest, however, were also found outside the palisade including seven human skulls, a bronze bowl, a bronze mirror and tweezers, a decorated wooden box and two iron currency bars (Coles and Minnitt 2000, 61, 143, 203). As Coles and Minnitt (2000, 143) comment, it is unlikely such items were thrown away or lost and they probably, therefore, represent structured deposits. The two lower stones may also have been dropped into the swampy water as deliberate offerings of some form. The casting of metalwork into rivers and bogs is a well-known phenomenon of the Iron Age and it may be that the items found outside the palisade at Glastonbury were made with a similar watery intent. However, Hingley's research noted that iron currency bars, for example, are also frequently met with on dry land, at settlement boundaries (Hingley 1990, 101). The items at Glastonbury may, therefore, represent boundary rather than watery deposits, or perhaps a conjoining of the two as both forms of depositional context represent liminal states.

8.3.12 Quern quarries
Finally, two unfinished lower stones from a quern quarry at Ashton Court Park, Bristol are also included on the database. The location of the two roughouts, at the foot of a steep-sided hill, appeared to be of fairly recent date as piles of waste flakes showed signs of recent scattering (Barford 1984, 13-14). It seems, therefore, that they had originally been left amongst other waste material at the quarry. Quern roughouts and blanks are not uncommon finds at quern quarries, examples having been found at Rivelin and Wharncliffe in South Yorkshire and Lodsworth in West Sussex (Wright 1988; Peacock 1987). These have generally been taken at face value, as broken and/or unwanted stones. However, it has been recently suggested (Heslop 2008, 45) that the leaving of apparently still usable roughouts at quarries should also be seen as a form of structured deposit. Heslop further suggests that some partly-made querns were also deliberately broken and left, such actions firmly locating the manufacture of querns within the ideology and behavioural practices of contemporary society (Heslop 2008, 45-46). The leaving of both complete and fragmentary stones at quarries, therefore, follows or rather prequels similar practices seen on settlement and other sites. These depositions were made at the very start of a quern's life history and are not so much to be related to the quern as a milling tool but rather to the process of its manufacture. This is a potentially dangerous task and as suggested in Chapter Three offerings may have been made for the safe working of the quarry or as an act of propitiation after an accident. Alternatively, they were thank offerings for the gift of the stone itself.

8.3.13 Associated artefacts
The nature of the other artefacts found in association with quern depositions has been touched upon in the sections above, particularly with reference to pits. As in the Bronze Age the majority of artefacts are broadly domestic in nature including animal bone, baked clay, charcoal, flints, plant remains, pottery, rubbing stones, slingstones, spindle whorls and whetstones. The association in some contexts such as occupation layers, cobbled surfaces and middens can only be described as loose and is probably largely unintentional. However, there are also several notable combinations of objects.

1. Craftworking deposits
The broad association of a chipped and burnt rotary quernstone with the remains of a smithing hearth or furnace, slag, a tuyère and fragments of crucible in the lower levels of Mound 5 at Glastonbury suggest that the stone had been used as a work surface (Bulleid 1917, 615; Coles and Minnitt 2000, 36-37). A similar collection of artefacts comprising metalworking debris including tuyère fragments, a broken crucible, pottery and a very hard quartz cobble rubber were also found in the gully of Structure 6 within the later Iron Age open settlement at Higher Besore, Truro while in Structure 1 the density of hearths and pits together with fragments of iron ore found in one of the hearths and rubber, whetstone and other rubbing stone fragments in another suggest that the building was used for metalworking and other industrial and craft processes (Quinnell and Taylor forthcoming; Gossip forthcoming). Bone and antler tools, fragments of bronze and iron, a whetstone, charcoal and burnt stone found with a complete saddle quern in a Middle Iron Age gully N954(E724) at Cadbury Castle likewise demonstrate the industrial nature of the working area that the gully bounded (Barrett *et al* 2000, 166, figure 84). Slag, a crucible fragment and hearth lining together with a fragment of saddle quern were also found in pit F303 and evidence from other nearby pits including terret and bridle bit moulds are indicative of bronze casting on this part of the plateau (Barrett *et al* 2000, 298; Cadbury Castle Archive). At Chun Castle, Cornwall, evidence for both bronze and tin

smelting was found and it is possible that a worn rubber[6] found near the furnaces had been used for grinding ore (Leeds 1926-1927, 222, 239).

2. Deposits of stone

The collection of stone artefacts in a pit at Trenowah in Cornwall (Johns forthcoming), as mentioned above, probably represents a craftsman's tools (Figure 8.7). A stone-filled pit that also contained two fragments of rotary quern and a whetstone was found at Mount Folly Farm in Devon. The positioning of the quern fragments, as indicated above, on the east side of the pit and the fact that only part of the quern was included suggests that this is a purposeful deposit of some form although its meaning eludes us now (Figure 8.8) (Watts, S. 2007a).

3. Animal and human burials

The placement of querns with animal skulls in the fill of disused storage pits are notable features at Ham Hill and Cadbury Castle (Leivers *et al* 2007; Cadbury Castle Archive). It is not an inevitable association, however, and it may be of import that it occurs towards the later Iron Age. Such a combination may have been symbolic of death and fertility. The raven and quern burial at Sigwells possibly had a similar symbolism (Figure 8.6) (Watts 2008b). Different again and different to each other are the combinations of artefacts including animal bone found in pits F040 and F011 also at Sigwells. Pit F040 is seen as a foundation deposit containing sherds from a large storage jar, a burnt ammonite and a bag of cremated sheep bone. The deposit is reminiscent in character of the foundation deposit recorded beneath the post ring of a Middle Bronze Age roundhouse at Scarcewater, Cornwall (Tabor 2008, 133; Tabor pers. corresp.; Jones and Taylor 2010, 19, 73). Pit F011 represents the only pit in the study area to contain a human burial and quern together. A lamb and neonatal infant were placed at the bottom of the pit and their bodies covered with rubble stone over which two, probably broken, pots were laid followed by a fragment of quern. The pit then appears to have been left and gradually filled in before an old brooch was placed some time later in a depression in the top of the pit (Tabor 2008, 135; Tabor pers. corresp.). A human burial and quern were also found in a rampart ditch at Ham Hill but appear to have been placed at different times, the quern being much higher in the ditch fill.

The different combinations of artefacts demonstrate that not only are we witnessing different levels of structured deposit but also that depositions were made within the same form of context for different reasons. Each deposition, although all will have drawn from the same underlying cosmology, has a different story to tell. Subsequent depositions in multi-layered pits represent later placements although each may have drawn upon the memories or invested power of earlier deposits. The brooch at the top of pit F011 at Sigwells, for example, is likely to have been placed with reference to the infant and lamb burial below it.

8.4 Discussion

Given the increase in cereal production in the Iron Age, a corresponding increase in the number of querns recovered from Iron Age contexts compared to those of the preceding Bronze Age is perhaps to be expected. The number of sites producing querns in structured contexts is also higher, 64 compared to 46. The barrenness of a large tract of the south-west, namely east Cornwall, west and north Devon and Exmoor, in terms of quern deposition was commented upon in Chapter Five. Distribution maps of hillforts and enclosures show that the land was generally well occupied during the Iron Age and into the Roman period (Griffith and Quinnell 1999c, figures 7.1, 7.4; Riley and Wilson-North 2001, figure 3.1) and the absence of querns from these areas could, therefore, be largely due to a lack of excavation. However, the possibility that the absence could prove to be genuine must also be considered. The Culm Measures which underlie much of mid and west Devon and eastern Cornwall, for example, give rise to heavy, difficult to work soils traditionally used for pasture rather than arable while Dartmoor is considered to have been largely deserted at the beginning of the 1st millennium BC, perhaps due to climatic deterioration and thereafter used mainly for summer grazing (Welldon Finn 1967, 292; Hesketh 2008, 8; Quinnell 1994, 76; Fitzpatrick 2008, 125).

The high number of Iron Age querns, which at 633 is almost twice the total of the 322 querns found within Bronze Age contexts, is, however, largely the result of archaeological causation. Extensive excavations at the two Meare Lake Villages and Cadbury Castle recovered 279 and 129 querns from Iron Age contexts respectively. Without those sites the number of Iron Age querns is actually lower than the number of Bronze Age querns which, coupled with the increase in the number of sites from 46 to 64, suggests a decrease in the number of querns in use, or rather being deposited in the archaeological

---

6. The rubber is not included in the database as no details of the context in which it was found are given.

record, during the Iron Age [7]. These figures, however, have more to do with excavation strategies than reality. Comparatively small areas have been excavated at some sites, particularly the larger promontory forts and hillforts such as The Rumps, Cranbrook Castle and Blaise Castle Hill. At other sites, such as Berrywood Hillfort near Newton Abbot, Devon and Gurnards Head on the north Cornish coast, the lack of primary contextual detail led to the exclusion of querns from the database. The decrease is in any case belied by the concentration of querns at just a few key sites of very different character which implies that querns continued to play an integral and important role in the lives of Iron Age peoples.

A greater proportion of the querns found in Iron Age structured contexts were broken (at least 65%), compared to the Bronze Age (48.7%). This suggests an increased tendency towards the deliberate breakage of quernstones in the Iron Age given that they are not items easily broken by accident (the proportion of fragmentary Neolithic querns was also incidently higher than that for the Bronze Age at 57%). The fragmentation of querns appears part of a wider general practice. Curwen, for example, noted the small size of the fragments of Iron Age querns at The Trundle, Sussex and suggested that this was the result of deliberate breakage (Curwen 1929, 63) while at Danebury, Hampshire two pieces from the same quernstone were found in different pits (Poole 1995, 262).

Most finds are of individual quernstones, a feature noted also of Neolithic and Bronze Age depositions. Fragments from different querns, or non-matching upper and lower stones are also, as implied above, occasionally found within the same context but only seven pairs of stones are recorded. These depositions can be seen as particularly significant, therefore. One of the most important depositions appears to be a foundation deposit at Glastonbury comprising a saddle quern and rubber, of a stone type unique to the site, placed almost within the centre of the settlement. Only one of the pairs comprised a complete rotary quern which was placed at the entrance to a small cavity in Wookey Hole. The quern was still usable when found and had clearly been chosen as a sealing deposit, although the reason why the cavity was closed is unknown. The deposition of the upper and lower stones from two different rotary querns in a pit at Ham Hill can also be seen as particularly important and meaningful, doubly so as they were placed in an inverted position near the bottom of the pit. Similarly, at Blaise Castle Hill a saddle quern was placed upside down at the base of a pit. These are gestures of closure, their inversion taking them out of the everyday realm. Several complete stones were also incorporated within the make-up of floors at Glastonbury and Meare. As in the Bronze Age it appears that querns and other artefacts were left broadly *in situ* rather than be retrieved when restructuring and rebuilding took place. Again contrasts can be made between the deposition of complete and fragmentary stones. The former, although worn, are generally not worn out and were clearly removed from their primary milling role for use as structured deposits. The latter may also have been taken out of circulation but were broken, probably deliberately, given the size of some of the fragments, prior to deposition.

It is also noticeable that the greater proportion of rotary quernstones found in structured contexts are upper stones. The higher number of upper stone fragments, which account for 56% of the total number of rotary querns, may be due to the fact that upper stones, with their larger and completely perforating central eyes, are comparatively easier to break than lower stones. Many upper stones also evidence wear on the grinding surface through to the handle hole. At this point the stone may have been determined to have reached the end of its use-life. Alternatively, the deposition could have more symbolic than practical connotations; the upper stone is the live, moveable stone potentially representative of the task in hand, the person who used it, of transformation or the circular movement of the heavens.

Saddle querns and rubbers are found in structured contexts throughout the Iron Age but there does appear to be a drop in their deposition in the Late Iron Age which coincides with the introduction and gradually increasing use of the rotary quern. The complete saddle quern found in a Late Iron Age pit (D838) at Cadbury Castle may, however, have still been in use prior to its deposition. Likewise, the two complete saddle querns from the late and final phase contexts of Mounds 6 and 32 at Glastonbury Lake Village suggest that they were left *in situ* when the site was abandoned (Cadbury Castle Archive; Coles and Minnitt 2000, 38, 62; Bulleid 1917, 616, 618). Indeed, although beyond the scope of this book, finds from sites such as Trethurgy, Cornwall demonstrate well that saddle querns continued to be used in the south-west into the Roman period (Quinnell 2004, 151). Fragments of saddle querns and rotary querns are also occasionally found together in Mid-Late Iron Age contexts. Kiln E982 and pits L152 and P758 at Cadbury Castle, for example, all contained

7. These figures do not include find spots.

fragments of both suggesting that their deposition and by extension their use ran concurrently, although quernstones could have been kept aside once they went out of use for deposition at a later date (Bellamy 2000, 313; Cadbury Castle Archive).

Many of the contexts appropriated in the Bronze Age such as pits, ditches, gullies and postholes continued to be used in the Iron Age. Querns also continue to be found in occupational layers and deposits. Barrows ceased to be used for burial in the Late Bronze Age but fragments of rotary quern found in the ditch surrounding a barrow at Crig-a-Mennis in north Cornwall indicates that these sites were still venerated. On the other hand the formalised abandonment processes seen on Bronze Age sites which frequently included querns do not seem to be apparent on Iron Age settlements. Nevertheless there is evidence, as noted above, for the leaving and covering over of occupation layers. Some regional variation is apparent, largely dictated by geology. Large storage pits are only found in the east of the region. The location of two new depositional contexts that come into play in the Iron Age are also determined by geology: Cornish fogous and the caves of Somerset and Devon. Their underground settings may have been considered significant (after Hill 1995, 110-111).

Some patterning is also apparent in the location of quern deposits with a trend towards deposition in postholes within the northern half of structures and in the southern half of roundhouse gullies and enclosure ditches. However, the dataset is rather small at present and more evidence is needed to confirm or refute this theory. Elsewhere in the country at Dalton Parlours, Yorkshire and Beaumont Leys, Leicester, for example, querns have been found in postholes in both the north and south sides of roundhouses and particularly in entranceways (Buckley and Major 1990, table 2 and 3; Thomas 2008b). In the south-west, however, a lower proportion of the querns is found in association with roundhouses and instead more emphasis seems to have been placed on depositions within the wider settlement. This trend is also noticeable at Glastonbury where querns tend to be located in association with working areas rather than dwellings. Likewise at Meare there are concentrations of querns within particular mounds which are interpreted as communal activity and food producing areas. On other sites the majority of pit and posthole deposits are external to roundhouses and more querns are found in boundary ditches and banks compared to the Bronze Age. Two lower stones found outside the palisade at Glastonbury are also interpreted as boundary deposits. This increase coincides with the wider growing importance placed on boundaries in the Iron Age as shown by depositions of metal hoards elsewhere in the country (Bradley 1987, 351; Hingley 1997, 15). Heslop (2008, 75) also noted an increased emphasis on boundary features in the deposition of beehive querns in the north-east of England in the Iron Age.

The occupation mounds of the Lake Villages of Glastonbury and, in particular, Meare account for a large number of querns, 55 and 279 respectively. These high figures are in part due to the extensive excavations that were carried out in the late 19th and 20th centuries but also show how important querns were in the lives of the people who occupied these sites. Most of the querns from these two sites are thought to have been reused in the construction of the clay floors but evidence for discrete groupings, the leaving of apparently reusable stones when new floors were laid and, importantly, a foundation deposit all point to individual depositions. Elsewhere, pits continue to be important depositional contexts, despite the fact that querns are found in just a small proportion of the total number of excavated pits within the study area. The pits were dug for a variety of reasons, including storage, cooking or for various industrial processes and, as examples from Sigwells and Trenowah show, some were dug purely to receive the artefacts placed within them.

The state of the querns as found and the accompanying artefacts also demonstrate well that once again different levels or categories of deposit can be found within the same or similar features. This is shown particularly well in the fill(s) of pits. Some pits were filled as a single event, others have distinct layers (these latter are found only within the larger storage pits in the east of the region). Querns and artefacts found in the same layer or within a single fill are clearly related in some way whereas those from other layers may belong to quite separate depositional events. This could well explain why querns are found in some pits and not others and with certain objects in some pits but not others. Nevertheless, in the eastern part of the study area it is not uncommon to find animal skulls and querns in the same storage pit, a combination that has been noted (Hill 1995) on other sites in southern England although this was not an invariable practice. There is also evidence to suggest that these tend towards the later Iron Age. However, on present evidence the placement of a quernstone in the same storage pit as an inhumation is a rare occurrence in the study area.

The only example currently known is that of an infant and quern fragment in a pit at Sigwells.

8.5 Conclusions

As in the Neolithic and Bronze Ages the depositional locations utilised for the structured deposition of querns in the Iron Age appear to follow the development and changing trends of society with an increased emphasis on depositions in the wider community and on communal sites such as hillforts.

Depositions of complete and potentially reusable stones appear to be of particular import although unusual combinations of artefacts that include fragments of quern show that the latter could also form part of significant deposits. It is also notable that, as in the preceding Neolithic and Bronze Ages, the quernstones are generally deposited as single items. Although several stones or fragments thereof may be found in the same context they are rarely from the same pair. Consequently, the deposition of paired stones can be seen as of especial import. Once again, the fragmentary or complete state of the quernstone(s) upon deposition, the feature in which it was placed and the accompanying artefacts all point to depositions made with differing levels of intent and meaning. These differences are also apparent within the same type of feature and, in the case of multi-layered storage pits, even within the same feature. With the latter it is possible that each deposition, although relating to a separate event, was made with reference to that preceding. Each separate deposition has its own story to tell, even if we may not now understand that story. Such depositions may be:

- Made on a personal or collective basis.
- Made as offerings in gratitude, penitence, propitiation, exhortation.
- Made in memoriam or to mark an event.
- Made with reference to earlier depositional events.
- Safe storage.
- Constructional material.

The final chapter now looks back at the evidence presented in this and previous chapters for the structured deposition of querns and their importance to the communities that used them on practical and symbolic levels. Conclusions are drawn as to the extent to which querns recovered from prehistoric sites and structures were deliberately placed in the positions in which they were found and whether different categories or levels of deposit are discernible in the archaeological record. The chapter concludes by looking forward, suggesting topics and methods for future research that will further our understanding of the place of querns in prehistoric societies and their use as structured deposits.

9

CONCLUSIONS AND FUTURE DIRECTIONS

9.1 Looking Back

This research opened with a discussion of the concept of structured deposition, that is, the meaningful placement of objects in the archaeological record. It was acknowledged that there are reasons for the position of all artefacts as found in that record. It was also established that not all deposits were made with equal significance or levels of intent. Depositions can vary from the disposal of rubbish to abandoned occupation detritus to artefacts buried in response to, or as a result of, particular events and which were probably made with due ceremony. The latter deposits are likely to show a corresponding recognisable formality or structure in the choice of artefact(s) and/or their placement. Not all artefacts are deposited in structured meaningful ways, however. Those whose final resting places are due to chance loss or to contemporary environmental occurrences such as flooding or to post-depositional processes and movement whether man-made or natural cannot be considered as structured deposits.

A review of the published literature showed that quernstones are included amongst the categories of artefacts that were apparently deposited in structured, meaningful ways in the prehistoric period. A quern, however, comprises two stones but the literature suggests that the two are rarely found together and were, therefore, separated at some point prior to deposition. The literature also demonstrated that quernstones may be found complete or broken. It is suggested, therefore, that quernstones were deposited with different levels and layers of meaning and intent which can be determined by the condition of the querns as found in the archaeological record.

The reinvestigation of the history and development of the quern in Chapter Two highlighted the fact that the increase in the use of the saddle quern in the Levant *circa* 12,800-9,300BP coincided not only with the development of agriculture in that region but also with a shift to the consumption of meal-based products (Adams 1999; Wright 2000, 98; Dubreuil 2004, 1626).

This has potentially great significance regarding the symbolic meanings of querns. The saddle quern spread with farming across Europe and appears to have been amongst the suite of changes and innovations that marked the onset of the Neolithic period in Britain *circa* 4000BC, there being little evidence for querns in the Mesolithic period. The saddle quern, the form and size of which varies greatly, was to be the main means of grinding grain in Britain for over 2000 years. In the Middle Iron Age, however, *circa* 400BC the rotary quern was introduced. This was literally a technological revolution marking a change from forward and back to rotary motion that was to underpin the subsequent development of milling with stones.

Although the manufacture of querns is/was frequently undertaken by men, their operation, as illustrated in Chapter Three is/was very much the province of women. This chapter, which explored the object biography of querns showed that although they are personal tools, each with its own unique life history, all have points of commonality. They may be used for grinding many different products but are of vital importance at a daily subsistence level for grinding grains and other essential food stuffs. Consequently, it is easy to understand why in the prehistoric period querns were amongst the categories of artefacts frequently used in structured deposits. However, as explored in Chapter Four, there are a number of other potential meanings behind these depositions which again suggest that querns were deposited with different levels of meaning. Such depositions may, for example, be related to transformation, the turning of raw materials into usable products, symbolising the transition from one state to another as witnessed in agricultural and human lifecycles. Alternatively, they may be expressions of gender or denote the making or breaking of a relationship. They may also be offerings related to a specific event such as the harvest. In addition the adoption of the rotary quern is likely to have led to profound changes in the perceived moral value of the saddle quern and also to the creation of new mythologies and traditions related to its circular motion. The deposition of a quernstone may have drawn upon one or more unique or common values related to the circumstances of its manufacture and acquisition, its use or its symbolical meanings.

With these points in mind an analysis was undertaken of the querns and the contexts in which they are found on prehistoric sites in the south-west of England in order to investigate the extent to which they appear to have been deliberately placed. Is it possible to identify different categories of deposit that could be indicative of different levels of meaning and intent and can changes be perceived that may relate to spatial or temporal variations in practice?

9.2 Sites and Querns

The analysis was based on a dataset of 990 querns of which 33, 324 and 633 were dated to the Neolithic, Bronze and Iron Ages respectively. They were recovered from 104 sites and again an increase can be seen in the numbers of sites bearing querns from 12 in the Neolithic to 47 in the Bronze Age to 64 in the Iron Age (some sites are multi-period). The bias in the locations of sites in western Cornwall, Dartmoor and north-east Somerset was commented upon in Chapter Five. It was suggested that although the general lack of querns in areas such as north-east Cornwall, west and mid Devon could be due to the underlying geology the bias is also probably due to a lack of fieldwork. That gaps in the archaeological record can be quickly filled is well-demonstrated by the line of sites producing querns along the route of the new A30 in east Devon.

The low number of Neolithic querns appears to fit the suggestion that grain was not grown in any large quantities at this time. However, the ochre stain on a saddle quern from Ben Bridge, Somerset indicates that querns were also used for grinding products other than grain. In addition, the lack of visible settlements means that sites and consequently querns are frequently recovered through chance rather than design and it is likely, therefore, that the number of currently known querns is but the tip of the iceberg. Similarly, only one quern has been found in a securely dated late Neolithic context, at Tremough, Cornwall. This appears in keeping with the evidence from elsewhere in the country that querns are rarely found in grooved ware deposits (Quinnell 2007, 83). This could reflect a decrease in the use of querns in the late Neolithic which is thought to coincide with a reduction in cereal cultivation at this time. On the other hand, it could also indicate that it was generally not appropriate to include quernstones with depositions of grooved ware. This could be due perhaps to the uses to which grooved ware was put or to the time of year that such depositions were made. Undated querns such as the pair from Ben Bridge or the fragment found in Sperris Quoit, Cornwall could also be later Neolithic in date.

It is also noticeable, however, that just 9 out of 324 querns, were securely dated to the Early Bronze Age. Although some 34 querns can only be broadly dated to the Bronze Age, the majority of Bronze Age querns are dated to the Middle or Middle-Late Bronze Age. The large rise in both sites and numbers can be ascribed to the development and increase in visible, permanent settlements and cultivation at this time. The number of Iron Age querns, on the other hand, is much enhanced by the large numbers recovered from Meare Village West (199) and Cadbury Castle (129) in Somerset and without these two sites the average number of querns per site is actually less than for the Bronze Age, 4.75 compared to 7, with 2.75 querns per site for the Neolithic. However, it should be borne in mind that these figures are based on querns found in structured contexts; a number of querns from Berrywood Hillfort, Devon and Gurnards Head promontory fort in Cornwall for example were not included in the database due to the lack of original contextual information. Also, many large Iron Age hillforts and promontory forts such as The Rumps, Cornwall and Cranbrook Castle, Devon have only seen small-scale excavation. The figures are probably due, therefore, more to archaeological causation than prehistoric practice. What they do reflect, however, is the development of large communal sites in the Iron Age on which querns played an important part in the lives of the people using those sites.

The quernstones include 311 saddle querns, 352 rubbers and 140 rotary quernstones together with 187 indeterminate fragments (Figure 5.3). The higher numbers of saddle querns and rubbers compared to rotary querns does not occasion surprise given the 4000 years of their existence in the British prehistoric period compared to the mere 400 years or so of the rotary quern. The rotary quern was probably first used in the east of the region in the 4th century BC; a few were found in Early-Middle Iron Age contexts at Cadbury Castle (Cadbury Castle Archive), a date similar to that suggested for Danebury, Hampshire (Cunliffe 1995a, 69). However, present evidence suggests that it made a later appearance in Devon and Cornwall, in the 3rd-2nd century BC, or possibly even later. Interestingly, as mentioned in Chapter 2 a later Iron Age date is also currently proposed for the introduction of the rotary quern to Wales, Scotland and Ireland. The overall reduction in the numbers of saddle querns and rubbers found in structured contexts in the later Iron Age coincides with the introduction of the rotary quern.

9.3 Contexts of Deposition

The 990 querns derived from a total of 530 different contexts which can be grouped into 26 broad types. Most relate to settlement, occupation or activity sites but there are a small number of contexts from tombs and barrows suggesting that querns, domestic tools associated with the living, occasionally pervaded the realm of the dead. Querns are not only found in below ground, liminal features such as pits, postholes and ditches but also in upstanding, above ground features including walls, banks and ramparts and also in hearths and occupational layers. In addition, deposits may be open or closed. In those deposits that are open the artefacts may be removed or interacted with subsequent to their deposition. Caches fall into this category as may Iron Age storage pits containing several layers of deposit. Closed deposits necessitate the permanent removal of objects from sight and circulation.

Regional variations in the type of context used for the deposition of querns are largely dicated by geological and topographical factors. Certain features such as occupation layers and hearths appear universal. Pits are also found across the region with the exception of the low lying, water-logged sites of Glastonbury and Meare in Somerset and they are also uncommon on sites located on the granite bosses of Dartmoor, Bodmin Moor, West Penwith and the Isles of Scilly. The deeper, storage pits, so familiar on Iron Age sites in southern England, are only found on sites in the east of the region. Stone walled structures in upland areas such as Dartmoor, Bodmin Moor and West Penwith have stone walls that provide opportunities for above ground deposition not available in timber structures. Fogous are peculiar to Cornwall and cave dwellings are found in the limestone hills of the Mendips and in Torbay.

Querns from the Neolithic, Bronze and Iron Ages were found in 8, 21 and 21 of the 26 broad depositional contexts respectively (Figure 5.5). Given the low number of Neolithic querns together with the fact that half were recovered from pits or hollows a comparatively wide range of depositional contexts was embraced. Some forms of depositional context, such as pits, hollows, middens, occupation layers and hearths are found throughout the prehistoric period but others appear exclusive to one period. Depositions of querns in caves and drains, for example, are only known for the Iron Age and fogous too are Iron Age features. Comparison of the contexts of deposition between the Neolithic, Bronze and Iron Ages shows a broad change in the location of depositions on ephemeral activity areas related perhaps to short-term occupation coupled with those made on more permanent hilltop, tor and causewayed enclosures, to the concentration on settlements and particularly in association with roundhouses in the Middle Bronze Age to an increase in depositions made within the wider settlement and community in the Iron Age.

The 4000 years or so between the Neolithic period and the end of the Iron Age in Britain witnessed great changes in terms of human cultural development, encompassing the beginnings of pottery production and agriculture, the introduction of metalwork, firstly of copper and bronze and later of iron, and development and growth of small farming settlements and the construction of large earthen monuments from causewayed enclosures to henges to barrows to hillforts. It is also likely that the underlying cosmology that governed societies will have changed over time leading to alterations in the processes of deposition. The changes in depositional location preferences can be seen, therefore, to reflect those changes.

Hill (1995, 110-111) has suggested that it was the placing of objects within the ground that was important not necessarily the location. However, certain features provide opportunities for depositional events that are not possible within other features. Compare boundary ditches, for example, with storage pits. Similar objects may be present in each but their associated symbolism would have been different. Depositions in the former may have been related to the delineation and protection of boundaries and the crossing of one side to another, the latter to agricultural production, to plenty or want, to life and death. The location of particular features also appears to be important in their choice as depositional locations. A preference for postholes in the western and southern half of structures and in entranceways, for example, was noted in the location of quern deposits in Bronze Age roundhouses. It was also noted that certain Neolithic pit deposits were made in reference to landscape features such as those at Tregarrick Farm, Cornwall and Milsoms Corner, Somerset which focussed on Roche Rock and Cadbury Castle respectively (Coles and Jones 2002-2003, 136-

137; Tabor 2008, 44). Some later depositions appear to focus on earlier monuments. A pit at Meacombe near Chagford, Devon which contained neatly arranged pottery sherds beneath a fragment of saddle quern (Figure 7.8) appears to have been dug in relation to a Neolithic chambered tomb located 50m to the north-west, and a small Early Iron Age pit at Trenowah, Cornwall which contained a cache of stone tools (Figure 8.7) was situated close to a Bronze Age ritual hollow. The location of the latter, at a point where the sea is just visible, is seen as an important factor in the choice of site (Dyer and Salvatore 2011, 4; Johns forthcoming).

Most depositions of querns throughout the prehistoric period, however, were made in sites, structures and features related to the living. Very few querns, only 24 (2.4% of the total dataset) were found in or related to burial features. It appears, therefore, that there were certain aspects of prehistoric life in which querns were generally not considered as appropriate artefacts for use in associated depositional events. Where querns are found in funerary contexts they are the exception rather than the rule and must be considered important deposits on this basis. However, human bone has been found in conjunction with quern fragments on both Bronze and Iron Age settlement sites suggesting that the world of the dead occasionally crossed into the world of the living.

9.4 Categories of Deposition

In terms of the actual placement of querns in the archaeological record two primary depositional practices are consistently noticeable across the south-west throughout the prehistoric period and which accord with the evidence presented in the literature review for the wider picture beyond the study area. Firstly, although paired stones are occasionally found, upper and lower stones tend to be separated prior to deposition. Secondly, quernstones may be deposited as complete or broken stones. Following the criteria set out in Chapter One further categories of deposition can be determined from the condition of quernstones as found in the archaeological record together with the artefacts with which they were found. These it is suggested are indicative of depositions made with different levels of meaning and intent. Depositions of complete but individual stones, for example, imply differences in choice and pre-depositional treatment compared to those say of broken stones or paired stones.

9.4.1 Separation of upper and lower stones

The majority of quern deposits in the south-west are of upper or lower stones with few examples of paired stones being found. Stones from more than one quern, however, may be found within the same deposit such as the upper and lower stones from two different rotary querns in the same pit at Ham Hill, Somerset (Leivers *et al* 2007, 44). The separation of upper from lower stone appears to be deliberate, rendering the quern inoperative. This is demonstrated at Mount Folly Farm, Devon where two joining fragments from the upper stone of a rotary quern were found in one pit and a fragment of lower stone, thought to be from its partner, was found in another (Watts, S. 2007a). Although ethnographic evidence (Graham 1994, figure 26) indicates that saddle querns and rubbers may be stored in different places until they are brought together for the act of milling, a single stone cannot function without its partner. There are several reasons to account for the permanent separation of upper from lower stones. It may be to break the power of the quern or to protect the quern from unfriendly spirits or one stone may represent the whole. Alternatively, the stone may be representative of a particular person or gender. In 10th century Welsh law, in the event of a divorce, the husband was to receive the upper stone and the wife the lower (Bennett and Elton 1898, 162).

It is also noticeable that a far greater number of rotary upper stones are represented in the archaeological record compared to lower stones. This may be because upper stones wear quicker than lower stones – a number showed evidence of the grinding surface having worn through to the handle hole. Alternatively, the upper stone may be seen as representing a woman, the lower stone a man. It is also the live, working part of the quern, its rotary motion also potentially symbolising the turning of the heavens.

9.4.2 Pairs of stones

It follows, therefore, that deposits of paired stones were made with different reasons and meanings to those of individual quernstones. Only eight paired stones are recorded on the database of which only one pair is a rotary quern. At Ben Bridge a complete saddle quern of probable Neolithic date was found lying on its side with its rubber beside it (Rahtz and Greenfield 1972, 85). These were isolated finds with no associated contextual details but it is possible that they had been left at a campsite for future use, the saddle quern turned on its side in a position of protection. Moving to the Bronze Age, a saddle quern and two rubbers left in a pit at Trethellan Farm, Cornwall when a new floor was laid over the top are likely to have comprised a domestic milling kit. However, they were covered over when a new floor was laid suggesting they were left as a closure deposit (Nowakowski 1991, 21, 23). Several pairs of saddle querns and rubbers were also found at Glastonbury and Meare where they appear to have been incorporated within the make up of various mounds despite being potentially still usable. Of particular import is the saddle quern and rubber from the foundations of Mound 38 (Bulleid 1917, 617). Their location close to the centre of the site and their material, a non-local igneous rock, the only stones of this rock type found on the site, suggest that they were a foundation deposit. A saddle quern and rubber found, presumably together, in the Iron Age occupation levels at Wookey Hole, Somerset appear to have been left broadly *in situ*. However, the stones of a rotary quern were used to block off the entrance to a small cavity in the Great Cave at Wookey Hole (Balch 1914, 181). The quern was still in a usable condition when found (Long 1931, 24) and had clearly been taken out of use to close off the cavity. As the above examples show, depositions of paired stones were made for a variety of reasons within a range of different locations. Together they form a small, discrete group indicating a rather unusual, infrequent and variable but nevertheless consistent practice throughout the prehistoric period.

9.4.3 Quern hoards

In addition to pairs of stones, hoards of rubbers are also known from several sites in Cornwall dating to the Bronze or Early Iron Age and again the nature of their depositions indicates more than rubbish disposal. Six rubbers, of varying types of granite and elvan were found in a Middle Bronze Age pit at Scarcewater and three were found in another while another collection of six were found together with a broken saddle quern in a pit of similar date at Truro College. A collection of stone tools was also found in a small Early Iron Age pit at Trenowah (Figures 8.3, 9.7) (Jones and Taylor 2010; Gossip forthcoming 21, 25; Johns forthcoming). These can be seen as a specific form of deposition representing either a cache or an offering; the pit at Trenowah was dug in the same vicinity as a Bronze Age ritual hollow. Related depositions include the six or seven rubbers beneath a saddle quern in a pit within one of the roundhouses at Trethellan Farm which were placed as one of the final acts in the demolition and abandonment of the site (Figure 1.6) (Nowakowski 1991, 25). Again these could be a cache, symbolising the inhabitants' intention to return to the site. However, the site of the house was then covered with soil and it is perhaps more likely that the deposit was symbolic of the death of the settlement (Nowakowski 1991, 2008; after Brück 1999b, 155). Six rubbers were also found in one of the compartments of the main room of an Early Iron Age house on Nornour, Isles of Scilly. These were probably used with the three saddle querns found *in situ* in the adjoining 'kitchen' room (Dudley 1967, 5, 7) but the nature of their deposition is unknown and may relate to the subsequent use of the site in the Roman period.

9.4.4 Fragmentary versus complete quernstones

The number of fragmentary querns (657) recorded from structured contexts is almost twice the number of complete or nearly complete stones (333) (Figure 5.3). Quernstones are heavy, durable objects which do not break easily unless the rock from which they are made is flawed or they have worn exceptionally thin. Many of the quern fragments from the south-west, however, are from stones that although worn are not worn out and, therefore, appear to have been deliberately broken prior to deposition. How such fragmentation was achieved needs further research and empirical testing. It has been noted that many fragments of Devonian and Cornish querns show no apparent impact marks (R. Taylor pers. comm.). Heating a stone and then dousing it with cold water is one possible option. At the Trundle, Sussex, Curwen suggested that the quernstones may have been burnt to make breaking them easier, while at Trethellan Farm, Cornwall fragments from a burnt saddle quern were found in the levelling layers within one of the roundhouses (Curwen 1931, 145; Nowakowski 1991, 73). The contexts in which fragments are found such as pits, ditches, postholes, extant walls and stratified occupation layers preclude the possibility of post-depositional breakage caused by ploughing (topsoil and general surface finds were not included in the analysis). It is possible that some querns had been used in their fragmented state prior to deposition, others may have been broken up for practical reuse as building stone or as posthole packing but fragments are also found in larger features such as pits and ditches which raises the question of why they should have been broken, particularly as most had already been 'broken' by the separation of upper from lower stone.

With the location of some fragments in the archaeological record such as those recorded as found in occupation layers it is difficult to gainsay the nature of their deposition other than they represent everyday detritus. Their presence in these contexts is likely to be due to chance rather than planned in that they were probably simply left on or near to where they were last used or thrown. As such they cannot truly be called structured deposits. However, an occupation layer, and thus the artefacts within it, is transformed into a structured deposit when covered over as part of a rebuilding or abandonment exercise. Likewise, the use of midden material to fill a pit or ditch, for example, or as a levelling layer is also structured, although again the quern fragment within it may be accidental.

Other deposits, however, such as the fragments of a burnt saddle quern strewn through the levelling and demolition layers of a roundhouse at Trethellan Farm, the fragment of saddle quern found inverted in the centre of the infill of the ritual structure at Callestick, Cornwall or the fragment of rotary upper stone buried with a raven in an Iron Age pit at Sigwells, Somerset more clearly represent deliberate depositions made with meaning and intent (Nowakowski 1991, 73; Jones 1998-1999, 15; Tabor 2008, 139).

It is also noticeable that most depositions are of incomplete quernstones such as the three joining fragments of saddle quern found in different parts of the wall of an Iron Age roundhouse on Dainton Common, Devon or the two fragments of upper rotary quernstone placed in an Iron Age pit at Mount Folly Farm (Figure 7.8) (Willis and Rogers 1948-1952, 87; Watts, S. 2007a). This raises further questions of what happened to the missing pieces and why, if this were a simple matter of breaking up and disposing of/ reusing an unwanted item were they not all deposited/ reused together? Examples of fragments from the same quernstone being found in different features such as the joining fragments of saddle quern found in two different postholes within the Bronze Age metalworking structure at Sigwells or the joining pieces of rotary quern found in two different Iron Age pits at Cadbury Castle (a third piece was found within in the 'gunge' layer) further suggest that such breakage and separation was a deliberate act with pieces retained for subsequent use and deposition (Watts 2008b; Cadbury Castle Archive). Beyond the study area examples of joining fragments in separate pits at Boscombe Down West, Wiltshire and Danebury indicate that this was part of a wider practice (Richardson 1951, 161; Poole 1995, 262). Although it is possible that missing pieces remain buried in unexcavated areas of sites, it has been suggested (Chapman 2000b, 95) that quernstones were broken and pieces shared and taken off site thus creating links between people and place. If this was the case then it was potentially a practice with a long history originating in the Neolithic period. However, to date, no joining fragments from disparate sites have been identified.

Although the numbers of complete versus fragmentary stones is broadly comparable for the Neolithic and Bronze Ages there is a noticeable increase in the number of fragmentary stones, particularly saddle querns, deposited in the Iron Age compared to the number of complete stones (Figure 5.3). It was suggested in Chapter Eight that this increase suggests a greater tendancy towards deliberate breakage in the Iron Age and which may be part of a wider general practice. Curwen (1929, 63) commented on the small size of the fragments of Iron Age querns found at The Trundle, Sussex compared to those of the Neolithic period. However, of the 453 fragmentary querns from the south-west 173 come from the twin sites of Meare Village East and West of which at least 63 are saddle querns. Without these two sites the figures become more even. Meare is considered to be the site of a summer meeting place and the stones, either left from previous gatherings or brought specifically to site, may have been broken up for reuse in the construction and repair of the clay floors (Coles 1987, 143). It is also noticeable that 82% of upper rotary quernstones were broken compared to 53% of lower stones. The former are probably comparatively easier to break given the larger and completely perforating central eye but their fragmentation may have more to do with their symbolic meanings as mentioned above.

9.4.5 Complete quernstones

It is the deposition of complete stones, whether as individual stones or as part of a pair or hoard, that state most clearly that they represent more than the casual disposal of rubbish. Many although worn do not appear to be worn out and were, therefore, taken from their prime task of milling for use as structured deposits. Several types of deposit can be identified, in addition to pairs and hoards. Some complete lower stones of saddle querns or rotary querns, for example, appear to have been left *in situ* in their working positions (see below). The complete saddle quern found in a Neolithic cairn on Carn Brea, Cornwall may have been cached or intended as a special deposit, the cairn contained many stones of different, although local, geological origin (Mercer 1981, 79, 81). A single saddle quern found in a pit on the Neolithic site at Milsoms Corner is also thought to be cached (Figure 6.3). The upper and lower stones from two separate rotary querns in an Iron Age pit on Ham Hill or the red and green saddle querns placed side by side in the ditch of the Bronze Age metalworking enclosure at Sigwells, on the other hand, represent closed, permanent deposits (Figure 4.2). The bringing together of two separate stones is thought to represent a relationship of some form (Leivers *et al* 2007, 58; Tabor 2008, 44).

More complete rubbers, however, were found in structured contexts than saddle querns, 187 compared to 111. The difference is most noticeable for the Bronze Age with only 42 complete saddle querns compared to 102 complete rubbers (Figure 5.3). Many rubbers may have been deposited in a complete state by virtue of their small size or by the fact that they are more easily replaced than saddle querns although as mentioned above, hoards of rubbers are a feature of the Bronze Age. Also, more complete or near complete rotary lower stones were found (21) than upper stones (14). Their complete state may be due to the fact that they are harder to break than upper stones given their more solid nature.

It should also be noted that although many complete stones appear still capable of grinding a number have edges or corners knocked off them. Rather than wear and tear this could be deliberate slighting representing another form of fragmentation, perhaps rendering the quern 'safe'.

9.4.6 Querns in situ
Several saddle querns were found *in situ* in their primary working positions in roundhouses on Middle-Late Bronze and Early Iron Age sites. These include Stannon Down and Bodrifty in Cornwall and Nornour, Isles of Scilly (Figure 3.10) (Mercer 1970; Dudley 1956, 12; Dudley 1967, 5). In each case the quern was situated close to a hearth and it is this that appears to have determined their location rather than any cosmological influence (after Webley 2007). These querns appear to have been left when their respective houses were abandoned, perhaps with the intention of returning. The saddle quern found on the floor of a Middle-Late Bronze Age structure at Gwithian, Cornwall together with two wooden bowls and collections of stone tools were possibly in *situ* (Sturgess and Lawson-Jones 2006, 168). All were covered over by the floor of a new building suggesting they were left where they lay as a closure deposit. Similarly, at Glastonbury a saddle quern found on floor 4 of Mound 4 appears also to have been left *in situ* when the area in which it lay was covered over by part of another clay spread and a stone path (Coles and Minnitt 2000, 34-35). The complete lower stones of saddle querns and rotary querns dated to the late and final phases of occupation at Glastonbury Lake Village may also have been left *in situ* as activity on the site decreased. The lower stone of a rotary quern found in a round house in Cranbrook Castle may also have been left on or near to its last place of use while another from Trevisker in Cornwall was found inverted over its emplacement (Coles and Minnitt 2000, 38, 61-63, 33, 68, 71, 80; Baring-Gould 1901, 132; ApSimon and Greenfield 1972, 323). It is suggested that there was a taboo against retrieving apparently workable stones for reuse and that they were deliberately left as a form of memoriam.

9.4.7 Stone type
The majority of south-western querns are of rock types from within a 25km radius of the sites where they were found with many deriving from sources considerably nearer. Consequently, it is generally unlikely that the deposition of these querns in the archaeological record will have depended upon their material. There is an exception, of course. A saddle quern of local granite was found in a Neolithic cairn at Carn Brea which comprised stones of different geological sources (Mercer 1981, 79). The cairn may not have been a simple field clearance cairn, therefore and the saddle quern not stored within it for use in the field, as originally suggested (Mercer 1981, 81). Instead it may have been intended as a special form of stone deposit. Where querns derive from distant sources their deposition may be more clearly ascribed to their rock type, as representative of a relationship of some form. This is well-demonstrated at Sheep Slait, Dorset where a fragment of rhyolite saddle quern from either Dartmoor or north Cornwall was found in a Bronze Age ring ditch (Figure 7.4). Granite querns also from either Dartmoor or Cornwall were found at Cadbury Castle while at Glastonbury the complete saddle quern and rubber recovered from near the centre of the site and which, it is suggested, were a foundation deposit were likewise of an igneous rock from Devon or Cornwall. Similarly, at Sigwells a small saddle quern of igneous rock from a source some 40km to the west was found in the ditch of a Bronze Age metalworking enclosure together with another, larger, saddle quern of greensand from 15km to the east (Figure 4.2) (Tabor 2008, 65, 98; Roe 2000, 264; Bulleid 1917, 617). Generally, the means by which particular querns found their way to their respective sites, whether through trade/exchange mechanisms, by personal acquirement

or as part of a dowry, is unknown although the presence of quernstones of igneous or granitic rock on sites in Somerset is suggestive of a connection with the tin trade. A rubber of Corallian sandstone from the Westbury district of Wiltshire found with a more local saddle quern of Old Red Sandstone at Ben Bridge (Rahtz and Greenfield 1977, 202) is also suggestive of a relationship. The different colours of the two stones would have made a striking, potentially powerful and symbolic, combination as did the colours of the two saddle querns in the ditch at Sigwells mentioned above. The deposition of different coloured stones has been noted elsewhere, within the ditches of the Neolithic causewayed enclosure at Etton, Cambridgeshire and in a Bronze Age pit at Winnall, Hampshire for example (Pryor 1998a, 260; Chadwick Hawkes 1969, 6). Such stones, as discussed in Chapter Four, may have signified a relationship, the different colours denoting their origins or they may have been brought together to tell a particular story or symbolise a transformation of some form. Whatever the meaning behind their deposition, however, it is clear, that they were placed with deliberate intent.

9.4.8 Associated artefacts

That querns were deposited in the archaeological record with different levels of meaning and intent is shown not only by their location and condition but also through the artefacts found with them. The meaning behind the deposition of a particular object can potentially vary according to the other artefacts with which it is associated (Jones 2004-2005, 124-125). Artefact assemblages can be linked in a number of different ways. They can, for example, resemble one another in form, material or colour or represent a task or, more elusively, a person or place. Although the artefacts found in contiguity with querns were generally domestic in nature a number of depositions were also associated with craft activities such as metalworking or pottery manufacture such as at Combe Hay, Somerset and Gwithian suggesting that the quernstones found in those contexts may also have been utilised for grinding ore or temper (Price and Watts 1980, 13, microfiche 6.2; Sturgess and Lawson-Jones 2006, 168). Thus it appears that the contiguity of artefacts as seen during their use lives continued with their deposition in the archaeological record. However, querns are occasionally also found with more unusual, exotic or esoteric objects which raise the particular deposition and, therefore, the quern out of the ordinary, everyday. The quern fragment with a macehead and large pot sherds in a Bronze Age enclosure ditch at Old Rydon Lane, Exeter, the saddle quern fragment placed over neatly arranged pottery sherds in a Bronze Age pit at Meacombe, the rhyolite quern and quartz crystal in the terminal of a ring ditch at Sheep Slait and the raven and quern burial in a pit within an Iron Age enclosure at Sigwells and the querns found with animal skulls at Ham Hill are good examples (Figures 7.8, 7.4, 8.6) (John Moore Heritage Services 2010, 7, 55; Dyer and Salvatore 2011, 4; Tabor 2008, 98, 139; Leivers *et al* 2007). These unusual combinations of objects each relate to a specific depositional event, each telling a different story and although we may not understand what they are saying they nevertheless clearly signify that they are more than refuse deposits.

9.5 Part of the Wider Picture

As indicated in the literature review the use of querns as structured deposits is a world-wide phenomenon of the prehistoric and early historic periods. The practice of placing quernstones in the ground or reusing them in hearths or walls can be seen, therefore, to have a long history stretching back to the earliest use of saddle querns in the Neolithic of the Near East. Although there has been little comparative research on the scale of this research, other work in Britain on the structured deposition of querns and on structured deposition in general by Buckley (1993), Heslop (2008), Watts, S. (2008a), Hill (1995), Brück (2001; 2006), Webley (2207) and Pope (2008), for example, together with the information presented in individual site reports suggests that the depositional events observed in the archaeological record for the south-west represent localised applications and interpretations of a wider practice.

The choice of depositional locations observed elsewhere in the country appears determined by the organisation of, and changes and developments in, local social structure and in associated monumental construction together with the opportunities and restrictions enabled by local geology and topography. As in the south-west most depositions of querns occur on sites and settlements related to the living with few finds in relation to funerary monuments. Querns have been found reused in the construction of a number of Neolithic tombs in southern Britain, however, such as at Hampnett in Gloucestershire, Waylands Smithy in Wiltshire and Gwernvale, South Wales (Grimes 1960, 75; Whittle 1991, 87; Britnell and Savory 1984, 134). Although more research is needed they may prove to be an important exception. The lack of known depositions of Late Neolithic and Early Bronze Age querns commented upon for the south-west also appears to be part of a wider picture. Exceptions include a saddle quern on its side just within the edge of a pit containing Fengate Ware at Thirlings, Northumberland and a saddle quern and rubbers together with flint tools in a pit at Maddle Farm, Berkshire (Miket 1976, 119; Gaffney and Tingle 1989, 82, 86). These nevertheless seem to confirm the theory that querns are rarely found in contiguity with grooved ware deposits (Quinnell 2007, 83). Moving to the Middle-Late Bronze Age and Early Iron Age, Pope's research in northern England has shown that quernstones were often placed in the walls of stone-built roundhouses (Pope 2008) while in southern England evidence suggests that depositions of artefacts were made during the formalised demolition and abandonment of roundhouses (Webley 2007). Both practices are evident in the structured deposition of querns in the south-west implying that the use of querns in such processes is again part of a much wider practice. It is further argued (Webley 2007; Pope 2007; 2008) that the location of daily activities within Bronze and Iron Age roundhouses across Britain was governed more by practicalities than cosmology. This appears to be the case also in the south-west where quernstones found *in situ* are generally located close to a hearth.

One aspect of depositional practice that has been noticed in north-east England, however, but cannot currently be confirmed in the south-west is the deposition of one or more complete rotary quernstones in off-site locations (Heslop 2008, 68-80). It is possible that some stray finds of complete stones such as that from Thorn Farm, Chagford in Devon are examples of the practice but as Heslop (2008, 75) rightly states 'care should be taken when speculating about…less-securely provenanced finds'. Consequently, it is not possible to determine if the mutual exclusivity of off-site depositions of quernstones and Iron Age metal hoards noted by Heslop (2008, 79) in the north-east and also by Waddell (1998, 323) in Ireland also prevails in the south-west. However, both quernstones and currency bars were found outside the palisade of Glastonbury Lake Village (Coles and Minnitt 2000, 61, 143, 203). That such exclusivity may not be a universal pattern is also suggested by the complete upper and lower stones of a rotary quern found in loose association with an Iron Age sword at Willington, Derbyshire (Wheeler 1979, 144).

As in the south-west evidence can be found across England and Wales for structured deposits comprising complete or fragmentary quernstones and for single or multiple finds in the same context. Fragments from a broken quern in a pit within a roundhouse at Rowden, Dorset, for example, appear to relate to the clearing and demolition of the structure upon its abandonment (Woodward 1991, 45, 46). Fourteen fragments from at least two saddle querns were found in the posthole of a four-post structure within an Iron Age settlement at Sutton Common, Yorkshire while at Humberstone, Leicestershire an almost complete saddle quern and rubber together with several other quern fragments were found in the entrance posthole of an Iron Age roundhouse (Watts, S. 2007b; Thomas 2008c). Pieces from the same rotary quernstone have been found in two different pits at Boscombe Down West and Danebury (Richardson 1951, 161; Cunliffe and Poole 1995, 83, 262). At Bryn Eryr, Gwynedd the lower stone of a rotary quern together with a mortar were found *in situ* on the floor in the north-west quadrant of a roundhouse close to the central hearth (Longley 1998, 236). And finally, Heslop (2008, 75) noted that whereas beehive querns found off-site in the north-east tended to be complete those on settlements were more likely to be broken. These examples together with those above suggest that, in common with evidence from the south-west of England that the condition of quernstones upon deposition and the contexts in which they are found are indicative of deposits made with different levels of intent and meaning. However, there is more that can be done to further our understanding of the role that querns played within prehistoric society and their place in structured deposits.

9.6 Looking Forward
9.6.1 First impressions
In the past many details concerning a deposit were simply not recorded. It was enough to comment that a quern was found within a certain feature, details of the type, condition, size, orientation or location of the quern within that feature were often not considered. With modern standards of excavation and recording the situation is now much improved but there is still more that could be gleaned. Not only is the practical and technical on-site recording at the time of excavation of import but (following Pollard 2001, 317) observations concerning the aesthetic nature of the deposition should also be noted which may provide clues to its cause and intent. Does it, for example, have any 'alerting' qualities in terms of associated artefacts, the arrangement of objects or colour either of the artefacts or the surrounding soil matrix? At Sigwells, for example, a general red theme was noted to the objects found in the postholes of the structure within the Bronze Age

metalworking enclosure, while at Meacombe near Chagford, Devon it was seen that the large pot sherds beneath a fragment of saddle quern had been carefully stacked and arranged (Figure 7.8) (Tabor 2008, 69; Dyer and Salvatore 2011). The location of the feature within the site or in relation to the surrounding landscape may also be important. It is thought, for example, that the Neolithic pits at Tregarrick Farm, Cornwall were dug with reference to Roche Rock (Coles and Jones 2002-2003, 136-137).

It is appreciated, however, that within development-led archaeology, budget and time constraints may often make such impressionistic recording unviable. The location and orientation of a quernstone within the context or feature in which it is found should nevertheless be recorded as standard regardless of the completeness of the stone. It was the location of two fragments from the same (incomplete) rotary quern on the east side and at different levels within a pit at Mount Folly Farm that indicated that this was more than a pit simply back-filled with rubble when it went out of use (Figure 8.8) (Watts, S. 2007a).

9.6.2 Comparable surveys
As shown in the literature review the use of querns as structured deposits is a world-wide phenomenon of the prehistoric and later periods. The subsequent analysis of the contexts of deposition of querns in the south-west of England touched upon comparable examples elsewhere in Britain indicating, as mentioned above, that the practices observed are local enactments of a wider custom. However, also as mentioned above, there has been little comparable research elsewhere, although Heslop's (2008) work in north-east England has provided much useful comparanda. Analysis of the contexts in which querns are found and the condition in which they are found is also needed, however, for other areas. This would enable a more definitive observation of patterns and changes at regional and national levels.

9.6.3 Joining fragments
Chapman (2000b, 94) has suggested that quernstones were broken and the pieces shared, creating a link between people and place, a process he refers to as enchainment. This, he says, explains why querns found in the archaeological record are often incomplete. Fragments will have been retained for subsequent depositions made on the same site or taken off site for deposition elsewhere. Several examples of joining fragments from the same quern deriving from different features on the same site have been found within the study area and elsewhere, at Sigwells, Cadbury Castle, Boscombe Down West and Danebury, for example (Watts, S. 2008b; Cadbury Castle Archive; Richardson 1951, 161; Poole 1995, 262). The matching and rejoining of quern fragments from different sites is, however, a rather more difficult and time-consuming task and as yet no joining fragments from disparate sites have been located. It is suggested that in order to pursue this line of enquiry, a well-investigated study area be chosen, such as that covered by the Cadbury Castle Environs Project, where quern fragments from sites in the environs of the hillfort could be potentially matched with those found during excavations on the hillfort itself. The failure of such a project would not refute Chapman's theory. However, the rejoining of fragments from different sites would certainly prove that quern fragments were, on occasion, dispersed although the reason for that dispersal may continue to elude.

9.6.4 Use-wear analysis
The prime function of querns is as milling tools for grain but as mentioned in Chapter Three they can be used for grinding many different materials, vegetable, mineral and animal. Thus to automatically equate querns with agriculture is to under-represent the wealth of potential meanings associated with their deposition. Within the study area, the saddle quern found at Ben Bridge had the remains of ochre upon it (Rahtz and Greenfield 1977, 85). At sites such as Combe Hay and Gwithian the contiguity of quernstones and fragments to tools and equipment associated with metalworking and pottery manufacture respectively suggest that these particular stones were used for grinding ore or temper or were used as work surfaces (Price and Watts 1980, 13, microfiche 6.2; Sturgess and Lawson-Jones 2006, 19, 168, 187-188). Further analyses are needed, however, to clarify the use of querns in these and other cases. As Craddock (1995, 162) points out regarding the presence of querns on metalworking sites, 'even miners have to eat'.

One such method of determining past use is use-wear analysis. This is currently an undeveloped study in Britain but has been successfully used in the analysis of querns from sites in France, the Near East and Arizona (Adams 1988; Adams 1999; Dubreuil 2004; Hamon 2008b; Adams *et al* 2009). Use-wear analysis comprises the macro- and microscopic examination of the grinding surface and comparing it with those of a control sets of stones that have each been used for grinding a specific material such as wheat, ochre or dried meat. It can also be used to determine the different types of wear induced by dehusking grain compared to milling it, a useful resource for domestic sites in determining what particular tasks individual querns were used for. As ethnographic research indicates, certain rock types or textures were preferred for certain tasks (David 1998, 23; Schneider 2002).

9.6.5 Backtracking the Neolithic

It has been suggested (Watts 2008a, 110) that the origin of the use of querns for structured deposits in Britain has its roots in the spread of agriculture across Europe in the Neolithic period. Current research favours a single origin for the onset of agriculture, that is deliberate cultivation as opposed to the gathering of wild grains. This occurred in the valley of the Euphrates *circa* 13,000-12,000 BC and by the beginning of the 7th millennium BC agriculture had spread to the Aegean and Greece. Over the course of the next 1000 years the practice of agriculture was adopted by peoples in the Balkans and also in south-eastern Europe. It continued to expand westwards in the 6th millennium BC around the Mediterranean to Italy and southern France and also inland to eastern and central Europe and thence to north-western Europe. Here the adoption of agriculture and other aspects of the Neolithic slowed, taking another 1500 years to reach the Atlantic and Baltic coasts and to cross the channel to Britain (Moore 2000; 492; Moore 2004, 61; Dubreuil 2004, 1626; Price 2000a).

The methods by which agriculture spread across Europe, whether by migration, diffusion or acculturation, are still under debate (Thomas 2008a; Cummings and Harris 2011). Whatever its causes and modes of transmission and adoption may have been, however, agriculture was ultimately successful (Price 2000b, 317). The cyclic rhythm of birth, death and regeneration of the natural world exploited by hunter-gather societies gave way to that of the cultured nature of the farming year. The cultivation of grain is seen as symbolising man's triumph over nature (Ramminger 2008, 42). With that cultivation, however, came a new regime of preparing the ground, sowing the seed and harvesting and storing the grain both for consumption and as seed corn for the following year. As Gimbutas (1982, 11) states, communities became 'bound…to the soil', a fact also recorded in the Old Testament, 'In the sweat of thy face shalt thou eat bread' (Genesis 3:19). Querns, other uses not withstanding, which transformed the grain from an indigestible material into a usable, edible product are symbols of that enslavement.

By whatever means the expansion of agriculture took place, it is likely that the techniques, technologies and practices both functional and symbolic associated with the cultivation and processing of grain were adapted and changed in response to local conditions (Curtis 2001, 74-75). Tools such as querns, therefore, have their part to play in the debate being found in turn on Early Neolithic sites across Anatolia and Europe such as at Aratashen and Aknashen in Armenia, Aşikli Huyuk and Coşkuntepe in Turkey, Karanovo and Azmak in Bulgaria, Bylany in the Czech Republic, Göttingen in north-west Germany, Berry-au-Bac in north-eastern France, Skogsmossen in eastern central Sweden, and Windmill Hill and Waylands Smithy in England (Hovsepyan and Willcox 2008, 64; Takaoğlu 2005, 424; Dennell 1978, 3; Pavlů 2008; Graefe 2008; Lidström Holmberg 2008, 76; Smith 1965; Whittle 1991). Consequently, the location of querns as found in the archaeological record may be indicative of different areas of adoption and adaptation.

There are three main avenues of research in this area. Firstly, points of commonality can be seen in the deposition of querns in Britain and in northern and north-western Europe, both in terms of location, in causewayed enclosures and funerary contexts for example, in the fragmentation of quernstones and the separation of upper from lower stones (Graefe *et al* 2009). But there are also differences, domestic settlements not being a feature of the British Neolithic as they are on the continent (those on Orkney and Shetland being important exceptions). Can the evidence for the structured deposition of querns on Neolithic sites in Britain be related more closely to depositional practises witnessed on the continent and thus the route(s) by which the Neolithic reached Britain be ascertained? Or, as mooted in Chapter One, is the use of querns as structured deposits a universal norm, to be expected in agricultural societies that engaged in the practice?

Secondly, there appears to be a change in the locations in which querns are found in the archaeological record and thus in Neolithic depositional practices between the areas east and west of the Rhine. To the east it has been noted that querns are placed in graves whereas to the west, in northern France and Belgium in particular, querns tend to be deposited in relation to domestic sites (Hamon 2008a, 25). Hamon (2008a, 25) suggests this is the result of changes in the symbolic status of querns as the Linearbandkeramik culture expanded from Central Europe to the north-west of the continent in the 6th millennium BC. Further research is needed, therefore, to determine where the borders of change lie, both chorographically and chronologically. Thirdly, the location of querns in the archaeological record needs to be back-tracked across Europe to Anatolia and the Near East to ascertain if changes occur in depositional practises in other areas. Gimbutas (1982, 13, 17) has observed that the peoples of eastern and central Europe developed their own cultural traditions that were different not only to those of Anatolia and the Near East but also to those that subsequently developed in western and northern Europe. Are there comparisons to be made with the querns that were used in these regions both in terms of form and depositional context that could also be indicative of cultural differences and consequently provide clues as to the means by which agricultural and associated practices expanded into different areas?

9.7 Conclusions

Analysis of the features and contexts in which querns are found in the south-west of England shows that the depositons of some querns within the archaeological record were clearly made with purpose and forethought. Their location, orientation, condition and/or associated artefacts indicate that they were not randomly discarded but placed with due consideration and intent. Indeed if one is looking for evidence of structured deposition one need look no further than the complete red and green saddle querns placed upside down in the ditch of a Middle Bronze Age metalworking enclosure at Sigwells (Figure 4.2) (Tabor 2008, 65). Other prime examples include the hoards of rubbers in Bronze Age pits in Cornwall, the combination of querns and horse skulls in Iron Age pits at Ham Hill and the quern fragment on top of stones and pottery sherds which had been placed over the bodies of a neonatal infant and a lamb in an Iron Age pit at Sigwells (Jones and Taylor 2010; Gossip forthcoming; Leivers *et al* 2007, 42-44; Tabor 2008, 135; SCEP Archive). Quern fragments left within occupation layers on the other hand may not be so obvious in their depositional qualities but that is not to say that they were not also placed, or rather left, without due care and forethought. If one accepts the existence of special, structured deposits one must also allow for the possibility that other depositions, if less glamorous to our eyes, were also made with intent and meaning.

To reiterate the point, even the disposal of unwanted, waste material will have been undertaken with some level of thought and consideration. Thus rubbish can also be considered as a structured deposit, there being a purpose to the deposit albeit just the disposal of unwanted items. Only those querns whose final resting place in the prehistoric archaeological record is due to loss, casual discard or post-depositional movement cannot be considered as structured deposits. In addition the fact that upper and lower stones are usually found separately and also that many appear to have been broken prior to deposition or conversely deposited in an apparently still workable state further implies that querns were deposited in the archaeological record with different levels of meaning and intent. At least 14 different types of deposit can be identified:

1. Complete paired stones. These may be cached, open deposits, buried with the intention of reclaim and reuse or permanent closed deposits.
2. A complete, or near complete, upper or lower stone. This may be deposited as a single stone or with another stone(s) in the same context.
3. Lower stones left *in situ* in their primary working positions. These may have been left with the intention of return or as an open abandonment deposit.
4. Quernstones, either complete or fragmentary, of non-local rock or of different/striking colours.
5. Quernstones, either complete or fragmentary, placed with unusual artefacts.
6. Quernstones, either complete or fragmentary arranged with other artefacts.
7. Quernstones, either complete or fragmentary, placed with craftworking tools.
8. Quernstones, complete or fragmentary, in noteworthy locations.
9. Quernstones, complete or fragmentary, utilised as part of a foundation, or a closure, demolition or abandonment deposit.
10. Quern fragments. May be one or more in the same context or feature, from one or more stones.
11. Quernstones, either complete or fragmentary, reused as building material or as hearths. Such reuse may be practical and/or symbolic.
12. Quern fragments in deposits that appear to all intents and purposes to be nothing more than, occupation detritus, domestic refuse or midden material.
13. Querns recovered from topsoil deposits and unstratfied site finds about which nothing can be said regarding the nature of their original deposition.
14. Querns whose final resting place in the archaeological record is due to post-depositional movement.

Of course, in reality the dividing line between each type of deposit may be blurred with some quern depositions falling into more than one category. Also, one type of deposition may not necessarily have been more important than another. Much will have depended upon the circumstances, location and composition of the deposit. A quern fragment found on the floor of a roundhouse, for example, may appear as nothing more than occupation detritus and yet it becomes a structured deposit when a new floor is laid over it. Likewise, a quern fragment in a midden deposit also becomes part of a structured deposit when that midden material is utilised as 'symbolic manure' and placed within a Scillonian entrance grave (Ashbee 1976, 21-23; Bradley 1984, 14). However, it is the deposition of complete quernstones and those fragments in combination with unusual artefacts or in noteworthy locations that demonstrate most clearly the importance of querns to prehistoric communities on both practical and symbolic levels.

Quernstones can also be deposited in the same type of feature with different levels or categories of intent. The placement of quern fragments within the postholes of Bronze Age roundhouses, for example, may be associated with the foundation, occupation or abandonment of those buildings. Pits were also dug for a variety of reasons, for storage, as kilns or hearth pits or for various industrial uses. The artefacts found within them may be related to these functions, such as the Bronze Age pit kiln at Combe Hay which contained, in addition to a saddle quern, clay, charcoal, burnt and unburnt stone and a burnishing or polishing stone (Price and Watts 1980, 13, Microfiche 6). On the other hand pits were also dug purely to receive the objects placed within them. Many Neolithic pits fall into this category but pits continued to be dug as receptacles in the Bronze and Iron Age periods, perhaps related to the foundation or closure of a building or a means of safe storage or to receive an offering. These include the rubbers, quartz crystal, pestles and unusual pottery sherds in a pit within a Bronze Age roundhouse at Scarcewater, the stone tools in an Early Iron Age pit at Trenowah and the burnt rubber and ammonite, cremated sheep bone, charcoal and pottery in a small pit in an Iron Age enclosure at Sigwells (Jones and Taylor 2010, 19, 73; Johns forthcoming; Tabor 2008, 133; Tabor pers. corresp.). Querns may also have been deposited for different reasons within the same type of pit or even the same pit as suggested not only by their complete or incomplete state but also by their position and the artefacts found in contiguity with them within the single or multiple layered fills of Iron Age storage pits. Such depositions may, as suggested by Hill (1995, 110-111), be totally unrelated to the prime use of the pit for the storage of grain. However, given the strong link between grain and querns, it is nevertheless tempting to suggest that depositions of querns, particularly those placed on or near the bottom of pits, were made in relation to the latter's function as storage pits, perhaps as part of a thank offering for a good harvest or a propitiatory offering following a bad harvest or a spoiled pit.

In the south-west the structured deposition of querns can be seen as a form of behavioural practice initiated in the Neolithic period with the beginnings of agriculture in the region and the introduction of the saddle quern. Deposition increased in the Middle Bronze Age with the development and spread of settled farming communities. The increase in depositions of saddle querns in the Iron Age appears to coincide with the introduction of the rotary quern in the 4th century BC but depositions of rotary querns as early as the 4th-3rd century BC show that it too was quickly utilised as a structured deposit. The depositional locations and categories of deposition observed in the south-west broadly reflect those recorded in other areas of England and Wales. Evidence, however, also indicates regional differences, determined by the local topography and geology or by particular social requirements. This suggests that in each case we are looking at regional variations upon a wider theme.

Querns are not of precious materials nor are they exotic objects, they are everyday tools made of stone. Yet through the course of studying the structured deposition of querns one is confronted by some of the most important aspects of prehistoric life and society. These include not only directly related subjects such as the beginnings and spread of agriculture, changes in farming practice, domestic organisation and the role of women but also indirect and even more vast topics such as the cosmology and ideology that underpinned society and governed the orientation (or not) of roundhouses and the place of the dead within society. Each of these issues is a research agenda in its own right and this book can do little more than brush the surface of them. However, the presence of querns in each of these aspects demonstrates the integral and vital role that these seemingly innocuous tools played in the lives of prehistoric peoples.

The ubiquity of querns and their apparent utilitarian function of grinding everyday foodstuffs, however, coupled with their simplicity of design and the use of local, unprecious materials in their manufacture has often led to them being overlooked in the past. In fact it is these very facets that form the core of the meaning behind their importance to prehistoric communities. Querns are personal tools, closely associated with the people, generally women as indicated by historic and ethnographic evidence, who used them. They were used on an almost daily basis over a period of many years leading to a special form of relationship with their users. They are more, however, than the humble tools of slave women and prisoners (Exodus 11:5; Judges 16:21). Far from being simple utilitarian items used on a daily, practical basis as a tool for grinding grain and other materials querns can be seen to have multiple meanings and values operating on entwined functional and symbolic levels. They are symbols not only of women, the home and the provision of food but also potentially of life and death seen in the transforming process of grain into meal between the two stones. In addition the movement of the rotary quern can be related to the turning of the heavens. Querns can thus be seen as ideal artefacts for use in depositional events through which different and often difficult concepts such as the place of men and women in the world and the cycle of life and death can be both controlled and explained. Their physical properties also make quernstones suitable for alternative functions such as hearths or building stones but even these uses may be seen as examples of structured deposits. The use of old material within new creates a sense of place and belonging, linking the present to the past.

Each deposition was made as a result of or in response to a specific event, place, person or circumstance. Each captured the essence of or harnessed the situation that gave rise to the deposit (after Brück 2006, 305). It has to be accepted, however, that it is not possible to understand the exact nature of the motive(s) and meaning(s) behind particular depositions or to explain the circumstances of all deposits. That said it can be recognised that different depositions were made with different intents as shown by their location, composition and circumstances. Depositions in roundhouses, for example, were made in response to the foundation, occupation/rebuilding, closure or abandonment of a structure while those in boundary ditches represent place/people and those in pits may have been made as offerings or as foundation, occupation or closure deposits or have been left in safe storage. Every deposition has its own story to tell even though we may not understand that story now. What is clear is that querns, as found in the archaeological record, were placed there with different levels and layers of meaning and intent. This is manifest in their complete/fragmentary, single/paired state, the artefacts with which they are found and the location, type and circumstances of the context in which they are found.

If this book has done one thing it is to demonstrate the importance of querns to prehistoric communities, an importance that is witnessed in their use as structured deposits. In order to further our understanding of the role of querns within prehistoric society in general and as structured deposits in particular it is now vital that more attention be paid to them, to the contexts in which they are found, the condition in which they are found and what they are found with.

APPENDICES

Appendix One

Sites included on the main database and numbers of querns found within structured contexts on those sites.

Site ID	Site Name	Parish	Site Type	Date	No. of Querns
1	Castle Hill	Feniton	Settlement	Bronze Age	1
2	Hayne Lane	Gittisham	Settlement	Bronze Age	2
3	Langland Lane	Ottery St. Mary	Settlement	Bronze Age	1
4	Long Range	Ottery St. Mary	Settlement	Iron Age	3
5	Blackhorse	Sowton	Settlement	Iron Age	5
6	Berrywood	High Week	Hillfort	Iron Age	1
9	Cranbrook Castle	Moretonhampstead	Hillfort	Iron Age	1
11	Dean Moor	Dean Prior	Settlement	Bronze Age	2
12	Shapley Common	North Bovey	Settlement	Bronze Age	1
13	Holworthy Farm	Parracombe	Enclosure	Middle-Late Bronze Age	1
14	Dainton Common	Ipplepen	Settlement	Bronze Age-Iron Age	13
17	Hazard Hill	Harberton	Settlement	Neolithic	5
18	Kestor	Gidleigh	Settlement	Bronze Age	1
20	Mount Folly	Bigbury	Settlement	Iron Age	3
21	Scadbrook	Ugborough	Settlement	Bronze Age	2
24	Kents Cavern	Torbay	Cave dwelling	Iron Age	1
25	Heatree	Manaton	Settlement	Bronze Age	1
26	Shaugh Moor	Shaugh Prior	Settlement	Bronze Age-Iron Age	24
27	White Ridge	Lydford	Settlement	Bronze Age	1
29	Raddick Hill	Walkhampton	Settlement	Bronze Age	1
31	Hembury	Payhembury	Causewayed enclosure	Neolithic	5
34	Cadbury Castle	Cadbury Castle	Hillfort	Neolithic-Iron Age	141
35	Glastonbury Lake Village	Godney	Crannog	Iron Age	55
36	Meare Village East	Meare	Summer gathering place	Iron Age	80
37	Meare Village West	Meare	Summer gathering place	Iron Age	199
38	Milsoms Corner	Cadbury Castle	Occupation site	Neolithic-Iron Age	4
39	Sigwells Farm	Charleton Horethorne	Enclosure(s)	Bronze Age-Iron Age	20
40	Crissells Green	Cadbury Castle	Occupation site	Bronze Age	2
41	Home Ground	Cadbury Castle	Settlement	Iron Age	3
42	Moor	Cadbury Castle	Occupation site	Iron Age	3
43	Sheep Slait	Poyntington	Occupation site	Bronze Age-Iron Age	2
44	Ham Hill	Montacute	Hillfort	Iron Age	17
45	Tyning Quarry	Radstock	Settlement	Iron Age	3

Appendices

Site ID	Site Name	Parish	Site Type	Date	No. of Querns
46	Wookey Hole	St Cuthbert Out	Cave dwelling	Iron Age	4
54	Blaise Castle	Bristol	Hillfort	Iron Age	4
56	Dibbles Farm	Christon	Settlement	Iron Age	1
61	Ben Bridge	Compton Martin	Occupation site	Neolithic	2
62	Chew Park	Stowey Sutton	Occupation site	Neolithic-Early Bronze Age	2
64	Solisbury Hill Camp	Batheaston	Hillfort	Iron Age	2
66	Reads Cavern	Priddy	Cave dwelling	Iron Age	1
67	Tynings Barrows	Cheddar	Barrow cemctcry	Bronze Age	5
71	Cadbury Camp	Tickenham	Hillfort	Iron Age	1
72	Camerton	Camerton	Occupation site	Neolithic-Iron Age	2
73	Encie Farm	Penselwood	Occupation site	Iron Age	1
76	Cannards Grave	Shepton Mallet	Settlement	Iron Age	2
77	Field Farm	Shepton Mallet	Ditched enclosure	Neolithic-Iron Age	8
81	Higher Boden	St. Anthony-in-Meneage	Settlement	Bronze Age-Iron Age	4
83	Bodrifty	Gulval	Settlement	Bronze Age	9
87	Burledge Camp	West Harptree	Hillfort	Iron Age	1
91	Twinyeo	Kingsteignton	Enclosure	Iron Age	2
93	Boscawen-un	92	Barrow	Bronze Age	1
94	Boleigh	St. Buryan	Barrow cemetery	Bronze Age	3
95	Higher Bussow	St. Ives	Settlement	Bronze Age	3
96	Bussow	St. Ives	Barrow	Bronze Age	1
97	Callestick	Perranzabuloe	Structure	Late Bronze Age	12
98	Carn Brea	Illogan	Defended Hilltop Settlement	Neolithic	3
99	Carn Euny	Sancreed	Settlement	Iron Age	4
100	Harlyn Bay	St. Merryn	Midden	Iron Age	1
101	Porth Bean House	St. Columb Minor	Unknown	Iron Age	1
102	Trevilson	Newlyn	Round house	Middle Bronze Age	2
103	The Rumps	St. Minver	Promontory Fort	Iron Age	3
104	Sperris Croft	Zennor	Settlement	Iron Age	2
105	Stannon Down	St. Breward	Settlement & cemetery	Middle Bronze Age-Iron Age	13
108	Tremough	Penryn	Occupation site	Late Neolithic-Iron Age	3
113	Trevarnon	Gwithian	Round	Iron Age	1
114	Treveneague	St. Hilary	Fogou	Iron Age	4
115	Trye	Gulval	Cairn	Bronze Age	1
116	Trevisker	St. Eval	Settlement	Middle Bronze Age-Iron Age	14
117	Trewey Downs	Zennor	Settlement	Late Bronze Age	1
118	Vynyeck	St. Buryan	Fogou	Iron Age	3
119	Castallack	Paul	Round	Iron Age	2
122	Goughs Old Cave	Cheddar	Cave dwelling	Iron Age	4
123	Davidstow	Davidstow	Barrow cemetery	Bronze Age	1
124	Castle Gotha	St. Austell	Round	Iron Age	3
126	Threemilestone	Kenwyn	Round	Iron Age	1

The Life and Death of Querns

Site ID	Site Name	Parish	Site Type	Date	No. of Querns
138	Tredrennen	St. Levan	Round	Iron Age	1
146	Bodwen	Lanlivery	Round	Iron Age	1
150	Gurnards Head	Zennor	Promontory Fort	Iron Age	1
163	Castle Dore	St. Sampson	Hillfort	Iron Age	1
171	Chun Castle	Madron	Hillfort	Iron Age	2
172	Helman Tor	Lostwithiel	Hilltop Enclosure	Neolithic	2
173	Carvinack	Kenwyn	Barrow	Bronze Age	1
174	Crig-a-Mennis	Perranporth	Barrow	Bronze Age-Iron Age	1
177	St. Columb Porth	St. Columb Minor	Unknown	Iron Age	1
181	North Hill	Samson	Entrance grave	Neolithic	1
186	Bants Cairn	St. Marys	Barrow	Bronze Age	1
191	Sperris Quoit	Zennor	Chambered tomb	Bronze Age	1
196	Little Arthur	St. Martins	Settlement	Iron Age	1
199	Nornour	St. Martins	Settlement	Middle Bronze Age-Roman	20
200	Halangy Porth	St. Marys	Settlement	Bronze Age-Early Iron Age	3
201	Halangy Down	St. Marys	Settlement	Iron Age	10
203	Gwithian	Gwithian	Settlement	Bronze Age	47
204	Trethellan	Newquay	Settlement	Middle Bronze Age-Iron Age	56
205	Trenowah	St. Austell	Occupation site	Bronze Age-Iron Age	13
206	Scarcewater	St. Stephen-in-Brannel	Settlement	Middle-Late Bronze Age	51
207	Penhale Farm	St. Stephen-in-Brannel	Settlement	Bronze Age	1
208	Higher Besore & Truro College	Kenwyn	Settlement	Late Bronze Age-Iron Age	24
209	Tregarrick Farm	Roche	Occupation site	Neolithic	1
212	Old Rydon Lane	Exeter	Enclosure	Bronze Age	1
213	Porthleven		Occupation Site	Bronze Age	1
214	Ashton	Bristol	Quarry	Iron Age	2
215	Meacombe	Chagford	Occupation Site	Bronze Age	1
217	Holne Moor	Holne	Occupation Site	Bronze Age	2

Appendices

Appendix Two

Additional find spots and the type and date of the quern found.

Site ID	Site Name	Parish	Nature of Find	Quern Type	Date
7	Crossways Farm	Bratton Fleming	Reused in hedge bank	Saddle quern	Prehistoric
8	Coffin Wood	Peter Tavy	Chance find nr hut circle & field system	Rotary lower stone	Iron Age
10	Court Gate Farm	South Brent	Field walking find	Rubber?	Prehistoric
15	East Hill	Ogwell	Find within field system	Saddle quern	Prehistoric
16	Walls Hills	St. Marychurch	Find	Rotary upper stone	
19	Cloggshill Cross	Alverdiscott	Find	Saddle quern	Prehistoric
22	Lee Abbey	Lynton	Chance find near BA settlement	Saddle quern	Prehistoric
23	Thorn Farm	Chagford	Find	Rotary upper stone	Iron Age/Roman
28	Stanlake Farm	Walkhampton	Reused in post-prehistoric enclosure bank?	Saddle quern	Prehistoric
30	Leighon	Manaton	Found buried in peat	Rubber	Prehistoric
32	North Tawton	North Tawton	Found nr site of Nemeto Statio	Rotary upper stone	Iron Age/Roman
33	Bitbeare Farm	Winkleigh	Nature of find unknown	Rotary upper stone	Iron Age/Roman
47	Landacre Bridge	Withypool	Find nr Bronze Age settlement	Saddle quern	Bronze Age
48	Barrington Hill	Ashill	Plough find	Rotary upper stone	Iron Age/Roman
49	Tedbury Camp	Elm	Found during clearance at E end of hillfort	Rotary quernstone	Iron Age
51	East Woodlands	Selwood	Found in garden	Rotary upper stone	Iron Age
52	Priddy Hill Farm	Priddy	Field walking find	Saddle quern	Neolithic
53	Clapton	Stogumber	Chance find	Rotary quern	Iron Age
55	Tower Hill	St. Cuthbert Out	Field walking finds	Saddle quern & 5 rubbers/pounders	Neolithic
58	Penselwood	Pen Selwood	Found in rectory garden	Rotary quern	Iron Age/Roman
59	Merriott	Merriott	No information	Lower stone of quern	Unknown
60	Halse	Halse	No information	Upper stone of quern	Unknown
63	Castle Hill Farm	Withiel Florey	No information	Rotary lower stone	Iron Age/Roman
65	Moat House Farm	Wraxall	Unstratified site find	Rotary lower stone	Iron Age
69	Combwich	Combwich	Find	Saddle quern	Prehistoric
70	Portishead	Portishead	Found during groundworks for new building	Rubber	Iron Age/Roman
71	Cadbury Camp	Tickenham	Found during ploughing	Quernstone	Iron Age/Roman
74	Sharcott	Exford	No information	Rotary lower stone	Prehistoric
75	Stoke St. Mary	Stoke St. Mary	Find	Rotary lower stone	Iron Age
78	Atley	Lanivet	Find	Saddle quern	Bronze Age
79	Ballowall	St. Just	Associated with settlement	Querns & rubbers	Prehistoric
84	Sandford Hill	Winscombe	Find	Saddle quern	Neolithic

The Life and Death of Querns

Site ID	Site Name	Parish	Nature of Find	Quern Type	Date
85	Clevedon	Clevedon	Found in garden	Rotary lower stone & rubbers	Iron Age/Roman
86	Old Farm Cottage	Norton Radstock	Found during quarry working	Quernstone	Unknown
89	Pickwick	Norton Malreward	Found on site of IA/RB settlement	Quern	Iron Age/Roman
92	Boleigh Fogou	St. Buryan	Fogou	Rubbers	Iron Age
107	Talskiddy	St. Columb Major	Found in barn and garden	Saddle quern	Prehistoric
109	Tredarvah	Penzance	Find in association with BA settlement	Saddle quern	Bronze Age
110	Tregeseal	St. Just	Find in field	Rotary upper stone	Iron Age/Roman
111	Tresawsen	Perranzabuloe	Find within site of Round	Rubber	Iron Age/Roman
120	Trewavas Head	Germoe	Find within promontory fort	2 Saddle querns	Iron Age
125	Trebarveth	St. Keverne	Found nr possible hut circle	Quern	Iron Age
127	Tregerthen	Zennor	Find	Upper stone of quern	Prehistoric/Roman
128	Priddy Rd Fm	Priddy	Find	Saddle quern	Neolithic
129	Tolmennor	Breage	Find in association with settlement	Querns	Prehistoric/Roman
132	Trevorian	Sennen	Find	Quern	Prehistoric
133	Trevornick	Cubert	No information	Quern	Unknown
136	Bojewyans	Sancreed	Found during ploughing	Saddle quern	Prehistoric
137	Chyenhal	Paul	Found in hedges	Rotary upper and lower stones	Iron Age/Roman
139	Tremewan	Penzance	Find	Saddle quern	Bronze Age
141	Tredavoe	Penzance	Find	Quernstones	Unknown
142	Boswarthen	Sancreed	Built into field walls	2 Saddle querns	Bronze Age
143	Bunkers Hill Fm	St. Buryan	Find	Saddle quern	Bronze Age
144	Lower Trevowan	Morvah	Find	2 Saddle querns	Later prehistoric
145	Trewey	Zennor	Built into hedge	Saddle quern	Later Prehistoric
148	Henver	St. Allen	Find, possibly associated with Round	Quern	Prehistoric
149	Bosporth-ennis	Zennor	Found nr settlement	Saddle quern	Later Prehistoric/Roman
152	Catchall	Sancreed	Find	Saddle quern	Bronze Age
153	Penzance	Penzance	Find	Querns	Later Prehistoric/Roman
154	Morvah	Morvah	No information	Quern	Prehistoric
155	Towednack	Towednack	No information	2 Saddle querns	Later Prehistoric
156	Hendra	Cury	Found during ploughing	Quern?	Iron Age
157	Mawla	St. Agnes	Find	Quernstone	Iron Age
158	Camborne	Camborne	Find	Rubber	Neolithic/Bronze Age

Appendices

Site ID	Site Name	Parish	Nature of Find	Quern Type	Date
159	Knave Go By	Camborne	Find	Rubber	Neolithic/ Bronze Age
160	Reskadinnick	Camborne	Find	Rubber	Neolithic/ Bronze Age
164	Boscarne	Lanivet	Find	2 Rotary upper stones	Iron Age/ Roman
165	Trevissick	St. Agnes	Find	Rotary quernstone	Iron Age/ Roman
167	Redruth	Redruth	Find	Rotary quernstone	Iron Age/ Roman
168	Trevu Farm	Camborne	Find	Rotary upper and lower	Iron Age/ Roman
170	Trewern	Madron	Find	Rotary upper and lower	Iron Age/ Roman
178	Pentle Bay	Tresco	Found in association with structure	Saddle quern	Prehistoric/ Roman
179	Porth Killier	St. Agnes	Find from cliff face associated with settlement	Rubber	Prehistoric
180	Cliff Fields	Tresco	Find	Rotary quernstone	Iron Age/ Roman
182	Periglis	St. Agnes	Find	Saddle quern	Prehistoric
183	St. Agnes Churchyard	St. Agnes	Find	Saddle quern	Prehistoric
184	Lawrences Brow	St. Martins	Find associated with settlement	Rubber	Bronze Age
185	Little Bay	St. Martins	Find on beach associated with settlement	Saddle querns	Bronze Age/ Iron Age
187	Holy Vale	St. Marys,	Find	2 Saddle querns	Prehistoric
188	Town Beach	Bryher	Field wall	Saddle quern	Prehistoric
189	Bar Point	St. Marys	In hut adjoining wall	Saddle quern	Prehistoric/ Roman
190	Pendrathen Beach	St. Marys	Find	Saddle quern	Prehistoric
192	Telegraph Hill	St. Marys	Find	Saddle quern	Prehistoric
193	Top Rock Hill	St. Martins	Find	Quern	Prehistoric
194	Porth Cressa East	St. Martins	Find	Quern	Prehistoric
195	English Island Carn	St. Martins	Find	Quern	Bronze Age
197	Porth Cressa	St. Marys	House exposed in cliff	Quern	Bronze Age
198	St. Warnas Cove	St. Agnes	Find	Quern	Prehistoric
210	Middleworth Farm	Burrator	Find	Saddle quern	Prehistoric
211	Shipley Cottage	South Brent	Find	Saddle quern	Prehistoric
216	Middle Rocombe		Find	Saddle quern	Prehistoric

Appendix Three

Tables derived from the database giving details of the querns and associated artefacts found in postholes, pits, ditches, funerary and other contexts for the Neolithic, Bronze Age and Iron Age periods.

<u>Key</u>

S	Saddle quern	Neo	Neolithic
Ru	Rubber	BA	Bronze Age
Q	Quern	IA	Iron Age
Ro	Rotary quern	E	Early
RoU	Upper stone of rotary quern	M	Middle
RoL	Lower stone of rotary quern	L	Late
frag(s)	Fragment(s)	U	Unknown
obj(s)	Object(s)	N/A	Not applicable
c/u	Condition Unknown		

Table 6.1: Neolithic pits with querns (Information from database, derived from Liddell 1929-1932; Houlder 1963; Tabor 2008; Cadbury Castle Environs Project Archive; Tabor pers. corresp.; Rahtz and Greenfield 1977; Wedlake 1958; Cole and Jones 2002-2003; Cadbury Castle Archive; Gossip and Jones 2007).

Details (Context No)	QuernType (Database Id No)	Associated Finds	Site Name (Database Id No)	Date
1 of 5 pits (28N pit 4)	Ru frag (122)	flint; pottery; pounder	Hembury (31)	4000-3000BC
Storage pit. No details recorded (1)	Ru (49); Ru frags (50)	no other finds recorded	Hazard Hill (17)	3890-3480BC
Storage pit. Fill of earth, ash, charcoal and occupation debris (5)	Ru (51)	stone axe frag; charcoal; flint; pebble; pottery	Hazard Hill (17)	3890-3480BC
Quarry pit. Large sterile pit (8)	Ru (48)	none	Hazard Hill (17)	3890-3480BC
Middle of line of 3 pits. Charcoal rich fill (F619)	Ru frag (733)	flint; plant remains; pottery	Milsoms Corner (38)	Earlier Neolithic
East end and largest of a line of 3 pits (F737)	S frags (735)	bone; baked clay; charcoal; flint; plant remains; pottery; stone	Milsoms Corner (38)	Earlier Neolithic
Off set from line of 3 (F726)	S (734)	bone; baked clay; charcoal; flint; plant remains; pottery; stone	Milsoms Corner (38)	Earlier Neolithic
Irregular oval pit. Dark charcoal flecked soil	Q frag (840)	burnt bone; charcoal; flint; plant remains (poss modern intrusion); pottery; stone	Chew Park (62)	Neolithic
Fill of black earth	S (987)	charcoal; flint; pottery; 2 pounders/rubbing stones	Camerton (72)	Neolithic
Bowl shaped pit, 1 of 2, part of larger group of 10. Dark silty clay fill. In situ burning (19(20))	S (1410)	flints; pottery	Tregarrick Farm (209)	3710-3520BC
Clean red earth fill (B436)	Q frag (241)	flint; slingstones	Cadbury Castle (34)	3600-3400BC
Clean red earth fill (B410)	Q frag (245)	bone; flint blade and arrowhead; pottery; slingstone	Cadbury Castle (34)	3600-3400BC
Red clay fill (T269)	Q frag (154)	bone; flint; pottery; stone	Cadbury Castle (34)	3600-3400BC
Red clay fill (T260)	SQ frag (311); Q frag 296)	bone; flint scraper; pottery; stone	Cadbury Castle (34)	3600-3400BC
Hollow with clean red earth fill (G180)	SQ frags (1390-1); Q frag (336	pottery	Cadbury Castle (34)	3600-3400BC
Silt fill	SQ frag (945)	cobbles; flint; pottery	Tremough (108)	2570-2290BC

Appendices

Table 6.2: *Other Neolithic features with querns (Information from database, derived from Liddell 1929-1932, 118; Liddell 1933-1936, 160; Rahtz and Greenfield 1977; Mercer 1997; Houlder 1963; Mercer 1981; Thomas and Wailes 1967).*

Context Form (Context No)	Quern Type (Database Id No)	Associated Finds	Site Name (Database Id No)	Date
Occupation layer	Ru c/u (118)	unknown	Hembury (31)	4000-3000BC
Occupation layer (28H)	Ru c/u (120, 121); Q c/u (119)	unknown	Hembury (31)	4000-3000BC
Occupation layer (BB41)	S (838) Ru (839)	none	Ben Bridge (61)	Unknown
Occupation layer (?Layer 6)	Ru frag (1080)	flint; pottery; stone axe	Helman Tor (172)	3970-2700BC
Hearth (3)	S (47)	unknown	Hazard Hill 917)	3890-3480BC
Clearance cairn	S (919)	stone	Carn Brea (98)	4000-3000BC
Wall (98)	S c/u (920); Ru c/u (921)	unknown	Carn Brea (98)	4000-3000BC
Midden (Layer 6-9)	Ru frag (1079)	flint;pottery	Helman Tor (172)	3970-2700BC
Chambered tomb	S frag (1103)	flint; pottery; slate; whetstone/hone	Sperris Quoit (191)	Unknown

Table 7.1: *Bronze Age postholes with querns (Information from database, derived from Jones and Taylor 2010; Jones forthcoming; Tabor 2008; Cadbury Castle Environs Project Archive; ApSimon and Greenfield 1972; Nowakowski 1991; Trethellan Farm Archive; Sturgess and Lawson Jones 2006; Fitzpatrick et al 1999a; Gossip and Jones 2007; Gossip forthcoming; Masson Phillips 1982; Cadbury Castle Archive; Watts, S. 2011b).*

Posthole Location	Roundhouse Quadrant	Quern Type (Database Id No)	Associated Finds	SiteName (Database Id No)	Date
Metalworking structure (F043)	W	S frags (752-3); Ru frag (754)	bone awl; pottery; burnt stone; stone	Sigwells Farm (39)	Early MBA
Roundhouse A (a.83)	SW	Ru (956)	bronze waste; packing stones	Trevisker (116)	MBA
Roundhouse 1250 (1319)	SW	S frag (1330)	none	Scarcewater (206)	MBA
Roundhouse 1250 (1300)	SW	S frag (1329)	none	Scarcewater (206)	MBA
H142/3022 (111)	SW	Q frags (1243)	pottery	Trethellan Farm (204)	MBA
Structure 1134 (1086)	SW	Ru frag (1166)	none	Gwithian (203)	M-LBA
Ancilliary structure 459 (241)	SE, S side of porch	Q frag (3)	charcoal; pottery	Hayne Lane (2)	M-LBA
Metalworking structure (F021)	SE, W side of entrance corridor	S frag (758)	animal bone; human bone	Sigwells Farm (39)	Early MBA
Structure 1642 (1527)	SE, S side of entrance	S frag (1211)	animal teeth and bone; charcoal; mussel shells; pebble packing	Gwithian (203)	EBA
H2222 (2364)	SE, W side of entrance	Ru (1271)	pebble	Trethellan Farm (204)	MBA
Ancilliary structure 459 (58)	SE, N side of Porch	Q frag (2)	charcoal; plant remains; pottery; spindlewhorl	Hayne Lane (2)	M-LBA
Roundhouse 392 (485)	SE, N side of entrance	Ru frag (946)	pottery	Tremough (108)	MBA

The Life and Death of Querns

Roundhouse 1500 (1160)	NW	S frag (1335-6)	none	Scarcewater (206)	MBA
H2222 (2249)	NW	Ru (1262-3); Ru frag (1280)	none	Trethellan Farm (204)	MBA
H2010 (2545)	NW	Ru frag (1275); Q frag (1279)	slate; stone	Trethellan Farm (204)	MBA
Metalworking structure (F036)	Centre	Q frag (755-7)	bone point; hammerstone; pottery	Sigwells Farm (39)	Early MBA
Round house centre	Centre	S (58)	pottery?	Scadbrook (21)	LBA
H2001 (2365)	Unknown	Ru (1257)	unknown	Trethellan Farm (204)	MBA
Roundhouse 1500 (1585) Non structural	W	S frag (1340)	none	Scarcewater (206)	MBA
Roundhouse A (a.11) (non structural)	NE	Ru (957)	unknown	Trevisker (116)	MBA
HB Structure 1 (windbreak) (6585)	SE	Ru (1436-8); Ru frag (1439	pottery; stone	Higher Besore & Truro College (208)	LBA
HB Structure 1 (windbreak) (6583)	NE	S frag (1440)	pottery; stone	Higher Besore & Truro College (208)	LBA
P305	Unknown	Q frag (26)	bone; flint; pottery; burnt stone	Cadbury Castle (34)	LBA
K/X016	N/A	S frag (261)	pottery; slingstones; whetstone	Cadbury Castle (34)	BA
In pit adjacent to other pits (135)	N/A	Ru frags (1423)	stone; worked stone	Porthleven (213)	LBA

Table 7.2: Bronze Age pits, cooking pits, pit kilns and hearths in roundhouses with querns (Information from database, derived from Nowakowski 1991; Jones and Taylor 2010; ApSimon and Greenfield 1972; Sturgess and Lawson-Jones 2006; Gossip forthcoming).

Pit Location (Context Id No)	Roundhouse Quadrant	Quern Type (Database Id No)	Associated Finds	Site Name (Database Id No)	Date
H2222 (2289)	SW of centre	Q frag (1288)	charcoal; complete but broken pot	Trethellan Farm (204)	MBA
H2001 (2527)	SW	S (1264); Ru (1273-4)	pottery	Trethellan Farm (204)	MBA
H2001 (2541)	SW	Ru (1281-2)	clay; pottery; slates; unworked stone	Trethellan Farm (204)	MBA
H648 (617)	SW	Ru frag (1294)	pottery	Trethellan Farm (204)	MBA
Roundhouse 1500 (1901)	SW	Ru frag (1341-2)	pestles; pottery; quartz crystal; slate slab	Scarcewater (206)	MBA
Roundhouse A (a.1)	SE	Ru (958); Ru c/u(973)	holed pebble; pebbles;	Trevisker (116)	MBA
H2222 (2601)	SE of centre	Q frag (1277)	animal teeth; plant remains; pottery; perforated slate	Trethellan Farm (204)	MBA
H2001 (2027)	NW	S (1250); Ru (1245, 1251-3,5, 1278); Q frag (1254)	none	Trethellan Farm (204)	MBA
Structure 725 (425)	NE	Ru (1172-3)	antler; pebbles; rubbing stones; scallop shell	Gwithian (203)	M-LBA
H142/3022 (3140)	NE	Q frag (1296)	pottery	Trethellan Farm (204)	MBA

Appendices

Roundhouse 1100 (1137)	NE	Ru (1323)	pottery	Scarcewater (206)	MBA
H2222 (2267)	N	Ru c/u (1289)	pottery; stone slab	Trethellan Farm (204)	MBA
TC Stucture 2 (2067)	N	Ru frag (1444)	plant remains; pottery	Higher Besore & Truro College (208)	LBA
HB Structure 1 (6581)	E	S (1435)	plant remains; quartz crystals	Higher Besore & Truro College (208)	LBA
Structure 3084 (3030)	Centre	S frag (1379)	none	Scarcewater (206)	LBA
Roundhouse 1500 Hearth/cooking pit (1715)	SE of centre	Ru (1339); Ru frag (1336)	none	Scarcewater (206)	MBA
H142/3022 Hearth/cooking pit (3035)	N	Ru c/u (1292)	pottery; burnt stone	Trethellan Farm (204)	MBA
H142/3022 Pit kiln (3047)	N	Q frag (1293)	burnt clay; pottery; burnt wood	Trethellan Farm (204)	MBA
TC Structure 3 Hearth pit (2009)	N of centre	Ru frag (1445)	anvil stones; charcoal; flint pebble; pottery; whetstone	Higher Besore & Truro College (208)	LBA
H2010 Hearth/cooking pit (2715)	Centre	Ru frags (1286)	pottery; burnt wood	Trethellan Farm (204)	MBA
H2010 Hearth/cooking pit (2371)	Centre	S frag (1287)	flint; pottery; unworked stone	Trethellan Farm (204)	MBA
Roundhouse 1500 Hearth (1170)	W of centre	Ru (1324)	none	Scarcewater (206)	MBA

Table 7.3: Bronze Age pits external to roundhouses with querns (Information from database, derived from Jones and Taylor 2010; Cadbury Castle Archive; Gossip forthcoming; Leach 2008; Dyer and Salvatore 2011; Watts, S. 2008b; Price and Watts 1980).

Pit Location (Context No)	**QuernType (Database Id No)**	**Associate Finds**	**Site Name (Database Id No)**	**Date**
SE of pit group 1650 (1665)	S (1361)	pottery	Scarcewater (206)	MBA
NW of pit group 1650 (1018)	Ru (1358-60)	flint knife; pottery	Scarcewater (206)	MBA
NW of pit group 1650	Ru frag (1688)	rubbing stone	Scarcewater (206)	MBA
NE of pit group 1600 (1618)	Ru frag (1376)	none	Scarcewater (206)	MBA
E of entrance (NW) Site 1 (F119)	Ru frag (1403)	animal bone; stone	Field Farm (77)	MBA
Centre of pit group 1600 (1601)	S (1366-7); Ru (1368) Ru frag (1365, 69)	none	Scarcewater (206)	MBA
Centre of pit group 1600 (1610)	Ru 1372-5; Ru frag (1370-1)	none	Scarcewater (206)	MBA
Centre E of pit group 1402 (1405)	S frag (1363)	none	Scarcewater (206)	MBA
Site N (N763)	S frag (202)	bone; bone tool; bronze frag; charcoal; flint; iron frag; pottery; shale bracelet frag; stone; burnt stone	Cadbury Castle (34)	LBA

Area D East (5027)	S frags (1387); Ru (1381, 83-6); Ru frags (1382)	pottery	Higher Besore & Truro College (208)	LBA
Site 3 (F47)	S frag (1408)	animal bone; flint flakes; hammerstone frag; pottery	Field Farm (77)	EBA
Area D East (5030)	Ru (1424-5)	plant remains; pottery; rubbing stone	Higher Besore & Truro College (208)	LBA
NW pit group (5035)	S frag (1441)	pottery; stone disc	Higher Besore & Truro College (208)	LBA
NW pit group (5033)	S (1442)	pottery	Higher Besore & Truro College (208)	LBA
TC Area C (2045)	Ru frag (1443)	pottery	Higher Besore & Truro College (208)	LBA
S of burial chamber (531)	S frag (1450)	burnt bone; charcoal; burnt clay; burnt flint; plant remains; pottery; stone	Meacombe (215)	MBA
S of house 1500 Hearth/cooking pit (1040)	S frag (1419)	chert flake; burnt clay; plant remains	Scarcewater (206)	BA
Centre SW of enclosure Cooking pit (F013)	S frag (740)	animal bone; pottery; stone	Sigwells (39)	Early MBA
Pit kiln (IVA)	S (823)	burnt clay; pottery; stone; burnishing stone	Combe Hay (57)	LBA
Site E Pit kiln (E700	Q frag (1229)	pottery	Cadbury Castle (34)	BA

Table 7.4: Bronze Age ditches with querns (Information from database, derived from John Moore Heritage Services 2010; Tabor pers. corresp.; Tabor 2008, 65, 98; Fitzpatrick et al 1999a; Leach 2008).

Ditch Type	Location of Quern (Context No)	Quern Type (Database Id No)	Associated Finds	Site Name (Database Id No)	Date
Ditch section Part of enclosure	W terminal, SE end of enclosure (01/013)	Q frag (1421)	pebble mace head; pottery	Old Rydon Lane (212)	BA
Enclosure	W side (F002)	S (738-9)	stone	Sigwells Farm (39)	MBA
Enclosure	SE (5026)	Q frags (1)	charcoal; flint; plant remains; pottery; quartz; whetstone	Castle Hill (1)	M-LBA
Ditch section	S terminal (F5)	Ru frags (1405)	flint flakes	Field Farm (77)	LBA
Ditch section	Site 2 S of entrance (F8)	Q frags (1404)	animal bone; flint flakes; stone	Field Farm (77)	MBA
Ditch section	Site 1 NW (F120)	Q frag (1402)	animal bone; anvil (lower in ditch); charcoal; flint; pottery	Field Farm (77)	MBA
Enclosure	NW corner (F003)	Q frags (736)	burnt stone	Sigwells Farm (39)	MBA
Ring ditch	N Terminal (F025)	S frag (768)	pottery; quartz crystal; stone	Sheep Slait (43)	LBA
Ditch section	N terminal (F7)	S frag (1406)	pottery	Field Farm (77)	LBA
Enclosure	Unknown (F004)	S frag (761) Ru (760)	unknown	Crissells Green (40)	EBA
Linear	?Centre (F054)	S frag (759)	none	Sigwells Farm (39)	EBA
Linear	Towards W end (F009)	Q frag (737)	animal bone; pottery	Sigwells Farm (39)	BA

Appendices

Table 7.5: Bronze Age barrows and graves with querns (Information from database, derived from Dudley 1961-1964; Russell and Pool 1964; Jones 2004-2005; Harris et al 1984; Hencken 1933; Borlase 1872; Daniel 1950).

Site Name (Database Id No)	Barrow quadrant	Context (No)	Quern Type (Database Id No)	Associated Finds	Date
Carvinack (173)	SW	?Quartz ring	Ru (1081)	none	BA
Trye (115)	SW quadrant	Cairn	S frag (955)	none	BA
Cairn 9 Stannon Down (105)	SW	Inner bank (205)	Ru (1043)	flint; pottery	BA
Cairn 2 Stannon Down (105)	SW	Kerb (29)	S (1041)	worked slate (flint; pebble; quartz)	BA
Cairn 9 Stannon Down (105)	SE	Inner ditch (206)	Ru frag (1044)	flint; pottery	BA
Cairn 6 Stannon Down (105)	S	Cairn wall (89)	S frag (1042)	plant remains	BA
Barrow 8 Davidstow (123)	NE	Cairn enclosure	Q c/u (995)	none	BA
Cairn 3 Stannon Down (105)	NE	Cairn stones	Ru (942)	none	MBA
Boscawen-un (93)	NE	Cairn enclosure	S frag (898)	cremated bone; pottery; stone	BA
Cairn 9 Stannon Down (105)	NE	Cairn stones (212)	Ru (1045)	whetstones (flint; pebbles/cobbles; pottery; slickstones; spindlewhorl; whetstone)	BA
Chew Park (62)	NE	Part of grave goods	Ru (843)	cremation; flint; pottery; stone axes; stone	EBA
Bants Carn (186)	ENE	Entrance passage	Ru c/u (1097)	pottery	BA
Chambered cairn H1-D5 North Hill (181)	Centre	Floor of entrance grave	Ru (1090)	animal bone; charcoal; pebbles; pottery; shells; worked stones	BA
South barrow T.11 Tynings Barrow Group (67)	Unknown	Barrow ditch	S (848-9, 851-2); S frag (850)	pottery; spindlewhorl	BA
Barrow E Boleigh (94)	Unknown	Cairn stones	S (901); Ru (899-900)	none	BA
Bussow (96)	Unknown	?Cairn stones	Q c/u (905)	unknown	LBA

The Life and Death of Querns

Table 8.1: Iron Age postholes with querns (Information from database, derived from Fitzpatrick et al 1999a; Barrett et al 2000; Cadbury Castle Archive; ApSimon and Greenfield 1972; Valentin pers. corresp.; Tabor pers. corresp.; ApSimon 1977; Johns forthcoming).

Posthole Location (Context No)	Quadrant	Quern Type (Database Id No)	Associated Finds	Site Name (Database Id No)	Date
4 or 12 post structure 61 (33)	SE or E side	RoU frag (8)	plant remains; pottery	Blackhorse (5)	M-LIA
4 post structure L5 (L355)	NW	S frag (194)	unknown	Cadbury Castle (34)	MIA
4 post structure P9 (P009)	NW	S (223); S frag (222)	bone; bronze frag; charcoal; flint; pottery; burnt stone	Cadbury Castle (34)	EIA
6 post structure T5 (T002)	NE	Ru frag (153)	bone; charcoal; flint; iron slag; pottery	Cadbury Castle (34)	MIA
NE 6 post structure T4 (T012)	NE	Q frag (150)	bone; pottery	Cadbury Castle (34)	E-MIA
3 post structure 276 (144)	N	Q frag (6)	unknown	Long Range (4)	M-LIA
6 post structure T2 (T345)	Centre of N side	Ro frag (237); S frag (236)	bone; daub; flint; pottery; slag; slingstones	Cadbury Castle (34)	MIA
Roundhouse 137 (654)	NW	Ru frag (12)	unidentified object	Blackhorse (5)	M-LIA
Roundhouse T6 (T348)	NE	Q frag (147)	bone; daub; flint; pottery	Cadbury Castle (34)	M-LIA
Roundhouse 1 entrance (F.37)	E	S (961)	burnt post; packing stones	Trevisker (116)	IA
N side of entrance to structure 2 (780)	E	S frag (893)	stone	Twinyeo (91)	EIA
Arc of round house (F045)	Unknown	S frags (732)	animal bone; pottery; stone	Milsoms Corner (38)	IA
Within hillfort (K623)	Unknown	RoU frag (373)	bone; bronze frag; pottery; slingstones; stone	Cadbury Castle (34)	IA
Within hillfort (PH2)	Unknown	Ru c/u (889)	animal bone; iron brooch; pottery	Burledge Camp (87)	IA
Within hillfort (N654)	Unknown	RoU frag (358)	bone; flint; pottery; slingstones	Cadbury Castle (34)	MIA
Enclosure 401 palisade (224)	Unknown	Ru frag (1319)	none	Trenowah (205)	MIA
Enclosure 401 palisade (206)	Unknown	Ru frag (1317)	none	Trenowah (205)	MIA
Enclosure 401 palisade (247)	Unknown	S frag (1318)	none	Trenowah (205)	MIA

Appendices

Table 8.2: Iron Age drains and gullies with querns (Information from database, derived from ApSimon and Greenfield 1972; Jones 2004-2005; Birbeck 2000; Barrett et al 2000; Cadbury Castle Archive; Tabor pers. corresp.; Schwieso 1976; Fitzpatrick et al 1999a; Gossip forthcoming).

Context Form (Context No)	Roundhouse quadrant	Quern Type (Database Id No)	Associated Finds	Site Name (Database Id No)	Date
Drain House 2 (M.29)	N	RoU (964)	pottery	Trevisker (116)	IA
Drain Site 9 (214)	S	SQ frag (1046-7)	charcoal; flint; pebble; plant remains; pottery; quartz	Stannon Down (105)	MIA
Drain House 2 (M.25)	S	RoL (963)	unknown	Trevisker (116)	IA
Pennanular gully P2 (P803)	?SW	Q frag (230)	bone; daub; flint; pottery; slingstones; stone; burnt stone	Cadbury Castle (34)	LIA
Pennanular gully (130)	E	Q frag (865)	animal bone; charcoal; plant remains; pottery	Cannards Grave (76)	MIA
Pennanular gully (269)	S terminal	Q frags (7)	charcoal; flint; pottery	Long Range (4)	M-LIA
Pennanular Gully (203)	S	Q frag (10)	charcoal; flint; pebble; plant remains; pottery	Blackhorse (5)	M-LIA
Pennanular gully C4 (C758)	S	Ru frag (287)	pottery; slag; slingstones; stone	Cadbury Castle (34)	M-LIA
Pennanular gully L2 (L758)	SE	Q frag (141)	bone; glass; iron obj; pottery	Cadbury Castle (34)	M-LIA
Pennanular gully House 6 (4500)	W (close to entrance)	Ru (1448)	crucible; metalworking waste; pottery; tuyere frags	Higher Besore (208)	M-LIA
Pennanular gully (304)	-	Q frags (862)	animal bone; charcoal; fired clay; glass bead; plant remains; pottery	Cannards Grave (76)	MIA
Pennanular gully	-	SQ (frag) (1000)	unknown	Threemilestone Round (126)	LIA
Gully (F009)	-	Q frag (762)	unknown	Homeground (41)	IA
Linear Gully (N954)	N/A	SQ (213)	antler tool; bone; bone tool; bronze frags; charcoal; daub; flint; iron frags; pottery; slingstones; polishing stone; stone; burnt stone; whetstone	Cadbury Castle (34)	MIA
Linear gully (F003)	N/A	RoU frag (765-6)	unknown	Moor (42)	LIA

The Life and Death of Querns

Table 8.3: Iron Age pits with querns (Information from database, derived from Johns forthcoming; Cadbury Castle Archive; Morris 1988; Watts, S. 2008b; Tabor 2008; Anon 1930; Adkins and Adkins 1991; McKinley 1999; Leivers et al 2007; McMurtrie 1899; Rahtz and Clevedon Brown 1958-1959; Cornwall Historic Environment Record No. 465; Brooks 1974; Russell 1971; Gordon 1940; Sheppard and Wolf 1982; Newman et al 1999; Fitzpatrick et al 1999a.; Saunders and Harris 1982; Watts, S. 2007a; Wilkes pers. corresp.).

SiteName (Database Id No)	Pit Number	Quern Type (Database Id No)	Layer (1 = bottom)	Associated Finds (finds in brackets from other layers/ association unknown)	Date
Trenowah (205)	345	SQ (1309); SQ frag (1308)	Single fill	pebbles; pottery; rubbing stone; stone	EIA
Cadbury Castle (34)	B853	RoU frags (314, 372)	Single fill	bone; charcoal; flint; slingstones; charcoal	E-MIA
Cadbury Castle (34)	E988	Q frags (335)	Unknown	(jet/shale bead; pottery)	E-MIA
Dibbles Farm (56)	XLVIII	SQ frags (822)	Unknown	(animal bone; baked clay; burnt stone; flint; grinder; pottery; whetstone)	E-MIA
Cadbury Castle (34)	N/A	Ro frag (1156)	Unknown	pottery	IA
Cadbury Castle (34)	A150	SQ frag (300)	1 of 3 layers	bone; flint; pottery; stone (bone; flint; iron obj; plant remains; pottery; stone; burnt stone)	IA
Cadbury Castle (34)	B092	RoU frags (381)	2 of 2 layers	(bone; flint; slingstones)	IA
Cadbury Castle (34)	EB8	Ru frag (327)	Single fill	bone; bronze pins; dog skull; pottery; slingstone; stone	IA
Sigwells Farm (39)	TR12/F011	Q frag (742)	Main layer	Lamb; neonatal infant; stone; pottery (brooch)	IA
Ham Hill (44)	-	Q state unknown (796-7)	Unknown	(antler; iron; pottery; slingstones)	IA
Ham Hill (44)	-	Q c/u (798)	Unknown	(antler; iron; pottery; slingstones)	IA
Ham Hill (44)	70	RoU frag (782)	Single fill	animal bone; charcoal; flint; pottery; slingstone; whetstone	IA
Ham Hill (44)	211	RoL (211)	Unknown. Pit not fully excavated	(horse skull)	IA
Ham Hill (44)	316	Q frag (784)	Unknown (3 layers)	(animal bone; burnt clay; burnt stone; charcoal; plant remains; pottery; slingstone)	IA
Tyning Quarry (45)	1	RoU (803)	Unknown	(animal teeth & bone; burnt clay; burnt stone; charcoal; flint; iron; pottery; spindlewhorl)	IA
Tyning Quarry (45)	2	SQ (982); Ru (983)	Unknown	(animal jaw & teeth; charcoal; pottery;stone)	IA

Appendices

Blaise Castle Hill (54)	Pit A	SQ (814); Ru (984-6)	1 (814, 986), 2 (985) and 3 (984) of 4 layers	1: iron nail; quartzite pebble animal bone; antler;bronze; brooches; burnt clay; charcoal; flint; hammerstone; hone; iron; pottery;; slingstones; spindlewhorls; weaving combs 2: animal bone; antler knife handle; bronze brooch; hammerstone; pottery; slingstones; spindlewhorl; weaving combs; whetstone 3: bronze wire; flint flakes; iron slag; Roman pottery; slingstone	IA
Porth Bean House (101)		Q c/u (929)	Unknown	(pottery; hammerstones)	IA
The Rumps (103)		Ro frag (932)	Single fill	pottery	IA
Trendrennen (138)		RoU (1016)	Found on top of pit	unknown	IA
Gurnards Head (150)		Ru (1032)	Single fill	none	IA
St Columb Porth (177)		Q c/u (1086)	Unknown	pottery; stone hammers	IA
Cadbury Castle (34)	C061	Q frag (1226)	Single fill	pottery; slingstones	MIA
Cadbury Castle (34)	F658	SQ frag (1233); Q frag (342)	Single fill	bone; flint; pottery; slag; slingstones; whetstone	MIA
Cadbury Castle (34)	N204	Q frag (180, 1225)	1 of 3 layers (180) Other unknown	ash; bone; charcoal; pottery; burnt stone (bone; bone tool; charcoal; flint; loomweight; pottery; burnt stone; stone)	MIA
Cadbury Castle (34)	B131	RoU frag (272)	1 of 3 layers	1: bone; stone (pottery; slingstones; stone)	MIA
Cadbury Castle (34)	B431	Q frag (359)	Unknown (7 layers)	(bone; charcoal; flint; pottery; slingstones; stone; burnt stone)	MIA
Sigwells Farm (39)	TR13/ F040	Ru (750)	Lower fill (main layer)	burnt ammonite; burnt animal bone; charcoal; pottery	MIA
Ham Hill (44)	126	RoU frag (781)	Unknown (3 layers)	(animal bone; burnt clay; flint; plant remains; slingstone; whetstone)	MIA
Ham Hill (44)	133	RoU frag (781)	Unknown (2 layers)	(animal bone; pottery; whetstone)	MIA
Encie Farm (73)	117	SQ frags (858)	Lower fill	(plant remains; pottery; stone)	MIA
Long Range (4)	41	SQ frag (5)	Unknown ?Single layer	none recorded	M-LIA
Cadbury Castle (34)	B866	Q frag (251)	Pit cutting two postholes Unknown (7 layers in all)	(bone; flint; iron knife; pottery; stone)	M-LIA
Cadbury Castle (34)	C102	RoU frag (217)	Small pit cut into larger pit. Single fill	(bone; flint; pottery; ox/horse skull; stone)	M-LIA
Cadbury Castle (34)	C202	Q frag (1451)	2 of 4 layers	bone; pottery; ox skull (bone; pottery; ox skull; slingstones)	M-LIA

The Life and Death of Querns

Cadbury Castle (34)	C203	Q frag (270)	Excavated as one layer	(bone; charcoal; pottery; slag; slate; slingstones; stone; whetstone)	M-LIA
Cadbury Castle (34)	C206	Ru frag (264)	Pit cut by another but top half excavated as one pit. No layers distinguished	(bone; bronze frag; pottery; slingstones; stone)	M-LIA
Cadbury Castle (34)	C409	Q frag (265)	Unknown (7 layers)	(bone and teeth; worked bone; bronze frag; charcoal; flint arrowhead; iron nave bands; pottery; slingstones)	M-LIA
Cadbury Castle (34)	C606	SQ frag (286)	Single fill	bone handle; clay; pottery; slingstones	M-LIA
Cadbury Castle (34)	C655	SQ (221); RoU frag (377)	1 of 2 (221) Other unknown	clay; iron tools; loomweights; 4 ox skulls (bone; bronze brooch; pottery; horse skull; stone)	M-LIA
Cadbury Castle (34)	C661	Ru frag (1228)	2 intercutting pits, quern from earlier pit (B)	(bone; bronze frags; clay; flints; pottery)	M-LIA
Cadbury Castle (34)	C766	Q frag (262, 269, 1227)	2 intercutting pits 1. 4 of 4 layers (262) 2. Smaller pit C766E with single fill cut into larger pit (269) Other unknown	(worked bone; bronze frag; cattle skull frag; charcoal; clay; dog skull; iron nail; pottery; slag; slingstones; stone; burnt stone)	M-LIA
Cadbury Castle (34)	C814	SQ frag (271)	2 intercutting pits each with ?single fill	(bone; pottery)	M-LIA
Cadbury Castle (34)	E982	RoU frags (218,349,380 1230); RoL frag (162,165,191,328); Ro frag (345,6); SQ frag (344); Q frag (166, 258, 334, 351)	Querns part of the structure of a stone-lined pit kiln	(finds within pit include bone; bronze frag; flint; pottery)	M-LIA
Cadbury Castle (34)	F303	SQ frag (343)	Unknown	(crucible frag; hearth lining; slag)	M-LIA
Cadbury Castle (34)	G192	RoU frag (215)	Unknown (6 layers)	(bone; bone tool; charcoal; flint arrowhead; iron saw; iron obj; mould; pottery; slingstones; whetstone)	M-LIA

Cadbury Castle (34)	L002	RoU frag (379)	Unknown (3 layers)	(ash; bone; bone tool; clay; flint; iron slag; iron awl; pottery; skull; slingstone; spindlewhorl; stone)	M-LIA
Cadbury Castle (34)	L012	Q frags (137, 277)	2 intercutting pits each with single layer. Pit B (277) cut into A (137)	(ash; bone; bronze frag; charcoal; fired clay; pottery; slag; spindlewhorl)	M-LIA
Cadbury Castle (34)	L076	RoU frag (356)	Unknown (3 layers)	(bronze frag; charcoal; pottery; slag; slingstones)	M-LIA
Cadbury Castle (34)	L108	RoU frag (281)	2 of 3 layers	iron object (bone; clay; iron objects; loomweight: pottery; slingstones; stone)	M-LIA
Cadbury Castle (34)	L152	SQ frag (193); RoU frag (362)	Single fill	ammonite fossil; pottery; slag; slingstones	M-LIA
Cadbury Castle (34)	L403	RoU frag (125)	?4 of 4 layers	bone; brooch; pin; pottery; slingstone; weaving comb (bone; bone tool; charcoal; clay; flint; iron nail; pottery; slingstones; spindlewhorl; burnt stone)	M-LIA
Cadbury Castle (34)	L404	Q frags (155-6)	Single fill	bone; bone tools; bronze slag; charcoal; clay bead; daub; iron nail; oyster shells; pottery; slingstones; stone; burnt stone; weaving comb frags	M-LIA
Cadbury Castle (34)	N280	Q frags (171, 176)	Remnants of large pit	(bone; bronze slag; charcoal; crucible frag; daub; flint; pottery; slingstones; stone; burnt stone)	M-LIA
Cadbury Castle (34)	P256	Q frag (308)	4 of 4 layers	bone; bronze sheeting; flint; iron obj; pottery; slingstones (bone; bronze frags; charcoal; clay; flint; fossil; iron obj; plant remains; pottery; slingstones; burnt stone)	M-LIA
Cadbury Castle (34)	P758	SQ frag (227); RoL (385); Q frag (376; 1232)	2 (227, 376) and 4 (385) of 6 layers. Other unknown	4: chalk disc; clay; flint; iron bucket loop; iron saw; small iron sickle; human cranium; pottery;slingstones; stone some burnt; whetstone 2: bone; chalk; charcoal; clay; flint; iron objects; slingstones; stone some burnt (bone; bronze objects; clay; flint; iron sickle and saw; pottery; stone some burnt; whetstone)	M-LIA
Cadbury Castle (34)	P905	Q frag (233)	2 of 3 layers	bone; flint; pottery; slingstones; weaving comb (worked bone;iron point; perforated stone; weaving comb)	M-LIA
Cadbury Castle (34)	S043	Q frags (158-9, 1223)	Unknown (2 layers with stones at top of pit)	(bone; bronze; charcoal; crucible frags; clay; flint; iron; loomweight; pottery; rubbing stones; slag; slingstones; spindlewhorl)	M-LIA

The Life and Death of Querns

Cadbury Castle (34)	S053/L103	Q frag (144)	2 of 2 layers	crucible frags; pottery; slag; slingstones (bone point; bronze brooch; bronze pin; charcoal; clay; flint scraper; iron obj and slag; loomweight frags; pottery; slingstones; stone; burnt stone)	M-LIA
Cadbury Castle (34)	S153	RoU frag (136)	2 of 4 layers	(bone; charcoal; clay; flint; pottery; slingstones; stone; burnt stone)	M-LIA
Cadbury Castle (34)	S203	Q frag (149)	Single fill	bone; charcoal; flint scraper; pottery; slingstones; burnt stone	M-LIA
Cadbury Castle (34)	S207	RoU frags (379)	1 of 4 layers	(crucible frags; pottery; whetstone)	M-LIA
Cadbury Castle (34)	T254	RoU frags (126; 352); Ro frag (369); Q frag (140)	2 of 4 layers (126, 352) Others unknown	charcoal; dog bone; cattle and horse skull frags; pottery (animal bone; bone tools; bronze obj; bronze spear; charcoal; clay; flint;iron obj; loomweight; pottery; slingstones; stone; burnt stone; whetstone)	M-LIA
Cadbury Castle (34)	T325	Ru frag (151); Ro frag (255)	Unknown (6 layers)	(bone; bronze frags; charcoal; clay; iron obj; pottery; slingstones	M-LIA
Cadbury Castle (34)	W076/B715	Q frag (259)	5 of 6 layers	rubble stone (bone; bronze frags; clay bead; iron obj; loomweight; pebbles; pottery; slingstones; spindlewhorl)	M-LIA
Cadbury Castle (34)	C255	RoU frag (366)	1 of 4 layers in secondary pit	(bone; charcoal; pottery; slag; slingstones; stone)	LIA
Cadbury Castle (34)	C457	RoU frag (187)	Unknown (4 layers)	(bone and teeth; bronze pin; charcoal; flint; iron knife; pottery; slag; slingstones; stone; burnt stone)	LIA
Cadbury Castle (34)	D838	SQ (384)	5 of 5 layers	whetstone; worked stone (clay; glassbead; pottery; slag; spindlewhorl)	LIA
Cadbury Castle (34)	F609	Q frags (338-9)	Single fill	bronze tweezers; bronze obj; flint; iron nail; pottery; slingstones	LIA
Cadbury Castle (34)	L452	SQ frag (195)	Pit cut by posthole Single fill	bone; bone tool; flint; pottery; slingstones; stone; burnt stone; whetstone	LIA
Cadbury Castle (34)	L649	RoL frag (364)	Unknown (?2 layers)	(bone; bronze ring; charcoal; iron objs; pottery; slingstone; stone; whetstone)	LIA
Cadbury Castle (34)	N007	Q frag (178)	Single fill	bone; pottery; stone; burnt stone; articulated cow skeleton at bottom of pit	LIA
Cadbury Castle (34)	P822	SQ frag (225)	Unknown (2 layers)	(bone; bronze frags; crucible frag; clay; flint; iron obj and slag; loomweight; pottery; slingstones; stone; burnt stone)	LIA
Cadbury Castle (34)	P826	SQ frag (224)	2 of 2 layers with thin layer of charcoal at base	(bone; charcoal; flint; iron obj; pottery; slingstones; stone; burnt stone; whelk shell)	LIA

Appendices

Cadbury Castle (34)	W035	Ru frag (316); RoU frags (324)	?Single fill	bone; charcoal; clay; pottery; stone; burnt stone	LIA
Cadbury Castle (34)	W058	RoU frag (365)	Unknown (4 layers)	(bone; charcoal; flint; pottery; slag; slingstones; burnt stone; whetstone)	LIA
Cadbury Castle (34)	W094	Ru frag (313)	Single fill	pottery; slingstones	LIA
Sigwells Farm (39)	TR13/F108	RoU frag (747); Q frag (748)	Lower fill (main layer)	raven; stones	LIA
Sigwells Farm (39)	TR13/F155	SQ frag (749)	Upper silt		LIA
Ham Hill (44)	1	RoU frags (785)	Unknown Pit not fully excavated	(animal bone; burnt stone; flint; pottery; slingstones)	LIA
Ham Hill (44)	73	RoU (780)	4 of 4 layers	animal bone; burnt flint; pottery; burnt stone (burnt animal bone; iron nave hoops and currency bar; plant remains; pottery; burnt stone	LIA
Ham Hill (44)	108	RoU (771); RoL (772)	1 of 3 layers	animal bone; burnt stone; iron sickle; plant remains; pottery; slingstones; whetstones (animal bone; ash; pottery; slingstones)	LIA
Ham Hill (44)	136	RoL (774); Q frag (778)	Single fill	animal bone including 7 horse skulls; iron billhook; pottery; slingstones	LIA
Ham Hill (44)	149	Q state unknown (779)	2 of 5 layers	horse skull; burnt stone (animal bone; baked clay; plant remains; pottery; slag; slingstones	LIA
Ham Hill (44)	185	RoU frags (777)	Unknown	(animal bone; baked clay; burnt stone; pottery; slingstone)	LIA
Castle Gotha (124)	RK358	RoL frag (998)	Unknown	pottery	LIA
Mount Folly (20)	859	RoU frag (1160)	Single fill	unknown	IA/Roman
Mount Folly (20)	F707	RoL frag 956)	Single fill	stone	IA/Roman
Mount Folly (20)	F755	RoU frags (55)	Single fill	stone; whetstone	IA/Roman
Cadbury Castle (34)	B454	RoU frag (130)	2 of 3 layers	charcoal; stone (bone;daub;pottery)	IA/Roman
Cadbury Castle (34)	W047	Ru frag (309)	5 of 6 layers	bronze frags (bone; bronze ring; bronze lump; flint; iron obj; pottery; slag; slingstones)	IA/Roman

The Life and Death of Querns

Table 8.4: Iron Age ditches with querns (Information from database derived from Watts, S. 2008a; Tabor pers. corresp.; Leach 2008; Gossip and Jones 2007; Gossip forthcoming; Saunders and Harris 1982; Fitzpatrick et al 1999a; Harris 1977; Leach 2002; Horne 1937; Hencken 1932; Johns forthcoming; Gray 1922; Gray 1925).

Ditch type (Context No)	Location within ditch	Quern Type (Database Id No)	Associated Finds	SiteName (Database Id No)	Date
Ditch (F010)	Unknown	Ru frag (764)	unknown	Homeground (41)	M-LIA
Ditch (F001)	Unknown	Q frag (767)	stone (animal bone; human bone; bronze and iron fragments)	Moor (42)	MIA
Ditch (F1)	Unknown	Ro frag (1407)	charcoal; flint flakes; beaker pottery sherd	Field Farm (77)	IA
Field (19)	S end of field	S frag (947)	pottery	Tremough (108)	LIA
Field/enclosure (2010)	Unknown	Ru (1449)	pottery	Higher Besore (208)	M-LIA
Enclosure (A7)	SSE	S frag (997)	unknown	Castle Gotha (124)	LIA/Roman
Enclosure (132)	SE	Ro frag (9)	pottery; whetstones	Blackhorse (5)	M-LIA
Enclosure (132)	S	Q frag (11)	flint; plant remains; pottery; spindle whorl	Blackhorse (5)	M-LIA
Enclosure (F003)	S	Q frag (741)		Sigwells Farm (39)	LIA
Enclosure (Cutting C)	SW quadrant	Ru frag (1026)	pebbles; pottery	Bodwen (146)	IA
Enclosure	SW quadrant	S frag (866)	animal bone; flint flakes; pottery	Field Farm (77)	IA
Enclosure	Unknown	Q frags (857)	unknown	Camerton (72)	EIA
Enclosure	E (end of fogou)	S c/u (954)	bone; charcoal; flint; mortar; pottery	Treveneague (114)	IA
Linear (167) (NE-SW)		Q frags (4)	chert	Langland Lane (3)	IA
Linear (122) (N-S)		Q frag (1310)	pottery; rubbing stone	Trenowah (205)	EIA
Linear (NW-SE)		S frag (1314, 1316); Ru (1315)	pottery	Trenowah (205)	EIA
Linear (163) (NW-SE)		S frag (1313)	pottery	Trenowah (205)	EIA
Rampart	E side of N entrance	Q frag (981)	charcoal; iron; pottery; whetstones	Cadbury Camp (71)	IA
Rampart (Cutting XIV)	Middle of east side of spur	RoU frag (788); Q frag (789)	Dog jaw bone; flint; iron slag; hammerstone; human burial; ox skull; pottery; spindlewhorl; stone disc; whetstone fragment	Ham Hill (44)	IA

Appendices

Table 8.5: Iron Age funerary contexts and human bone deposits with querns (Information from database, derived from Christie 1960; Palmer 1919-20; Tabor pers. corresp.; Trethellan Farm Archive; Hencken 1932; Gray 1925; Tabor 2008, 135; Cadbury Castle Archive).

Funerary Context (Context No)	Quern Type (Database Id No)	Associated Human Bone Type	Site Name (Database Id No)	Date
Barrow ditch	Ro frags (1082)	None directly associated	Crig-a-Mennis (174)	IA
Cave floor	Ru frag (847)	Human bone	Reads (Keltic) Cavern (66)	LIA
Ditch (F001)	Q frag (767)	Human bone	Moor (42)	MIA
Grave (2064)	Ru frags (1247)	None directly associated	Trethellan Farm (204)	IA
Fogou infill (114)	SQ c/u (953); c/u, Ru c/u (1030-1)	Human bone	Treveneague	IA
Rampart ditch (E side of spur)	RoU frags (788), Q frag (789)	Articulated adult burial	Ham Hill (44)	IA
Pit (F011)	Q frag (742)	Articulated infant burial	Sigwells Farm (39)	IA
Pit (P758 – layer 4)	RoL (385) SQ frag (227); Q frags (376, 1232)	Human cranium	Cadbury Castle (34)	M-LIA

BIBLIOGRAPHY

Adams, J. 1993: Toward Understanding the Technological Development of Manos and Metates, *Kiva*, 58.3, 331-344.

Adams, J., Delgade, S., Dubreuil, L., Hamon, C., Plisson, H. & Risch, R. 2009: Functional Analysis of Macro-Lithic Artefacts. A Focus on Working Surfaces. In, Sternke, F., Eigeland, L. & Costa, L-J. (Eds.), *Non-Flint Raw Material Use in Prehistory*, 43-66.

Adams, J.L. 1988: Use-Wear Analyses on Manos and Hide-Processing Stones, *Journal of Field Archaeology*, 15.3, 307-315.

Adams, J.L. 1999: Refocusing the Role of Food-Grinding Tools as Correlates for Subsistence Strategies in the U.S. Southwest, *American Antiquity*, 64.3, 475-498.

Adams, J.L. 2002: *Ground Stone Analysis*, Salt Lake City, University of Utah Press.

Adkins, L. & Adkins, R. 1991: Excavations at Ham Hill, 1991, *Proceedings of the Somerset Archaeological and Natural History Society*, 135, 89-94.

Albek, S. 2005: VIII. Stone Tools, *Acta Archaeologica*, 76.1, 117-123.

Alcock, L. 1960: Castell Odo. An Embanked Settlement on Mynydd Ystum, Near Aberdaron, Caernarvonshire, *Archaeologia Cambrensis*, 109, 78-135.

Alcock, L. 1972: *'By Cadbury Castle is that Camelot...' The Excavation of Cadbury Castle 1966-1970*, London, Thames & Hudson.

Alcock, L. 1995: *Cadbury Castle Somerset. The Early Medieval Archaeology*, Cardiff, University of Wales Press.

Allen, H. 1974: The Bagundji of the Darling Basin. Cereal Gatherers in an Uncertain Environment, *World Archaeology*, 5.3, 309-322.

Alonso, N. 1997: Oriegen y Expansion del Molino Rotativo Bajo en el Mediterraneo Occidental. In, Meeks, D. & Garcia, D. (Eds.), *Techniques et Economie Antiques et Médiévales. Le Temps de L'innovation*, Paris, Editions Errance, 15-19.

Alonso, N. 2002: Le Moulin Rotatif Manuel au Nord-est de la Péninsule Ibérique. In, Procopiou, H. & Treuil, R. (Eds.), *Moudre et Broyer*, Paris, CTHS, 183-196.

Alonso, N., Aulinas, M., Garcia, M., Martin, F., Prats, G. & Vila, S. 2009: *Manufacturing Rotary Querns During 4th C.BC. Els Vilars Fortress (Arbeca, Catalonia, Spain)*, Poster presented at Bread for the People. A Colloquium on the Archaeology of Mills and Milling, The British School at Rome, 4th-7th November 2009.

Ambrose, K. 2006: The 'Mystic Mill' Capital at Vézelay. In, Walton, S.A. (Ed.), *Wind & Water in the Middle Ages*, Tempe, Arizona Centre for Medieval and Renaissance Studies, 235-258.

Anon 1834: Bread in the East, *The Penny Magazine*, 4th January, 2-4.

Anon 1848: Archaeological Intelligence, *The Archaeological Journal*, 5, 322-337.

Anon 1850: Proceedings at the Meeting of the Archaeological Institute. December 6, 1850, *The Archaeological Journal*, 7, 391-398.

Anon 1868-1870: Chronological Memoranda 1867, *Journal of the Royal Institution of Cornwall*, 3, 68-76.

Anon 1874: Women Grinding Corn, *Illustrated London News*, 375.

Anon 1895: Japanese Domestic Milling, *The Miller*, XXI No. 864, 5th August 1895, 412.

Anon 1901: House Mills in Posen, *The Miller*, 3rd June 1901, 227.

Anon 1930: Additions to the Museum, *Proceedings of the Somerset Natural History and Archaeological Society*, 76.1, lxxxix-xc.

Anon 1974: Carn Euny, *Current Archaeology*, 44, 262-268.

Anon 2010: *Encyclopedia of Myths*, http://www.mythencyclopedia.com, 29th January 2010.

Anon 2011: Teigncombe Pottery Seminar, *A.C.E Archaeological Club Newsletter*, March, 15.

ApSimon, A.M. 1977: Burledge Camp (Notes on the Trial Excavations, 1955). In, Rahtz, P.A. and Greenfield, E., *Excavations at Chew Valley Lake, Somerset*, Department of Environment Archaeological Report, 8, 168-170.

Bibliography

ApSimon, A.M. & Greenfield, E. 1972: The Excavation of Bronze Age and Iron Age Settlements at Trevisker, St. Eval, Cornwall, *Proceedings of the Prehistoric Society*, 38, 302-381.

Aquilué, X., Castanyer, P., Santos, M. & Tremoleda, J. 2000: *Guidebooks to the Museu d'Arqueologia de Catalunya*. Empúries Edicions El Mèdol, Generalitat de Catalunya.

Aranguren, B., Becattini, R., Lippi, M.M. & Revedin, A. 2007: Grinding Flour in Upper Palaeolithic Europe (25,000 Years BP), *Antiquity*, 81, 845-855.

Armit, I. 1991: The Atlantic Scottish Iron Age. Five Levels of Chronology, *Proceedings of the Society of Antiquaries of Scotland*, 121, 181-214.

Arnold, B. 2001: Power Drinking in Iron Age Europe, *British Archaeology*, 57, 12-19.

Aschmann, H. 1949: A Metate Make of Baja, California, *American Anthropologist*, 51.4, 682-686.

Ashbee, P. 1976: Bant's Carn, St. Marys, Isles of Scilly. An Entrance Grave Restored and Reconsidered, *Cornish Archaeology*, 15, 11-26.

Ashbee, P. 1983: Halangy Porth, St. Mary's, Isles of Scilly, Excavations 1975-76, *Cornish Archaeology*, 22, 3-42.

Ashbee, P. 1996: Halangy Down, St. Mary's, Isle of Scilly, Excavations 1964-1977, *Cornish Archaeology*, 35.

Auel, J.M. 2002: *The Shelters of Stone*, London, BCA.

Balch, H.E. 1914: *Wookey Hole. Its Caves and Cave Dwellers*, Oxford, Oxford University Press.

Barber, A. 2000: *Hayes Farm, Clyst Honiton Nr. Exeter, Devon. Archaeological Excavation Phase 1 (1999)*, Cotswold Archaeological Trust Report, 001127.

Barber, M. 2003: *Bronze and the Bronze Age*, Stroud, Tempus Publishing Ltd.

Barford, P.M. 1984: Some Possible Quern Quarries in the Bristol Area. A Preliminary Survey, *Bristol and Avon Archaeology*, 3, 13-17.

Baring-Gould, S., Burnard, R., Worth, R.N., Gray, W.A.G. & Worth, R.H. 1894: The Exploration of Grimspound, *Transactions of the Devonshire Association*, 26, 101-121.

Baring-Gould, S. (ed) 1901: Seventh Report of the Dartmoor Exploration Committee, *Transactions of the Devonshire Association*, 33, 129-138.

Baring-Gould, S. (ed) 1902: Eighth Report of the Dartmoor Exploration Committee, *Transactions of the Devonshire Association*, 34, 160-165.

Barker, G 1985: *Prehistoric Farming in Europe*, Cambridge, Cambridge University Press.

Barnwell, E.L. 1881: Querns, *Archaeologia Cambrensis*, 30-43

Barrett, J.C. 1987: The Glastonbury Lake Village. Models and Source Criticism, *The Archaeological Journal*, 144, 209-423.

Barrett, J.C. 1994: *Fragments from Antiquity. An Archaeological of Social Life in Britain, 2900-1200BC*, Oxford, Blackwell.

Barrett, J.C. 2000: Material Culture. The Artefact Categories. In, Barrett, J.C., Freeman, P.W.M. & Woodward, A., *Cadbury Castle Somerset. The Later Prehistoric and Early Historic Archaeology*, London, English Heritage Archaeological Report, 20, 44-45.

Barrett, J.C., Freeman, P.W.M. & Woodward, A. 2000: *Cadbury Castle Somerset. The Later Prehistoric and Early Historic Archaeology*, London, English Heritage Archaeological Report, 20.

Baudais, D. & Lundström-Baudais, K. 2002: Enquête Ethnoarchéologique dans un Village du Nord-Oest du Népal. In, Procopiou, H. & Treuil, R. (Eds.), *Moudre et Broyer, 1, Méthodes*, Paris, CTHS, 155-180.

Bauer, A.J. 1990: Millers and Grinders. Technology and Household Economy in Meso-America, *Agricultural History*, 64.1, 1-17.

Baug, I. & Løland, T. 2009: *The Geologist, the Archaeologist and the Craftsman. An Interdisciplinary Research in Quernstone Quarries in Hyllestad in Western Norway*, Paper presented at Bread for the People. A Colloquium on the Archaeology of Mills and Milling, The British School at Rome, 4th-7th November 2009.

Bayliss, A., Whittle, A. & Healy, F. 2008: Timing, Tempo and Temporailities in the Early Neolithic of Southern England. In, Fokkens, H., Coles, B.J., Vian Gijn, A.L., Kleijne, H.P., Hedwig, H.P. & Slappendel, C.G. (Eds.), *Between Foraging and Farming*, Leiden, 25-42.

Baysal, A. & Wright, K.I. 2005: Cooking, Crafts and Curation. Ground-stone Artefacts from Çatalhöyük. In, Hodder, I. (Ed.), *Changing Materialities at Çatalhöyük. Reports from the 1995-99 Seasons*, Cambridge and London, McDonald Institute and British Institute at Ankara, 307-324.

Beaune, S.A. de 2003: Origine du Matériel de Mouture. Innovation et Continuité du Paléolithique au Néolithique. In, Barboff, M., Griffin-Kremer, C., Kremer, R. & Sigaut, F. (Eds.), *Meules à Grains.*, Paris, Ibis Press, 17-30.

Beckett, S.C. 1981: Pollen Analysis of the Peat Deposits. In, Smith, K., Coppen, J., Wainwright, C.J. & Becket, S., The Shaugh Moor Project: Third Report -Settlement and Environment Investigations, *Proceedings of the Prehistoric Society*, 47, 205-273.

Behre, K. 2007: Evidence for Mesolithic Agriculture in and around Central Europe, *Vegetation History and Archaeobotany*, 16, 203-219.

Bell, M. 1977: Excavations at Bishopstone, Sussex, *Sussex Archaeological Collections*, 115.

Bellamy, P.S. 2000: Querns. In, Barrett, J.C., Freeman, P.W.M. & Woodward, A. (Eds.), *Cadbury Castle Somerset. The Later Prehistoric and Early Historic Archaeology*, 206-211, 313-314.

Bellavia, G., Downes, J.M. & Ferris, I. 2000: The Pits. In, Barrett, J.C., Freeman, P.W.M. & Woodward, A. (Eds.), *Cadbury Castle, Somerset. The Later Prehistoric and Early Historic Archaeology*, London, English Heritage Archaeological Report, 20, 203-206.

Bennett, J.A. 1890: Camelot, *Proceedings of the Somerset Archaeological and Natural History Society*, 36.2, 1-19.

Bennett, R. & Elton, J. 1898: *History of Corn Milling, 1, Handstones, Slave & Cattle Mills*, London, Simpkin, Marshall and Company Ltd.

Beresford, G. 1971: Tresmorn, St. Gennys, *Cornish Archaeology*, 10, 55-72.

Bersu, G. 1940: Excavations at Little Woodbury, Wiltshire, *Proceedings of the Prehistoric Society*, 6, 30-111.

Binford, L.R. 1973: Interassemblage Variability. The Mousterian and the 'Functional' Argument In, Renfew, C. (Ed.), *The Explanation of Culture Change. Models in Prehistory*, London, Duckworth, 227-254.

Birbeck, V. 2000: Excavations on Iron Age and Romano-British Settlements at Cannards Grave, Shepton Mallet, *Proceedings of the Somerset Archaeological and Natural History Society*, 144, 41-116.

Birley, E. 1932: Excavations at Chesterholm-Vindolanda, *Archaeologia Aeliana*, 9, 216-221.

Black, M.E. 1984: Maidens and Mothers. An Analysis of Hopi Corn Metaphors, *Ethnology*, 23.4, 279-288.

Blight, J.T. 1864-1867: *Proceedings of the Society of Antiquaries of London*, 3,

Bloxam, E. 2011: Visualising the Invisible. Re-discovering the Ancient Grinding Stone Quaries of the Aswan West Bank, Egypt. In, Williams, D. & Peacock, D. (Eds.), *Bread for the People. The Archaeology of Mills and Millng*, University of Southampton, Series in Archaeology Monograph, 3, Oxford, Archaeopress, 43-53.

Borlase, W. 1756 (reprinted 1966): *Observations on the Ancient and Present State of the Islands of Scilly*, Newcastle, Frank Graham.

Borlase, W.C. 1872: *Naenia Cornubiae*, London, Longmans, Green, Reader and Dyer.

Bowen, H.C. & Wood, P.D. 1968: Experimental Storage of Corn Underground and its Implications for Iron Age Settlements, *London University Institute of Archaeology Bulletin*, 7, 1-14.

Bradfield, R.M. 1973: *A Natural History of Associations, 2*, London, Gerald Duckworth & Company Limited.

Bradley, R. 1984: *The Social Foundations of Prehistoric Britain*, London, Book Club Associates.

Bradley, R. 1987: Stages in the Chronological Development of Hoards and Votive Deposits, *Proceedings of the Prehistoric Society*, 53, 351-362.

Bradley, R. 1998: *The Significance of Monuments*, London, Routledge.

Bradley, R. 2005a: *Ritual and Domestic Life in Prehistoric Europe*, London, Routledge.

Bradley, R. 2005b: *The Moon and the Bonfire*, Edinburgh, Society of Antiquaries of Scotland.

Bremness, L. 1988: *The Complete Book of Herbs*, London, Guild Publishing.

Britnell, W.J. & Savory, H.N. 1984: *Two Neolithic Long Cairns in the Black Mountains of Brecknock*, Bangor, Cambrian Archaeological Monograph, 2.

Brooks, R.T. 1974: The Excavation of The Rumps Cliff Castle, St. Minver, Cornwall, *Cornish Archaeology*, 13, 7-50.

Brown, A. 2007: Dating the Onset of Cereal Cultivation in Britain and Ireland. The Evidence from Charred Cereal Grains, *Antiquity*, 81, 1042-1052.

Brück, J. 1995: A Place for the Dead. The Role of Human Remains in Late Bronze Age Britain, *Proceedings of the Prehistoric Society*, 61, 245-277.

Brück, J. 1999a: Ritual and Rationality. Some Problems of Interpretation in European Archaeology, *European Journal of Archaeology*, 2.3, 313-344.

Brück, J. 1999b: Houses, Lifecycles and Deposition on Middle Bronze Age Settlements in Southern England, *Proceedings of the Prehistoric Society*, 65, 145-166.

Brück, J. 2001: Body Metaphors and Technologies of Transformation in the English Middle and Late Bronze Age. In, Brück, J. (Ed.), *Bronze Age Landscapes. Tradition and Transformation*, Oxford, Oxbow, 149-160.

Brück, J. 2006: Fragmentation, Personhood and the Social Construction of Technology in Middle and Late Bronze Age Britain, *Cambridge Archaeological Journal*, 16.3, 297-315.

Brudenell, M. & Cooper, A. 2008: Post-Middenism. Depositional Histories on Later Bronze Age Settlements at Broom, Bedfordshire, *Oxford Journal of Archaeology*, 27.1, 15-36.

Brumfield, E.M. 1991: Weaving and Cooking. Women's

Production in Aztec Mexico. In, Gero, J.M. & Conkey, M.W. (Eds.), *Engendering Archaeology. Women and Prehistory*, Oxford, Basil Blackwell Ltd., 224-251.

Brun, A. Le 2001: At the Other End of the Sequence. The Cypriot Aceramic Neolithic as seen from Khirokitia. In, Swiny, S. (Ed.), *The Earliest Prehistory of Cyprus. From Colonization to Exploitation*, Boston, American Schools of Oriental Research, 109-117.

Buckley, D. 1993: Querns in Ritual Contexts, *Quern Study Group Newsletter*, 3, 2-5.

Buckley, D.G. 1979: The Stone. In, Wainwright, G.J. (Ed.), *Gusage All Saints. An Iron Age Settlement in Dorset*, 89-97.

Buckley, D.G. & Major, H. 1988: Quernstones. In, Crummy, N. (Ed.), *The Post Roman Small Finds from Excavations in Colchester 1971-1985*, Colchester Archaeological Report, 5, 36-39.

Buckley, D.G. & Major, H. 1990: Quernstones. In, Wrathmell, S. & Nicholson, A. (Eds.), *Dalton Parlours. Iron Age Settlement and Roman Villa*, Yorkshire Archaeology, 3, West Yorkshire Archaeology Service, 105-120.

Bulleid, A. 1917: Millstones and Querns. In, Bulleid, A. & Gray, H. St. George (Eds.), *The Glastonbury Lake Village, 2*, Glastonbury, Glastonbury Antiquarian Society, 608-620.

Bulleid, A. 1924 (reprinted 1980): *The Lake Villages of Somerset*, Glastonbury, Glastonbury Antiquarian Society.

Bulleid, A. 1936: *The Twenty-fifth Long Fox Memorial Lecture. Somerset Lake Villages*, Reprinted from The Bristol Medico-Chirurgical Journal, Winter, 1936, Vo. LIII, No. 202.

Bulleid, A. & Gray, H. St. George 1948: *The Meare Lake Village, 1*, Taunton, Taunton Museum.

Bullen, R.A. 1930: *Harlyn Bay and the Discoveries of its Prehistoric Remains*, Padstow, Colonel Bellers.

Burnard, R. 1897: Dartmoor Stone Implements and Weapons, *Transactions of the Devonshire Association*, 29, 378-385.

Burnham, B. & Burnham, H. 2004: *Dolaucothi-Pumpsaint. Survey and Excavations at a Roman Gold-Mining Complex 1987-1999*, Oxford, Oxbow Books.

Burstow, G.P. & Holleyman, G.A. 1957: Late Bronze Age Settlement on Itford Hill, Sussex, *Proceedings of the Prehistoric Society*, 23, 167-212.

Butcher, S.A. 1978: Excavations at Nornour, Isles of Scilly, 1967-73. The Pre-Roman Settlement, *Cornish Archaeology*, 17, 29-112.

Calder, C.S.T. 1955-1956: Report on the Discovery of Numberous Stone Age House-Sites in Shetland, *Proceedings of the Society of Antiquaries of Scotland*, 89, 340-397.

Campbell, E. 1987: A Cross-Marked Quern from Dunadd and Other Evidence for Relations Between Dunadd and Iona, *Proceedings of the Society of Antiquaries of Scotland*, 17, 105-117.

Campbell, J.G. 1990: *Superstitions of the Highlands and Islands of Scotland*, Glasgow, James MacLehose and Sons.

Cane, S. 1989: Australian Aboriginal Seed Grinding and its Archaeological Record. A Case Study from the Western Desert. In, Harris, D.R. & Hillman, G.C. (Eds.), *Foraging and Farming. The Evolution of Plant Exploitation*, London, Unwin Hyman Ltd., 99-119.

Carruthers, W.J. 2006: The Charred Plant Remains. In, Tingle, M., Excavations of a Possible Causewayed Enclosure and Roman Site at Membury 1986 and 1994-2000, *Proceedings of the Devon Archaeological Society, 64*, 42-45.

Carruthers, W.J. 2007: Plant Remains. In, Gossip, J. & Jones, A.M. (Eds.), *Archaeological Investigations of a Later Prehistoric and a Romano-British Landscape at Tremough, Penryn, Cornwall*, Oxford, BAR British Series, 443, 100-106.

Carruthers, W.J. 2010: The Charred Plant Remains. In, Cotswold Archaeology, *South-West Reinforcement Project. Ottery St. Mary to Aylesbeare, Aylesbeare to Kenn, Fishacre to Choakford Gas Pipelines, Devon. Post-Excavation Assessment and Updated Project Design, 1. Text*, Cotswold Archaeology Report, 09106, Appendix 15.

Carruthers, W.J. forthcoming: The Charred Plant Remains from Truro College. In, Gossip, J., Life Outside the Round. Bronze Age and Iron Age Settlement at Higher Besore and Truro College, Threemilestone, Truro, *for submission to Cornish Archaeology*.

Carter, G.F. 1977: The Metate. An Early Grain-Grinding Implement in the New World. In, Reed, C.A. (Ed.), *Origins of Agriculture*, The Hague, Mouton Publishers, 693-712.

Casalis, E. 1861: *The Basutos. Or, Twenty-Three Years in South Africa*, London, James Nisbet & Co.

Cassel, K. 2005: Sojvide. In, Hoops, J., *Reallexikon der germanischen Altertumskunde*, 29, Berlin, Walter de Gruyter GMBH & Co., 220-223.

Caulfield, S. 1977: The Beehive Quern in Ireland, *Journal of the Royal Society of Antiquaries of Ireland*, 107, 104-138.

Chadwick Hawkes, S. 1969: Finds from Two Middle Bronze Age Pits at Winnall, Winchester, Hants,

Hampshire Field Club and Archaeological Society, 26, 5-18.

Champion, T., Gamble, C., Shennan, S. & Whittle, A. 1984: *Prehistoric Europe*, London, Academic Press.

Chapman, J. 2000a: 'Rubbish-dumps' or 'Places of Deposition'? Neolithic and Copper Age Settlements in Central and Eastern Europe. In, Ritchie, A. (Ed.), *Neolithic Orkney in its European Context*, Cambridge, McDonald Institute for Archaeological Research, 347-362.

Chapman, J. 2000b: *Fragmentation in Archaeology*, London, Routledge.

Chapman, J. 2000c: Pit-digging and Structured Deposition in the Neolithic and Copper Age, *Proceedings of the Prehistoric Society*, 66, 61-87.

Chapman, J. & Gaydarska, B. 2007: *Parts and Wholes. Fragmentation in Prehistoric Context*, Oxford, Oxbow Books.

Chapman, J.W. (ed.) 1970: *Johnson's Journey to the Western Islands of Scotland and Boswell's Journal of a Tour to the Hebrides with Samuel Johnson, LL.D.*, Oxford, Oxford University Press.

Childe, V.G. 1943: Rotary Querns on the Continent and in the Mediterranean Basin, *Antiquity*, 17, 19-26.

Christie, P.M. 1960: Crig-a-Mennis. A Bronze Age Barrow at Liskey, Perranzabuloe, Cornwall, *Proceedings of the Prehistoric Society*, 26, 76-97.

Christie, P.M. 1965: Carn Euny Excavations. Interim Report on the 1964 Season, *Cornish Archaeology*, 4, 24-30.

Christie, P.M. 1988: A Barrow Cemetery on Davidstow moor, Cornwall. Wartime Excavations by C.K. Croft Andrew, *Cornish Archaeology*, 27, 27-169.

Christie, P.M.L. 1978: The Excavation of an Iron Age Souterrain and Settlement at Carn Euny, Sancreed, Cornwall, *Proceedings of the Prehistoric Society*, 44, 309-433.

Clapham, A.J. 1999: Charred Plant Remains. In, Fitzpatrick, A.P., Butterworth, C.A. & Grove, J. (Eds.), *Prehistoric and Roman Sites in East Devon. The A30 Honiton to Exeter Improvement DBFO Scheme, 1996-9. 1. Prehistoric Sites*, Wessex Archaeology Report 16, 51-59, 85, 112-119, 152-158, 184-191.

Clapham, A.J. & Stevens, C.J. 1999: The Charred Plant Remains. Environmental and Economic Evidence. In, Fitzpatrick, A.P., Butterworth, C.A. & Grove, J. (Eds.), *Prehistoric & Roman Sites in East Devon. The A30 Honiton to Exeter Improvement DBFO Scheme, 1996-9. 1. Prehistoric Sites*, Wessex Archaeology Report 16, 196-207.

Clark, E 1961: *Cornish Fogous*, London, Methuen & Co. Ltd.

Clarke, D. & Maguire, P. 1989: *Skara Brae*, Edinburgh, Historic Scotland.

Cleary, K. 2006: Irish Bronze Age Settlements. More Than meets the Eye? *Archaeology Ireland*, 20.2, 18-21.

Close-Brooks, J. 1983: Some Early Querns, *Proceedings of the Society of Antiquaries of Scotland*, 113, 282-289.

Cobbett, W. 1979 (reprint): *Cottage Economy*, Oxford, Oxford University Press.

Cole, D. & Jones, A.M. 2002-2003: Journeys to the Rock. Archaeological Investigatins at Tregarrick Farm, Roche, Cornwall, *Cornish Archaeology*, 41-42, 107-143.

Coles, B. & Coles, J. 1986: *Sweet Track to Glastonbury*, London, Thames & Hudson.

Coles, D. 2009: Note. In, Green, T., Excavation of a Hillslope Enclosure at Holworthy Farm, Parracombe Displaying Bronze Age and Iron Age Activity, *Proceedings of the Devon Archaeological Society*, 67, 79.

Coles, J. & Minnitt, S. 2000: *'Industrious and Fairly Civilized'. The Glastonbury Lake Village*, Taunton, Somerset Levels Project and Somerset County Council Museums Service.

Coles, J.M. 1987: Meare Village East. The Excavations of A. Bulleid and H. St. George Gray 1932-1956, *Somerset Levels Papers*, 13, 1-253.

Collard, M., Edinborough, K., Shennan, S. & Thomas, G. 2010: Radiocarbon Dating Evidence Indicates Migrants Introduced Farming to Britain, *Journal of Archaeological Science*, 37, 866-870.

Colville, J. 1892: The Rural Economy of Scotland in the Time of Burns, *Proceedings of the Philosophical Society of Glasgow*, 23, 120-152.

Cook, S. 1970: Price and Output Variability in a Peasant-Artisan Stoneworking Industry in Oaxaca, Mexico. An Analytical Essay in Economic Anthropology, *American Anthropologist*, 72.4, 776-801.

Cook, S. 1973: Stone Tools for Steel-Age Mexicans? Aspects of Production in a Zapotec Stoneworking Industry, *American Anthropologist*, 75.5, 1485-1503.

Cookson, M.M. 2003: Practical Experience in Using French Millstones. In, Barboff, M., Griffin-Kremer, C., Kremer, R. & Sigaut, F. (Eds.), *Meules à Grains*, Paris, Ibis Press, 344-353.

Cool, H. 2007: Coarse Stone Tools. In, Dunnell, A. (Ed.), *Cist Burials and an Iron Age Settlement at Dryburn Bridge, Innerwick, East Lothian*, 75-78.

Bibliography

Cornwall Council Historic Environment Service 2009: *Flying Through Cornwall's Past*, http://www.historic-cornwall.org.uk/flyingpast.html, 11th August 2009.

Cotswold Archaeology 2010: *South-West Reinforcement Project. Ottery St. Mary to Aylesbeare, Aylesbeare to Kenn, Fishacre to Choakford Gas Pipelines, Devon. Post-Excavation Assessment and Updated Project Design, 1. Text*, Cotswold Archaeology Report, 09106.

Craddock, P.T. 1995: *Early Metal Mining and Production*, Edinburgh, Edinburgh University Press.

Crangle, R. 2002: *Access 2000*, Unpublished course notes, University of Exeter, IT Services.

Crawford, H.S. 1909: Some Types of Quern, or Handmill, *The Journal of the Royal Society of Antiquaries of Ireland*, 39, 393-396.

Crawford, O.G.S. 1953: *Archaeology in the Field*, London, Phoenix House Ltd.

Crawford, O.G.S. & Röder, J. 1955: The Quern-Quarries of Mayen in the Eifel, *Antiquity*, 29, 68-76.

Crofts, C.B. 1952-1953: Bodrifty, Mulfra. Interim Report 1950-1952, *Proceedings of the West Cornwall Field Club*, NS 1.1, 15-19.

Cummings, V. & Harris, O. 2011: Animals, People and Places. The Continuity of Hunting and Gathering Practices Across the Mesolithic-Neolithic Transition in Britain, *European Journal of Archaeology*, 14.3, 361-382.

Cunliffe, B. 1984a: Iron Age Wessex. Continuity and Change. In, Cunliffe, B. & Miles, D. (Eds.), *Aspects of the Iron Age in Central Southern Britain*, Oxford, Oxford University Committee for Archaeology, Monograph 2, 12-45.

Cunliffe, B. 1984b: *Danebury. An Iron Age Hillfort in Hampshire, 2. Excavations 1969-1978. The Finds*, CBA Research Report, 52.

Cunliffe, B. 1988: *Greeks, Romans and Barbarians*, London, Guild Publishing.

Cunliffe, B. 1991: *Iron Age Communities in Britain*, London, Routledge.

Cunliffe, B. 1992: Pits, Preconceptions and Propitiation in the British Iron Age, *Oxford Journal of Archaeology*, 11.1, 69-83.

Cunliffe, B. 1993: *Book of Danebury*, London, BT Batsford Ltd./English Heritage.

Cunliffe, B. 1995a: *Danebury. An Iron Age Hillfort in Hampshire, 6, A Hillfort Community in Perspective*, CBA Research Report, 102.

Cunliffe, B. 1995b: *Book of Iron Age Britain*, London, B.T. Batsford Ltd.

Cunliffe, B. 2003: *Danebury Hillfort*, Stroud, Tempus Publishing Ltd.

Cunliffe, B. 2005: *Iron Age Communities in Britain (4th edition)*, London, Routledge.

Cunliffe, B. & Poole, C. 1991: *Danebury. An Iron Age Hillfort in Hampshire, 5, Excavations 1979-1988*, CBA Research Report, 73.

Cunliffe, B. & Poole, C. 1995: Pits and Propitiation. In, Cunliffe, B. *Danebury. An Iron Age Hillfort in Hampshire, 6, A Hillfort Community in Perspective*, CBA Research Report, 102,

Cunningham, J.J. 2003: Transcending the 'Obnoxious Spectator'. A Case for Processual Pluralism in Ethnoarchaeology, *Journal of Anthropological Archaeology*, 22, 389-410.

Cunnington, M. 1930-1932: The 'Sanctuary' on Overton Hill Near Avebury, *Wiltshire Archaeological Magazine*, 45, 300-335.

Curtis, R.L. 2001: *Ancient Food Technology*, Leiden, Brill.

Curwen, E.C. 1929: Excavations in The Trundle, Goodwood, 1928, *Sussex Archaeological Collections*, 70, 33-85.

Curwen, E.C. 1931: Excavations in The Trundle. Second Season, 1930, *Sussex Archaeological Collections*, 72, 100-150.

Curwen, E.C. 1934: A Late Bronze Age Farm and a Neolithic Pit-dwelling on New Barn Down, Clapham, nr. Worthing, *Sussex Archaeological Collections*, 75, 137-170.

Curwen, E.C. 1937: Querns, *Antiquity*, 11, 133-150.

Curwen, E.C. 1941: More About Querns, *Antiquity*, 15, 15-32.

Curwen, E.C. 1950: The Querns. In, Norris, N.E.S. and Burstow, G.P., A Prehistoric and Romano-British Site at West Blatchington, Hove, *Sussex Archaeological Collections*, 89, 50-52.

Da Re, M.G. 2003: Le Moulin à Ane en Sardaigne. D'objet Exemplaire à Objet D'afffection. In, Barboff, M., Griffin-Kremer, C., Kremer, R. & Sigaut, F. (Eds.), *Meules à Grains*, Paris, Ibis Press, 98-114.

Damp, J.E. 1984: Architecture of the Early Valdiva Village, *American Antiquity*, 49.3, 573-585.

Daniel, G.E. 1950: *The Prehistoric Chamber Tombs of England and Wales*, Cambridge, Cambridge University Press.

Dant, T. 2005: *Materiality and Society*, Maidenhead, Open University Press.

Dark, P. & Gent, H. 2001: Pests and Diseases of Prehistoric Crops. A Yield 'Honeymoon' for Early Grain Crops in Europe, *Oxford Journal of Archaeology*, 20, 59-78.

Darvill, T. 2002: White on Blonde. Quartz Pebbles and the use of Quartz at Neolithic Monuments in the Isle of Man and Beyond. In, Jones, A. & Macgregor, G. (Eds.), *Colouring the Past*, Oxford, Berg, 73-91.

Darvill, T. 2008: *The Concise Oxford Dictionary of Archaeology*, Oxford Reference Online, Oxford University Press, http://www.oxfordreference.com, 2008-2011.

David, N. 1998: The Ethnoarchaeology and Field Archaeology of Grinding at Sukur, Adamawa State, Nigeria, *The African Archaeological Review*, 15.1, 13-63.

Dennell, R.W. 1978: *Early Farming in South Bulgaria from the VI to the III Millennia B.C.*, Oxford, BAR International Series (Supplementary), 45.

Depla, A. 1994: Women in Ancient Egyptian Wisdom Literature. In, Archer, L.J., Fischler, S. & Wyke, M. (Eds.), *Women in Ancient Societies. An Illusion of the Night*, Basingstoke, The Macmillan Press, 24-52.

Dineley, M. & Dineley, G. 2000: Neolithic Ale. Barley as a Source of Malt Sugars for Fermentation. In, Fairbairn, A.S. (Ed.), *Plants in Neolithic Britain and Beyond*, Oxford, Oxbow Books, 137-153.

Domergue, C., Béziat, D., Cauuet, G., Jarrier, C., Landes, C., Morasz, J.-G., Oliva, P., Pulou, R. & Tollon, F. 1997: Les Moulins Rotatifs dans les Mines et le Centre Métalurgiques Antiques. In, Garcia, D. & Meeks, D. (Eds.), *Techniques et Economie Antiques et Médiévales. Le Temps de L'innovation*, Paris, Editions Errance, 48-61.

Drennen, R.D. 1976: Religion and Social Evolution in Formative Mesoamerica. In, Flannery, K.V. (Ed.), *The Early Mesoamerican Village*, New York, Academic Press, 345-364.

Dubreuil, L. 2004: Long-term Trends in Natufian Subsistence. A Use Wear Analysis of Ground Stone Tools, *Journal of Archaeological Science*, 31, 1613-1629.

Dubreuil, L. 2005: Mortars Versus Grinding-Slabs and the Neolithization Process in the Near East. *Prehistoric Technology 40 Years Later. Functions Studies and the Russian Legacy. Book of Abstracts*, Verona, Comune de Verona, 55-56.

Dudley, D. 1956: An Excavation at Bodrifty, Mulfra Hill, near Penzance, Cornwall, *The Archaeological Journal*, 113, 1-32.

Dudley, D. 1961-1964: The Excavation of the Carvinack Barrow, Tregavethan, Nr Truro, Cornwall, *Journal of the Royal Institution of Cornwall*, 4.4, 414-451.

Dudley, D. 1967: Excavations on Nor'nour in the Isles of Scilly, 1962-1966, *The Archaeological Journal*, 124, 1-64.

Dunning, G.C. 1966: Neolithic Occupation Sites in East Kent, *The Antiquaries Journal*, 46.1, 1-25.

Dyer, M.J. & Salvatore, J.P. 2011: *Archaeological Watching Brief on the SWW Pipeline Route from the Reservoir South West of Bovey Cross, North Bovery to Sandy Park, Drewsteignton, Devon*, Exeter Archaeology Report, 11.20.

Ede, J. 1990: Carbonised Seeds. In, Smith, G., Excavations at Ham Hill, 1983, *Proceedings of the Somerset Archaeological and Natural History Society*, 134, 39-43.

Ede, J. 1999: Charred Seeds. In, McKinley, J.I., Excavations at Ham Hill, Montacute, Somerset 1994 and 1998, *Proceedings of the Somerset Archaeological and Natural History Society*, 142, 116-.

Englund, R.K. 1991: Hard Work Where will it Get You? Labor Management in Ur III Mesopotamia, *Journal of Near Eastern Studies*, 50.4, 255-280.

Ertug-Yaras, F. 2002: Pounders and Grinders in a Modern Central Anatolian Village. In, Procopiou, H. & Treuil, R. (Eds.), *Moudre et Broyer, I, Méthodes*, Paris, CTHS, 211-225.

Evans, J. 1897: *The Ancient Stone Implements, Weapons and Ornaments of Great Britain*, London, Longmans, Green, and Co.

Fairbairn, A.S. 1999: Charred Plant Remains. In, Whittle, A., Pollard, J. & Grigson, C. (Eds.), *The Harmony of Symbols. The Windmill Hill Causewayed Enclosure, Wiltshire*, Oxford, Oxbow Books, 139-156.

Falconer, J.P.E. & Adams, S.B. 1935: Recent Finds at Solisbury Hill Camp, near Bath, *Proceedings of the Bristol Speleological Society*, 4.3, 183-222.

Fasham, P.J., Farwell, D.E. & Whinney, R.J.B. 1989: *The Archaeological Site at Easton Lane, Winchester*, Hampshire Field Club Monograph, 6.

Fell, C.I. 1936: The Hunsbury Hillfort. A New Survey of Material, *Archaeological Journal*, 93, 57-100.

Fendin, T. 2000: Fertility and the Repetive Partition, *Lund Archaeological Review*, 6, 85-97.

Fendin, T. 2006: Grinding Processes and Reproductive Metaphors. In, Andrén, A., Jennbert, K. & Raudvere, C. (Eds.), *Old Norse Religion in Long-Term Perspectives*, Lund, Nordic Academic Press, 159-163.

Firth, J. 1974: *Reminiscences of an Orkney Parish*, Stromness, Orkney Natural History Society.

Fitzpatrick, A.P. 1997: Everyday Life in Iron Age Wessex. In, Gwilt, A. & Haselgrove, C. (Eds.), *Reconstructing Iron Age Societies*, Oxford, Oxbow Monograph, 71, 73-86.

Fitzpatrick, A.P., Butterworth, C.A. & Grove, J. (Eds.) 1999a: *Prehistoric and Roman Sites in East Devon. The*

Bibliography

A30 Honiton to Exeter Improvement DBFO, 1996-9. 1. Prehistoric Sites, Wessex Archaeology Report, 16.

Fitzpatrick, A.P., Butterworth, C.A. & Grove, J. (Eds.) 1999b: *Prehistoric and Roman Sites in East Devon. The A30 Honiton to Exeter Improvement DBFO, 1996-9. 2. Romano-British Sites*, Wessex Archaeology Report, 16.

Fitzpatrick, A.P. (Ed.) 2008: Late Bronze Age and Iron Age. In, Webster, C.J. (Ed.), *The Archaeology of South West England*, Taunton, Somerset County Council, 117-144.

Fleming, A. 1988: *The Dartmoor Reaves. Investigating Prehistoric Land Divisions*, London, Batsford.

Fox, A. 1954: Excavations at Kestor, an Early Iron Age Settlement near Chagford, Devon, *Transactions of the Devonshire Association*, 86, 21-62.

Fox, A. 1957: Excavations on Dean Moor, in the Avon Valley, 1954-1956. The Late Bronze Age Settlement, *Transactions of the Devonshire Association*, 89, 18-77.

Fox, A. 1973: *South-West England 3500BC – AD600*, Newton Abbot, David & Charles.

Frankel, R. 2003: The Olynthus Mill. Its Origin, and Diffusion. Typology and Distribution, *American Journal of Archaeology*, 107, 1-21.

Frere, S. 1972: *Verulamium Excavations*, 1, Reports of the Research Committee of the Society of Antiquaries of London, 28.

Freshwater, T. 1996: A Lava Quern Workshop in Late Saxon London, *London Archaeologist*, 8.2, 39-45.

Fulford, M. 2001: Links with the Past. Pervasive 'Ritual' Behaviour in Roman Britain, *Britannia*, 32, 199-218.

Fullagar, R. & Field, J. 1997: Pleistocene Seed-Grinding Implements from the Australian Arid Zone, *Antiquity*, 71, 300-307.

Fullard, H. & Darby, H.C. (Eds.) 1964: *The University Atlas*, London, George Philip and Son Limited.

Gaffney, V. & Tingle, M. 1989: *The Maddle Farm Project. An Intergrated Survey of Prehistoric and Roman Landscapes on the Berkshire Downs*, Oxford, BAR British Series 200.

Gage, J., Jones, A., Bradley, R., Spence, K., Barber, E.J.W. & Taçon, P.S.C. 1999: Viewpoint. What Meaning Had Colour in Early Societies?, *Cambridge Archaeological Journal*, 9.1, 109-126.

Gallant, L. & Silvester, R.J. 1985: An Excavation on the Iron Age Hillfort at Berry Down, Newton Abbot, *Proceedings of the Devon Archaeological Society*, 43, 39-58.

Garrow, D. 2007: Placing Pits. Landscape Occupation and Depositional Practice During the Neolithic in East Anglia, *Proceedings of the Prehistoric Society*, 73, 1-24.

Garrow, D., Beadsmore, E. & Knight, M. 2005: Pit Clusters and the Temporality of Occupation. An Earlier Neolithic Site at Kilverstone, Thetford, Norfolk, *Proceedings of the Prehistoric Society*, 71, 139-157.

Garwood, P., Jennings, D., Skeates, R. & Toms, J. 1991: Preface. In, Garwood, P., Jennings, D., Skeates, R. & Toms, J. (Eds.), *Sacred and Profane*, Oxford, Oxford University Committee for Archaeology, v-x.

Gast, M. 2003: Meules et Molettes Sahariennes. In, Barboff, M., Griffin-Kremer, C., Kremer, R. & Sigaut, F. (Eds.), *Meules à Grains*, Paris, Ibis Press, 61-66.

Gaucheron 1990: *Buckwheat Handmills in Brittany*, Reading, The International Molinological Society.

Gerrard, C. 2003: *Medieval Archaeology*, London, Routledge.

Gerrard, S. 2000: *The Early British Tin Industry*, Stroud, Tempus Publishing Ltd.

Gibson, J.J. 1986: *The Ecological Approach to Visual Perception*, New Jersey, Lawrence Erlbaum Associates.

Giles, M. 2008: Identity, Community and the Person in Later Prehistory. In, Pollard, J. (Ed.), *Prehistoric Britain*, Oxford, Blackwell Publishing Ltd., 330-350.

Gillard, M., Morris, B. & Walls, S. 2010: *Middle Burrow Farm, East Worlington, Devon. Results of Archaeological Monitoring and Excavation*, Southwest Archaeology Report, 100916.

Gimbutas, M. 1982: *The Goddesses and Gods of Old Europe. Myths and Cult Images*, London, Thames & Hudson.

Gimbutas, M. 1987: The Earth Fertility Goddess of Old Europe, *Dialogues D'histoire Ancienne*, 13.1, 11-69.

Gimbutas, M. 1991: *The Civilization of the Goddess. The World of Old Europe*, San Francisco, Harper.

Goody, J. 1982: *Cooking, Cuisine and Class. A study in Comparative Sociology*, Cambridge, Cambridge University Press.

Gordon, A.S.R. 1940: The Excavation of Gurnard's Head, an Iron Age Cliff Castle in Western Cornwall, *Archaeological Journal*, 97, 96-111.

Gosden, C. 2001: Making Sense. Archaeology and Aesthetics, *World Archaeology*, 33.2, 163-167.

Gosden, C. & Marshall, Y. 1999: The Cultural Biography of Objects, *World Archaeology*, 31.2, 169-178.

Gossip, J. forthcoming: Life Outside the Round. Bronze Age and Iron Age Settlement at Higher Besore and Truro College, Threemilestone, Truro, *for submission to Cornish Archaeology*.

Gossip, J. and Johns, C. in press: The Evaluation of a Multi-Period Prehistoric Site and Fogou at Boden Vean, St. Anthony-in-Meneage, Cornwall 2003, *Cornish Archaeology*.

Gossip, J. & Jones, A.M. (Eds.) 2007: *Archaeological Investigations of a Later Prehistoric and a Romano-British Landscape at Tremough, Penryn, Cornwall*, Oxford, BAR British Series, 443.

Gould, R.A., Koster, D.A. & Sontz, A.H.L. 1971: The Lithic Assemblage of the Western Desert Aborigines of Australia, *American Antiquity*, 36.2, 146-169.

Graefe, J. 2008: Trade and Use of Raw Material for Neolithic Querns in North-Western Germany. In, Hamon, C. & Graefe, J. (Eds.), *New Perspectives on Querns in Neolithic Societies*, Bonn, DGUF, 23-32.

Graefe, J., Hamon, C., Lidström Holmberg, C., Tsoraki, C. & Watts, S. 2009: Subsistence, Social and Ritual Practices. Quern Deposits in the Neolithic Societies of Europe. In, Bonnardin, S., Hamon, C., Lauwers, M. & Quilliec, B. (Eds.), *Réalités Archéologiques et Historiques des 'Dépôts' de la Préhistoire à nos Jours XXIX*, Antibes, Editions APDCA, 87-96.

Graham, M. 1993: Settlement Organization and Residential Variability Among the Rarámuri. In, Cameron, C.M. & Tomka, S.A. (Eds.), *Abandonment of Settlements and Regions. Ethnoarchaeological and Archaeological Approaches*, Cambridge, Cambridge University Press, 25-42.

Graham, M. 1994: *Mobile Farmers. An Ethnoarchaeological Approach to Settlement Organization among the Rarámuri of Northwestern Mexico*, Ethnoarchaeological Series, 3, Ann Arbor, International Monographs in Prehistory.

Graves, R. 1959: Introduction. In, Guirand, F. (Ed.), *Larousse Encyclopedia of Mythology*, London, Batchworth Press Limited, v-viii.

Gray, A. 1972: Prehistoric Habitation Sites on the Isles of Scilly, *Cornish Archaeology*, 11, 19-49.

Gray, H. St. George 1922: Trial Excavations at Cadbury Camp, Tickenham, Somerset, 1922, *Proceedings of the Somerset Archaeological and Natural History Society*, 68.2, 8-20.

Gray, H. St. George 1925: Excavations at Ham Hill, Somerset. Part 2, *Proceedings of the Somerset Archaeological and Natural History Society*, 71.2, 57-75.

Gray, H. St. George & Bulleid, A. (deceased) 1953: *The Meare Lake Village*, 2, Taunton, Privately printed.

Gray, H. St. George & Cotton, M.A 1966: *The Meare Lake Village*, 3, Taunton, Privately printed.

Green, C. 2011: Hertfordshire Puddingstone Querns. Working with a Difficult Rock. In, Williams, D. & Peacock, D. (Eds.), *Bread for the People. The Archaeology of Mills and Milling*, University of Southampton, Series in Archaeology Monograph, 3, Oxford, Archaeopress, 123-130.

Green, M.J. 1997: *Exploring the World of the Druids*, London, Thames and Hudson Ltd.

Green, M.J. 1999: Back to the Future. In, Gazin-Schwartz, A. & Holtorf, C.J. (Eds.), *Archaeology and Folklore*, London, Routledge, 48-66.

Green, T. 2009: Excavation of a Hillslope Enclosure at Holworthy Farm, Parracombe Displaying Bronze Age and Iron Age Activity, *Proceedings of the Devon Archaeological Society*, 67, 39-97.

Greene, K. 1997: Reflections on 'Le Temps de L'innovation'. A Personal Response to the Colloquium's Principal Themes. In, Meeks, D. & Garcia, D. (Eds.), *Les Moulins Rotatifs dans les Mines et le Centre Métalurgiques Antiques*, Paris, Editions Errance, 227-229.

Greene, K. 1998: *Archaeology. An Introduction*, London, Routledge.

Griffith, F. & Quinnell, H. 1999a: Barrows and Ceremonial Sites in the Neolithic and Earlier Bronze Age. In, Kain, R. & Ravenhill, W. (Eds.), *Historical Atlas of South-West England*, Exeter, Exeter University Press, 55-61.

Griffith, F. & Quinnell, H. 1999b: Neolithic Settlement, Land Use and Resources. In, Kain, R. & Ravenhill, W. (Eds.), *Historic Atlas of South-West England*, Exeter, Exeter University Press, 51-54.

Griffith, F. & Quinnell, H. 1999c: Settlement c.2500BC to c.AD600. In, Kain, R. & Ravenhill, W. (Eds.), *Historic Atlas of South-West England*, Exeter, Exeter University Press, 62-88.

Griffith, W.E. 1951: Decorated Rotary Querns from Wales and Ireland, *Ulster Journal of Archaeology*, 14, 49-61.

Grimes, W.F. 1960: *Excavations on Defence Sites, 1939-1945, 1. Mainly Neolithic-Bronze Age*, London, Ministry of Works Archaeological Report, 3.

Grinsell, L.V. 1961: The Breaking of Objects as a Funerary Rite, *Folklore*, 72.3, 475-491.

Gwilt, A. & Heslop, D. 1995: Iron Age and Roman Querns from the Tees Valley. In, Vyner, B. (Ed.), *Moorland Monuments. Studies in the Archaeology of North-East Yorkshire in Honour of Raymond Hayes and Don Spratt*, CBA Research Report, 101, 38-45.

Bibliography

Haaland, R. 1995: Sedentism, Cultivation and Plant Domestication in the Holocene Middle Nile Region, *Journal of Field Archaeology*, 22.2, 157-174.

Haaland, R. 1997: Emergence of Sedentism. New Ways of Living, New Ways of Symbolizing, *Antiquity*, 71, 374-385.

Hack, B. 1982: Tower Hill, St. Cuthbert Out, *Proceedings of the Somerset Archaeological and Natural History Society*, 126, 72.

Hamilakis, Y. 1999: Food Technologies/Technologies of the Body. The Social Context of Wine and Oil Production and Consumption in Bronze Age Crete, *World Archaeology*, 31.1, 38-54.

Hamilton, A. 1980: Dual Social Systems. Technology, Labour and Women's Secret Rites in the Eastern Desert of Australia, *Oceania*, 51.1, 4-16.

Hamilton, J.R.C. 1956: *Excavations at Jarlshof, Shetland*, Ministry of Works Archaeological Report, 1, Edinburgh, HMSO.

Hamilton, S. 2002: Between Ritual and Routine. Interpreting British Prehistoric Pottery Production and Distribution. In, Woodward, A. & Hill, J.D. (Eds.), *Prehistoric Britain. The Ceramic Basis*, Oxford, Prehistoric Ceramics Research Group, Occasional Publication 3, Oxbow Books, 38-53.

Hamon, C. 2008a: The Symbolic Value of Grindingstones Hoards. Technical Properties of Neolithic Examples. In, Hamon, C. & Quilliec, B. (Eds.), *Hoards from the Neolithic to the Metal Ages: technical and codified practices: session of the XIth Annual Meeting of the European Association of Archaeologists BAR international series; 1758*.

Hamon, C. 2008b: Functional Analysis of Stone Grinding and Polishing Tools from the Earliest Neolithic of North-Western Europe, *Journal of Archaeological Science*, 35, 1502-1520.

Hamon, C. 2008c: Lifecycle of a Neolithic Quern. Limits and Contribution of a Combined Technical and Functional Analysis on Grinding Tools. In, Hamon, C. & Graefe, J. (Eds.), *New Perspectives on Querns in Neolithic Societies*, Bonn, DGUF, 45-54.

Hamon, C. & Gall, V. Le 2011: Les Meules en Pays Minyanka (Mali). Étude des Carrières et Techniques de Production Actuelles. In, Williams, D. & Peacock, D. (Eds.), *Bread for the People. The Archaeology of Mills and Milling*, University of Southampton, Series in Archaeology Monograph, 3, Oxford, Archaeopress, 19-28.

Hamon, C. & Gall, V. Le 2013: Millet and Sauce. The Uses and Functions of Querns among the Minyanka (Mali), Journal of Anthropological Archaeology, 32, 109-121.

Hamon, C. & Graefe, J. 2008: New Perspectives on Querns in Neolithic Societies. In, Hamon, C. & Graefe, J. (Eds.), *New Perspectives on Querns in Neolithic Societies*, Bonn, DGUF, 9-10.

Hamond, F.W. 1979: Settlement, Economy and Environment on Prehistoric Dartmoor, *Proceedings of the Devon Archaeological Society*, 37, 146-175.

Hardy, K. 2007: Food for Thought. Starch in Mesolithic Diet, *Mesolithic Miscellany*, 18.2, 2-11.

Harlan, J.R. 1995: *The Living Fields. Our Agricultural Heritage*, Cambridge, Cambridge University Press.

Harris, D. 1977: Bodwen, Lanlivery. A Multi-Period Occupation, *Cornish Archaeology*, 16, 43-59.

Harris, D., Hooper, S. & Trudgian, P. 1984: Excavation of Three Cairns on Stannon Downs, St. Breward, *Cornish Archaeology*, 23, 141-154.

Harrison, R. 2003: The Magical Virtue of these Sharp Things, *Journal of Material Culture*, 8.3, 311-336.

Haselgrove, C. 1999: The Iron Age. In, Hunter, J. & Ralston, I. (Eds.), *The Archaeology of Britain*, 113-134.

Haselgrove, C., Armit, I., Champion, T., Creighton, J., Gwilt, A., Hill, J.D., Hunter, F. & Woodward, A. 2001: *Understanding the British Iron Age. An Agenda for Action*, Salisbury, Trust for Wessex Archaeology.

Hastorf, C.A. 1991: Gender, Space, and Food in Prehistory. In, Gero, J.M. & Conkey, M.W. (Eds.), *Engendering Archaeology. Women and Prehistory*, Oxford, Basil Blackwell Ltd., 132-159.

Hayden, B. 1987a: Traditional Metate Manufacturing in Guatemala Using Chipped Stone Tools. In, Hayden, B. (Ed.), *Lithic Studies Among the Contemporary Highland Maya*, Tuscon, University of Arizona Press, 8-119.

Hayden, B. 1987b: Past to Present Uses of Stone Tools and their Effects on Assemblage Characteristics in the Maya Highlands. In, Hayden, B. (Ed.), *Lithic Studies Among the Contemporary Highland Maya*, Tuscon, University of Arizona Press, 160-234.

Hayden, B. & Nelson, M. 1981: The Use of Chipped Lithic Material in the Contemporary Maya Highlands, *American Antiquity*, 46.4, 885-898.

Healy, F. 2009: *Refining the Dating of South-Western Neolithic Enclosures*, Conference Paper presented at Current Research in the Prehistory of South-West England. A Day to Celebrate the Work of Henrietta Quinnell. Devon and Cornwall Archaeological Socieites Joint Symposium, Tavistock.

Healy, J.F. 1978: *Mining and Metallurgy in the Greek and Roman World*, London, Thames & Hudson.

Hencken, H. O'Neill 1932: *The Archaeology of Cornwall and Scilly*, London, Methuen & Co. Ltd.

Hencken, H. O'Neill 1933: Notes on the Megalithic Monuments in the Isles of Scilly, *The Antiquaries Journal*, 13, 13-29.

Henshall, A.S. 1955-1956: Long Cist Cemetery at Parkburn Sandpit, Lasswade, Midlothian, *Proceedings of the Society of Antiquaries of Scotland*, 89, 252-283.

Hesketh, R. 2008: *Devon's Geology*, Launceston, Bossiney Books Ltd.

Heslop, D. 1987: *The Excavation of an Iron Age Settlement at Thorpe Thewles, Cleveland, 1980-1982*, CBA Research Report, 65.

Heslop, D.H. 2008: *Patterns of Quern Production, Acquisition and Deposition. A Corpus of Beehive Querns from Northern Yorkshire and Southern Durham*, Yorkshire Archaeological Society, Occasional Paper, 5.

Hill, J.D. 1995: *Ritual and Rubbish in the Iron Age of Wessex*, BAR British Series, 242, Oxford.

Hillman, G. 1977: Grain. In, Miles, H., Excavation at Killibury Hillfort, Egloshayle 1975-6, *Cornish Archaeology*, 16, 110.

Hilton-Simpson, M.W. 1922: The Berbers of the Aures Mountains, Algeria. A Study of a Primitive People, *The Scottish Geographical Magazine*, 38, 145-163.

Hingley, R. 1990: Iron Age 'Currency Bars'. The Archaeological and Social Context, *Archaeological Journal*, 147, 91-117.

Hingley, R. 1997: Iron, Ironworking and Regeneration. A Study of the Symbolic Meaning of Metalworking. In, Gwilt, A. & Haselgrove, C. (Eds.), *Reconstructing Iron Age Societies*, 9-18, Oxbow Monograph, 71, 9-18.

Hodder, I. 1982: *The Present Past. An Introduction to Anthropology for Archaeologists*, London, B.T. Batsford.

Hodder, I. (Ed.) 2005: *Changing Materialities at Çatalhöyük. Reports from the 1995-99 Seasons*, Çatalhöyük Research Project, 5, Cambridge and London, McDonald Institute for Archaeological Research and the British Institute at Ankara.

Hoffner, H.A. 2000: Legal and Social Institutions of Hittite Anatolia. In, Sasson, J.M. (Ed.), *Civilizations of the Ancient Near East*, 1 and 2, Peabody, Massachusetts, Hendrickson Publishers Inc., 555-569.

Holbrook, N. (Ed.) 2008: Roman. In, Webster, C.J. (Ed.), *The Archaeology of South West England*, Taunton, Somerset County Council, 151-161.

Holden, T.G. 1995: The Last Meals of the Lindow Bog Men. In, Turner, R.C. & Scaife, R.G. (Eds.), *Bog Bodies*, London, 76-82.

Hollinrake, C. and N. 2003: Doulting Abbey Quarry. In, Webster, C., Somerset Archaeology 2001, *Proceedings of the Somerset Archaeological and Natural History Society*, 145, 137.

Horne, D.E. 1937: An Early Iron Age Site at Camerton, Somerset, *Proceedings of the Somerset Archaeological and Natural History Society*, 83.2, 155-165.

Horsfall, G.A. 1987: A Design Theory Perspective on Variability in Grinding Stones. In, Hayden, B. (Ed.), *Lithic Studies among the Contemporary Highland Maya*, Tuscon, The University of Arizona Press,

Houlder, C.H. 1963: A Neolithic Settlement on Hazard Hill, Totnes, *Proceedings of the Devon Archaeological Exploration Society*, 21, 2-31.

Hovsepyan, R. & Willcox, G. 2008: The Earliest Finds of Cultivated Plants in Armenia. Evidence from Charred Remains and Crop Processing Residues in Pisé from the Neolithic Settlements of Aratashen and Aknashen, *Vegetation History and Archaeobotany*, 17.1, 63-71.

Howard, J. 2006: *Bread in Ancient Egypt*, http://www.touregypt.net/featurestories/bread, 28th June 2006.

Hurcombe, L. 2007: *Archaeological Artefacts as Material Culture*, London, Routledge.

Ingle, C. 1987: The Production and Distribution of Beehive Querns in Cumbria. Some Initial Considerations, *Transactions of the Cumberland and Westmoreland Archaeological Society*, 87, 11-17.

Ingle, C. 1993-1994: The Quernstones from Hunsbury Hillfort, Northamptonshire, *Northamptonshire Archaeology*, 25, 21-33.

Ingold, T. 2007: Materials Against Materiality, *Archaeological Dialogues*, 14.1, 1-16.

Jaccottey, L. 2009: *Les Carrières due Massif due Massif de la Serre (Jura, France). 6700 ans de Production de meules*, Paper presented at Bread for the People. A Colloquium on the Archaeology of Mills and Milling, The British School at Rome, 4th-7th November 2009.

Jaccottey, L. 2011: Seven Thousand Years of Millstone Producion in the Serre Mountain Range of the French Jura. In, Williams, D. & Peacock, D. (Eds.), *Bread for the People. The Archaeology of Mills and Milling*, University of Southampton, Series in Archaeology Monograph, 3, Oxford, Archaeopress, 293-307.

Jacob, H.E. (trans. Winston, R. & C.) 2007: *Six Thousand Years of Bread. Its Holy and Unholy History*, New York, Skyhorse Publishing.

Bibliography

Jarvis, K. and Maxfield, V. 1975: The Excavation of a First-Century Roman Farmstead and a Late Neolithic Settlement, Topsham, Devon, *Proceedings of the Devon Archaeological Society*, 33, 209-266.

Jefferies, J.S. 1979: The Pits. In, Wainwright, G.J. (Ed.), *Gussage All Saints. An Iron Age Settlement in Dorset*, London, Department of Environment Archaeological Report, 10, 9-15.

Jodry, F. & Féliu, C. 2009: Nouvelles Données sur les Dépôts de Meules Rotatives. Deux Exemples de La Tène Finale en Alsace In, Bonnardin, S., Hamon, C., Lauwers, M. & Quilliec, B. (Eds.), *Réalités Archéologiques et Historiques des 'Dépôts' de la Préhistoire à nos Jours XXIX*, Antibes, Editions APDCA, 69-76.

John Moore Heritage Services 2010: *An Archaeological Excavation in the Corridor of the Proposed Road Linking the A379 to Old Rydon Lane, Topsham, Exeter*.

Johns, C. (Ed.) 2011: *SHERF Resource Assessment: Chapter 4 Neolithic and Early Bronze Age Working Draft for Consultation*, http://www.scilly.gov.uk/environment/conservation/SHERF, 7th December 2011.

Johns, C. forthcoming: The Excavation of a Multi-Period Archaeological Landscape at Trenowah, St. Austell, Cornwall, 1997, *for submission to Cornish Archaeology*.

Johnston, A.W. 1910: Grotti Finnie and Grotti Minnie, *Old-Lore Miscellany*, 3, 8-10.

Jones, A. 1998-1999: The Excavation of a Later Bronze Age Structure at Callestick, *Cornish Archaeology*, 37-38, 5-55.

Jones, A. 2000: Life After Death. Monuments, Material Culture and Social Change in Neolithic Orkney. In, Ritchie, A. (Ed.), *Neolithic Orkney in its European Context*, Cambridge, McDonald Institute for Archaeological Research, University of Cambridge, 127-138.

Jones, A. 2002: A Biography of Colour. Colour, Material Histories and Personhood in the Early Bronze Age of Britain and Ireland. In, Jones, A. & Macgregor, G. (Eds.), *Colouring the Past*, Oxford, Berg, 159-174.

Jones, A. & MacGregor, G. 2002: *Colouring the Past*, Oxford, Berg.

Jones, A.M. 2004-2005: Settlement and Ceremony. Archaeological Investigations at Stannon Down, St. Breward, Cornwall, *Cornish Archaeology*, 43-44, 1-140.

Jones, A.M. forthcoming: Ritual, Rubbish or Everyday Life? Evidence from a Middle Bronze Age Settlement in Mid Cornwall. In, Morris, J. & Randall, C. (Eds.), *Ritual in Context. Explaining Ritual Complexity in Archaeology*, Oxford, Oxbow Monograph.

Jones, A.M. & Quinnell, H. 2011: The Neolithic and Bronze Age Periods in Cornwall, c4000 Cal BC to c1000 Cal BC. An Overview of Recent Developments, *Cornish Archaeology*, 50, 197-229.

Jones, A.M. & Reed, S.J. 2006: By Land, Sea and Air. An Early Neolithic Pit Group at Portscatho, Cornwall, and Consideration of Coastal Activity During the Neolithic, *Cornish Archaeology*, 45, 1-130.

Jones, A.M. & Taylor, S.R. 2004: *What Lies Beneath...St. Newlyn East & Mitchell*, Truro, Cornwall County Council.

Jones, A.M. & Taylor, S.R. 2010: *Scarcewater, Pennance, Cornwall. Archaeological Excavation of a Bronze Age and Roman Landscape*, Oxford, BAR British Series, 516.

Jones, G. & Rowley-Conwy, P. 2007: On the Importance of Cereal Cultivation in the British Neolithic. In, Colledge, S. & Conolly, J. (Eds.), *The Origin and Spread of Domestic Plants in Southwest Asia and Europe*, Walnut Creek, California, Left Coast Press, Inc., 391-419.

Jones, H.L (trans) 1923: *The Geography of Strabo*, 2, London, William Heinemann.

Jones, J. 2006: Charred Plant Remains. In, Jones, A.M. and Reed, S.J., By Land, Sea and Air. An Early Neolithic Pit Group at Portscatho, Cornwall, and Consideration of Coastal Activity During the Neolithic, *Cornish Archaeology*, 45, 14-15.

Jordan, M. 2002: *Encyclopedia of gods*, London, Kyle Cathie Limited.

Jørgensen, A.B. 2000: Investigations of Danish Rotary Querns from the Iron Age. In, Procopiou, H. & Treuil, R. (Eds.), *Moudre et Broyer, 2*, Paris, CTHS, 183-196.

Katz, E. 2003: Le Metate, Meule Dormante due Mexique. In, Barboff, M., Griffin-Kremer, C., Kremer, R. & Sigaut, F. (Eds.), *Meules à Grains*, Paris, Ibis Press, 32-50.

Kawakami, K. 2005: *Japanese Watermills*, Tokyo, Office HANS.

Keates, S. 2002: The Flashing Blade. Copper, Colour and Luminosity in North Italian Copper Age Society. In, Jones, A. & Macgregor, G. (Eds.), *Colouring the Past*, Oxford, Berg, 109-125.

Keller, P.T. 1989: Quern Production at Folkestone, South-East Kent. An Interim Note, *Britannia*, 20, 193-200.

Kelly, J. 2002: Querns and the Cosmos, *Quern Study Group Newsletter*, 6, 9-14.

Kirk-Greene, A.H.M. 1957: A Lala Initiation Ceremony, *Man*, 57, 9-11.

Knappett, C. 2005: *Thinking Through Material Culture*, Philadelphia, University of Pennsylvania Press.

Knappett, C. & Leeuw, S. van der forthcoming: The Space of Innovation. Cognitive, Social and Physical Considerations, *for submission to Current Anthropology*,

Kopytoff, I. 1986: The Cultural Biography of Things. Commoditization as Process. In, Appadurai, E. (Ed.), *The Social Life of Things, Commodities in Cultural Perspective*, Cambridge, Cambridge University Press, 64-91.

Kosambi, D.D. 1965: *The Culture and Civilisation of Ancient India in Historical Outline*, London, Routledge and Kegan Paul.

Kraybill, N. 1977: Pre-Agricultural Tools for the Preparation of Foods in the Old World. In, Reed, C.A. (Ed.), *Origins of Agriculture*, The Hague, Mouton Publishers, 485-521.

Ladle, L. 1998: Bestwall Quarry Excavations 1998. Interim Report, *Proceedings of the Dorset Natural History and Archaeological Society*, 120, 110.

Laidlaw, M. 1999a: Other Objects of Worked Stone. In, Fitzpatrick, A.P., Butterworth, C.A. & Grove, J. (Eds.), *Prehistoric and Roman Sites in East Devon. The A30 Honiton to Exeter Improvement DBFO Scheme, 1996-9. 1. Prehistoric Sites*, Wessex Archaeology Report 16, 43, 108, 147-148, 178.

Laidlaw, M. 1999b: The Stone. In, McKinley, J.I., Excavations at Ham Hill, Montacute, Somerset 1994 and 1998, *Proceedings of the Somerset Archaeological and Natural History Society*, 142, 108-109.

Lange, F.W. & Rydberg, C.R. 1972: Abandonment and Post-Abandonment Behavior at a Rural Central American House Site, *American Antiquity*, 37.3, 419-432.

Laws, K., Brown, L. & Roe, F. 1991: Objects of Stone. In, Cunliffe, B. (Ed.), *Danebury. An Iron Age Hillfort in Hampshire. 5. The Excavations 1979-1988. The Finds*, CBA Research Report, 73, 382-404.

Lawson-Jones, A. 2007: Flint. In, Gossip, J. & Jones, A.M. (Eds.), *Archaeological Investigations of a Later Prehistoric and a Romano-British Landscape at Tremough, Penryn, Cornwall*, Oxford, BAR British Series, 443, 88-96.

Leach, P. 2002: Shepton Mallet, Field Farm, *Proceedings of the Somerset Archaeological and Natural History Society*, 146, 141-142.

Leach, P. 2008: Prehistoric Ritual Landscapes and other Remains at Field Farm, Shepton Mallet, *Proceedings of the Somerset Archaeological and Natural History Society*, 152, 11-68.

Leeds, E.T. 1926-1927: Excavations at Chun Castle, in Penwith, Cornwall, *Archaeologia*, 76, 205-240.

Leivers, M., Chisham, C., Knight, S. & Stevens, C. 2007: Excavations at Ham Hill Quarry, Hamdon Hill, Montacute, *Proceedings of the Somerset Archaeological and Natural History Society*, 150, 39-62.

Leone, M.P. 1981: Archaeology's Relationship to the Present and the Past. In, Gould, R.A. & Schiffer, M.B. (Eds.), *Modern Material Culture. The Archaeology of Us*, London, Academic Press, 1-14.

Leverett, M. and Quinnell, H. 2010: An Early Neolithic Assemblage from Wayland's, Tiverton, *Proceedings of the Devon Archaeological Society*, 68, 1-14.

Lewis, O. 1963: *Life in a Mexican Village. Tepoztlán Restudied*, Urbana, University of Illinois Press.

Liddell, D.M. 1929-1932: A Report on the Excavations at Hembury Fort, Devon, *Proceedings of the Devon Archaeological Exploration Society*, 1, 40-63.

Liddell, D.M. 1933-1936: Report on the Excavations at Hembury Fort, *Proceedings of the Devon Archaeological Exploration Society*, 2, 134-175.

Lidström Holmberg, C. 2004: Saddle Querns and Gendered Dynamics of the Early Neolithic in Mid Central Sweden, *Arrival. Coast to Coast*, 10, 199-231.

Lidström Holmberg, C. 2008: Grinding Technologies, Social Relations and the becoming of the Northernmost TRB. In, Hamon, C. & Graefe, J. (Eds.), *New Perspectives on Querns in Neolithic Societies*, Bonn, DGUF, 69-92.

Lionái, C.N. 2010: *Life, Death and Food Production in Bronze Age Ireland. Recent Excavations at Stamullin, Co. Meath*, http://www.arch-tech.ie/stamullinarticle.html, 24th September 2010.

Literary Digest 1929: *The Complete Works of William Shakespeare*, London, Funk & Wagnalls Co.

Livingstone, D. 1887: *A Popular Account of Dr. Livingstone's Expedition to the Zambesi and its Tributaries and of the Discoveries of Lakes Shirwa and Nyassa 1858-1864*, London, John Murray.

Long, G. 1931: *The Mills of Man*, London, Herbert Joseph.

Longley, D. 1998: Bryn Eryr. An Enclosed Settlement of the Iron Age on Anglesey, *Proceeding of the Prehistoric Society*, 64, 225-273.

Mackenzie, D.A. 1912: *Teutonic Myth and Legend*, http://www.sacred-texts.com/neu/tml/tml28.htm 2nd June 2010.

Bibliography

MacKie, E.W. 1971: English Migrants and Scottish Brochs, *Glasgow Archaeological Journal*, 2, 39-71.

MacKie, E.W. 1971-1972: Some New Quernstones from Brochs and Duns, *Proceedings of the Society of Antiquaries of Scotland*, 104, 137-146.

Macleod Banks, M. 1941: *British Calendar Customs. Scotland*, 3, Publications of the Folk-Lore Society, 104, London, William Glaisher Ltd.

Macleod Banks, M. 1946: *British Calendar Customs. Orkney and Shetland*, Publications of the Folk-Lore Society, 112, London, William Glaisher Ltd.

Madureri, E. 1984: Storia della Costruzione dei Molini, parte 3, *Tecnica Molitoria*, October 1984, 733-743.

Magnússon, E. 1910: Gróttasongr. The Stone of the Quern Grotte, parts 1 and 2, *Old-Lore Miscellany*, 3, 139-150, 237-253.

Major, H. 1987: A Roman Lava Quernstone from Takeley Church, *Transactions of the Essex Society of Archaeology and History*, 18.3, 114-115.

Masson Phillips, E.N. 1982: The Excavation of a Dartmoor Hut, *Transactions of the Devonshire Association*, 114, 57-62.

Maudlin, R. 1993: The Relationship Between Ground Stone and Agricultural Intensification in Western New Mexico, *Kiva*, 58.3, 317-330.

McKinley, J.I. 1999: Excavations at Ham Hill, Montacute, Somerset 1994 and 1998, *Proceedings of the Somerset Archaeological and Natural History Society*, 142, 77-137.

McLaren, F.S. 2000: Revising the Wheat Crops of Neolithic Britain. In, Fairbairn, A.S. (Ed.), *Plants in Neolithic Britain and Beyond*, Oxford, Oxbow Books, 91-100.

McMurtrie, J. 1899: Notes on Ancient British and Romano-British Remains Discovered in the Tyning and Kilmersdon Road Quarries at Radstock, *Proceedings of the Somerset Archaeological and Natural History Society*, 45.2, 108-124.

McOmish, D. 1996: East Chisenbury. Ritual and Rubbish at the British Bronze Age-Iron Age Transition, *Antiquity*, 70, 68-76.

Meadows, J., Barclay, A. & Bayliss, A. 2007: A Short Passage of Time. The Dating of the Hazleton Long Cairn Revisited, *Cambridge Archaeological Journal*, 17, Supplement S1, 45-64.

Mears, R. & Hillman, G. 2007: *Wild Food*, London, Hodder and Stoughton.

Megaw, J.V.S. 1976: Gwithian, Cornwall. Some Notes on the Evidence for Neolithic and Bronze Age Settlement. In, Burgess, C. & Miket, R. (Eds.), *Settlement and Economy in the Third and Second Millennia BC*, Oxford, BAR British Series, 33, 51-79.

Menasanch, M., Risch, R. & Soldevilla, J.A. 2002: Las Tecnologias del Procesade de Cereal en el Sudeste de la Peninsula Ibérica Durante el III ye el II Milenio A.N.E. In, Procopiou, H. & Treuil, R. (Eds.), *Moudre et Broyer*, 1, Paris, CTHS, 81-109.

Mepham, L. 1999: Other Objects of Worked Stone. In, Fitzpatrick, A.P., Butterworth, C.A. & Grove, J. (Eds.), *Prehistoric and Roman Sites in East Devon. The A30 Honiton to Exeter Improvement DBFO, 1996-9. 1. Prehistoric Sites*, Wessex Archaeology Report, 16, 134.

Mercer, R.J. 1970: The Excavation of a Bronze Age Hut Settlement at Stannon Down, St. Breward, Cornwall, 1968, *Cornish Archaeology*, 9, 17-46.

Mercer, R.J. 1981: *Excavations at Carn Brea, Illogan, Cornwall, 1970-73*, Reprinted from Cornish Archaeology, 20.

Mercer, R. 1997: The Excavation of a Neolithic Enclosure Complex at Helman Tor, Lostwithiel, Cornwall, *Cornish Archaeology*, 36, 5-63.

Merrifield 1987: *The Archaeology of Ritual and Magic*, London, B.T. Batsford Ltd.

Miket, R. 1976: The Evidence for Neolithic Activity in the Milfield Basin, Northumberland. In, Burgess, C. & Miket, R. (Eds.), *Settlement and Economy in the Third and Second Millennium BC*, Oxford, BAR British Series, 33, 113-142.

Minnitt, S. & Coles, J. 1996: *The Lake Villages of Somerset*, Taunton, Glastonbury Antiquarian Society, Somerset Levels Project and Somerset County Council Museums Service.

Moffett, M. 2003: The Mystic Mill from Vézelay. In, Moffett, M., Fazio, M.W. & Wodehouse, L. (Eds.), *A World History of Architecture*, London, Laurence King Publishing Ltd., 215.

Molleson, T. 1994: The Eloquent Bones of Abu Hureyra, *Scientific American*, August, 60-65.

Moore, A.M.T., Hillman, G.C. & Legge, A.J. 2000: *Village on the Euphrates. From Foraging to Farming at Abu Hureyra*, Oxford, Oxford University Press.

Moore, A.M.T. 2004: Abu Hureyra and the Development of Farming in Western Asia. Directions of Future Research. In, Peltenburg, E. and Wasse, A. (Eds.), *Neolithic Revolution. New Perspectives in Southwest Asia in Light of Recent Discoveries on Cyprus*, Oxford, Oxbow Books, 61-69.

Moore, H.L. 1996: *Space, Text and Gender*, London, The Guildford Press.

Moore, H.L. 2006: The Interpretation of Spatial Patterning in Settlement Residues. In, Hodder, I. (Ed.), *Symbolic and Structural Archaeology*, Cambridge, Cambridge University Press, 74-79.

Moore, T. 2007: Perceiving Communities. Exchange Landscapes and Social Networks in the Later Iron Age of Western Britain, *Oxford Journal of Archaeology*, 26.1, 79-102.

Moritz, L.A. 1958: *Grain-Mills and Flour in Classical Antiquity*, Oxford, Clarendon Press.

Morris, E.L. 1988: The Iron Age Occupation at Dibbles Farm, *Proceedings of the Somerset Archaeological and Natural History Society*, 132, 23-81.

Morris, J. 1973: *The Age of Arthur*, London, Weidenfield and Nicolson.

Much, M. 1893: *Die Kupferzeit in Europa*, Jena, Hermann Costenoble.

Mulville, J. 2008: Foodways and Social Ecologies from the Middle Bronze Age to Late Iron Age. In, Pollard, J. (Ed.), *Prehistoric Britain*, Oxford, Blackwell Publishing Ltd, 225-247.

Murray, P. 1980: Discard Location. The Ethnographic Data, *American Antiquity*, 45.3, 490-502.

Nash Williams, V.E. 1939: A New Roman Mining Site at Lower Machen, Monmouthshire, *Archaeologia Cambrensis*, 94, 108-110.

Natural England 2009: *England's Geology by County*, http://www.naturalengland.org.uk/ourwork/conservation/geodiversity/englands/counties, 22nd May 2009.

Neal, D.S. 2001: Gadebridge Revisited. Excavations on the Roman Villa 2000, *The Antiquaries Journal*, 81, 109-129.

Neal, D.S., Wardle, A. & Hunn, J. 1990: *Excavation of the Iron Age, Roman and Medieval Settlement at Gorhambury, St. Albans*, English Heritage Archaeological Report, 14, London, Historic Buildings and Monuments Commission for England.

Needham, S. & Spence, T. 1997: Refuse and the Formation of Middens, *Antiquity*, 71, 77-90.

Nelson, M.C. & Lippmeier, H. 1993: Grinding-Tool Design as Conditioned by Land-Use Pattern, *American Antiquity*, 58.2, 286-305.

Nesbitt, M. & Samuel, D. 1996: From Staple Crop to Extinction? The Archaeology and History of the Hulled Wheats. In, Padulosi, S., Hammer, K. & Heller, J. (Eds.), *Hulled Wheats. Proceedings of the First International Workshop on Hulled Wheats*, Rome, International Plant Genetic Resources Institute, 41-100.

Newman, C., Morris, E.L. & Bonner, D. 1999: Iron Age and Romano-British Sites along the Bowden Reservoir Link Pipeline, South-East Somerset, *Proceedings of the Somerset Archaeological and Natural History Society*, 143, 1-27.

Newman, P. 1998: *The Dartmoor Tin Industry. A Field Guide*, Newton Abbot, Chercombe Press.

Noall, R.J. 1971: Bussow Bronze Age Village and its Last Inhabitants, *Cornish Archaeology*, 10, 29-31.

Nowakowski, J. 1991: Trethellan Farm, Newquay. The Excavation of a Lowland Bronze Age Settlement and Iron Age Cemetery, *Cornish Archaeology*, 30, 5-242.

Nowakowski, J. 2001: Leaving Home in the Cornish Bronze Age. Insights into Planned Abandonment Processes. In, Brück, J. (Ed.), *Landscapes. Tradition and Transformation*, Oxford, Oxbow, 139-148.

O'Neil, H.E. 1964: Excavation of a Celtic Hermitage on St. Helens, Isles of Scilly 1956-60, *The Archaeological Journal*, 121, 40-69.

Osborne, R. 2004: Hoards, Votives, Offerings. The Archaeology of the Dedicated Object, *World Archaeology*, 36.1, 1-10.

O'Sullivan, A. & Kenny, N. 2008: A Matter of Life and Death, *Archaeology Ireland*, 22.4, 8-11.

Oswald, A. 1997: A Doorway on the Past. Practical and Mystic Concerns in the Orientation of Roundhouse Doorways. In, Gwilt, A. & Haselgrove, C. (Eds.), *Reconstructing Iron Age Societies*, Oxford, Oxbow Monograph 71, 87-95.

Pailler, Y. & Sheridan, A. 2009: Everything You Always Wanted to Know About...La Néolithisation de la Grande-Bretagne et de l'Irlande, *Bullet de la Société Préhistorique Française*, 106.1, 25-56.

Palmer, L.S. 1919-1920: The Keltic Cavern, *Proceedings of the Bristol Speleological Society*, 1.1, 9-20.

Parker Pearson, M. 1996: Food, Fertility and Front Doors in the First Millennium BC. In, Champion, T. & Collis, J.R. (Eds.), *The Iron Age in Britain and Ireland. Recent Trends*, Sheffield, J.R. Collis Publications, Department of Archaeology and Prehistory, University of Sheffield, 117-132.

Parker Pearson, M. & Ramilisonina 1998: Stonehenge for the Ancestors. The Stones Pass on the Message, *Antiquity*, 72, 308-326.

Paston, A.G. 1974: Preliminary Ethnoarchaeological Investigations Among the Tarahumara. In, Donnan, C.B. & Clewlow, C.W. (Eds.), *Ethnoarchaeology*, Los Angeles, Institute of Archaeology, University of California, Monograph 4, 93-114.

Pavlů, I. 2008: Dimensions of Grinding Stones Between Anatolia and Central Europe. In, Hamon, C. & Graefe, J. (Eds.), *New Perspectives on Querns in Neolithic Societies*, Bonn, DGUF, 11-22.

Peacock, D.P.S 1987: Iron Age and Roman Quern Production at Lodsworth, West Sussex, *The Antiquaries Journal*, 67, 61-85.

Bibliography

Peacock, D. & Cutler, L. 2010: A Neolithic Voyage, *The International Journal of Nautical Archaeology*, 39.1, 116-124.

Pearce, S.M. 1981: *The Archaeology of South West Britain*, London, Collins.

Pearce, S.M. & Padley, T. 1977: The Bronze Age Find from Tredarvah, Penzance, *Cornish Archaeology*, 16, 25-41.

Pessolana, S. 2007: *Hamer People*, http://www.pbase.com/sergio_pes/hamer_people, 5th April 2007.

Pfaffenberger, B. 1988: Fetishised Objects and Humanised Nature. Towards an Anthropology of Technology, *Man*, NS 23.2, 236-252.

Piperno, D.R. & Pearsall, D.M. 1998: *The Origins of Agriculture in the Lowland Neotropics*, London, Academic Press.

Piperno, D.R., Weiss, E., Holst, I. & Nadel, D. 2004: Processing of Wild Cereal Grains in the Upper Palaeolithic Revealed by Starch Grain Analysis, *Nature*, 430, 670-673.

Pitts, M. 2007: Ancient Trading Power Near Inverness, *British Archaeology*, 92, 6.

Pollard, J. 2001: The Aesthetics of Depositional Practice, *World Archaeology*, 33.2, 315-333.

Pollard, J. 2002: *Neolithic Britain*, Princes Risborough, Shire Publications Ltd.

Pollard, J. & Healy, F. (Eds.) 2008: Neolithic and Early Bronze Age. In, Webster, C. (Ed.), *The Archaeology of South West England*, Taunton, Somerset County Council, 75-102.

Poole, C. 1995: Study 12. Pits and Propitiation. In, Cunliffe, B. (Ed.), *Danebury. An Iron Age Hillfort in Hampshire, 6, A Hillfort Community in Perspective*, CBA Research Report, 102, 249-275.

Pope, R. 2007: Ritual and the Roundhouse. A Critique of Recent Ideas on the Use of Domestic Space in Later Prehistory. In, Haselgrove, C. & Pope, R. (Eds.), *The Earlier Iron Age in Britain and the Near Continent*, Oxford, Oxbow Books, 204-228.

Pope, R. 2008: Roundhouses. 3000 Years of Prehistoric Design, *Current Archaeology*, 222, 14-21.

Price, J.E. 1871: Notes on a Roman Quern Discovered in St. Martin's Le Grand, *Transactions of the London and Middlesex Archaeological Society*, 4, 124-130.

Price, R. & Watts, L. 1980: Rescue Excavations at Combe Hay, Somerset 1968-1973, *Proceedings of the Somerset Archaeological and Natural History Society*, 124, 1-49.

Price, T.D. 2000a: Europe's First Farmers. An Introduction. In, Price, T.D. (Ed.), *Europe's First Farmers*, Cambridge, Cambridge University Press, 1-18.

Price, T.D. 2000b: Lessons in the Transitions to Agriculture. In, Price, T.D. (Ed.), *Europe's First Farmers*, Cambridge, Cambridge University Press, 301-318.

Procopiou, H. 2011: *Millstones in Bronze Age Crete. Diversity and Change*, Paper presented at Seen Through A Millstone. Geology and Archaeology of Quarries and Mills, Bryggens Museum, Bergen, Norway, 19th - 21st October 2011.

Proctor, J. 2002: Late Bronze Age/Early Iron Age Placed Deposits from Westcroft Road, Carshalton, *Surrey Archaeological Collections*, 89, 65-103.

Pryor, F. 1998a: *Etton. Excavations at a Neolithic Causewayed Enclosure near Maxey, Cambridgeshire*, London, English Heritage Archaeological Report, 18.

Pryor, F. 1998b: *Farmers in Prehistoric Britain*, Stroud, Tempus Publishing Ltd.

Pryor, F. 2003: *Britain BC*, London, Harper Collins.

Quinnell, H. 1986: Cornwall during the Iron Age and the Roman Period, *Cornish Archaeology*, 25, 111-132.

Quinnell, H. 1988: The Local Character of the Devon Bronze Age and its Interpretation in the 1980s, *Proceedings of the Devon Archaeological Society*, 46, 1-14.

Quinnell, H. 1991: The Late Mrs. E.M. Minter's Excavation of Hut Circles at Heatree, Manaton in 1968, *Proceedings of the Devon Archaeological Society*, 49, 1-24.

Quinnell, H. 1994: Becoming Marginal? Dartmoor in Later Prehistory, *Proceedings of the Devon Archaeological Society*, 52, 75-83.

Quinnell, H. 1998: *Later Prehistoric Pottery Survey*, Unpublished.

Quinnell, H. 2002-2003: Stone Artefacts. In, Cole, D. and Jones, A.M., Journeys to the Rock. Archaeological Investigations at Tregarrick Farm, Roche, Cornwall, *Cornish Archaeology*, 41-42, 121-123.

Quinnell, H. 2004: *Trethurgy. Excavations at Trethurgy Round, St. Austell. Community and Status in Roman and Post-Roman Cornwall*, Truro, Cornwall County Council.

Quinnell, H. 2004-2005: The Stone Artefacts. In, Jones, A.M., Settlement and Ceremony. Archaeological Investigations at Stannon Down, St. Breward, Cornwall, *Cornish Archaeology*, 43-44, 87-99.

Quinnell, H. 2007: Stonework. In, Gossip, J. & Jones, A.M. (Eds.), *Archaeological Investigations of a Later Prehistoric and a Romano-British Landscape at Tremough, Penryn, Cornwall*, Oxford, BAR British Series, 443, 81-88.

Quinnell, H. 2010: Prehistoric and Roman Stonework. In, Jones, A.M. & Taylor, S.R. (Eds.), *Scarcewater, Pennance, Cornwall*, Oxford, BAR British Series, 516, 113-130.

Quinnell, H. 2011a: Prehistoric Pottery and Other Finds from Pit 531. In, Dyer, M.J. & Salvatore, J.P. (Eds.), *Archaeological Watching Brief on the SWW Pipeline Route from the Reservoir South West of Bovey Cross, North Bovey to Sandy Park, Drewsteignton, Devon*, Exeter Archaeology Report, 11.20, 6-7.

Quinnell, H. 2011b: A Summary of Cornish Ceramics in the First Millennium BC, *Cornish Archaeology*, 50, 231-240.

Quinnell, H. forthcoming: Stone Artefacts. In, Johns, C., The Excavation of a Multi-Period Archaeological Landscape at Trenowah, St. Austell, Cornwall, *for submission to Cornish Archaeology*.

Quinnell, H. in press a: The Stonework. In, Gossip, J. and Johns, C., The Evaluation of a Multi-Period Prehistoric Site and Fogou at Boden Vean, St. Anthony-in-Meneage, Cornwall 2003, *Cornish Archaeology*.

Quinnell, H. in press b: The Pottery. In, Gossip, J. and Johns, C., The Evaluation of a Multi-Period Prehistoric Site and Fogou at Boden Vean, St. Anthony-in-Meneage, Cornwall 2003, *Cornish Archaeology*.

Quinnell, H. & Taylor, R. 1998-1999: Stone Artefacts. In, Jones, A.M., The Excavation of a Later Bronze Age Structure at Callestick, *Cornish Archaeology*, 37-38, 26-36.

Quinnell, H. & Taylor, R. forthcoming: Stonework. In. Gossip, J., Life Outside the Round. Bronze Age and Iron Age Settlement at Higher Besore and Truro College, Threemilestone, Truro, *for submission to Cornish Archaeology*.

Raftery, B. 1984: *La Tene in Ireland. Problems of Origin and Chronology*, Marburg, Vorgeschichtliches Seminar.

Rahtz, P.A. & Clevedon Brown, J. 1958-1959: Blaise Castle Hill, Bristol. 1957, *Proceedings of the Bristol Speleological Society*, 8.3, 147-171.

Rahtz, P.A. & Greenfield, E. 1977: *Excavations at Chew Valley Lake, Somerset*, Department of Environment Archaeological Report, 8.

Ramminger, B. 2008: Quern Requirement and Raw Material Supply in Linearbandkeramik Settlements of the Mörlener Bucht, NW Wetterau, Hesse. In, Graefe, J. & Hamon, C. (Eds.), *New Perspectives on Querns in Neolithic Societies*, Bonn, DGUF, 33-44.

Ratcliffe, J. 1991: *Lighting up the Past in Scilly*, Truro, Cornwall Archaeological Unit.

Reille, J. 2000: L'apparition des Meules Rotatives en Languedoc Oriental (Ive s.avant J.-C) d'apres L'etude du Site de Lattes, *Gallia*, 57, 261-272.

Renfrew, C. 2003: *Figuring It Out*, London, Thames & Hudson.

Renfrew, C. and Bahn, P. 1996: *Archaeology. Theories, Methods and Practice*, London, Thames and Hudson Ltd.

Renfrew, J. 1973: *Palaeoethnobotany. The Prehistoric Food Plants of the Near East and Europe*, London, Methuen & Co. Ltd.

Renfrew, J.M. 2000: Vegetables in the Ancient Near Eastern Diet. In, Sasson, J.M. (Ed.), *Civilizations of the Ancient Near East,* 1 and 2, Peabody, Massachusetts, Hendrickson Publishers Inc., 191-202.

Reynolds, P.J. 1967: Experiment in Iron Age Agriculture, *Transactions of the Bristol and Gloucestershire Archaeological Society*, 86, 60-73.

Reynolds, P.J. 1969: Experiment in Iron Age Agriculture. Part Two, *Transactions of the Bristol and Gloucestershire Archaeological Society*, 88, 29-33.

Reynolds, P.J. 1974: Experimental Iron Age Storage Pits. An Interim Report, *Proceedings of the Prehistoric Society*, 40, 118-131.

Reynolds, P.J. 1979: *Iron-Age Farm. The Butser Experiment*, London, Colonnade Books.

Richards, A.I. 1939: *Land, Labour and Diet in Northern Rhodesia*, London, Oxford University Press.

Richards, C. & Thomas, J. 1984: Ritual Activity and Structured Deposition in Later Neolithic Wessex. In, Bradley, R. & Gardiner, J. (Eds.), *Neolithic Studies. A Review of Some Current Research*, 189-218.

Richardson, K.M. 1951: The Excavation of Iron Age Villages on Boscombe Down West, *Wiltshire Archaeological Magazine*, 54, 123-168.

Richmond, A. 1999: *Preferred Economies. The Nature of the Subsistence Base Throughout Mainland Britain During Prehistory*, Oxford, BAR British Series 290.

Richmond, I. 1968: *Hod Hill, 2, Excavations Carried out Between 1951 and 1958 for the Trustees of the British Museum*, 2, London, The Trustees of the British Museum.

Riley, H. & Wilson-North, R. 2001: *The Field Archaeology of Exmoor*, Swindon, English Heritage.

Ritchie, A. 1983: Excavation of a Neolithic Farmstead at Knap of Howar, Papa Westray, Orkney, *Proceedings of the Society of Antiquaries of Scotland*, 113, 40-121.

Roberts, N. 2005: Some Eucharistic Mills, *Proceedings of the Twentieth Mill Research Conference*, 3-10.

Robinson, G. 2007: *The Prehistoric Landscape of Scilly*, BAR British Series, 447.

Robinson, M. 1993: The Importation and Use of Stone.

In, Allen, T.G. & Robinson, M.A. (Eds.), *The Prehistoric Landscape and Iron Age Enclosed Settlement at Mingies Ditch, Hardwick-with-Yelford, Oxon. Thames Valley Landscapes. The Windrush Valley, 2*, Oxford, Oxford University Committee for Archaeology, 79-80.

Robinson, M.A. 2000: Further Considerations of Neolithic Charred Cereals, Fruit and Nuts. In, Fairbairn, A.S. (Ed.), *Plants in Neolithic Britain and Beyond*, Oxford, Oxbow Books, 85-90.

Roe, F.E.S. 1997: Stone Axes and Rubbers. In, Mercer, R., The Excavation of a Neolithic Enclosure Complex at Helman Tor, Lostwithiel, Cornwall, *Cornish Archaeology*, 36, 53-54.

Roe, F.E.S. 2000: Worked Stone. In, Barrett, J.C., Freeman, P.W.M. & Woodward, A. (Eds.), *Cadbury Castle, Somerset. The Later Prehistoric and Early Historic Archaeology*, London, English Heritage Archaeological Report, 20, 262-269.

Rogerson, A. 1977: Excavations at Scole, 1973, *East Anglian Archaeology*, 5, 97-224.

Rohl, D.M. 1999: *Legend. The Genesis of Civilisation*, London, Century.

Ross, A. 1986: Lindow Man and the Celtic Tradition. In, Stead, I.M., Bourke, J.B. & Brothwell, D. (Eds.), *Lindow Man. The Body in the Bog*, London, British Museum Publications, 162-169.

Rostovtzeff, M. 1937: Two Homeric Bowls in the Louvre, *American Journal of Archaeology*, 41.1, 86-96.

Runnels, C. 1990: Rotary Querns in Greece, *Journal of Roman Archaeology*, 3, 147-154.

Russell, V. 1971: West Penwith Survey, Truro, Cornwall Archaeological Society.

Russell, V. & Pool, P.A.S. 1964: Excavation of a Menhir at Trye, Gulval, *Cornish Archaeology*, 3, 15-26.

Samuel, D. 1993: Ancient Egyptian Cereal Processing. Beyond the Artistic Record, *Cambridge Archaeological Journal*, 3.2, 276-283.

Samuel, D. 1999: Bread Making and Social Interactions at the Amarna Workmen's Village, Egypt, *World Archaeology*, 31.1, 121-144.

Samuel, D. 2000: Brewing and Baking. In, Nicholson, P.T. & Shaw, I. (Eds.), *Ancient Egyptian Materials and Technology*, Cambridge, Cambridge University Press, 537-576.

Samuel, D. 2001: Bread. In, Redford, D.B. (Ed.), *The Oxford Encyclopedia of Ancient Egypt, 1*, Oxford, Oxford University Press, 196-198.

Samuel, D. 2002: Bread in Archaeology, *Civilisations*, 49.1-2, 27-36.

Samuel, D. 2010: Experimental Grinding and Ancient Egyptian Flour Production. In, Ikram, S. & Dodson, A. (Eds.), *Beyond the Horizon. Studies in Egyptian Art, Archaeology and History in Honour of Barry J. Kemp*, Cairo, University of Cairo Press, 456-477.

Sankalia, H.D. 1959: Rotary Querns from India, *Antiquity*, 33, 128-130.

Santillana, G. de & Dechend, H. von 1969: *Hamlet's Mill*, http://www.bibliotecapleyades.net/hamlets_mill/hamletmill06.htm, 25th June 2010.

Saunders, A. & Harris, D. 1982: Excavations at Castle Gotha, St. Austell, *Cornish Archaeology*, 21, 109-153.

Saville, A. 1990: *Hazleton North, Gloucestershire, 1979-82. The Excavation of a Neolithic Long Cairn of the Cotswold-Severn Group*, English Heritage Archaeological Report, 13.

Scarre, C. 2002: Epilogue. Colour and Materiality in Prehistoric Society. In, Jones, A. & Macgregor, G. (Eds.), *Colouring the Past. The Significance of Colour in Archaeological Research*, Oxford, Berg, 227-242.

Schamberger, K., Sear, M., Wehner, K., Wilson, J. & Team, The Australian Journeys Gallery Development 2009: *Transnational Ties. Australian Lives in the World*, National Museum of Australia. http://epress.anu.edu.au/anu_lives/transnational/mobile-devices/ch17.html, 21st May 2009.

Schiffer, M.B. 1983: Towards the Identification of Formation Processes, *American Antiquity*, 48, 675-706.

Schiffer, M.B. 1987: *Formation Processes of the Archaeological Record*, Albuquerque, University of New Mexico Press.

Schiffer, M.B. 1995: *Behavioral Archaeology*, Salt Lake City, University of Utah Press.

Schiffer, M.B. 1999: *The Material Life of Human Beings*, London, Routledge.

Schiffer, M.B. & Skibo, J.M. 1997: The Explanation of Artifact Variability, *American Antiquity*, 62.1, 27-50.

Schlanger, S.H. 1991: On Manos, Metates and the History of Site Occupations, *American Antiquity*, 56.3, 460-474.

Schneider, J.S. 1996: Quarrying and Production of Milling Implements at Antelope Hill, Arizona, *Journal of Field Archaeology*, 23.3, 299-311.

Schneider, J.S. 2002: Milling Tool Design, Stone Textures and Function. In, Procopiou, H. & Treuil, R. (Eds.), *Moudre et Broyer, 1, Méthodes*, Paris, CTHS, 31-53.

Schulting, R. 2004: An Irish Sea Change. Some Implications for the Mesolithic-Neolithic

Transition. In, Cummings, V. & Fowler, C. (Eds.), *The Neolithic of the Irish Sea, Materiality and Traditions of Practice*, Oxford, 22-28.

Schwieso, J. 1976: Excavations at Threemilestone Round, Kenwyn, Truro, *Cornish Archaeology*, 15, 51-67.

Scullard, H.H. 1981: *Festivals and Ceremonies of the Roman Republic*, London, Thames & Hudson Ltd.

Seager Thomas, M. 1999: Stone Finds in Context, *Sussex Archaeological Collections*, 137, 39-48.

Shaffrey, R. 2003: The Rotary Querns from the Society of Antiquaries' Excavations at Silchester, 1890-1909, *Britannia*, 34, 143-174.

Shaffrey, R. 2006: Review of Recent Finds in Southern England, *Quern Study Group Newsletter*, 7.

Sharples, N.M. 1991: Warfare in the Iron Age of Wessex, *Scottish Archaeological Review*, 8, 79-89.

Sharples, N. 2012: Ham and Mustard, *British Archaeology*, March/April 2012, 35-39.

Sheppard, P. & Woolf, C. 1982: Parochial Check-Lists of Antiquities. Hundred of Pydar. 9. Parish of St. Columb Minor, *Cornish Archaeology*, 21, 197-204.

Sheridan, A., Schulting, R., Quinnell, H. and Talor, R. 2008: Revisiting a Small Passage Tombe at Broadsands, Devon, *Proceedings of the Devon Archaeological Society*, 66, 1026.

Sheridan, A. 2011: The Early Neolithic of South-West England. New Insights and New Questions. In, Pearce, S. (Ed.), *Recent Archaeological Work in South-Western Britain. Papers in Honour of Henrietta Quinnell*, Oxford, BAR British Series 548, 21-39.

Silvester, R.J. 1980: The Prehistoric Open Settlement at Dainton, South Devon, *Proceedings of the Devon Archaeological Society*, 38, 17-48.

Silvester, R.J. 1986: The Later Prehistoric and Roman Material from Kent's Cavern, Torquay, *Proceedings of the Devon Archaeological Society*, 44, 9-38.

Simpson, F.G. & Richmond, I.A. 1935: Randylands Milecastles, 54, *Transactions of the Cumberland and Westmoreland Antiquarian and Archaeological Society*, 35, 236-244.

Simpson, J.A. & Weiner, E.S.C. (prepared by) 1989a: *The Oxford English Dictionary. Second Edition*, 13, Oxford, Clarendon Press.

Simpson, J.A. & Weiner, E.S.C. (prepared by) 1989b: *The Oxford English Dictionary. Second Edition*, 9, Oxford, Clarendon Press.

Sinclair, A. 2000: Constellations of Knowledge. In, Dobres, M. & Robb, J. (Eds.), *Agency in Archaeology*, London, Routledge,

Smith, G. 1987: *Dainton Excavations, 1986*, Unpublished manuscript in Devon Historic Environment Service.

Smith, I.F. 1965: *Windmill Hill Avebury. Excavations by Alexander Keiller 1925-1939*, Oxford, Oxford University Press.

Société Jersiaise 1977: *La Hougue Bie, Jersey, Channel Islands. Prehistoric Tomb and Ancient Chapels*, St. Helier, Société Jersiaise.

Sørensen, M.L. 2000: *Gender Archaeology*, Cambridge, Polity Press.

Stanley, P.R. 1975: *The Querns from Cadbury Castle*, University College Cardiff, Department of Archaeology, Undergraduate Thesis.

Stevens, C.J. 2007: Reconsidering the Evidence. Towards as Understanding of the Social Contexts of Subsistence Production in Neolithic Britain. In, Colledge, S. & Conolly, J. (Eds.), *The Origins and Spread of Domestic Plants in Southwest Asia and Europe*, Walnut Creek, California, Left Coast Press, Inc., 375-389.

Stone, A. 2008: *The Cosmic Mill*, http://www.indigogroup.co.uk/edge/cmill.htm, 2nd June 2010.

Stone, J.F.S 1941: The Deverel-Rimbury Settlement on Thorny Down, Winterbourne Gunner, South Wiltshire, *Proceedings of the Prehistoric Society*, 7, 114-133.

Storck, J. & Teague, W.D. 1952: *Flour for Man's Bread*, Minneapolis, University of Minnesota Press.

Straker, V. 1991: Charred Plant Macrofossils. In, Nowakowski, J., Trethellan Farm, Newquay. The Excavation of a Lowland Bronze Age Settlement and Iron Age Cemetery, *Cornish Archaeology*, 30, 161-179.

Straker, V., Brown, A., Fyfe, R., Jones, J. & Wilkinson, K 2008: Later Bronze Age and Iron Age Environmental Background. In, Webster, C.J. (Ed.), *The Archaeology of South West England*, Taunton, Somerset County Council, 103-116.

Sturgess, J. 2007: Bronze Age Gwithian, *Cornish Archaeology*, 46, 23-33.

Sturgess, J. & Lawson-Jones, A. 2006: *Bronze Age Gwithian Revisited. Archaeological Excavations Between 1956 and 1961 in Cornwall*, 1, Historic Environment Service (Projects) Report, 2006R067, Truro, Cornwall Country Council.

Tabor, R. 2008: *Cadbury Castle. The Hillfort and Landscape*, Stroud, The History Press.

Takaoğlu, T. 2005: Coşkuntepe. An Early Neolithic Quern Production Site in NW Turkey, *Journal of Field Archaeology*, 30.4, 419-433.

Taylor, H. 1949-1950: The Tynings Barrow Group. Third Report, *Proceedings of the Bristol Speleological Society*, 6.2, 111-172.

Tewolde, B.G.E. 1993: The Impact of Modern Science

and Technology on Human Rights in Ethiopia. In, Weeramantry, C.G. (Ed.), *The Impact of Technology on Human Rights*, Tokyo, United Nations University Press, 189-242.

Thomas, C. 1964: Minor Sites in the Gwithian Area, *Cornish Archaeology*, 3, 37-62.

Thomas, C. 1985: *Exploration of a Drowned Landscape*, London, B.T. Batsford Ltd.

Thomas, C. 1991: Beacon Hill Re-visited. A Re-assessment of the 1969 Excavations, *Reports of the Lundy Field Society*, 42, 43-54.

Thomas, C. & Wailes, B. 1967: Sperris Quoit. The Excavation of a New Penwith Chamber Tomb, *Cornish Archaeology*, 6, 9-22.

Thomas, J. 1999: *Understanding the Neolithic*, London, Routledge.

Thomas, J. 2008a: The Mesolithic-Neolithic Transition in Britain. In, J. Pollard (Ed.), *Prehistoric Britain*, Oxford, Blackwell Publishing Ltd., 58-89.

Thomas, J. 2008b: Excavation of an Iron Age Settlement Adjacent to Beaumont Leys Lane, Beaumont Leys, Leicester, Unpublished ULAS Report, 2008-114.

Thomas, J. 2008c: Excavation of an Iron Age 'Aggregated' Settlement at Manor Fam, Humberstone, Leicester, Unpublished ULAS Report, 2008-133.

Thomas, J. 2010: The Worked Stone, In, Speed, G., *The Excavation of an Enclosed Iron Age Settlement at Hallam Fields, Birstall, Leicester, Transactions of the Leicestershire Archaeological and Historical Society*, 84, 27-75.

Thompson, F.H. 1979: Three Surrey Hillforts. Excavations at Anstiebury, Holmbury and Hascombe, 1972-1977, *The Antiquaries Journal*, 59, 245-318.

Thomson, J. 1924: *The Book of Silchester*, II, London, Simpkin, Marshall, Hamilton, Kent & Co. Ltd.

Thomsom, W.M. 1877 (New Impression 1985): *The Land and the Book*, London, Darf Publishers Limited.

Thomson, W.M. 1877: *The Land and the Book*, London, Darf Publishers Limited (new impression 1985).

Thorpe, B. 1844: *The Homilies of the Anglo-Saxon Church*, 1, London, The Aelfric Society.

Tilley, C. 1999: *Metaphor and Material Culture*, Oxford, Blackwell Publishers Ltd.

Tilley, C. 2007: Materiality in Materials, *Archaeological Dialogues*, 14.1, 16-20.

Tilley, C. 2009: Jacob's Well, Black Hill. A Bronze Age Water Shrine on Woodbury Common, *Proceedings of the Devon Archaeological Society*, 67, 23-37.

Tingle, M. 2006: Excavations of a Possible Causewayed Enclosure and Roman Site at Membury 1986 and 1994-2000, *Proceedings of the Devon Archaeological Society*, 64, 1-52.

Tooley, A.M.J. 1995: *Egyptian Models and Scenes*, Princes Risborough, Shire.

Tratman, E.K. 1959-1960: Gough's Old Cave, Cheddar, Somerset, *Proceedings of the Bristol Speleological Society*, 1.9, 7-21.

ULAS 2007: *Projects. Husbands Bosworth, Leicestershire*, University of Leicester Archaeological Services. http://www.le.ac.uk/ulas/projects/husbands_bosworth.html, 27th July 2007.

Vaughan Williams, R. & Lloyd, A.L. 1959: *The Penguin Book of English Folk Songs*, Harmondsworth, Penguin Books Ltd.

Van der Veen, M. 1989: Charred Grain Assemblages from Roman-Period Corn Driers in Britain, *Archaeological Journal*, 146, 302-319.

Van der Veen, M. & Jones, G. 2006: A Re-analysis of Agricultural Production and Consumption. Implications for Understanding the British Iron Age, *Vegetation History and Archaeobotany*, 15, 217-228.

Waddell, J. 1998: *The Prehistoric Archaeology of Ireland*, Galway, Galway University Press.

Wainwright, G.J. 1979: *Gussage All Saints. An Iron Age Settlement in Dorset*, DoE Archaeological Report, 10.

Wainwright, G.J. & Smith, K. 1980: The Shaugh Moor Project. Second Report. The Enclosure, *Proceedings of the Prehistoric Society*, 46, 65-122.

Walker, W.H. & Lucero, L.J. 2000: The Depositional History of Ritual and Power. In, Dobres, M. & Robb, J. (Eds.), *Agency in Archaeology*, London, Routledge, 130-147.

Walton, J. 1974: *Water-mills, Windmills and Horse-mills of South Africa*, Cape Town and Johannesburg, C. Struik Ltd.

Warre, F. 1851: Worle Camp, *Proceedings of the Somerset Archaeological and Natural History Society*, 2.2, 64-85.

Watts, M. 2002: *The Archaeology of Mills & Milling*, Stroud, Tempus Publishing Ltd.

Watts, M. 2008: *Corn Milling*, Oxford, Shire Publications Ltd.

Watts, S. 1996: The Rotary Quern in Wales. Part One, *Melin*, 12, 26-35.

Watts, S. 1999: *An Examination of the Changes in the Intensity of use of Storage Pits in the Iron Age*, Unpublished Individual Study Module, Certificate in Archaeology, Exeter University.

Watts, S. 2003: The Longis Querns Uncovered, Alderney Society Bulletin, 67-75.

Watts, S. 2006a: *Deconstructing the Function of Querns*, Paper

Watts, S. 2006b: Rotary Querns c.700-1700, *Finds Research Group AD700-1700 Datasheet*, 38.

Watts, S. 2007a: *Querns from Mount Folly, Bigbury, Devon*, Unpublished report for E. Wilkes, Bournemouth University.

Watts, S. 2007b: Querns. In Noort, R. van de, Chapman, H.P. &Collis J. (eds) *Sutton Common. The excavation of an Iron Age 'marsh-fort'*, CBA report 154, York, 96-7.

Watts, S. 2008a: Object Biography and its Importance in Furthering our Understanding of the Structured Deposition of Querns in Neolithic Britain. In, Hamon, C. & Graefe, J. (Eds.), *New Perspectives on Querns in Neolithic Societies*, Bonn, DGUF, 93-102.

Watts, S. 2008b: *Querns from the Cadbury Castle Environs Project. Overview and Catalogue*, Unpublished report for R. Tabor, SCEP.

Watts, S. 2009: The Saddle Quern. In, Green, T. (Ed.), Excavation of a Hillslope Enclosure at Holworthy Farm, Parracombe Displaying Bronze Age and Iron Age Activity, *Proceedings of the Devon Archaeological Society*, 67, 78-79.

Watts, S. 2011a: The Function of Querns. In, Williams, D. & Peacock, D. (Eds.), *Bread for the People. The Archaeology of Mills and Milling*, University of Southampton Series in Archaeology Monograph, 3, Oxford, Archaeopress, 341-348.

Watts, S. 2011b: *Quern Fragments from Porthleven, Cornwall*, Unpublished Report for Southwest Archaeology.

Webley, L 2007: Using and Abandoning Roundhouses. A reinterpretation of the Evidence from Late Bronze Age-Early Iron Age Southern England, *Oxford Journal of Archaeology*, 26.2, 127-144.

Webster, C. & Mayberry, T. 2007: *The Archaeology of Somerset*, Wellington, Somerset County Council.

Webster, C.J. (Ed.) 2008: *The Archaeology of South West England*, Taunton, Somerset County Council.

Wedlake, W.J. 1958: *Excavations at Camerton, Somerset*, Camerton, Camerton Excavation Club.

Welldon Finn, R. 1967: Devonshire. In, Darby, H.C. & Welldon Finn, R. (Eds.), *The Domesday Geography of South-West England*, Cambridge, University Press, 223-295.

Welldon Finn, R. & Wheatley, P. 1967: Somerset. In, Darby, H.C. & Welldon Finn, R. (Eds.), *The Domesday Geography of South-West England*, Cambridge, University Press, 132-222.

Wheeler, H. 1979: Excavations (of a Multiperiod Complex) at Willington, Derbyshire 1970-2, *Derbyshire Archaeological Journal*, 99, 58-220.

Wheeler, R.E.M. 1925: *Prehistoric and Roman Wales*, Oxford, Clarendon Press.

Wheeler, R.E.M. 1943: *Maiden Castle, Dorset*, Reports of the Research Committee of the Society of Antiquaries of London, 12.

Whimster, R. 1977: Iron Age Burial in Southern Britain, *Proceedings of the Prehistoric Society*, 43, 317-327.

Whittle, A. 1991: Waylands Smithy, Oxfordshire. Excavations at the Neolithic Tomb in 1962-63 by R.J.C. Atkinson and S. Piggott, *Proceedings of the Prehistoric Society*, 57.2, 61-101.

Whittle, A. 1996: *Europe in the Neolithic*, Cambridge, Cambridge University Press.

Whittle, A., Pollard, J. & Grigson, C. 1999: *The Harmony of Symbols. The Windmill Hill Causewayed Enclosure, Wiltshire*, Oxford, Oxbow Books.

Whittle, A., Bayliss, A. & Wysocki, M. 2007: Once in a Lifetime. The Date of the Wayland's Smithy Long Barrow, *Cambridge Archaeological Journal*, 17, Supplement S1, 103-121.

Whittle, A., Bayliss, A. & Healy, F. 2008: The Timing and Tempo of Change. Examples from the Fourth Millennium cal. BC in Southern England, *Cambridge Archaeological Journal*, 18.1, 65-70.

Wilkinson, K & Straker, V. 2008: Neolithic and Early Bronze Age Environmental Background. In, Webster, C. (Ed.), *The Archaeology of South West England*, Taunton, Somerset County Council, 63-74.

Williams, B.B. 1978: Excavations at Lough Eskragh, County Tyrone, *Ulster Journal of Archaeology*, 41, 37-48.

Williams, M. 2003: Growing Metaphors, *Journal of Social Archaeology*, 3.2, 223-255.

Williams-Thorpe, O. & Thorpe, R.S. 1990: Millstone Provenancing used in Tracing the Route of a Fourth-Century BC Greek Merchant Ship, *Archaeometry*, 32.2, 115-137.

Willis, L. & Rogers, E.H. 1951: Dainton Earthworks, *Proceedings of the Devon Archaeological Exploration Society*, 4.4, 79-101.

Wilson, H. 2001: *Egyptian Food and Drink*, Princes Risborough, Shire Publications Ltd.

Winbolt, S.E. 1929-1930: Excavations at Holmbury Camp, Surrey, *Surrey Archaeological Collections*, 38, 156-170.

Wood, J. 2000: Food and Drink in European Prehistory, *European Journal of Archaeology*, 3.1, 89-111.

Woodman, P. 2000: Getting Back to Basics. Transitions to Farming in Ireland and Britain. In, Price, T.D. (Ed.), *Europe's First Farmers*, Cambridge, Cambridge University Press, 219-259.

Bibliography

Woodward, A. 2000: Depositional Processes. In, Barrett, J.C., Freeman, P.M.W., & Woodward, A., *Cadbury Castle Somerset. The Later Prehistoric and Early Historic Archaeology*, London, English Heritage Archaeological Report, 20, 20-22.

Woodward, P.J. 1991: *The South Dorset Ridgeway. Survey and Excavations 1977-84*, Dorset Natural History and Archaeological Society Monograph, 8.

Worthen, S. 2006: Of Mills and Meaning. In, Walton, S.A. (Ed.), *Wind & Water in the Middle Ages*, Tempe, Arizona Centre for Medieval and Renaissance Studies, 259-281.

Wright, K.I. 1994: Ground-stone Tools and Hunter-Gatherer Subsistence in Southwest Asia Implications for the Transition to Farming, *American Antiquity*, 59, 238-263.

Wright, K.I. 2000: The Social Origins of Cooking and Dining in Early Villages of Western Asia, *Proceedings of the Prehistoric Society*, 66, 89-121.

Wright, M.E. 1988: Beehive Quern Manufacture in the South-East Pennines, *Scottish Archaeological Review*, 5.1,2, 65-77.

Young, D. 2006: The Colours of Things. In, Tilley, C., Keane, W. & Küchler, S. (Eds.), *Handbook of Material Culture*, London, Sage Publications, 173-186.

Zvelebil, M. 1994: Plant Use in the Mesolithic and its Role in the Transition to Farming, *Proceedings of the Prehistoric Society*, 60, 35-74.

INDEX

Numbers in bold refer to figures.

A

abandonment deposits 7, 10-11, 13, 41, 51, 62, 79, 81-2, 84-90, 97, 99, 101, 108, 110, 117, 137, 139
Aelfric 50
affordance 25, 41
Africa 18, 28, 37
Alderney **31**, 31, 42
al-Farghani 50
Algeria 32
Amberley Mount, Sussex 94
Anatolia 21, 33, 34, 36, 136-7
Anglesey Abbey, Cambridgeshire 54
animal
  bone 8,-9, 13, 47 ,66, 72, 91-2, 97, 111, 113-4, 117-8, 121-2
  cattle/ox 111, 117, 120
  dog 107, 113-4
  horse 8-9, 92, 111, 113-4, 117, 137
  sheep/lambs 48, 114, 120, 122, 137-8
  skulls 63, 113-5, 122, 124, 133, 137
Arizona 30, 46, 136
Armenia 136
artefacts, associated 72, 97-8, 108, 121-2, 133, 134, 137
Ashton Court Park, Bristol 121
Australia 18, 31, 34, 45

B

bappirs 39, 102
Bants Carn, Isles of Scilly 94-5, **95**
Barleycorn, John 49
Barford, Warwickshire 8, 13, 68
barrows 51, 61-2, 74, 83, 88, 90, 94-7, 100, 102, 105, 117, 120, 124, 128
  long 10, 19, 64, 72
Beaumont Leys, Leicestershire 124
beehive quern 8, 10, 17, 21, **23**, 23, 29, 32, 103, 124, 134, 172
behavioural chain 25
Belgium 11, 136
Ben Bridge, Somerset 62, 65, 66, 70-3, 127, 129, 133, 136
Berrywood, Devon 16, 102-3, 123, 127
Bestwall Quarry, Dorset 75
Bishopstone, Sussex 23
Blackhorse, Devon 102, 108, 119
Black Patch, Sussex 7

Blaise Castle Hill, Bristol **113**, 116, 123
Boden Vean, Cornwall 117
Bodmin Moor 75, 79, 84, 94, 108, 128
Bodrifty, Cornwall 36, 74, 107, 109-10, 132
Boscawen-un, Cornwall 95, **96**, 118
Boscombe Down, Wiltshire 131, 134-5
boundaries 6, 10, 15, 57, 74, 80, 83, 91-3, 100-1, 118-9, 121, 124, 128, 139
Brean Down, Somerset 74
breccia 104, 58
Brent Knoll, Somerset 102
Broadsands, Devon 64
Brooklands, Surrey 22
Broom, Bedfordshire 3
Bulgaria 19, 38, 136
Bussow, Cornwall 79

C

Cadbury Castle, Somerset 6, 16, 24, 33, 58-9, 66-7, 69, 72, 75, 102-5, 107-8, 110-13, **111**, 115-23, 127, 131-2, 136
Cain and Abel 48
cairns 74, 77, 96, 101, 131-2
  burial 19, 64, 74, 94, 96
  clearance 62, 66, 71-3, 132
Callestick, Cornwall 74, 77-80, 88, 90, 96, 98-99, 131
Camerton, Somerset 65, 67-8
Caracalla, Emperor 35
Carn Brea, Cornwall 64, 70-3, 131-2
Carn Euny, Cornwall 16, 107, 117, 118n5
Carshalton, Surrey 9
Castallack, Cornwall 118,
Castle Gotha, Cornwall 103
Castle Hill, Devon 64-5, 75, 92
Catalonia 21-2
Cato 21
caves 61, 64, 102, 105, 109, 120, 124, 128
  Gough's Old Cave, Somerset 109
  Kent's Cavern, Devon 61, 109
  Read's Cavern, Somerset 109, 120
  Wookey Hole, Somerset 31, 61, 102, 109, 120, 123, 130
Chagford, Devon 90, 129, 134-5
châine opèratoire 25
Chaucer 17n1, 28
Chew Park, Somerset 64-5, 67, 94-5, **94**, 100

Index

child/ children   11, 46-7
Christie, Agatha   42
Chun Castle, Cornwall   107, 121
Chysauster, Cornwall   102
colour   7, 25, **29**, 40, 51, **52**, 56, 62, 69-70, 93, 98, 101, 112, 114, 133-4, 137
Combe Hay, Somerset   91, 97-8, 133, 136, 138
constellation of knowledge   27, **27**
Consus   48
Corallian sandstone   62, 66, 70, 133
cosmic mill   50
cosmology   1, 3-4, 9, 11, 13, 54, 83, 85, 87, 99, 109, 122, 128, 132, 134, 138
Costa Rica   52, **53**
Cranbrook Castle, Devon   61, 103, 109, 123, 127, 132
Crete   75
Crig-a-Mennis, Cornwall   124
Cyprus   47
Cyrus the Great   37
Czech Republic   36, 136

D

Dainton, Devon   74, 77, 96, 107, 131
Dalton Parlours, Yorkshire   22, 33, 124
Danebury, Hampshire   6, 7, 8, 12, 20, 22-3, 33, 111-12, 114, 116, 123, 127, 131, 134-5
Dartmoor   58, 60-2, 64, 74-5, 77-80, 92, 97-9, 101, 103, 107, 122, 127-8, 132
Deal, Kent   6, **6**
Dean Moor, Devon   61, 74, 79, 117
death   7, 9-10, 13, 26, 38, 41, 45, 47-50, 52, 54, 56-7, 61, 78, 85, 87-8, 93, 100-101, 114, 117, 122, 128, 130, 136, 139
Dibbles Farm, Somerset   111, 113-4
Diodorus   22, 35, 37, 38
ditches   3, 5, 15, 43, 57, 62, 128, 130-1, 139
  boundary   5, 15, 57, 92-3, 119, 124, 128, 139
  Bronze Age   51, 77n7, 78, 91-2, 97-8, 100-101, 132-3, 137
  enclosure   91-3, 100-1, 108, 114, 119, 124, 133
  Iron Age   6, 102, 105-6, 114, 119-120, 122, 124
  Neolithic   5, 9, 19, 51, 133
  rampart   119-20, 122
  ring   62, 77, 88, 90, 92, 98, 99, 132-3
donkey mill   21-2, 37
Doulting Abbey Quarry, Somerset   64, 69
drains   108-9, 128
Durrington Walls, Wiltshire   1

E

Easton Lane, Winchester, Hampshire   22
Egypt   18-19, 30, 34-6, 38-9
elvan   87, 90, 130
enchainment   9, 13, 43, 55, 68, 136
enclosure banks   105, 118
enclosure ditch   91-3, 100-1, 108, 114, 119, 124, 133
entrance grave   71, -2, 94, 118, 138
Etton, Cambridgeshire   9-10, **10**, 20, 33, 47, 51, 68, 70, 133
eucharistic mill   50
Exeter, Devon   60, 77, 92, 98, 133
Exmoor   58, 64, 74, 122

F

Fairfield, Bedfordshire   22
Fenia and Menia   50
fertility   3, 6-7, 9-10, 13, 45, 47, 49, 52, 56, 93-5, 111, 113-4, 118, 122
Field Farm, Somerset   91-2
Flag Fen, Cambridgeshire   7
fogous   62, 105, 117-8, 120, 124, 128
Folkestone, Kent   23
formation processes   2-4
foundation deposit   11, 41, 79, 81, 84, 87, 90, 98-9, 101, 106-7, 114, 117, 122-4, 130, 132, 137-9
fragmentation   9, 10, 13, 43, 45, 49, 54-6, 72, 100, 123, 130-132, 135
France   11-12, **12**, 22, 32, 51, 54, 64, 116, 136-7

G

Gadebridge Park, Hertfordshire   23
Germany   22, 30, 37, 51, 136
Glastonbury Lake Village, Somerset   15, 20, 24, 39-40, 61-2, 102-7, **106**, 109-10, 120-4, 128, 130, 132, 134
granite   29, **29**, 51, 62, 70-1, 74, 77, 84, 87-8, 90, 104, 117, 120, 128, 130, 132
greensand   30, 33, 51, 58, 62, 77, 92, 132
Greece   11, 22, 33-34, 136
greisen   87, 117
Grimes Graves, Norfolk   71
Grimspound, Devon   60
Grotta-Söngr   50
gullies   15, 62, 84, 88, 96, 105, 108-9, 119, 121, 124
Gurnards Head, Cornwall   123, 127
Gussage All Saints, Dorset   8, 20, 22-23, 112n3
Gwithian, Cornwall   58, 74-9, 81-5, 87-8, 93, 96-100, 118, 132-3, 136

H

Hadrian's Wall 23, 37
Halangy Down, Isles of Scilly 109
Halangy Porth, Isles of Scilly 71, 84, 93
Haldon Hill, Devon 64-5
Ham Hill, Somerset 77n2, 102-3, 111, 113-14, 116, 119-20, 122-3, 129, 132-3, 137
Hampnett, Gloucestershire 72, 133
Hangman Grit **29**
Harberton, Devon 64, 69
Harlyn Barn, Cornwall 118
harvest 11-13, 19, 38, 47-8, 52, 56-7, 65, 68, 71, 112, 126, 136, 138
Hayes Farm, Devon 67
Hayne Lane, Devon 74-5, 78-83, 97, 100
Hazard Hill, Devon 64, 66-72, 84
Hazleton, Gloucestershire 8, 19, 64
hearths 6-7, 11, 35-6, 41, 54, 62-7, 70-2, 84-5, 87, 93, 107-9, 110, 113, 118, 121, 128, 132-4, 137, 138-9
Heatree, Devon 61, 79
Helman Tor, Cornwall 64, 70-2
Hemsford, Devon 64-5, 69
Herodian 35
Hembury, Devon 64-5, 67, 70, 102
Hertfordshire puddingstone 23, **29**
Higher Besore, Cornwall 77, 80-2, 87, 90, 97-8, 108, 110, 121
Higher Boden, Cornwall 88
Holne Moor, Devon 61, 79
Holworthy, Devon 20, 58, 60, 75, 78, 88, **89**
Homeground, Somerset 107
Homer 34
hopper rubber 17, 33, 37
human bone deposits 8, 13, 69, 74, 82, 95-8, 107, 115, 117-121, 129
human burials 11, 47, 93-4, 111, 114, 119-20, 122
Humberstone, Leicestershire 134
Hunsbury, Northamptonshire 33, 38
Husbands Bosworth, Leicestershire 68, 70

I

igneous rock 32-3, 51, 77, 92, 104, 106, 130, 132-3
India 12, 47
Iran 48
Iraq 36
Ireland 8, 10-11, 19, 22-23, 28, 42, 48, 52, 75, 128, 134
Israel 18, 25, 36, 41
  Abimelech, king of 25, 41
Iraq 36

Italy 18, 22, **53**, 54, 136
Itford Hill, Sussex 5, 55, 123, 130-1

J

Jamieson, Robert 39
Japan 56, **57**
Jarlshof, Shetland **20**
Jersey vi

K

Kestor, Devon 61, 107
Killibury, Cornwall 102
kiln 11, 13, 39, 85, 91, 98, 105, 110-11, 113, 123, 138
Kilverstone, Norfolk 3

L

Lammas 48
Langland Lane, Devon 65, 102, 119
lava 29, 43, 51
  Mayen **29**, 30, 33, 51
  Permian 62, 77, 100
limestone 14, 29, 93, 104, 128
Lindow II, Cheshire 39, 102
Linearbandkeramik 47, 136
Lodsworth, Sussex 30-1, 33, 121
London 43, 54
Long Range, Devon 108
Lughnasadh 48
Lundy 109

M

Maddle Farm, Berkshire 36, 134
Maiden Castle, Dorset 33, 51, 64, 69
Mali 31, 39, 42, 46, 56, 70
Maperton Ridge, Somerset 64
Meacombe, Devon 90, **91**, 129, 133, 136
Meare, Somerset 15, 20, 58, 61-2, 102-7, 109-10, 122-4, 127-8, 130-1
  Village East 103, 107, 110, 131
  Village West 15, 103, 105, 107, 110, 127, 131
Membury, Devon 64-5, 67
men using querns 34-35, 37
Mesopotamia 34, 36, 39, 42
metalworking 22, 33, 38, 52, 74-5, 77, 96, 98, 101, 105, 110, 113, 117, 121, 135
metate 12, 31-2, 35, 37, 42, 52, 53, 68, 79
Mexico 2, 31, 35, 37, 68, 84, 93
middens 8-9, 62, 66, 71, 78, 80-1, 93-4, 101, 105, 113, 115, 118, 121, 128, 138
  East Chisenbury, Wiltshire 71, 93

Index

material 3, 9, 69, 88, 92-7, 99, 112-3, 118, 131, 137-8
  Potterne, Wiltshire 71, 93
Milsoms Corner, Somerset 47, 64-70, **69**, 72-73, 108, 115, 128, 131
Mingies Ditch, Oxfordshire 36
Moor, The, Somerset 119-20
Moretum 35, 37, 39
Moses 13, 32, 39, 48
Mot 49
Mount Folly, Devon 115, **116**, 122, 129, 131, 135
Mundilfoeri 50

N

Natufian 18, 36
Near East 20, 24, 34, 36, 49, 133, 136-7
New Barn Down, Sussex 20
Nicaragua 52
Normandy puddingstone 33, 64
Nornour, Isles of Scilly 36, **37**, 54, 79, 88, 93, 109, 130, 132
North Hill, Isles of Scilly 94-5
Norway 32

O

occupation deposits 3, 14, 62, 70-2, 78, 84-5, 88, 97, 101, 105, 109-110, 117, 117, 120-1, 124, 126, 128, 130-1, 137-8
Old Red Sandstone 33, 62, 66, 70, 77, 93, 98, 104, 107, 133
Olynthus mill 17, 22, 28, 37, **47**
Ops Consiua 47
Orkney 20, 71, 136
ovens 38-9, 72, 107, 110-11, 118

P

Panama 52
Penhale Farm, Cornwall 88
Penhale Moor, Cornwall 88
Penhale Round, Cornwall 65
Penryn, Cornwall 40, **40**
performance characteristic 25, 38-9
Petronius 50
pit 3, 5-6, **6**, 8, 15, 43, 54, 62, **113**, 128, 130-1, 138-9
  Bronze Age 3, 5-6, 11, 32, 51, 56, 75, 77-8, 81, 84-88, 90-1, 95-101, 129-30, 133-4, 137-8
  burials 8, 47, 111, 114, 120, 122
  cooking 36, 54, 67, 70, 85, 91, 109
  hearth 110, 138
  Iron Age 6, 8-9, 12, 23 103, 105, 110-117, 120-5, 129-35, 137-8
  kiln 91, 98, 105, 110, 113, 123, 138
  Neolithic 3, 6, **6**, 8-9, 11, 13, 15, 19, 33, 47, 51, 64-70, 72-3, 115, 128, 131, 134-5, 138
  storage 6-8, 13, 15, 47-9, 54, 57, 63, 102, 111-117, 120, 122, 124-5, 128, 138
Pliny 75, 111
Plutarch 34
Porthleven, Cornwall 81
Portscatho, Cornwall 65, 67
post-depositional processes 9, 15-16, 43, 56, 61n2, 62, 77n1, 120, 126, 137
posthole 11, 15, 43, 62, 128, 130
  Bronze Age 8, 51, 74, 80-6, 88, 90-1, 93, 96-101, 131, 134, 138
  Iron Age 105, 108, 124, 134
  Neolithic 64
pottery
  decorated 46, 69, 79, 82, 86, 90, 92, 103n1, 109, 117-8
  grooved ware 64-5, 69, 72-3, 127, 134

Q

quartz 51, 97, 121
  crystals **78**, 87, 90, 92, 97-8, 101, 133, 138
  porphyry 62, 77
quern
  buckwheat 30, **30**
  building stones 41, **42**, 71, 79, 107, 110, 130, 139
  decorated 31, 52-4, **53**, 56
  emplacement 19, 28, 35-**36**, 36, 109, 132
  hoards, 77, **77**, 97, 100, 130-2, 137
  Hunsbury **23**
  manufacture 30-2, 121
  medieval 10-11, 17, 52, **53**, 109, 111
  model **34**
  monument **57**
  mouldstones 41, **41**
  post-medieval **53**, 54, 111
  pot 17, 52, **53**
  proto rotary **21**
  puddingstone 23, **23**, **29**, 33, 51, 64
  quarries 23, 30-3, 42, 61-2, 121
  Roman 8, 16, 22-4, 28-33, 37, 40, **40**, 43, 50, 52, 109, 111, 123
  saucer 17, **18**, 20
  Saxon 17n1, 43
  sleeping fox 52-4, **53**
  Sussex **23**, 103
  trough 17-18, **18**, 20, 20
  Wessex **18**, **23**, 103
  Yorkshire **23**

R

Raddon, Devon 64
rampart ditch 119-20, 122
ramparts 16, 103n2, 118-19, 128,
raven burial 114, **114**, 120, 122, 131, 133
regeneration 9, 11, 38. 45, 47-8, 56, 87, 94, 136
rhyolite 62, 77, **78**, 92, 98, 101, 132-3
ring ditch 62, 77, 88, 90, 92, 97-9, 132-3
Roche Rock, Cornwall 67, 115, 128, 136
roundhouse orientation 54, 85,
Rowden, Dorset 78, 134
Rumps, The, Cornwall 103, 123, 127

S

Sanctuary, The, Wiltshire 33, 51
Scadbrook, Devon 61, 79-81
Scarcewater, Cornwall 74-8, **77**, 80-5, 87, 90, 97-101, 114, 122, 130, 138
Scotland *18*, 20, 22, 23, **23**, 32, 32, 39, 41, 41, 48, 51, 53, 128
Seneca 54
Shaugh Moor, Devon 61, 74-5, 77-9, 99, 103
Sheep Slait, Dorset 62, 77, **78**, 92, 97, 132-3
Shetland **20**, 34, 68, 79, 136
Sigwells, Somerset 20
  Bronze Age 33, 51-2, **52**, 74-8, 80-4, **82**, 91-3, 96-8, 100-101, 132-34, 137
  Iron Age 111, 113-14, **114**, 120, 122, 124-25, 131, 135, 137-38
Silchester, Berkshire 21, **21**
Solisbury Hill, Somerset 118
South Africa 18, 38
South America 19, 28
Spain 21-2
Sperris Quoit, Cornwall 65, 70-1, 73, 127
St. Helens, Isles of Scilly 109
St. Kilda 87, 110
Standon Down, Devon 60
Stannon Down, Cornwall 74, 79, 84-5, 94, 108, 132
Strabo 112
Sudan 19, 32
Sutton Common, Yorkshire 134
Sweden 11-12, 19, 47, 136
Syria 18, 34, 36, 49, 93
  Abu Hureyra 18, **19**, 34, 36
  Darius, king of 93

T

Tammuz 49
Thirlings, Northumberland 70, 134
Thorney Down, Wiltshire 20
Thorpe Thewles, Cleveland 22, 41

tomb
  chambered tombs 64-5, 71-4, 91, 129, 133
  passage 64
Topsham, Devon 64, 69
Tower Hill, Somerset 72
transformation 8-11, 38, 44-6, 49-51, 56, 87, 93-6, 101, 108, 117, 119, 123, 126, 133
Tregarrick Farm, Cornwall 66-9, 72, 115, 128, 136
Tremough, Cornwall 64, 67, 69, 72, 75, 80-1, 83, 127
Trenowah, Cornwall 97, 105, 113-14, 115, 118-19, 122, 124, 129-30, 138
Tresco Abbey Gardens, Isles of Scilly **16**
Trethellan Farm, Cornwall 7, **8**, 32, 36, 56, 58, 74-8, 80-4, 86-8, 90, 93, 97, 99-101, 120, 130-1
Trevarnon, Cornwall 118
Treveneague, Cornwall 117-8, 120
Trevilson, Cornwall 88
Trevisker, Cornwall 81, 83, 103, 108-9, 132
Tribes
  Basuto (South Africa) 38
  Bemba (Zambia) 33
  Betamaliba (West Africa) 54
  Dogon (Mali) **28**, 31
    Endo (Kenya) 3, **4**
    Hopi (Arizona) 46, 48
  La La (Nigeria) 46
  Minyanka (Mali) 31, 46, 70
  Quechan (Arizona) 30-1
  Rarámuri (Mexico) 2, 2, 31, 68, 92-3
Trimalchio 50
Trundle, The, Sussex 5, 55, 123, 130-1
Truro College, Cornwall 75, 77, **77**, 90, 97, 100, 114, 130
Turkey **21, 35**, 36, 136
Twinyeo, Devon 107-8
Tynings Farm, Somerset 97
Tynings Quarry, Somerset 116

V

Varro 112
Vyneck, Cornwall 118

W

Wales 13, 22-3, 52, **53**, 54, 72, 128-9, 133-4, 136
Walls 24, 28, 39, 41, 62, 66, 70, 78-9, 96, 110, 128, 130, 133
  enclosure 71, 96, 118-9
  ring ditch 88, 90, 99
  roundhouse 61, 74, 78-80, 88, 98-101, 107,

131, 134
Wanlip, Leicestershire   22
Waylands Smithy, Oxfordshire   10, **18**, 19, 72, 133, 136
Winnall Down, Hampshire   5, **6**, 51, 133
Windmill Hill, Wiltshire   **18**, 19, 136
woman/women   3-4, **21**, 28, 30-39, 42, 44-47, 49, 56-7, 70, 80, 87, 126, 129, 138-9

X

Xenophon   37

Y

Yarnton, Oxfordshire   38-9
Yorkshire Quern Survey   8, 10